THE LORD'S PRAYER

The Lord's Prayer

THOMAS WATSON

THE BANNER OF TRUTH TRUST

THE BANNER OF TRUTH TRUST

Head Office
3 Murrayfield Road
Edinburgh
EH12 6EL
UK

North America Office
PO Box 621
Carlisle
PA 17013
USA

banneroftruth.org

First published as part of *A Body of Practical Divinity*, 1692
Reprinted 1890
First Banner of Truth Trust edition from the 1890 edition, 1960
This revised edition 1965
Reprinted 1972, 1978, 1982, 1989, 1993, 1999,
2009, 2012, 2015, 2020

*

ISBN
Paperback: 978 0 85151 145 0
Clothbound: 978 0 85151 664 6

*

Printed in the USA by
Versa Press Inc.,
East Peoria, IL.

Contents

The Preface to the Lord's Prayer

'Our Father which art in Heaven '

HAVING gone over the chief grounds and fundamentals of religion, and enlarged upon the decalogue, or ten commandments, I shall speak now upon the Lord's prayer.

'After this manner therefore pray ye, Our Father which art in heaven, hallowed,' &c. Matt. vi 9.

In this Scripture are two things observable: the introduction to the prayer, and the prayer itself.

The introduction to the Lord's prayer is, 'After this manner pray ye.' Our Lord Jesus, in these words, gave to his disciples and to us a directory for prayer. The ten commandments are the rule of our life, the creed is the sum of our faith, and the Lord's prayer is the pattern of our prayer. As God prescribed Moses a pattern of the tabernacle (Exod xxv 9), so Christ has here prescribed us a pattern of prayer. 'After this manner pray ye,' &c. The meaning is, let this be the rule and model according to which you frame your prayers. *Ad hanc regulam preces nostras exigere necesse est* [We ought to examine our prayers by this rule]. Calvin. Not that we are tied to the words of the Lord's prayer. Christ says not, 'After these words, pray ye;' but 'After this manner:' that is, let all your petitions agree and symbolize with the things contained in the Lord's prayer; and well may we make all our prayers consonant and agreeable to this prayer. Tertullian calls it, *Breviarium totius evangelii*, 'a breviary and compendium of the gospel;' it is like a heap of massive gold. The exactness of this prayer appears in the dignity of the Author. A piece of work has commendation from its artificer, and this prayer has commendation from its Author; it is the Lord's prayer. As the moral law was written with the finger of God, so this prayer was dropped from the lips of the Son of God. *Non vox hominem sonat, est Deus* [The voice is not that of a man, but that of God]. The exactness of the prayer appears in the excellence of the matter. It is 'as silver tried in a furnace, purified seven times.' Psa xii 6. Never was prayer so admirably and curiously composed as this. As Solomon's Song, for its excellence is called the 'Song of songs,' so may this be well called the 'Prayer of prayers'. The matter of it is admirable, 1. For its comprehensiveness. It is short and pithy, *Multum in parvo*, a great deal said in a few words. It requires most art to draw the two globes curiously in a little map. This short prayer is a system or body of divinity.

2. For its clearness. It is plain and intelligible to every capacity. Clearness is the grace of speech. 3. For its completeness. It contains the chief things that we have to ask, or God has to bestow.

Use. Let us have a great esteem of the Lord's prayer; let it be the model and pattern of all our prayers. There is a double benefit arising from framing our petitions suitably to this prayer. Hereby error in prayer is prevented. It is not easy to write wrong after this copy; we cannot easily err when we have our pattern before us. Hereby mercies requested are obtained; for the apostle assures us that God will hear us when we pray 'according to his will.' 1 John v 14. And sure we pray according to his will when we pray according to the pattern he has set us. So much for the introduction to the Lord's prayer, 'After this manner pray ye.'

The prayer itself consists of three parts. 1. A Preface. 2. Petitions. 3. The Conclusion. The preface to the prayer includes, 'Our Father;' and, 'Which art in heaven.'

I. *The first part of the preface is* 'Our Father.' Father is sometimes taken personally, 'My Father is greater than I' (John xiv 28); but Father in the text is taken essentially for the whole Deity. This title, Father, teaches us that we must address ourselves in prayer to God alone. There is no such thing in the Lord's prayer, as, 'O ye saints or angels that are in heaven, hear us'; but, 'Our Father which art in heaven.'

In what order must we direct our prayers to God? Here the Father only is named. May we not direct our prayers to the Son and Holy Ghost also?

Though the Father only be named in the Lord's prayer, yet the other two Persons are not excluded. The Father is mentioned because he is first in order; but the Son and Holy Ghost are included because they are the same in essence. As all the three Persons subsist in one Godhead, so, in our prayers, though we name but one Person, we must pray to all. To come more closely to the first words of the preface, 'Our Father.' Princes on earth give themselves titles expressing their greatness, as 'High and Mighty.' God might have done so, and expressed himself thus, 'Our King of glory, our Judge:' but he gives himself another title, 'Our Father,' an expression of love and condescension. That he might encourage us to pray to him, he represents himself under the sweet notion of a Father. 'Our Father.' *Dulce nomen Patris* [Sweet is the name of Father]. The name Jehovah carries majesty in it: the name Father carries mercy in it.

In what sense is God a Father?

(1) By creation; it is he that hath made us: 'We are also his offspring.'

[2]

Acts xvii 28. 'Have we not all one Father?' Mal ii 10. Has not one God created us? But there is little comfort in this; for God is Father in the same way to the devils by creation; but he that made them will not save them.

(2) God is a Father by election, having chosen a certain number to be his children, upon whom he will entail heaven. 'He hath chosen us in him.' Eph i 4.

(3) God is a Father by special grace. He consecrates the elect by his Spirit, and infuses a supernatural principle of holiness, therefore they are said to be 'born of God.' 1 John iii 9. Such only as are sanctified can say, 'Our Father which art in heaven.'

What is the difference between God being the Father of Christ, and the Father of the elect?

He is the Father of Christ in a more glorious and transcendent manner. Christ has the primogeniture; he is the eldest Son, a Son by eternal generation; 'I was set up from everlasting, from the beginning, or ever the earth was.' Prov viii 23. 'Who shall declare his generation?' Isa liii 8. Christ is a Son to the Father, as he is of the same nature with the Father, having all the incommunicable properties of the Godhead belonging to him; but we are sons of God by adoption and grace, 'That we might receive the adoption of sons.' Gal iv 5.

What is that which makes God our Father?

Faith. 'Ye are all the children of God by faith in Christ Jesus.' Gal iii 26. An unbeliever may call God his Creator, and his Judge, but not his Father. Faith legitimizes us, and makes us of the blood-royal of heaven. 'Ye are the children of God by faith.' Baptism makes us church members, but faith makes us children. Without faith the devil can show as good a coat of arms as we can.

How does faith make God to be our Father?

As it is a uniting grace. By faith we have coalition and union with Christ, and so the kindred comes in; being united to Christ, the natural Son, we become adopted sons. God is the Father of Christ; faith makes us Christ's brethren, and so God comes to be our Father. Heb ii 11.

Wherein does it appear that God is the best Father?

(1) In that he is most ancient. 'The Ancient of days did sit.' Dan vii 9. A figurative representation of God, who was before all time, which may cause veneration.

(2) God is the best Father, because he is perfect. 'Your Father which is in heaven is perfect;' he is perfectly good. Matt v 48. Earthly fathers are subject to infirmities; Elias, though a prophet, 'was a man subject to like passions' (James v 17); but God is perfectly good. All the perfection we can arrive at in this life is sincerity. We may resemble God a little, but not equal him; he is infinitely perfect.

(3) God is the best Father in respect of wisdom. 'The only wise God.' 1 Tim i 17. He has a perfect idea of wisdom in himself; he knows the fittest means to bring about his own designs. The angels light at his lamp. In particular, one branch of his wisdom is, that he knows what is best for us. An earthly parent knows not, in some intricate cases, how to advise his child, or what may be best for him to do; but God is a most wise Father; he knows what is best for us; he knows what comfort is best for us: he keeps his cordials for fainting. 'God that comforteth those that are cast down.' 2 Cor vii 6. He knows when affliction is best for us, and when it is fit to give a bitter potion. 'If need be ye are in heaviness.' 1 Pet i 6. He is the only wise God; he knows how to make evil things work for good to his children. Rom viii 28. He can make a sovereign treacle of poison. Thus he is the best Father for wisdom.

(4) He is the best Father, because the most loving. 'God is love.' 1 John iv 16. He who causes bowels of affection in others, must needs have more bowels himself; *quod efficit tale* [for he accomplishes the same]. The affections in parents are but marble and adamant in comparison of God's love to his children; he gives them the cream of his love – electing love, saving love. 'He will rejoice over thee with joy; he will rest in his love; he will joy over thee with singing.' Zeph iii 17. No father like God for love; if thou art his child thou canst not love thy own soul so entirely as he loves thee.

(5) He is the best Father, for riches. He has land enough to give to all his children; he has unsearchable riches. Eph iii 8. He gives the hidden manna, the tree of life, rivers of joy. He has treasures that cannot be exhausted, gates of pearl, pleasures that cannot be ended. If earthly fathers should be ever giving, they would have nothing left to give; but God is ever giving to his children, and yet has not the less. His riches are imparted not impaired; like the sun that still shines, and yet has not less light. He cannot be poor who is infinite. Thus he is the best Father; he gives more to his children than any father or prince can bestow.

(6) God is the best Father, because he can reform his children. When his son takes bad courses, a father knows not how to make him better; but God knows how to make the children of the election better: he can change their hearts. When Paul was breathing out persecution against the saints, God soon altered his course, and set him praying. 'Behold, he prayeth.' Acts ix

11. None of those who belong to the election are so roughcast and unhewn but God can polish them with his grace, and make them fit for the inheritance.

(7) God is the best Father, because he never dies. 'Who only hath immortality.' 1 Tim vi 16. Earthly fathers die, and their children are exposed to many injuries, but God lives for ever. 'I am Alpha and Omega, the beginning and the ending.' Rev i 8. God's crown has no successors.

Wherein lies the dignity of those who have God for their Father?

(1) They have greater honour than is conferred on the princes of the earth; they are precious in God's esteem. 'Since thou wast precious in my sight, thou hast been honourable.' Isa xliii 4. The wicked are dross (Psa cxix 119), and chaff (Psa i 4); but God numbers his children among his jewels. Mal iii 17. He writes all his children's names in the book of life. 'Whose names are in the book of life.' Phil iv 3. Among the Romans the names of their senators were written down in a book, *patres conscripti* [the enrolled fathers]. God enrols the names of his children, and will not blot them out of the register. 'I will not blot his name out of the book of life.' Rev iii 5. God will not be ashamed of his children. 'God is not ashamed to be called their God.' Heb xi 16. One might think it were something below God to father such children as are dust and sin mingled; but he is not ashamed to be called our God. That we may see he is not ashamed of his children, he writes his own name upon them. 'I will write upon him the name of my God;' that is, I will openly acknowledge him before all the angels to be my child; I will write my name upon him, as the son bears his father's name. Rev iii 12. What an honour and dignity is this!

(2) God confers honourable titles upon his children. He calls them the excellent of the earth, or the magnificent, as Junius renders it. Psa xvi 3. They must needs be excellent who are *e regio sanguine nati*, of the blood-royal of heaven; they are the spiritual phœnixes of the world, the glory of the creation. God calls his children his glory. 'Israel, my glory.' Isa xlvi 13. He honours his people with the title of kings. 'And hath made us kings.' Rev i 6. All God's children are kings, though they have not earthly kingdoms. They carry a kingdom about them. 'The kingdom of God is within you.' Grace is a kingdom set up in the hearts of God's children. Luke xvii 21. They are kings to rule over their sins, to bind those kings in chains. Psa cxlix 8. They are like kings. They have their *insignia regalia*, their ensigns of royalty and majesty. They have their crown. In this life they are kings in disguise; they are not known, therefore they are exposed to poverty and reproach. 'Now are we the sons of God, and it doth not yet appear what we shall be.' 1 John iii 2. Why, what shall we be? Every son of God shall have

his crown of glory, and white robes. 1 Pet v 4; Rev vi 11. Robes signify dignity, and white signifies sanctity.

(3) The honour of those who have God for their Father is, that they are all heirs; the youngest son is an heir. God's children are heirs to the things of this life. God being their Father, they have the best title to earthly things, they have a sanctified right to them. Though they have often the least share, they have the best right; and with what they have they have the blessing of God's love and favour. Others may have more of the venison, but God's children have more of the blessing. Thus they are heirs to the things of this life. They are heirs to the other world. 'Heirs of salvation' (Heb i 14); 'Joint-heirs with Christ' (Rom viii 17). They are co-sharers with Christ in glory. Among men the eldest son commonly carries away all; but God's children are all—joint-heirs with Christ, they have a co-partnership with him in his riches. Has Christ a place in the celestial mansions? So have the saints. 'In my Father's house are many mansions. I go to prepare a place for you.' John xiv 2. Has he his Father's love? So have they. 'That the love wherewith thou hast loved me may be in them.' Psa cxlvi 8; John xvii 26. Does he sit upon a throne? So do God's children. Rev iii 21. What a high honour is this!

(4) God makes his children equal in honour to the angels. Luke xx 36. They are equal to the angels; nay, those saints who have God for their Father, are in some sense superior to the angels; for Jesus Christ having taken our nature, *naturam nostram nobilitavit*, says Augustine, has ennobled and honoured it above the angelic. Heb ii 16. God has made his children, by adoption, nearer to himself than the angels. The angels are the friends of Christ: believers are his members, and this honour have all the saints. What a comfort is this to God's children who are here despised, and loaded with calumnies and invectives! 'We are made as the filth of the world,' etc. 1 Cor iv 13. But God will put honour upon his children at the last day, and crown them with immortal bliss, to the envy of their adversaries.

How may we know that God is our Father? All cannot say, 'Our Father.' The Jews boasted that God was their Father. 'We have one Father, even God.' John viii 41. Christ tells them their true pedigree. 'Ye are of your father the devil;' ver 44. They who are of Satanic spirits, and make use of their power to beat down the power of godliness, cannot say, God is their Father; they may say, 'Our father who art in hell.' How then may we know that God is our Father?

(1) By having a filial disposition, which is seen in four things. [1] To melt in tears for sin as a child weeps for offending his father. When Christ looked on Peter, and Peter remembered his sin in denying him, he fell to weeping. Clemens Alexandrinus reports of Peter that he never heard a cock crow but he wept. It is a sign that God is our Father when the heart of stone

is taken away, and there is a gracious thaw in the heart; and it melts into tears for sin. He who has a childlike heart, mourns for sin in a spiritual manner, as it is sin he grieves for, as it is an act of pollution. Sin deflowers the virgin soul; it defaces God's image; it turns beauty into deformity; it is called the plague of the heart. 1 Kings viii 38. A child of God mourns for the defilement of sin; sin has to him a blacker aspect than hell.

He who has a childlike heart, grieves for sin, as it is an act of enmity. Sin is diametrically opposed to God. It is called walking contrary to God. 'If they shall confess their iniquity, and that they have walked contrary unto me.' Lev xxvi 40. It does all it can to spite God; if God be of one mind, sin will be of another; sin would not only unthrone God, but strike at his very being. If sin could help it, God would no longer be God. A childlike heart grieves for this; 'Oh!' say she, 'that I should have so much enmity in me, that my will should be no more subdued to the will of my heavenly Father!' This springs a leak of godly sorrow.

A childlike heart weeps for sin, as it is an act of ingratitude. It is an abuse of God's love; it is taking the jewels of his mercies, and making use of them to sin. God has done more for his children than others; he has planted his grace and given them some intimations of his favour; and to sin against kindness, dyes a sin in grain, and makes it crimson; like Absalom, who soon as his Father kissed him, and took him into favour, plotted treason against him. Nothing so melts a childlike heart in tears, as sins of unkindness. Oh, that I should sin against the blood of a Saviour, and the bowels of a Father! I condemn ingratitude in my child, yet I am guilty of ingratitude against my heavenly Father. This opens a vein of godly sorrow, and makes the heart bleed afresh. Certainly it evidences God to be our Father, when he has given us a childlike frame of heart, to weep for sin as it is sin, an act of pollution, enmity and ingratitude. A wicked man may mourn for the bitter fruit of sin, but only a child of God can grieve for its odious nature.

[2] A filial disposition is to be full of sympathy. We lay to heart the dishonours reflected upon our heavenly Father. When we see his worship adulterated, and his truth mingled with the poison of error, it is as a sword in our bones, to see his glory suffer. 'I beheld the transgressors and was grieved.' Psa cxix 158. Homer describing Agamemnon's grief when forced to sacrifice his daughter Iphigenia, brings in all his friends weeping and condoling with him; so, when God is dishonoured, we sympathise, and are as it were clad in mourning. A child that has any good nature, is cut to the heart to hear his father reproached; so an heir of heaven takes a dishonour done to God more heinous than a disgrace done to himself.

[3] A filial disposition, is to love our heavenly Father. He is unnatural that

[7]

does not love his father. God who is crowned with excellency, is the proper object of delight; and every true child of God says as Peter, 'Lord, thou knowest that I love thee.' But who will not say he loves God? If ours be a true genuine love to our heavenly Father, it may be known by the effects. Then we have a holy fear. There is the fear which rises from love to God, of losing the visible tokens of his presence. Eli's 'heart trembled for the ark.' 1 Sam iv 13. It is not said his heart trembled for his two sons Hophni and Phinehas; but his heart trembled for the ark, because the ark was the special sign of God's presence; and if that were taken, the glory was departed. He who loves his heavenly Father, fears lest the tokens of his presence should be removed, lest profaneness should break in like a flood, lest Popery should get head, and God should go from his people. The presence of God in his ordinances is the glory and strength of a nation. The Trojans had the image of Pallas, and they had an opinion that as long as that image was preserved among them, they should never be conquered; so, as long as God's presence is with a people they are safe. Every true child of God fears lest God should go, and the glory depart. Let us try by this whether we have a filial disposition. Do we love God, and does this love cause fear and jealousy? Are we afraid lest we should lose God's presence, lest the Sun of Righteousness should remove out of our horizon? Many are afraid lest they should lose some of their worldly profits, but not lest they should lose the presence of God. If they may have peace and trading, they care not what becomes of the ark of God. A true child of God fears nothing so much as the loss of his Father's presence. 'Woe to them when I depart from them.' Hos ix 12.

Love to our heavenly Father is seen by loving his day. 'If thou call the Sabbath a delight.' Isa lviii 13. The ancients called this *regina dierum*, the queen of days. If we love our Father in heaven, we spend this day in devotion, in reading, hearing, meditating; on this day manna falls double. God sanctified the Sabbath; he made all the other days in the week, but he has sanctified this day; this day he has crowned with a blessing. Love to our heavenly Father is seen by loving his children. 'Every one that loveth him that begat, loveth him also that is begotten of him.' 1 John v 1. If we love God, the more we see of him in any, the more we love them. We love them though they are poor, as a child loves to see his father's picture, though hung in a mean frame. We love the children of our Father, though they are persecuted. 'Onesiphorus was not ashamed of my chain.' 2 Tim i 16. Constantine kissed the hole of Paphnusius's eye, because he suffered the loss of his eye for Christ. They have no love to God, who have no love to his children; they care not for their company; they have a secret disgust and antipathy against them. Hypocrites pretend great reverence to departed saints; they canonize dead saints, but persecute living ones. I may say of these, as the apostle in Heb xii 8: they are 'bastards, not sons.'

If we love our heavenly Father, we shall be advocates for him, and stand up in the defence of his truth. He who loves his father will plead for him when he is traduced and wronged. He has no childlike heart, no love to God, who can hear his name dishonoured and be silent. Does Christ appear for us in heaven, and are we afraid to appear for him on earth? Such as dare not own God and religion in times of danger, God will be ashamed to be called their God; it will be a reproach to him to have such children as will not own him. A childlike love to God is known by its degree. We love our Father in heaven above all other things; above estate, or relations, as oil runs above the water. Psa lxxiii 25. A child of God seeing a supereminence of goodness and a constellation of all beauties in him, is carried out in love to him in the highest measure. As God gives his children electing love, such as he does not bestow upon the wicked, so his children give to him such love as they bestow upon none else. They give him the flower and spirits of their love; they love him with a love joined with worship; this spiced wine they keep only for their Father to drink of. Cant viii 2.

[4] A childlike disposition is seen in honouring our heavenly Father. 'A son honoureth his father.' Mal i 6.

We show our honour to our Father in heaven, by having a reverential awe of him upon us. 'Thou shalt fear thy God.' Lev xxv 17. This reverential fear of God, is when we dare do nothing that he has forbidden in his Word. 'How can I do this great wickedness, and sin against God?' Gen xxxix 9. It is part of the honour a son gives to a father, that he fears to displease him. We show our honour to our heavenly Father, by doing all we can to exalt him and make his excellencies shine forth. Though we cannot lift him up higher in heaven, yet we may lift him higher in our hearts, and in the esteem of others. When we speak well of God, set forth his renown, display the trophies of his goodness; when we ascribe the glory of all we do to him; when we are the trumpeters of his praise; this is honouring our Father in heaven, and a sure sign of a childlike heart. 'Whoso offereth praise, glorifieth me.' Psa l 23.

(2) We may know God is our Father by resembling him. The child is his father's picture. 'Each one resembled the children of a king'; every child of God resembles the king of heaven. Judg viii 18. Herein God's adopted children and man's differ. A man adopts one for his son and heir that does not at all resemble him; but whomsoever God adopts for his child is like him; he not only bears his heavenly Father's name, but his image. 'And have put on the new man, which is renewed after the image of him that created him.'

[9]

Col iii 10. He who has God for his Father, resembles him in holiness, which is the glory of the Godhead. Exod xv 11. The holiness of God is the intrinsic purity of his essence. He who has God for his Father, partakes of the divine nature; though not of the divine essence, yet of the divine likeness; as the seal sets its print and likeness upon the wax, so he who has God for his Father, has the print and effigies of his holiness stamped upon him. 'Aaron, the saint of the Lord.' Psa cvi 16. Wicked men desire to be like God hereafter in glory, but do not affect to be like him here in grace; they give it out to the world that God is their Father, yet have nothing of God to be seen in them; they are unclean: they are not only without his image, but hate it.

(3) We may know God is our Father by having his Spirit in us. [1] By having the intercession of the Spirit. It is a Spirit of prayer. 'Because ye are sons, God hath sent forth the Spirit of his Son into your hearts, crying Abba, Father.' Gal iv 6. Prayer is the soul's breathing itself into the bosom of its heavenly Father. None of God's children are born dumb. *Implet Spiritus Sanctus organum suum, et tanquam fila chordarum tangit Spiritus Dei corda sanctorum* [The Holy Spirit fills his instrument, and the Spirit of God touches the hearts of the saints like the threads of harp-strings]. Prosper. 'Behold, he prayeth.' Acts ix 11. But it is not every prayer that evidences God's Spirit in us. Such as have no grace may excel in gifts, and affect the hearts of others in prayer, when their own hearts are not affected; as the lute makes a sweet sound in the ears of others, but itself is not sensible.

How shall we know our prayers to be indited by the Spirit, and so he is our Father?

When they are not only vocal, but mental; when they are not only gifts, but groans. Rom viii 26. The best music is in concert: the best prayer is when the heart and tongue join together in concert.

When they are zealous and fervent. 'The effectual fervent prayer of a righteous man availeth much.' James v 16. The eyes melt in prayer, and the heart burns. Fervency is to prayer as fire to incense, which makes it ascend to heaven as a sweet perfume.

When prayer has faith mingled with it. Prayer is the key of heaven, and faith is the hand that turns it. 'We cry, Abba, Father.' Rom viii 15. 'We cry,' there is fervency in prayer; 'Abba, Father,' there is faith. Those prayers suffer shipwreck which dash upon the rock of unbelief. We may know God is our Father, by having his Spirit praying in us; as Christ intercedes above, so the Spirit intercedes within.

[2] By having the renewing of the Spirit, which is nothing else but regeneration, which is called a being born of the Spirit. John iii 5. This

regenerating work of the Spirit is a transformation, or change of nature. 'Be ye transformed by the renewing of your mind.' Rom xii 2. He who is born of God has a new heart: new, not for substance, but for qualities. The strings of a viol may be the same, but the tune is altered. Before regeneration, there are spiritual pangs, much heart-breaking for sin. It is called a circumcision of the heart. Col ii 11. In circumcision there was a pain in the flesh; so in spiritual circumcision there is pain in the heart; there is much sorrow arising from a sense of guilt and wrath. The jailor's trembling was a pang in the new birth. Acts xvi 29. God's Spirit is a spirit of bondage before it is a spirit of adoption. This blessed work of regeneration spreads over the whole soul; it irradiates the mind; it consecrates the heart, and reforms the life; though regeneration be but in part, yet it is in every part. 1 Thess v 23. Regeneration is the signature and engraving of the Holy Ghost upon the soul; the new-born Christian is bespangled with the jewels of the graces, which are the angels' glory. Regeneration is the spring of all true joy. At our first birth we come weeping into the world, but at our new birth there is cause of rejoicing; for now, God is our Father, and we are begotten to a lively hope of glory. 1 Pet i 3. We may try by this our relation to God. Has a regenerating work of God's Spirit passed upon our souls? Are we made of another spirit, humble and heavenly? This is a good sign of sonship, and we may say, 'Our Father which art in heaven.'

[3] We know God is our Father by having the conduct of the Spirit. We are led by the Spirit. 'As many as are led by the Spirit of God, they are the sons of God.' Rom viii 14. God's Spirit does not only quicken us in our regeneration, but leads us on till we come to the end of our faith. It is not enough that the child has life, but he must be led every step by the nurse. 'I taught Ephraim to go, taking them by their arms.' Hos xi 3. As the Israelites had the cloud and pillar of fire to go before them, and be a guide to them, so God's Spirit is a guide to go before us, and lead us into all truth, and counsel us in all our doubts, and influence us in all our actions. 'Thou shalt guide me with thy counsel.' Psa lxxiii 24. None can call God Father but such as have the conduct of the Spirit. Try then what spirit you are led by. Such as are led by a spirit of envy, lust, and avarice, are not led by the Spirit of God; it were blasphemy for them to call God Father; they are led by the spirit of Satan, and may say, 'Our father which art in hell.'

[4] By having the witness of the Spirit. 'The Spirit itself beareth witness with our spirit, that we are the children of God.' Rom viii 16. This witness of the Spirit, suggesting that God is our Father, is not a vocal witness or voice from heaven. The Spirit in the word witnesseth: the Spirit in the word says, he who is qualified, who is a hater of sin and a lover of holiness,

is a child of God, and God is his Father. If I can find such qualifications wrought, it is the Spirit witnessing with my spirit that I am a child of God. Besides, we may carry it higher. The Spirit of God witnesses to our spirit, by making more than ordinary impressions upon our hearts, and giving some secret hints and whispers that God has purposes of love to us, which is a concurrent witness of the Spirit with conscience, that we are heirs of heaven, and God is our Father. This witness is better felt than expressed; it scatters doubts and fears, and silences temptations. But what shall one do that has not this witness of the Spirit? If we want the witness of the Spirit, let us labour to find the work of the Spirit; if we have not the Spirit testifying, let us labour to have it sanctifying, and that will be a support to us.

(4) If God be our Father, we are of peaceable spirits. 'Blessed are the peacemakers: for they shall be called the children of God.' Matt v 9. Grace infuses a sweet, amicable disposition; it files off the ruggedness of men's spirits; it turns the lion-like fierceness into a lamb-like gentleness. Isa xi 7. They who have God to be their Father follow peace as well as holiness. God the Father is called the 'God of peace,' Heb xiii 20: God the Son, the 'Prince of Peace,' Isa ix 6: God the Holy Ghost, a Spirit of peace; 'the unity of the Spirit in the bond of peace.' Eph iv 3. The more peaceable, the more like God. God is not the Father of those who are fierce and cruel, as if, with Romulus, they had sucked the milk of a wolf. 'The way of peace have they not known.' Rom iii 17. They sport in mischief, and are of a persecuting spirit, as Maximinus, Diocletian, Antiochus, who, as Eusebius says, took more tedious journeys, and ran more hazards in vexing and persecuting the Jews, than any of his predecessors had done in obtaining victories. These furies cannot call God Father. If they do, they will have as little comfort in saying Father, as Dives had in hell, when he said, 'Father Abraham.' Luke xvi 24. Nor can those who are makers of division. 'Mark them which cause divisions, and avoid them.' Rom xvi 17. Such as are born of God, are makers of peace. What shall we think of such as are makers of divisions? Will God father these? The devil made the first division in heaven. They may call the devil father; they may give the cloven foot in their coat of arms; their sweetest music is in discord; they unite to divide. Samson's fox tails were tied together only to set the Philistines' corn on fire. Judges xv 4. Papists unite only to set the church's peace on fire. Satan's kingdom grows up by making divisions. Chrysostom observes of the church of Corinth, that when many converts were brought in, Satan knew no better way to dam up the current of religion than to throw in an apple of strife, and divide them into parties: one was for Paul, and another for Apollos, but few for Christ. Would Christ not have his coat rent, and can he endure to have his body rent? Surely, God will never father them who are not sons of peace.

Of all those whom God hates, he is named for one who is a sower of discord among brethren. Prov vi 19.

(5) If God be our Father, we shall love to be near him, and to have converse with him. An ingenuous child delights to approach near to his father, and go into his presence. David envied the birds that built their nest near to God's altars, when he was debarred his Father's house. Psa lxxxiv 3. True saints love to get as near to God as they can. In the word they draw near to his holy oracle, in the sacrament they draw near to his table. A child of God delights to be in his Father's presence; he cannot stay away long from God; he sees a Sabbath-day approaching, and rejoices; his heart has been often melted and quickened in an ordinance; he has tasted that the Lord is good, therefore he loves to be in his Father's presence; he cannot keep away long from God. Such as care not for ordinances cannot say, 'Our Father which art in heaven.' Is God the Father of those who cannot endure to be in his presence?

Use 1. For instruction. See the amazing goodness of God, that he is pleased to enter into the sweet relation of a Father to us. He needed not to adopt us, he did not want a Son, but we wanted a Father. He showed power in being our Maker, but mercy in being our Father. That when we were enemies, and our hearts stood out as garrisons against God, he should conquer our stubbornness, and of enemies make us children, and write his name, and put his image upon us, and bestow a kingdom of glory; what a miracle of mercy is this! Every adopted child may say, 'Even so, Father, for so it seemed good in thy sight.' Matt xi 26.

If God be a Father, then I infer that whatever he does to his children, is in love.

(1) If he smiles upon them in prosperity, it is in love. They have the world not only with God's leave, but with his love. He says to every child of his, as Naaman to Gehazi, 'Be content, take two talents.' 2 Kings v 23. So God says to his child, 'I am thy Father, take two talents.' Take health, and take my love with it; take an estate, and take my love with it: take two talents. His love is a sweetening ingredient in every mercy.

How does it appear that a child of God has worldly things in love?

Because he has a good title to them. God is his father, therefore he has a good title. A wicked man has a civil title to the creature, but no more; he has it not from the hand of a father; he is like one that takes up cloth at the draper's, and it is not paid for; but a believer has a good title to every foot of land he has, for his Father has settled it upon him.

A child of God has worldly things in love, because they are sanctified to him. They make him better, and are loadstones to draw him nearer to God. He has his Father's blessing with them. A little that is blest is sweet. 'He shall bless thy bread and thy water.' Exod xxiii 25. Esau had the venison, but Jacob got the blessing. While the wicked have their meat sauced with God's wrath, believers have their comforts seasoned with a blessing. Psa lxxviii 30, 31. It was a sacred blessing from God that made Daniel's pulse nourish him more, and made him look fairer than they that ate of the king's meat. Dan i 15.

A child of God has worldly things in love, because whatever he has is an earnest of more; every bit of bread is a pledge and earnest of glory.

(2) God being a Father, if he frown, if he dip his pen in gall, and write bitter things, if he correct, it is in love. A father loves his child as well when he chastises and disciplines him, as when he settles his land on him. 'As many as I love, I rebuke.' Rev iii 19. Afflictions are sharp arrows, says Gregory Nazianzen, but they are shot from the hand of a loving Father. *Correctio est virtutis gymnasium* [Correction is the school of character]. God afflicts with love: he doth it to humble and purify. Gentle correction is as necessary as daily bread; nay, as needful as ordinances, as word and sacraments. There is love in all: God smites that he may save.

(3) God being a Father, if he desert and hide his face from his child, it is in love. Desertion is sad in itself, a short hell. Job vi 9. When the light is withdrawn, the dew falls. Yet we may see a rainbow in the cloud – the love of a Father in all this. God hereby quickens grace. Perhaps grace lay dormant. Cant v 2. It was as fire in the embers, and God withdrew comfort to invigorate and exercise it. Faith as a star sometimes shines brightest in the dark night of desertion. Jonah ii 4. When God hides his face from his child, he is still a Father, and his heart is towards his child. As when Joseph spake roughly to his brethren, and made them believe he would take them for spies, his heart was full of love, and he was fain to go aside and weep; so God's bowels yearn towards his children when he seems to look strange. 'In a little wrath I hid my face from thee, but with everlasting kindness will I have mercy on thee.' Isa liv 8. Though God may have the look of an enemy, yet still he has the heart of a Father.

Learn hence the sad case of the wicked. They cannot say, 'Our Father in heaven;' they may say, 'Our Judge,' but not 'Our Father;' they fetch their pedigree from hell. 'Ye are of your father the devil.' John viii 44. Such as are unclean and profane, are the spurious brood of the old serpent, and it were blasphemy for them to call God Father. The case of the wicked is deplorable; if they are in misery, they have none to make their moan to. God is not their Father, he disclaims all kindred with them. 'I never knew you: depart from me, ye that work iniquity.' Matt vii 23. The wicked, dying in their sins, can expect no mercy from God as a Father. Many say, He that made them will save them; but 'It is a people of no understanding; therefore he that made them will not have mercy on them.' Isa xxvii 11. Though God was their Father by creation, yet because they were not his children by adoption, therefore He that made them would not save them.

Use 2. For invitation. Let all who are yet strangers to God, labour to come into this heavenly kindred; never cease till they can say, 'Our Father which art in heaven.'

But will God be a Father to me, who has profaned his name, and been a great sinner?

If thou wilt now at last seek God by prayer, and break off thy sins, he has the bowels of a Father for thee, and will in nowise cast thee out. When the prodigal arose and went to his father, 'his father had compassion, and ran and fell on his neck, and kissed him.' Luke xv 20. Though thou hast been a prodigal, and almost spent all upon thy lusts, yet if thou wilt give a bill of divorce to thy sins, and flee to God by repentance, know that he has the bowels of a Father; he will embrace thee in the arms of his mercy, and seal thy pardon with a kiss. What though thy sins have been heinous? The wound is not so broad as the plaister of Christ's blood. The sea covers great rocks; the sea of God's compassion can drown thy great sins; therefore be not discouraged, go to God, resolve to cast thyself upon his Fatherly compassion. He may be entreated of thee, as he was of Manasseh. 2 Chron xxxiii 13.

Use 3. For comfort. Here is comfort for such as can, upon good grounds, call God Father. There is more sweetness in this word Father than if we had ten thousand worlds. David thought it a great matter to be son-in-law to a king. 'What is my father's family, that I should be son-in-law to the king?' 1 Sam xviii 18. But what is it to be born of God, and have him for our Father?

Wherein lies the happiness of having God for our Father?

(1) If God be our Father, he will teach us. What father will refuse to counsel his son? Does God command parents to instruct their children, and will not he instruct his? Deut iv 10. 'I am the Lord thy God, which teacheth thee to profit.' Isa xlviii 17. 'O God, thou hast taught me from my youth.' Psa lxxi 17. If God be our Father, he will give us the teachings of his Spirit. 'The natural man receiveth not the things of God, neither can he know them.' 1 Cor ii 14. The natural man may have excellent notions in divinity, but God must teach us to know the mysteries of the gospel after a spiritual

manner. A man may see the figures upon a dial, but he cannot tell how the day goes unless the sun shines; so we may read many truths in the Bible, but we cannot know them savingly, till God by his Spirit shines upon our soul. God teaches not only our ear, but our heart; he not only informs our mind, but inclines our will. We never learn aught till God teach us. If he be our Father, he will teach us how to order our affairs with discretion (Psa cxii 5) and how to carry ourselves wisely. 'David behaved himself wisely.' 1 Sam xviii 5. He will teach us what to answer when we are brought before governors; he will put words into our mouths. 'Ye shall be brought before governors and kings for my sake; but take no thought how or what ye shall speak; for it is not ye that speak, but the Spirit of your Father which speaketh in you.' Matt x 18, 19, 20.

(2) If God be our Father, he has bowels of affection towards us. If it be so unnatural for a father not to love his child, can we think God can be defective in his love? All the affections of parents come from God, yet are they but a spark from his flame. He is the Father of mercies. 2 Cor i 3. He begets all the mercies and bowels in the creature; his love to his children is a love which passeth knowledge. Eph iii 19. It exceeds all dimensions; it is higher than heaven, it is broader than the sea. That you may see God's fatherly love to his children: Consider, God makes a precious valuation of them. 'Since thou wast precious in my sight.' Isa xliii 4. A father prizes his child above his jewels. Their names are precious, for they have God's own name written upon them. 'I will write upon him the name of my God.' Rev iii 12. Their prayers are a precious perfume; their tears he bottles. Psa lvi 8. He esteems his children as a crown of glory in his hands. Isa lxii 3. God loves the places where they were born in for their sakes. 'Of Zion it shall be said, This and that man was born in her'; this and that believer was born there. Psa lxxxvii 5. He loves the ground his children tread upon; hence, Judea, the seat of his children and chosen ones, he calls a delightsome land. Mal iii 12. It was not only pleasant for situation and fruitfulness, but because his children, who were his *Hephzibah*, or delight, lived there. He charges the great ones of the world not to injure his children, because their persons are sacred. 'He suffered no man to do them wrong; yea, he reproved kings for their sakes, saying, Touch not mine anointed.' Psa cv 14, 15. By anointed is meant the children of the high God, who have the unction of the Spirit, and are set apart for God. He delights in their company. He loves to see their countenance, and hear their voice. Cant ii 14. He cannot refrain long from their company; let but two or three of his children meet and pray together, he will be sure to be among them. 'Where two or three are gathered together in my name, there am I in the midst of them.' Matt xviii 20. He bears his children in his bosom, as a nursing father does the sucking

child. Numb xi 12; Isa xlvi 4. To be carried in God's bosom shows how near his children lie to his heart. He is full of solicitous care for them. 'He careth for you.' 1 Peter v 7. His eye is still upon them, they are never out of his thoughts. A father cannot always take care for his child, he sometimes is asleep; but God is a Father that never sleeps. 'He shall neither slumber nor sleep.' Psa cxxi 4. He thinks nothing too good to part with for his children; he gives them the kidneys of the wheat, and honey out of the rock, and 'wines on the lees well refined.' Isa xxv 6. He gives them three jewels more worth than heaven – the blood of his Son, the grace of his Spirit, and the light of his countenance. Never was there such an indulgent, affectionate Father. If he has one love better than another, he bestows it upon them; they have the cream and quintessence of his love. 'He will rejoice over thee, he will rest in his love.' Zeph iii 17. He loves his children with such a love as he loves Christ. John xvii 26. It is the same love, for the unchangeableness of it. God will no more cease to love his adopted sons than he will to love his natural Son.

(3) If God be our Father, he will be full of sympathy. 'As a father pitieth his children, so the Lord pitieth them that fear him.' Psa ciii 13. 'Is Ephraim my dear son? my bowels are troubled for him.' Jer xxxi 20. God pities his children in two cases.

[1] In case of infirmities. If the child be deformed, or has any bodily distemper, the father pities it; so, if God be our Father, he pities our weaknesses: and he so pities them as to heal them. 'I have seen his ways, and will heal him.' Isa lvii 18. As he has bowels to pity, so he has balsam to heal.

[2] In case of injuries. Every blow of the child goes to the father's heart; so, when the saints suffer, God sympathises. 'In all their affliction he was afflicted.' Isa lxiii 9. He did, as it were, bleed in their wounds. 'Saul, Saul, why persecutest thou me?' When the foot was trod on, the head cried out. God's soul was grieved for the children of Israel. Judges x 16. As when one string in a lute is touched, all the rest sound; so when God's children are stricken, his bowels sound. 'He that toucheth you toucheth the apple of his eye.' Zech ii 8.

(4) If God be our Father, he will take notice of the least good he sees in us; if there be but a sigh for sin, he hears it. 'My groaning is not hid from thee.' Psa xxxviii 9. If but a penitential tear comes out of the eye he sees it. 'I have seen thy tears.' Isa xxxviii 5. If there be but a good intention, he takes notice of it. 'Whereas it was in thine heart to build an house unto my name, thou didst well that it was in thine heart.' 1 Kings viii 18. He punishes intentional wickedness, and crowns intentional goodness. 'Thou didst well that it was in thine heart.' He takes notice of the least *scintilla*, the least spark of grace

[17]

in his children. 'Sara obeyed Abraham, calling him lord.' 1 Peter iii 6. The Holy Ghost does not mention Sara's unbelief, or laughing at the promise; he puts a finger upon the scar, winks at her failing, and only takes notice of the good that was in her, her obedience to her husband – she 'obeyed Abraham, calling him lord.' Nay, that good which the saints scarce take notice of in themselves, God in a special manner observes. 'I was an hungred, and ye gave me meat; I was thirsty, and ye gave me drink. Then shall the righteous answer, Lord, when saw we thee an hungred and fed thee?' Matt xxv 35, 37. They as it were overlooked and disclaimed their own works of charity, but Christ takes notice of them – 'I was an hungred, and ye fed me.' What comfort is this! God spies the least good in his children; he can see a grain of corn hid under chaff, grace hid under corruption.

(5) If God be our Father, he will take all we do in good part. Those duties which we ourselves censure he will crown. When a child of God looks over his best duties, he sees so much sin cleaving to them that he is confounded. 'Lord,' he says, 'there is more sulphur than incense in my prayers.' But for your comfort, if God be your Father, he will crown those duties which you yourselves censure. He sees there is sincerity in the hearts of his children, and this gold, though light, shall have grains of allowance. Though there may be many defects in the services of his children, he will not cast away their offering. 'The Lord healed the people.' 2 Chron xxx 20. The tribes of Israel, being straitened in time, wanted some legal purifications; yet because their hearts were right God healed them and pardoned them. He accepts of the good will. 2 Cor viii 12. A father takes a letter from his son kindly, though there are blots or bad English in it. What blottings are there in our holy things! Yet our Father in heaven accepts them. 'It is my child,' God says, 'and he will do better; I will look upon him, through Christ, with a merciful eye.'

(6) If God be our Father, he will correct us in measure. 'I will correct thee in measure.' Jer xxx 11. This he will do two ways. It shall be in measure, *for the kind.* He will not lay upon us more than we are able to bear. 1 Cor x 13. He knows our frame. Psa ciii 14. He knows we are not steel or marble, therefore will deal gently, he will not over-afflict. As the physician, who knows the temper of the body, will not give physic too strong for the body, nor give one drachm or scruple too much, so God, who has not only the title, but the bowels of a father, will not lay too heavy burdens on his children, lest their spirits fail before him. He will correct in measure, *for duration;* he will not let the affliction lie too long. 'The rod of the wicked shall not rest upon the lot of the righteous,' Psa cxxv 3. It may be there, but not rest. 'I will not contend for ever.' Isa lvii 16. Our heavenly Father will

love for ever, but he will not contend for ever. The torments of the damned are for ever. 'The smoke of their torment ascendeth up for ever and ever.' Rev xiv 11. The wicked shall drink a sea of wrath, but God's children only taste of the cup of affliction, and their heavenly Father will say, *transeat calix*, 'let this cup pass away from them.' Isa xxxv 10.

(7) If God be our Father, he will intermix mercy with all our afflictions. If he gives us wormwood to drink, he will mix it with honey. In the ark the rod was laid up and manna; so with our Father's rod there is always some manna. Asher's shoes were iron and brass, but his foot was dipped in oil. Deut xxxiii 24, 25. Affliction is the shoe of brass that pinches; but there is mercy in the affliction, there is the foot dipped in oil. When God afflicts the body, he gives peace of conscience; there is mercy in the affliction. An affliction comes to prevent falling into sin; there is mercy in an affliction. Jacob had his thigh hurt in wrestling; there was the affliction: but when he saw God's face, and received a blessing from the angel, there was mercy in the affliction. Gen xxxii 30. In every cloud a child of God may see a rainbow of mercy shining. As the painter mixeth dark shadows and bright colours together, so our heavenly Father mingles the dark and bright together, crosses and blessings; and is not this a great happiness, for God thus to chequer his providences, and mingle goodness with severity?

(8) If God be our Father, the evil one shall not prevail against us. Satan is called the evil one, emphatically. He is the grand enemy of the saints; and that both in a military sense, as he fights against them with his temptations; and in a forensic or law sense, as he is an accuser, and pleads against them; yet neither way shall he prevail against God's children. As for shooting his fiery darts, God will bruise Satan shortly under the saints' feet. Rom xvi 20. As for his accusing, Christ is an advocate for the saints, and answers all bills of indictment brought against them. God will make all Satan's temptations promote the good of his children. [1] As they set them praying. 2 Cor xii 8. Temptation is a medicine for security. [2] As they are a means to humble them. 'Lest I should be exalted above measure, there was given to me a thorn in the flesh, the messenger of Satan.' 2 Cor xii 7. The thorn in the flesh was a temptation; it was to prick the bladder of pride. [3] As they establish them more in grace. A tree shaken by the wind is more settled and rooted; so the blowing of a temptation does but settle a child of God more in grace. Thus the evil one, Satan, shall not prevail against the children of God.

(9) If God be our Father, no real evil shall befall us. 'There shall no evil befall thee.' Psa xci 10. It is not said, no trouble; but, no evil. God's children are privileged persons; they are privileged from being hurt of every thing. 'Nothing shall by any means hurt you.' Luke x 19. The hurt and malignity of the affliction is taken away. Affliction to a wicked man has evil in it; it

[19]

makes him worse. 'Men were scorched with great heat and blasphemed the name of God.' Rev xvi 9. But no evil befalls a child of God; he is bettered by affliction. 'That we might be made partakers of his holiness.' Heb xii 10. What hurt does the furnace to the gold? It only makes it purer. What hurt does affliction to grace? Only refine and purify it. What a great privilege it is to be freed, though not from the stroke, yet from the sting of affliction! No evil shall touch a saint. When the dragon, say they, has poisoned the water, the unicorn with his horn draws out the poison. Christ has drawn the poison out of every affliction, that it cannot injure a child of God. Again, no evil befalls a child of God, because no condemnation. 'No condemnation to them which are in Christ Jesus.' Rom viii 1. God does not condemn them, nor does conscience. When both jury and judge acquit, no evil befalls the accused; for nothing is really an evil but that which damns.

(10) If God be our Father, we may go with cheerfulness to the throne of grace. Were a man to petition his enemy, there were little hope; but when a child petitions his father, he may hope with confidence to succeed. The word 'Father' works upon God; it toucheth his very bowels. What can a father deny his child? 'If his son ask bread, will he give him a stone?' Matt vii 9. This may embolden us to go to God for pardon of sin, and further degrees of sanctity. We pray to a Father of mercy sitting upon a throne of grace. 'If ye then, being evil, know how to give good gifts to your children, how much more shall your heavenly Father give the Holy Spirit to them that ask him?' Luke xi 13. This quickens the church, and adds wing to prayer. 'Look down from heaven.' Isa lxiii 15. 'Doubtless thou art our Father'; ver 16. For whom does God keep his mercies but for his children? Three things may give boldness in prayer. We have a Father to pray to, and the Spirit to help us to pray, and an Advocate to present our prayers. God's children should in all their troubles run to their heavenly Father, as the sick child in 2 Kings iv 19: 'He said unto his father, My head, my head.' So pour out thy complaint to God in prayer. 'Father, my heart, my heart; my dead heart, quicken it; my hard heart, soften it in Christ's blood. Father, my heart, my heart.' Surely God, who hears the cry of ravens, will hear the cry of his children!

(11) If God be our Father, he will stand between us and danger. A father will keep off danger from his child. God calls himself *Scutum*, a shield. As a shield he defends the head, guards the vitals, and shields off dangers from his children. 'I am with thee, and no man shall set on thee to hurt thee.' Acts xviii 10. God is a hiding-place. Psa xxvii 5. He preserved Athanasius strangely; he put it into his mind to depart out of the house he was in, the night before the enemy came to search for him. As God has a breast to feed, so he has wings to cover his children. 'He shall cover thee with his feathers,

and under his wings shalt thou trust.' Psa xci 4. He appoints his holy angels to be a lifeguard about his children. Heb i 14. Never was any prince so well guarded as a believer. The angels [1] are a numerous guard. 'The mountain was full of horses of fire round about Elisha.' 2 Kings vi 17. 'The horses and chariots of fire' were the angels of God to defend the prophet Elisha. [2] A strong guard. One angel, in a night, slew a hundred and fourscore and five thousand. 2 Kings xix 35. If one angel slew so many, what would an army of angels have done? [3] The angels are a swift guard; they are ready in an instant to help God's children. They are described with wings to show their swiftness: they fly to our help. 'At the beginning of thy supplications the commandment came forth, and I am come.' Dan ix 23. Here was swift motion for the angel, to come from heaven to earth between the beginning and ending of Daniel's prayer. [4] The angels are a watchful guard; not like Saul's guard, asleep when their lord was in danger. 1 Sam xxvi 12. The angels are a vigilant guard; they watch over God's children to defend them. 'The angel of the Lord encampeth round about them that fear him.' Psa xxxiv 7. There is an invisible guardianship of angels about God's children.

(12) If God be our Father, we shall not want anything that he sees to be good for us. 'They that seek the Lord shall not want any good thing.' Psa xxxiv 10. God is pleased sometimes to keep his children on hard commons, but it is good for them. As sheep thrive best on short pasture, so God sees too much may not be good for his people; plenty might breed surfeit. *Luxuriant animi rebus secundis* [In prosperity men's characters run riot]. God sees it good sometimes to diet his children, and keep them short, that they may run the heavenly race the better. It was good for Jacob that there was a famine in the land; it was the means of bringing him to his son Joseph; so God's children sometimes see the world's emptiness, that they may acquaint themselves more with Christ's fulness. If God sees it to be good for them to have more of the world, they shall have it. He will not let them want any good thing.

(13) If God be our Father, all the promises of the Bible belong to us. His children are called 'heirs of promise.' Heb vi 17. A wicked man can lay claim to nothing in the Bible but the curses; he has no more to do absolutely with the promises than a ploughman has to do with the city charter. The promises are children's bread; they are *mulctralia evangelii*, the breasts of the gospel milking out consolations; and who are to suck these breasts but God's children? The promise of pardon is for them. 'I will pardon all their iniquities, whereby they have sinned against me.' Jer xxxiii 8. The promise of healing is for them. Isa lvii 19. The promise of salvation is for them. Jer xxiii 6. The promises are the supports of faith; they are God's sealed deed; they are a Christian's cordial. Oh, the heavenly comforts which are distilled

from the promises! Chrysostom compares the Scripture to a garden: the promises are the fruit trees that grow in this garden. A child of God may go to any promise in the Bible, and pluck comfort from it; he is an heir of the promise.

(14) God makes all his children conquerors. They conquer themselves; *fortior est qui se quam qui fortissima vincit moenia* [he who conquers himself is stronger than he who conquers the stoutest ramparts]. The saints conquer their own lusts; they bind these princes in fetters of iron. Psa cxlix 8. Though the children of God may be sometimes foiled, and lose a single battle, yet not the victory. They conquer the world. The world holds forth her two breasts of profit and pleasure, and many are overcome by it; but the children of God have a world-conquering faith. 'This is the victory that overcometh the world, even our faith.' 1 John v 4. They conquer their enemies. How can that be, when their enemies often take away their lives? They conquer, by not complying with them; as the three children would not fall down to the golden image. Dan iii 18. They would rather burn than bow. Thus they were conquerors. He who complies with another's lust, is a captive; he who refuses to comply, is a conqueror. God's children conquer their enemies by heroic patience. A patient Christian, like the anvil, bears all strokes invincibly. Thus the martyrs overcame their enemies by patience. God's children are more than conquerors. 'We are more than conquerors.' Rom viii 37. How are they more than conquerors? Because they conquer without loss, and because they are crowned after death, which other conquerors are not.

(15) If God be our Father, he will now and then send us some token of his love. His children live far from home, and meet sometimes with coarse usage from the unkind world; therefore, to encourage them, he sends them tokens and pledges of his love. What are these? He gives them an answer to prayer, which is a token of love; he quickens and enlarges their hearts in duty, which is a token of love; he gives them the first fruits of his Spirit, which are love tokens. Rom viii 23. As he gives the wicked the first fruits of hell, horror of conscience and despair, so he gives his children the first fruits of his Spirit, joy and peace, which are foretastes of glory. Some of his children, having received those tokens of love from him, have been so transported, that they have died for joy, as the glass often breaks with the strength of the wine put into it.

(16) If God be our Father, he will indulge and spare us. 'I will spare them, as a man spareth his own son that serveth him.' Mal iii 17. God's sparing his children, imports his clemency towards them. He does not punish them as he might. 'He hath not dealt with us after our sins.' Psa ciii 10. We often do which which merits wrath, grieve God's Spirit, and relapse into sin. God

passes by much and spares us. He did not spare his natural Son, and yet he spares his adopted sons. Rom viii 32. He threatened Ephraim to make him as the chaff driven with the whirlwind, but he soon repented. 'Yet I am the Lord thy God.' Hos xiii 4. 'I will be thy king;' ver 10. Here God spared him, as a father spares his son. Israel often provoked God with their complaints, but he used clemency towards them; he often answered their murmurings with mercies. Thus he spared them, as a father spares his son.

(17) If God be our Father, he will put honour and renown upon us at the last day. [1] He will clear the innocence of his children. His children in this life are strangely misrepresented. They are loaded with invectives – they are called factious, seditious; as Elijah, the troubler of Israel; and Luther, the trumpet of rebellion. Athanasius was accused to the Emperor Constantine as the raiser of tumults; and the primitive Christians were accused as *infanticidii, incestus rei*, 'killers of their children, guilty of incest.' Tertullus reported Paul to be a pestilent person. Acts xxiv 5. Famous Wycliffe was called the idol of the heretics, and reported to have died drunk. If Satan cannot defile God's children, he will disgrace them; if he cannot strike his fiery darts into their consciences he will put a dead fly to their names; but God will one day clear their innocence; he will roll away their reproach. As he will make a resurrection of bodies, so of names. 'The Lord God will wipe away tears from off all faces, and the rebuke of his people shall he take away.' Isa xxv 8. He will be the saints' vindicator. 'He shall bring forth thy righteousness as the light.' Psa xxxvii 6. The night casts its dark mantle upon the most beautiful flowers; but the light comes in the morning and dispels the darkness, and every flower appears in its orient brightness. So the wicked may by misreports darken the honour and repute of the saints; but God will dispel this darkness, and cause their names to shine forth. 'He shall bring forth thy righteousness as the light.' Thus God stood up for the honour of Moses when Aaron and Miriam sought to eclipse his fame. 'Wherefore then were ye not afraid to speak against my servant Moses?' Numb xii 8. So God will one day say to the wicked, 'Wherefore were ye not afraid to defame and traduce my children? Having my image upon them, how durst you abuse my picture?' At last his children shall come forth out of all their calumnies, as 'a dove covered with silver, and her feathers with yellow gold.' Psa lxviii 13. [2] God will make an open and honourable recital of all their good deeds. As the sins of the wicked shall be openly mentioned, to their eternal infamy and confusion; so all the good deeds of the saints shall be openly mentioned, 'and then shall every man have praise of God.' 1 Cor iv 5. Every prayer made with melting eyes, every good service, every work of charity, shall be openly declared before men and angels. 'I was an hungred, and ye gave me meat: thirsty, and ye

gave me drink: naked, and ye clothed me.' Matt xxv 35, 36. Thus God will set a trophy of honour upon all his children at the last day. 'Then shall the righteous shine forth as the sun in the kingdom of their Father.' Matt xiii 43.

(18) If God be our Father, he will settle a good inheritance upon us. 'Blessed be the God and Father of our Lord Jesus, which hath begotten us again unto a lively hope, to an inheritance incorruptible, and undefiled.' 1 Pet i 3, 4. A father may have lost his goods, and have nothing to leave his son but his blessing; but God will settle an inheritance on his children, and an inheritance no less than a kingdom. 'It is your Father's good pleasure to give you the kingdom.' Luke xii 32. This kingdom is more glorious and magnificent than any earthly kingdom; it is set out by pearls, precious stones, and the richest jewels. Rev xxi 19. What are all the rarities of the world, the coasts of pearl, the islands of spices, the rocks of diamonds, to this kingdom? In this heavenly kingdom is satisfying, unparalleled beauty, rivers of pleasure, and that for ever. 'At thy right hand are pleasures for evermore.' Psa xvi 11. Heaven's eminence is its permanence; and this kingdom God's children enter into immediately after death. There is a sudden transition and passage from death to glory. 'Absent from the body, present with the Lord.' 2 Cor v 8. God's children shall not wait long for their inheritance; it is but winking, and they shall see God. How should this comfort those of God's children who are low in the world! Your Father in heaven will settle a kingdom upon you at death, such a kingdom as eye hath not seen; he will give you a crown not of gold, but glory; he will give you white robes lined with immortality. 'It is your Father's good pleasure to give you the kingdom.'

(19) If God be our Father, it is a comfort in case of the loss of relations. Hast thou lost a father? If thou art a believer, thou art no orphan, thou hast a heavenly Father, a Father that never dies. 'Who only hath immortality.' 1 Tim vi 16. It is comfort in case of your own death. God is thy Father, and death is but going to thy Father. Well might Paul say death is yours. 1 Cor iii 22. It is your friend that will carry you home to your Father. How glad are children when they are going home! It was Christ's comfort at death that he was going to his Father. 'I leave the world, and go to the Father.' John xvi 28. 'I ascend unto my Father.' John xx 17. If God be our Father, we may with comfort, at the day of death, resign our souls into his hand. Thus did Christ. 'Father, into thy hands I commend my spirit.' Luke xxiii 46. If a child has any jewel, he will in time of danger put it into his father's hands, where he thinks it will be kept most safe; so the soul, which is our richest jewel, we may resign at death into God's hands, where it will be safer than in our own keeping. 'Father, into thy hands I commend my spirit.' What a comfort it is that death carries a believer to his Father's

house, where are delights unspeakable and full of glory! How glad was old Jacob when he saw the waggons and chariots to carry him to his son Joseph! 'The spirit of Jacob revived.' Gen xlv 27. Death is a triumphant chariot, to carry every child of God to his Father's mansion-house.

(20) If God be our Father, he will not disinherit us. He may for a time desert his children, but will not disinherit them. The sons of kings have sometimes been disinherited by the cruelty of usurpers; as the son of Alexander the Great was put out of his just right, through the violence and ambition of his father's captains; but what power on earth can hinder the heirs of the promise from their inheritance? Men cannot, and God will not, cut off the entail. The Arminians hold falling away from grace, so that a child of God may be deprived of his inheritance; but God's children can never be degraded or disinherited, and their heavenly Father will not cast them off from being children. It is evident that God's children cannot be finally disinherited, by virtue of the eternal decree of heaven. God's decree is the very pillar and basis on which the saints' perseverance depends. That decree ties the knot of adoption so fast, that neither sin, death, nor hell, can break it asunder. 'Whom he did predestinate, them he also called,' &c. Rom viii 30. Predestination is nothing else but God's decreeing a certain number to be heirs of glory, on whom he will settle the crown; for whom he predestinates, he glorifies. What shall hinder God's electing love, or make his decree null and void? Besides God's decree, he has engaged himself by promise, that the heirs of heaven shall never be put out of their inheritance. His promises are not like blanks in a lottery, but as a sealed deed which cannot be reversed; they are the saints' royal charter; and one promise is that their heavenly Father will not disinherit them. 'I will make an everlasting covenant with them, that I will not turn away from them; but I will put my fear in their hearts, that they shall not depart from me.' Jer xxxii 40. God's fidelity, which is the richest pearl of his crown, is engaged in this promise for his children's perseverance. 'I will not turn away from them.' A child of God cannot fall away while he is held fast in these two arms of God – his love, and his faithfulness. Jesus Christ undertakes that all God's children by adoption shall be preserved in a state of grace till they inherit glory. The heathens feigned of Atlas that he bore up the heavens from falling; but Jesus Christ is that blessed Atlas that bears up the saints from falling away.

How does Christ preserve the saints' graces, till they come to heaven?

(1) *Influxu Spiritus* [By the influence of the Spirit]. He carries on grace in the souls of the elect, by the influence and co-operation of his Spirit. He continually excites and quickens grace in the godly; he by his Spirit blows

up the sparks of grace into a holy flame. *Spiritus est vicarius Christi;* the Spirit is Christ's vicar on earth, his proxy, his executor, to see that all that he has purchased for the saints be made good. Christ has obtained for them an inheritance incorruptible, and the Spirit is his executor, to see that the inheritance be settled upon them. 1 Pet i 4, 5. (2) He carries on his work perseveringly in the souls of the elect, by the prevalence of his intercession. 'He ever liveth to make intercession for them.' Heb vii 25. He prays that every saint may hold out in grace till he comes to heaven. Can the children of such prayers perish? If the heirs of heaven should be disinherited, and fall short of glory, then God's decree must be reversed, his promise broken, and Christ's prayer frustrated, which would be blasphemy to imagine.

(3) That God's children cannot be disinherited, or put out of their right to the crown of heaven, is evident from their mystic union with Christ. Believers are incorporated into him; they are knit to him as members to the head, by the nerves and ligaments of faith, so that they cannot be broken off. 'The church, which is his body.' Eph i 22, 23. What was once said of Christ's natural body, is as true of his mystic body. 'A bone of it shall not be broken.' As it is impossible to sever the leaven and the dough when they are once mingled and kneaded together, so it is impossible, when Christ and believers are once united, that they should ever, by the power of death or hell, be separated. Christ and his spiritual members make one Christ. Is it possible that any part of Christ should perish? How can Christ want any member of his mystic body and be perfect? Every member is an ornament to the body, and adds to the honour of it. How can Christ part with any mystic member, and not part with some of his glory too? By all this it is evident that God's children must needs persevere in grace, and cannot be disinherited. If they could be disinherited, the Scripture could not be fulfilled, which tells us of glorious rewards for the heirs of promise. 'Verily there is a reward for the righteous.' Psa lviii 11. If God's adopted children should fall away finally from grace, and miss of heaven, what reward would there be for the righteous? Moses indiscreetly looked for the recompense of the reward, and a door would be opened to despair.

But the doctrine of final perseverance, and the certainty of the heavenly inheritance may lead to carnal security, and unholy walking.

Corrupt nature may suck poison from this flower; but he who has felt the efficacy of grace upon his heart, dares not abuse this doctrine. He knows that perseverance is attained in the use of means, and walks holily, that in the use of the means he may arrive at perseverance. Paul knew that he should not be disinherited, and that nothing could separate him from the love of Christ; but who more holy and watchful than he was? 'I keep under my body.' 1 Cor ix 27. 'I press toward the mark.' Phil iii 14. God's children have a holy fear which keeps them from self-security and wantonness; they believe the promise, therefore they rejoice in hope; they fear their hearts, therefore they watch and pray.

Thus you see what strong consolation there is for all the heirs of the promise. Such as have God for their Father are the happiest persons on earth; they are in such a condition that nothing can hurt them; they have their Father's blessing, all things conspire for their good; they have a kingdom settled on them, and the entail can never be cut off. How comforted should they be in all conditions, let the times be what they will! Their Father who is in heaven rules over all. If troubles arise, they carry them sooner to their Father. The more violently the wind beats against the sails of a ship, the sooner it is brought to the haven; and the more fiercely God's children are assaulted, the sooner they come to their Father's house. 'Wherefore comfort one another with these words.' 1 Thess iv 18.

Use 4. For exhortation. Let us behave ourselves as the children of such a Father.

(1) Let us depend upon him in all our straits and exigencies; let us believe that he will provide for all our wants. Children rely upon their parents for the supply of their wants. If we trust God for salvation, shall we not trust him for a livelihood? There is a lawful and prudent care to be used, but beware of being distrustful. 'Consider the ravens: for they neither sow nor reap; and God feedeth them.' Luke xii 24. Does God feed the birds of the air, and will he not feed his children? 'Consider the lilies how they grow: they spin not; yet Solomon in all his glory was not arrayed like one of these;' ver 27. Does God clothe the lilies, and will he not clothe his lambs? Even the wicked taste of his bounty. 'Their eyes stand out with fatness.' Psa lxxiii 7. Does God feed his slaves, and will he not feed his family? His children may not have a liberal share in the things of this life; they may have but little meal in the barrel; they may be drawn low, and almost dry; but they shall have as much as God sees to be good for them. 'They that seek the Lord shall not want any good thing.' Psa xxxiv 10. If God gives them not *ad voluntatem* [what they want], he will *ad sanitatem* [what is good for them]; if he gives them not always what they crave, he will give them what they need; if he gives them not a feast, he will give them a *viaticum* – a bait by the way. Let them depend upon his fatherly providence; let them not give way to distrustful thoughts, distracting cares, or indirect means. 'Casting all your care upon him; for he careth for you.' 1 Pet v 7. An earthly parent may have affection for his child, and would gladly provide for him, but may not be able; but God is never at a loss to provide for his children, and he has

C

promised an adequate supply. 'Verily thou shalt be fed.' Psa xxxvii 3. Will God give his children heaven, and will he not give them enough to bear their charges thither? Will he give them a kingdom, and deny them daily bread? O put your trust in him, for he has said, 'I will never leave thee, nor forsake thee.' Heb xiii 5.

(2) If God be our Father, let us imitate him. The child not only bears his father's image, but imitates him in his speech, gesture and behaviour. If God be our Father, let us imitate him. 'Be ye followers of God, as dear children.' Eph v 1. Imitate God in forgiving injuries. 'I have blotted out, as a thick cloud, thy transgressions.' Isa xliv 22. As the sun scatters not only thin mists, but thick clouds, so God pardons great offences. Imitate him in this. 'Forgiving one another.' Eph iv 32. Cranmer was a man of a forgiving spirit: he buried injuries and requited good for evil. He who has God for his Father, will have him for his pattern. Imitate God in works of mercy. 'The Lord looseth the prisoners.' Psa cxlvi 7. He opens his hand and satisfies the desire of every living thing. Psa cxlv 16. He drops his sweet dew upon the thistle as well as the rose. Imitate God in works of mercy; relieve the wants of others; be rich in good works. 'Be merciful, as your Father also is merciful.' Luke vi 36. Be not so hard hearted as to shut out the poor from all communication. Dives denied Lazarus a crumb of bread, and Dives was denied a drop of water.

(3) If God be our Father, let us submit patiently to his will. If he lay his strokes on us, they are the corrections of a Father, not the punishments of a judge. This made Christ himself patient. 'The cup which my Father hath given me, shall I not drink it?' John xviii 11. He sees we need affliction. 1 Pet i 6. He appoints it as a diet drink, to purge and sanctify us. Isa xxvii 9. Therefore dispute not, but submit. 'We have had fathers of our flesh which corrected us, and we gave them reverence.' Heb xii 9. They might correct out of ill humour, but God does it for our profit. Heb xii 10. Therefore say as Eli, 'It is the Lord: let him do what seemeth him good.' 1 Sam iii 18. What does the child get by struggling, but more blows? What got Israel by their murmuring and rebelling, but a longer and more tedious march, till, at last, their carcases fell in the wilderness?

(4) If God be our Father, let it cause in us a childlike reverence. 'If I be a father, where is mine honour?' Mal i 6. It is part of the honour we give to God to reverence and adore him; if we have not always a childlike confidence, let us always preserve a childlike reverence. How ready are we to run into extremes, either to despond or to grow wanton! Because God is a Father, do not think you may take liberty to sin; if you do, he may act as if he were no Father, and throw hell into your conscience. When David presumed upon God's paternal affection, and began to wax wanton under

mercy, God made him pay dear for it by withdrawing the sense of his love; and, though he had the heart of a Father, yet he had the look of an enemy. David prayed, 'Make me to hear joy and gladness.' Psa li 8. He lay several months in desertion, and it is thought never recovered his full joy to the day of his death. O keep alive holy fear! With childlike confidence, preserve an humble reverence. The Lord is a Father, therefore love to serve him; he is the mighty God, therefore fear to offend him.

(5) If God be our Father, let us walk obediently. 'As obedient children.' 1 Pet i 14. When God bids you be humble and self-denying, deny yourselves; part with your bosom sin. Be sober in your attire, savoury in your speech, grave in your deportment; obey your Father's voice; open to him as the flower to the sun. If you expect your Father's blessing, obey him in whatever he commands, both in first and second table duties. When a musician would make sweet music, he touches upon every string of the lute. The ten commandments are like a ten-stringed instrument, and we must touch every string, obey every commandment, or we cannot make sweet melody in religion. Obey your heavenly Father, though he commands things contrary to flesh and blood; when he commands to mortify sin, the sin which has been most dear: pluck out a right eye, that you may see better to go to heaven; when he commands you to suffer for sin. Acts xxi 13. Every good Christian has a spirit of martyrdom in him, and is ready to suffer for the truth rather than the truth should suffer. Luther said he had rather be a martyr than a monarch. Peter was crucified with his head downwards, as Eusebius relates. Ignatius called his chains his spiritual pearls, and wore his fetters as a bracelet of diamonds. We act as God's children, when we obey his voice, and count not our lives dear, so that we may show our love to him. 'They loved not their lives unto the death.' Rev xii 11.

(6) If God be our Father, let us show by our cheerful looks that we are the children of such a Father. Too much drooping and despondency disparages the relation in which we stand to him. What though we meet with hard usage in the world! We are now in a strange land, far from home; it will be shortly better with us when we are in our own country, and our Father has us in his arms. Does not the heir rejoice in hope? Shall the sons of a king walk dejected? 'Why art thou, being the king's son, lean?' 2 Sam xiii 4. Is God an unkind Father? Are his commands grievous? Has he no land to give his heirs? Why, then, do his children walk so sad? Never had children such privileges as they who are of the seed-royal of heaven, and have God for their Father. They should rejoice who are within a few hours of being crowned with glory.

(7) If God be our Father, let us honour him by walking very holily. 'Be ye holy; for I am holy.' 1 Pet i 16. A young prince, having asked a philo-

sopher how he should behave himself, the philosopher said, '*Memento te filium esse regis.*' 'Remember thou art a king's son; do nothing but what becomes the son of a king.' So let us remember we are the adopted sons and daughters of the high God, and do nothing unworthy of such a relation. A debauched child is the disgrace of his father. 'Is this thy son's coat?' said they to Jacob, when they brought it home dipped in blood. So, when we see a person defiled with malice, passion, drunkenness, we may say, Is this the coat of God's adopted son? Does he look like an heir of glory? It is blaspheming the name of God to call him Father, and yet live in sin. Such as profess God to be their Father and live unholily, slander and defraud; they are as bad to God as the heathen. 'Are ye not as children of the Ethiopians to me, O children of Israel? saith the Lord.' Amos ix 7. When Israel grew wicked, they were no better to God than Ethiopians, who were uncircumcised, a base and ill-bred people. Loose, scandalous livers under the gospel are no better in God's esteem than Pagans; nay, they shall have a hotter place in hell. Oh! let all who profess God to be their Father, honour him by their unspotted lives. Scipio abhorred the embraces of a harlot, because he was the general of an army. Abstain from all sin, because you are born of God, and have God for your Father. 'Abstain from all appearance of evil.' 1 Thess v 22. It was a saying of Augustus, that 'an emperor should not only be free from crimes, but from the suspicion of them.' By a holy life you should bring glory to your heavenly Father, and cause others to become his children. *Est pellax virtutis odor* [the fragrance of virtue is seductive]. Causinus, in his hieroglyphics, speaks of a dove, whose wings being perfumed with sweet ointments, drew the other doves after her; so the holy lives of God's children are a sweet perfume to draw others to religion, and make them to be of the family of God. Justin Martyr says, that which converted him to Christianity was beholding the blameless lives of the Christians.

(8) If God be our Father, let us love all that are his children. 'How pleasant it is for brethren to dwell together in unity!' Psa cxxxiii 1. It is compared to ointment for its sweet fragrance. 'Love the brotherhood.' 1 Peter ii 17. *Idem est motus animae in imaginem et rem* [The motion of the soul is the same towards the image and the reality]. The saints are the walking pictures of God. If God be our Father, we shall love to see his picture of holiness in believers; shall pity them for their infirmities, but love them for their graces; we shall prize their company above others. Psa cxix 63. It may justly be suspected that God is not Father of those who love not his children. Though they retain the communion of saints in their creed, they banish the communion of saints out of their company.

(9) If God be our Father, let us show heavenly-mindedness. They who

are born of God, set their affections on things that are above. Col iii 2. O ye children of the high God! do not disgrace your high birth by sordid covetousness. What, a son of God, and a slave to the world! What, sprung from heaven, and buried in the earth! For a Christian, who pretends to derive his pedigree from heaven, wholly to mind earthly things is to debase himself; as if a king should leave his throne to follow the plough. 'Seekest thou great things for thyself?' Jer xlv 5. As if the Lord had said, 'What, thou Barak, thou who art born of God, akin to angels, and by thy office a Levite, dost thou debase thyself, and spot the silver wings of thy grace by beliming them with earth! Seekest thou great things? Seek them not.' The earth chokes the fire; so earthliness chokes the fire of good affections.

(10) If God be our Father, let us own him as such in the worst times; stand up in his cause, and defend his truths. Athanasius owned God when most of the world turned Arians. If suffering come, do not deny God. He is a bad son who denies his father. Such as are ashamed to own God in times of danger, he will be ashamed to own for his children. 'Whosoever therefore shall be ashamed of me and of my words in this adulterous generation, of him also shall the Son of man be ashamed, when he comes in the glory of his Father, with the holy angels.' Mark viii 38.

II. *The second part of the preface is,* 'Which art in heaven.' God is said to be in heaven, not because he is so included there as if he were nowhere else; for 'the heaven of heavens cannot contain thee.' 1 Kings viii 27. But the meaning is, that he is chiefly resident in what the apostle calls 'the third heaven,' where he reveals his glory most to saints and angels. 2 Cor xii 2.

What may we learn from God being in heaven?

(1) That we are to raise our minds in prayer above the earth. God is nowhere to be spoken with but in heaven. He never denied that soul its suit that went as far as heaven to ask it.

(2) We learn his sovereign power. *Hoc vocabulo intelligitur omnia subesse ejus imperio* [By this word we learn that all things are under his rule]. Calvin. 'Our God is in the heavens: he hath done whatsoever he hath pleased.' Psa cxv 3. In heaven he governs the universe, and orders all occurrences here below for the good of his children. When the saints are in straits and dangers, and see no way of relief, he sends from heaven and helps them. 'He shall send from heaven, and save me.' Psa lvii 3.

(3) We learn his glory and majesty. He is in heaven; therefore he is covered with light. Psa civ 2. He is 'clothed with honour.' Psa civ 1. He is far above all worldly princes, as heaven is above earth.

(4) We learn his omniscience. All things are naked and unmasked to his eye. Heb iv 13. Men plot and contrive against the church; but God is in

heaven, and they do nothing but what he sees. If a man were on the top of a tower or theatre, he might see all the people below; God in heaven, as on a high tower or theatre, sees all the transactions of men. The wicked make wounds in the backs of the righteous, and then pour in vinegar; but God writes down their cruelty. 'I have surely seen the affliction of my people.' Exod iii 7. God can thunder out of heaven upon his enemies. 'The Lord thundered in the heavens; yea, he sent out his arrows, and scattered them; and he shot out lightnings, and discomfited them.' Psa xviii 13, 14.

(5) We learn comfort for the children of God. When they pray to their Father, the way to heaven cannot be blocked up. One may have a father living in foreign parts, but the way, both by sea and land, may be so blocked up, that there is no coming to him; but thou, saint of God, when thou prayest to thy Father, he is in heaven; and though thou art ever so confined, thou mayest have access to him. A prison cannot keep thee from thy God; the way to heaven can never be blocked up.

III. *I shall next speak of the pronoun* 'our.' There is an appropriation of the appellation, 'Father.' 'Our Father.' Christ, by the word 'our,' would teach us thus much: that in all our prayers to God, we should exercise faith. Father denotes reverence: Our Father, denotes faith. In all our prayers to God we should exercise faith. Faith baptizes prayer, and gives it a name; it is called 'the prayer of faith.' James v 15. Without faith, it is speaking, not praying. Faith is the breath of prayer; prayer is dead unless faith breathe in it. Faith is a necessary requisite in prayer. The oil of the sanctuary was made up of several sweet spices, pure myrrh, cassia, cinnamon. Exod xxx 23, 24. Faith is the chief spice or ingredient in prayer, which makes it go up to the Lord as sweet incense. 'Let him ask in faith.' James i 6. 'Whatsoever ye shall ask in prayer, believing, ye shall receive.' Matt xxi 22. *Invoco te, Domine, quanquam languida et imbecilla fide, tamen fide.* 'Lord,' said Cruciger, 'I pray, though with a weak faith, yet with faith.' Prayer is the gun we shoot with, fervency is the fire that discharges it, and faith is the bullet which pierces the throne of grace. Prayer is the key of heaven, faith is the hand that turns it. Pray in faith, 'Our Father.' Faith must take prayer by the hand, or there is no coming nigh to God. Prayer without faith is unsuccessful. If a poor handy-craftsman, who lives by his labour, has spoiled his tools so that he cannot work, how shall he subsist? Prayer is the tool we work with, which procures all good for us; but unbelief spoils and blunts our prayers, and then we get no blessing from God. A faithless prayer is fruitless. As Joseph said, 'Ye shall not see my face, except your brother be with you' (Gen xliii 3); so prayer cannot see God's face unless it bring its brother faith with it. What is said of Israel, 'They could not enter in because of unbelief,' is as true of prayer; it cannot enter into heaven because of unbelief. Heb iii 19. Prayer often suffers shipwreck because it dashes upon the rock of unbelief. O mingle faith with prayer! We must say, 'Our Father.'

What does praying in faith imply?

Praying in faith implies having faith, and the act implies the habit. To walk implies a principle of life; so to pray in faith implies a habit of grace. None can pray in faith but believers.

What is it to pray in faith?

(1) It is to pray for that which God has promised. Where there is no promise, we cannot pray in faith.

(2) It is to pray in Christ's meritorious name. 'Whatsoever ye shall ask in my name, that will I do.' John xiv 13. To pray in Christ's name, is to pray with confidence in Christ's merit. When we present Christ to God in prayer; when we carry the Lamb slain in our arms; when we say, 'Lord, we are sinners, but here is our surety; for Christ's sake be propitious,' we come to God in Christ's name; and this is to pray in faith.

(3) It is to fix our faith in prayer on God's faithfulness, believing that he hears and will help. This is taking hold of God. Isa lxiv 7. By prayer we draw nigh to God, by faith we take hold of him. 'They cried unto the Lord;' and this was the crying of faith. 2 Chron xiii 14. They 'prevailed, because they relied upon the Lord God of their fathers;' ver 18. Making supplication to God, and staying the soul on God, is praying in faith. To pray, and not rely on God to grant our petitions, *irrisio Dei est*, says Pelican; 'it is to abuse and put a scorn on God.' By praying we seem to honour God; by not believing we affront him. In prayer we say, 'Almighty, merciful Father;' by not believing, we blot out all his titles again.

How may we know that we truly pray in faith?

(1) When faith in prayer is humble. A presumptuous person hopes to be heard for some inherent worthiness in himself; he is so qualified, and has done God good service, therefore he is confident God will hear him. See an instance in Luke xviii 11, 12: 'The Pharisee stood and prayed thus, God, I thank thee, that I am not as other men are, extortioners, unjust. I fast twice in the week; I give tithes of all that I possess.' This was a presumptuous prayer; but a sincere heart evinces humility in prayer as well as faith. 'The publican, standing afar off, would not lift up so much as his eyes unto heaven, but smote upon his breast, saying, God be merciful to me a sinner.' 'God be merciful,' there was faith; 'to me a sinner,' there was humility and a sense of unworthiness. Luke xviii 13.

(2) We may know we pray in faith, when, though we have not the thing we pray for, we believe God will grant it, and are willing to stay his leisure. A Christian having a command to pray, and a promise, is resolved to follow God with prayer, and not give over; as Peter knocked, and when the door was not opened, continued knocking until at last it was opened. Acts xii 16. So when a Christian prays, and prays, and has no answer, he continues to knock at heaven's door, knowing an answer will come. 'Thou wilt answer me.' Psa lxxxvi 7. Here is one that prays in faith. Christ says, 'Pray, and faint not.' Luke xviii 1. A believer, at Christ's word, lets down the net of prayer, and though he catch nothing, he will cast the net again, believing that mercy will come. Patience in prayer is nothing but faith spun out.

Use 1. For reproof of those who pray in formality, not in faith; they who question whether God hears or will grant. 'Ye ask, and receive not, because ye ask amiss.' James iv 3. He does not say, ye ask that which is unlawful; but ye ask amiss, and therefore ye receive not. Unbelief clips the wings of prayer, that it will not fly to the throne of grace; the rubbish of unbelief stops the current of prayer.

Use 2. For exhortation. Let us set faith to work in prayer. The husband-man sows in hope; prayer is the seed we sow, and when the hand of faith scatters this seed, it brings forth a fruitful crop of blessing. Prayer is the ship we send out to heaven; when faith makes an adventure in this ship, it brings home large returns of mercy. O pray in faith; say, 'Our Father.' That we may exercise faith in prayer, consider:

(1) God's readiness to hear prayer. *Deus paratus ad vota exaudienda.* Calvin. Did God forbid all addresses to him, it would put a damp upon the trade of prayer; but his ear is open to prayer. One of the names by which he is known, is, 'O thou that hearest prayer.' Psa lxv 2. The ædiles among the Romans had their doors always open, that all who had petitions might have free access to them. God is both ready to hear and grant prayer, which should encourage faith in prayer. Some may say, they have prayed, but have had no answer. God may hear prayer, though he does not immediately answer it. We write a letter to a friend, he may have received it, though we have yet had no answer to it. Perhaps thou prayest for the light of God's face; he may lend thee an ear, though he does not show thee his face. God may give an answer to prayer, when we do not perceive it. His giving a heart to pray, and inflaming the affections in prayer, is an answer to prayer. 'In the day when I cried thou answeredst me, and strengthenedst me with strength in my soul.' Psa cxxxviii 3. David's inward strength was an answer to prayer. Therefore let God's readiness to hear prayer encourage faith in prayer.

(2) That we may exercise faith in prayer, let us consider that we do not pray alone. Christ prays our prayers over again. His prayer is the ground why our prayer is heard. He takes the dross out of our prayer, and presents nothing to his Father but pure gold. He mingles his sweet odours with the prayers of the saints. Rev v 8. Think of the dignity of his person, he is God; and the sweetness of his relation, he is a Son. Oh, what encouragement is here, to pray in faith! Our prayers are put into the hand of a Mediator. Christ's prayer is mighty and powerful.

(3) We pray to God for nothing but what is pleasing to him, and he has a mind to grant. If a son ask nothing but what his father is willing to bestow, it will make him go to him with confidence. When we pray to God for holy hearts, there is nothing more pleasing to him. 'This is the will of God, even your sanctification.' 1 Thess iv 3. We pray that God would give us hearts to love him, and there is nothing he more desires than our love. How should it make us pray in faith, when we pray for nothing but what is acceptable to God, and which he delights to bestow!

(4) To encourage faith in prayer, let us consider the many sweet promises that God has made to prayer. The cork keeps the net from sinking, so the promises are the cork to keep faith from sinking in prayer. God has bound himself to us by his promises. The Bible is bespangled with promises made to prayer. 'He will be very gracious unto thee at the voice of thy cry.' Isa xxx 19. 'The Lord is rich unto all that call upon him.' Rom x 12. 'Ye shall find me, when ye shall search for me with all your heart.' Jer xxix 13. 'He will fulfil the desire of them that fear him.' Psa cxlv 19. The Tyrians tied their god Hercules with a golden chain that he should not remove; God hath tied himself fast to us by his promises. How should these animate and spirit faith in prayer! Faith gets strength in prayer by sucking from the breast of a promise.

(5) That we may exercise faith in prayer, consider that Jesus Christ has purchased that which we pray for. We may think the things we ask for in prayer too great for us to obtain, but they are not too great for Christ to purchase. We pray for pardon. Christ has purchased it with his blood. We pray for the Spirit to animate and inspire us. The sending down of the Holy Ghost into our hearts, is the fruit of Christ's death. It should put life into our prayers, and make us pray in faith, to reflect that the things we ask, though more than we deserve, yet they are not more than Christ has purchased for us.

(6) To pray in faith, consider there is such bountifulness in God, that he often exceeds the prayers of his people. He gives them more than they ask! Hannah asked a son, and God not only gave her a son, but a prophet. Solomon asked wisdom, and God gave him not only wisdom, but riches

and honour besides. Jacob prayed that God would give him food and raiment, and he increased his pilgrim's staff into two bands. Gen xxxii 10. God is often better to us than our prayers, as when Gehazi asked but one talent, Naaman would needs force two upon him. 2 Kings v 23. We ask one talent, and God gives two. The woman of Canaan asked but a crumb, namely, to have the life of her child; and Christ gave her more, he sent her home with the life of her soul.

(7) The great success which the prayer of faith has found. Like Jonathan's bow, it has not returned empty. *Vocula pater dicta in corde* [The little word 'father' spoken in the heart], says Luther. The little word father, pronounced in faith, has overcome God. 'Deliver me, I pray thee.' Gen xxxii 11. This was mixed with faith in the promise. 'Thou saidst, I will surely do thee good;' ver 12. This prayer had power with God, and prevailed. Hos xii 4. The prayer of faith has opened prison doors, stopped the chariot of the sun, locked and unlocked heaven. James v 17. The prayer of faith has strangled the plots of enemies in their birth, and has routed their forces. Moses' prayer against Amalek did more than Joshua's sword; and should not this hearten and corroborate faith in prayer?

(8) If all this will not prevail, consider how heartless and comfortless it is not to pray in faith! The heart misgives secretly that God does not hear, nor will he grant. Faithless praying must needs be comfortless; for there is no promise made to unbelieving prayer. It is sad sailing where there is no anchoring, and sad praying where there is no promise to anchor upon. James i 7. The disciples toiled all night and caught nothing; so the unbeliever toils in prayer and catches nothing; he receives not any spiritual blessings, pardon of sin, or grace. As for the temporal mercies which the unbeliever has, he cannot look upon them as the fruit of prayer, but as the overflowings of God's bounty. Oh, therefore labour to exert and put forth faith in prayer!

But so much sin cleaves to my prayer, that I fear it is not the prayer of faith, and God will not hear it.

If thou mournest for this, it hinders not but that thy prayer may be in faith, and God may hear it. Weakness shall not make void the saint's prayers. 'I said in my haste, I am cut off.' Psa xxxi 22. There was much unbelief in that prayer: 'I said in my haste:' in the Hebrew, 'in my trembling,' David's faith trembled and fainted, yet God heard his prayer. The saints' passions do not hinder their prayers. James v 17. Therefore be not discouraged, for though sin will cleave to thy holy offering, yea, these two things may comfort, that thou mayest pray with faith, though with weakness; and God sees the sincerity, and will pass by the infirmity.

How shall we pray in faith?

Implore the Spirit of God. We cannot say, 'Our Father,' but by the Holy Ghost. God's Spirit helps us, not only to pray with sighs and groans, but with faith. The Spirit carries us to God, not only as to a Creator, but a Father. 'God hath sent forth the Spirit of his Son into your hearts, crying, Abba, Father.' Gal iv 6. 'Crying:' there the Spirit causes us to pray with fervency. 'Abba, Father:' there the Spirit helps us to pray with faith. The Spirit helps faith to turn the key of prayer, and then it unlocks heaven.

The First Petition in the Lord's Prayer

'Hallowed be thy name.' Matt vi 9

HAVING spoken of the introduction to the Lord's prayer, 'After this manner therefore pray ye,' and the preface, 'Our Father which art in heaven;' I come, thirdly, to the prayer itself, which consists of seven petitions. The first petition is:

'Hallowed be thy name.' In the Latin it is, *sanctificetur nomen tuum*, 'Sanctified be thy name.' In this petition, we pray that God's name may shine forth gloriously, and that it may be honoured and sanctified by us, in the whole course and tenor of our lives. It was the angels' song, 'Glory be to God in the highest;' that is, let his name be glorified and hallowed. This petition is set in the forefront, to show that the hallowing of God's name is to be preferred before all things. It is to be preferred before life. We pray, 'Hallowed be thy name,' before we pray, 'Give us this day our daily bread.' It is to be preferred before salvation. Rom ix 23. God's glory is more worth than the salvation of all men's souls. As Christ said of love in Matt xxii 38, 'This is the first and great commandment;' so I may say of this petition, 'Hallowed be thy name:' it is the first and great petition; it contains the most weighty thing in religion, which is God's glory. When some of the other petitions shall be useless and out of date, as we shall not need to pray in heaven, 'Give us our daily bread,' because there shall be no hunger; nor, 'Forgive us our trespasses,' because there shall be no sin; nor, 'Lead us not into temptation,' because the old serpent is not there to tempt: yet the hallowing of God's name will be of great use and request in heaven; we shall be ever singing hallelujahs, which is nothing else but the hallowing of God's name. Every Person in the blessed Trinity, God the Father, Son, and Holy Ghost, must have this honour, to be hallowed; their glory being equal, and their majesty co-eternal. 'Hallowed be thy name.' To admire God's name is not enough; we may admire a conqueror; but when we say, 'Hallowed be thy name,' we set God's name above every name, and not only admire him, but adore him; and this is proper to the Deity only. For the further explanation, I shall propound three questions.

I. *What is meant by God's name?*

[1] His essence. 'The name of the God of Jacob defend thee' (Psa xx 1); that is, the God of Jacob defend thee.

[2] Anything by which he may be known. As a man is known by his name; so by his attributes of wisdom, power, holiness, and goodness, God is known as by his name.

II. *What is meant by hallowing God's name?*

To hallow, is *a communi separare*, to set apart a thing from the common use, to some sacred end. As the vessels of the sanctuary were said to be hallowed, so, to hallow God's name, is to set it apart from all abuses, and to use it holily and reverently. In particular, hallowing God's name is to give him high honour and veneration, and render his name sacred. We can add nothing to his essential glory; but we are said to honour and sanctify his name when we lift him up in the world, and make him appear greater in the eyes of others. When a prince is crowned, there is something added really to his honour; but when we crown God with our triumphs and hallelujahs, there is nothing added to his essential glory. He cannot be greater than he is, only we may make him appear greater in the eyes of others.

III. *When may we be said to hallow and sanctify God's name?*

[1] When we profess his name. Our meeting in his holy assembly is an honour done to his name. This is good, but it is not enough. All that wear God's livery by profession are not true servants; there are some professors against whom Christ will profess at the last day. 'I will profess I never knew you.' Matt vii 23. Therefore, to go a little further:

[2] We hallow and sanctify God's name when we have a high appreciation and esteem of him, and set him highest in our thoughts. The Hebrew word to honour, signifies to esteem precious: we conceive of God in our minds as the most superexcellent and infinite good; we see in him a constellation of all beauties and delights; we adore him in his glorious attributes, which are the several beams by which his divine nature shines forth; we adore him in his works, which are bound up in three great volumes – creation, redemption, and providence. We hallow and sanctify his name when we lift him highest in our souls; we esteem him a supereminent and incomprehensible God.

[3] We hallow and sanctify his name when we trust in it. 'We have trusted in his holy name.' Psa xxxiii 21. No way can we bring more revenues of honour to God, or make his crown shine brighter, than by confiding in him. Abraham 'was strong in faith, giving glory to God.' Rom iv 20. Here was hallowing God's name. Unbelief stains God's honour and eclipses his name. 'He that believeth not God hath made him a liar' (1 John v 10); so faith glorifies and hallows his name. The believer trusts his best jewels in

God's hands. 'Into thine hand I commit my spirit.' Psa xxxi 5. Faith in a Mediator does more honour, and sanctifies God's name more, than martyrdom or the most sublime acts of obedience.

[4] We hallow and sanctify God's name when we never make mention of it but with the highest reverence. His name is sacred, and it must not be spoken of but with veneration. When the Scripture speaks of God, it gives him his titles of honour. 'Blessed be the most high God.' Gen xiv 20. 'Blessed be thy glorious name, which is exalted above all praise.' Neh ix 5. To speak vainly or slightly of God is profaning his name, and is taking his name in vain. By giving God his venerable titles, we hang his jewels on his crown.

[5] We hallow and sanctify God's name when we love his name. 'Let them that love thy name be joyful.' Psa v 11. The love which honours God's name must be special and discriminating love – the cream and flower of our love; such as we give to none besides; as the wife honours her husband by giving him such love as she gives to none else – a conjugal love. Thus we hallow God's name by giving him such love as we give to none else – a love joined with worship. 'He is thy Lord; and worship thou him.' Psa xlv 11.

[6] We hallow and sanctify God's name when we give him a holy and spiritual worship. (1) When we give him the same kind of worship that he has appointed. 'I will be sanctified in them that come nigh me:' that is, I will be sanctified with that very worship I have appointed. Lev x 3. It is the purity of worship that God loves better than the pomp. It dishonours his name to bring anything into his worship which he has not instituted; as if he were not wise enough to appoint the manner in which he will be served. Men prescribe to him and superadd their inventions; which he looks upon as offering strange fire, and as a high provocation. (2) When we give to God the same heart devotion in worship that he has appointed. 'Fervent in spirit; serving the Lord.' Rom xii 11. The word for fervent is a metaphor, which alludes to water that seethes and boils over; to signify that our affections should boil over in holy duties. To give God outside worship, and not the devotion of the heart, instead of hallowing and sanctifying him in an ordinance, is to abuse him; as if one calls for wine and you give him an empty glass. It is to deal with God as Prometheus did with Jupiter, who did eat the flesh and present Jupiter with nothing but bones covered over with skin. We hallow God's name and sanctify him in an ordinance when we give him the vitals of religion, and a heart flaming with zeal.

[7] We hallow and sanctify God's name when we hallow his day. 'Hallow ye the sabbath day.' Jer xvii 22. Our Christian Sabbath, which comes in the room of the Jews' Sabbath, is called the Lord's day. Rev i 10. It was anciently

called *dies lucis*, a day of light, wherein Christ the Sun of Righteousness shines in an extraordinary manner. It is an honour done to God to hallow his Sabbath. (1) We must rest on this day from all secular works. 'Bring in no burden on the sabbath day.' Jer xvii 24. As when Joseph would speak with his brethren he thrust out the Egyptians; so when we would converse with God on this day, we must thrust out all earthly employments. Mary Magdalene refused to anoint Christ's dead body on the sabbath day. Luke xxiii 56. She had before prepared her ointment and spices, but came not to the sepulchre till the Sabbath was past; she rested on that day from civil work, even the commendable and glorious work of anointing Christ's dead body. (2) We must in a solemn manner devote ourselves to God on this day; we must spend the whole day with God. Some will hear the word, but leave all their religion at church; they do nothing at home, they do not pray or repeat the word in their houses, and so rob God of a part of his day. It is lamentable to see how God's day is profaned. Let no man think God's name is hallowed while his Sabbath is broken.

[8] We hallow and sanctify God's name when we ascribe the honour of all we do to him. 'Give unto the Lord the glory due unto his name.' Psa xcvi 8. Herod, instead of hallowing God's name, dishonoured it by assuming that praise to himself which was due to God only. Acts xii 23. We ought to take the honour from ourselves and give it to God. 'I laboured more abundantly than they all;' one would think this had savoured of pride: but the apostle pulls the crown from his own head and sets it upon the head of free grace: 'Yet not I, but the grace of God which was with me.' 1 Cor xv 10. If a Christian has any assistance in duty, or victory over temptation, he rears up a pillar and writes upon it, *Hucusque adjuvavit Deus*. 'Hitherto the Lord hath helped me.' John the Baptist transferred all the honour from himself to Christ; he was content to be eclipsed that Christ might shine the more. 'He that cometh after me is preferred before me.' John i 15. I am but the herald, the voice of one crying; he is the prince. I am but a lesser star; he is the sun. I baptize with water only; he with the Holy Ghost. This is hallowing God's name, when we transfer all honour from ourselves to God. 'Not unto us, O Lord, not unto us, but unto thy name give glory.' Psa cxv 1. The king of Sweden wrote this motto on the battle at Leipsic, *Ista a Domino facta sunt* – the Lord has wrought this victory for us.

[9] We hallow and sanctify God's name by obeying him. How does a son more honour his father than by obedience? 'I delight to do thy will, O my God.' Psa xl 8. The wise men showed honour to Christ, not only by bowing the knee to him, but by presenting him with gold and myrrh. Matt ii 11. We hallow God's name, not only by lifting up our eyes and hands to

heaven and bowing the knee in prayer, but by presenting him with golden obedience. As the factor trades for the merchant, so we trade for God and lay out our strength in his service. It was a saying of Dr Jewel, 'I have spent and exhausted myself in the labours of my holy calling.' 'To obey is better than sacrifice.' The cherubims representing the angels are set forth with their wings displayed, to show how ready they are to do service to God. To obey is angelic; to pretend honour to God's name, and yet not obey, is but a devout compliment. Abraham honoured God by obedience; he was ready to sacrifice his son, though the son of his old age, and a son of the promise. 'By myself have I sworn, saith the Lord, for because thou hast done this thing, and hast not withheld thy son, thine only son: that in blessing I will bless thee.' Gen xxii 16, 17.

[10] We hallow and sanctify God's name when we lift up his name in our praises. God is said to sanctify, and man is said to sanctify. God sanctifies us by giving us grace; and we sanctify him by giving him praise. What were our tongues given for but to be organs of God's praise? 'Let my mouth be filled with thy praise and with thy honour all the day.' Psa lxxi 8. 'Blessing, and honour, and glory, and power, be unto him that sitteth upon the throne, and unto the Lamb for ever.' Rev v 13. Thus God's name is hallowed and sanctified in heaven; the angels and glorified saints are singing hallelujahs. Let us begin the work of heaven here. David sang forth God's praises and doxologies in a most melodious manner, and was, therefore, called the sweet singer of Israel. 2 Sam xxiii 1. Praising God is hallowing his name; it spreads his renown; it displays the trophies of his excellency; it exalts him in the eyes of others. 'Whoso offereth praise glorifieth me.' Psa l 23. This is one of the highest and purest acts of religion. In prayer we act like men; in praise we act like angels. Praise is the music of heaven, and a work fit for a saint. 'Let the saints be joyful: let the high praises of God be in their mouth.' Psa cxlix 5, 6. None but saints can in a right manner thus hallow God's name by praising him. As everyone has not skill to play on the viol and organ, so every one cannot rightly sound forth God's harmonious praises; only the saints can do it; they only can make their tongue and heart join in concert. 'I will praise the Lord with my whole heart.' Psa cxi 1. 'He was extolled with my tongue.' Psa lxvi 17. Here was joining in concert. This hallowing God's name by praise is very becoming a Christian. It is unbecoming to murmur, which is dishonouring God's name; but it becomes the saints to be spiritual choristers, singing forth the honour of his name. It is called the 'garment of praise.' Isa lxi 3. How comely and handsome is this garment of praise for a saint to wear! 'Praise is comely for the upright.' Psa xxxiii 1. Especially is it a high degree of hallowing God's name when we

can speak well of him and bless him in an afflicted state. 'The Lord hath taken away; blessed be the name of the Lord.' Job i 21. Many will bless God when he gives, but to bless him when he takes away, is in a high degree to honour him and hallow his name. Let us thus magnify God's name. Has he not given us abundant matter for praising him? He has given us grace, a mercy spun and woven out of his bowels; and he intends to crown grace with glory. This should make us hallow his name by being trumpets for his praise.

[11] We hallow and sanctify God's name when we sympathize with him; when we grieve when his name suffers. (1) We lay to heart his dishonour. How was Moses affected with God's dishonour! He broke the tables. Exod xxxii 19. We grieve to see God's Sabbaths profaned, his worship adulterated, the wine of truth mingled with error. (2) We grieve when God's church is brought low, because his name suffers. Nehemiah lays to heart the miseries of Sion; his complexion begins to alter, and he looks sad. 'Why is thy countenance sad?' Neh ii 2. What! sad, when the king's cup-bearer, and wine is so near! Oh! but it fared ill with the church of God, and religion seemed to lose ground, and God's name suffered; therefore Nehemiah grows weary of the court; he leaves his wine and mingles his drink with weeping. Such holy sympathy and grieving when God's name suffers, he esteems as honouring and sanctifying his name. Hezekiah grieved when the king of Assyria reproached the living God. He went to the temple, and spread the letter of blasphemy before the Lord. Isa xxxvii 17. He no doubt watered the letter with his tears; he seemed not to be so much troubled at the fear of losing his own life and kingdom, as that God should lose his glory.

[12] We hallow and sanctify God's name when we give the same honour to God the Son that we give to God the Father. 'That all men should honour the Son, even as they honour the Father.' John v 23. The Socinians deny Christ's divinity, saying that he is a mere man: which is to make him below the angels. The human nature, considered in itself, is below the angelic, and thus they reflect dishonour upon the Lord of glory. Psa viii 5. We must give equal honour to the Son as to the Father; we must believe Christ's deity; he is the picture of his Father's glory. Heb i 3. If the Godhead be in Christ, he must needs be God; but the Godhead shines in him. 'In him dwelleth all the fulness of the Godhead bodily;' therefore, he is God. Col ii 9. How could these divine titles be given to Christ as omnipotence, in Heb i 3; ubiquity, in Matt xxviii 20; a power of sealing pardons in Matt ix 6; co-equality with God the Father, both in power and dignity, in John v 21, 23, if he were not crowned with the Deity? When we believe Christ's Godhead, and build

D   [43]

our hope of salvation on the corner-stone of his merit; when we see neither the righteousness of the law, nor of angels, can justify, but flee to Christ's blood as to the altar of refuge; this is honouring and sanctifying God's name. God never thinks his name hallowed unless his Son be honoured.

[13] We hallow God's name by standing up for his truths. Much of God's glory lies in his truths. His truths are his oracles. He intrusts us with his truths as a treasure; we have not a richer jewel to intrust him with than our souls, nor has he a greater jewel to intrust us with than his truths. His truths set forth his glory. When we are zealous advocates for his truths, it is an honour done to his name. Athanasius was called the bulwark of truth; he stood up in the defence of God's truths against the Arians, and so was a pillar in the temple of God. We had better have truth without peace, than peace without truth. It concerns the sons of Zion to stand up for the great doctrines of the gospel; as the doctrine of the Trinity, the hypostatical union, justification by faith, and the saints' perseverance. We are bid to contend earnestly, to strive as in an agony for the faith, that is the doctrine of faith. Jude 3. This contending for the truth, brings great revenues to heaven's exchequer; and hallows God's name. Some can contend for ceremonies, but not for the truth. We should count him unwise that should contend for a box of counters more than for his box of title-deeds.

[14] We hallow and sanctify God's name by making as many proselytes as we can to him; when, by all holy expedients, counsel, prayer, example, we endeavour the salvation of others. How did Monica, Augustine's mother, labour for his conversion! She had sorer pangs in travail for his new birth than for his natural birth. It is hallowing God's name when we diffuse the sweet savour of godliness, and propagate religion to others; when not only we ourselves honour God, but are instruments to make others honour him. Certainly when the heart is seasoned with grace, there will be an endeavour to season others. God's glory is as dear to a saint as his own salvation; and that this glory may be promoted he endeavours the conversion of souls. Every convert is a new member added to Christ. Let us then hallow God's name by labouring to advance piety in others; especially let us endeavour that those who are nearly related to us, or are under our roof, may honour God. 'As for me and my house, we will serve the Lord.' Josh xxiv 15. Let us make our houses Bethels, places where God's name is called upon. 'Salute Nymphas, and the church that is in his house.' Col iv 15. Let the parent endeavour that his children may honour God, and the master that his servants may honour him. Read the Word, drop holy instruction, perfume your houses with prayer. The Jews had sacrifices in their families as well as in the tabernacle. Exod xii 3. This is hallowing God's

name when we make proselytes to him, and endeavour that all under our charge should honour and sanctify his name.

[15] We hallow God's name when we prefer the honour of his name before the dearest things. (1) When we prefer the honour of God's name before our own credit. The saints of old have, for the honour of God, been willing to endure reproach. 'For thy sake I have borne reproach.' Psa lxix 7. David cared not what reproach he suffered, so God's name might not suffer. The prophet Elijah was called in derision, the 'hairy prophet;' and the prophet Isaiah, 'the bearer of burdens;' and the prophet Zephaniah, 'the bitter prophet;' but they wound these reproaches as a crown about their head. The honour of God's name was dearer to them than their own honour. Moses esteemed the reproach of Christ greater riches than the treasures of Egypt. Heb xi 26. The apostles went away rejoicing that they were counted worthy to suffer shame for the name of Christ! that they were graced so far as to be disgraced for the name of Christ. Acts v 41. We hallow God's name when we are content to have our name eclipsed, that his name may shine the more. (2) When we prefer the honour of God's name before our worldly profit and interest. 'We have forsaken all, and followed thee.' Matt xix 27. When these two, God and estate, come in competition, we would rather let estate go than God's love and favour. Thus that noble Marquis of Vico parted with a fair estate, using these words, 'Let their money perish with them, that count all the gold and silver in the world worth one hour's communion with Jesus Christ.' (3) When we prefer the honour of God's name before our own life. 'For thy sake we are killed all the day long.' Rom viii 36. The honour done to God's name is not by bringing the outward pomp and glory to him as we do to kings, but it comes in another way, and that is by the sufferings of his people. When the world sees how entirely his people love him, that they will die in his service, it exalts and honours his name. God's crown flourishes in the ashes of his martyrs. Basil speaks of a virgin, condemned to the fire, who having her life and estate offered her, if she would bow to the idol, answered, *Valeat vita, pereat pecunia:* Let life and money go, welcome Christ. When God's glory weighs heaviest in the balance, and we are willing to suffer the loss of all rather than God's name should suffer, we do, in a high degree, hallow God's name.

[16] We hallow and sanctify God's name by a holy conversation. 'Ye are a royal priesthood, a peculiar people; that ye should shew forth the praises of him who hath called you.' 1 Pet ii 9. As an unholy life dishonours God's name, 'The name of God is blasphemed among the Gentiles through you;' Rom ii 24, so by our holy and Bible conversation we honour God's name.

A holy life speaks louder than all the anthems and praises in the world. Though the main work of religion lies in the heart, yet when our light so shines, that others behold it, we glorify God. When our lives shine, his name shines in us. The Macedonians used one day in the year to wear the picture of Alexander set with pearl and costly jewels; so when we carry the picture of Christ about us in our holy example, we bring honour to God's name.

Use 1. See the true note and character of a godly person: he is a sanctifier of God's name. A true saint ambitiously endeavours to advance God's name. The question he asks himself in everything he is going about is, Will this action tend to the honour of God's name? Will it exalt God? It was Paul's chief design that Christ might be magnified, that the crown upon his head might flourish. Phil i 20. A godly man thinks it scarce worth his while to live if he may not bring some revenues of honour to God's name.

Use 2. I may here take up a sad lamentation, and speak, as the apostle Paul, weeping. Phil iii 18. Consider how God's name, instead of being hallowed and sanctified, is dishonoured. His name, which is worth more than the salvation of all men's souls, suffers deeply. We are apt to speak of our sufferings; alas! what are all our sufferings! God's name suffers most. His name is the dearest thing he has. How do men stand upon their name and honour! God's name is this day dishonoured; it is like the sun in an eclipse. Theodosius took it heinously when they threw dirt upon his statue; but what is far worse, disgrace is thrown upon the glorious name of Jehovah. His name, instead of being hallowed, is dishonoured by all sorts; by heathens, by Turks, by Jews, by Papists, and by Protestants.

(1) By heathens; who have a knowledge of a godhead by the light of nature; yet dishonour him, and sin against the light of nature. Rom i 19. The Egyptians worship an ox; the Persians worship the sun; the Grecians and Romans, Jupiter; and the Parthians worship the devil.

(2) God's name is dishonoured by the Turks, who adore Mahomet their great prophet, as one divinely inspired. Mahomet was of an impure, vicious nature. He plucked the crown from Christ's head by denying his Deity.

(3) God's name is dishonoured by the Jews, who give not equal honour and adoration to God the Son, as to God the Father. They expect a Messiah yet to come, *saeculum futurum* [an age to come]. They believe not in Christ; they blaspheme him; they reject imputed righteousness; they vilify the Christian Sabbath.

(4) God's name is dishonoured by the Papists. Theirs is a God-dishonouring religion. They dishonour the name of God by their idolatry, which is spiritual adultery. Idolatry is to worship a false God, or the true God in a

false manner. They dishonour God by their idolatry, in making graven images, and giving the same honour to them that is due to God. Images are teachers of lies. They represent God in a bodily shape. Hab ii 18. They dishonour God by their idolatry in the mass; worshipping the host, and offering it up as a sacrifice for sin. The apostle says, 'By one offering [Christ] hath perfected forever them that are sanctified' (Heb x 14); but as if his offering on the cross were imperfect, they offer him up daily in the mass, which is a dishonour to Christ's priestly office. The Papist, instead of hallowing God's name, dishonours it by locking up the Scriptures in an unknown tongue. Like the Philistines, they pluck out people's eyes, and then make sport with them. The Bible is a shining light, but they draw a curtain over it; they take away the key of knowledge, and hinder God's glory by hindering men's salvation. Luke xi 52. Instead of hallowing God's name, they dishonour it by giving men indulgences. They say the Pope, as Peter's successor, has power to grant indulgences, by virtue whereof men are set free in the sight of God. This is to steal a flower from the crown of heaven. The Pope assumes a power to pardon which is God's royal prerogative. 'Who can forgive sins but God only?' Mark ii 7. The Pope, by his indulgence, encourages men to sin. What need the Papists care what sins they commit, when they have a licence and patent from the Pope to bear them harmless? Instead of hallowing God's name, they dishonour it by their invocation to saints. We are to pray to God only. 'Pray to thy Father;' not pray to a saint or the Virgin Mary, but pray to your Father in heaven. Matt vi 6. We may pray to none but whom we may believe in. Rom x 14. The saints in heaven are ignorant of our grievances. 'Abraham is ignorant of us.' Isa lxiii 16. Instead of hallowing God's name, they dishonour it, by their luxury and uncleanness. At Rome, fornication keeps open shop, and is in some cases preferred before honourable matrimony. *Urbs est jam tota lupanar* [The whole city is now a brothel]. Instead of hallowing God's name, they dishonour it, by their blasphemies. They give equal, nay, more honour to the Virgin Mary than to Christ; they ascribe more to her milk than to his blood; they call her *Scala Coeli*, the ladder of heaven; *Janua paradisi*, the gate of Paradise. In their doxologies they say, 'Praise be to the Virgin Mary, and also to Christ.' What blasphemy is this, to set the creature above the Creator! They say to her, O *felix puerpera, nostra piaris scelera!* O happy Mother of a Son, who purgest away our crimes! Instead of hallowing God's name, they dishonour it, by their lies. Their golden legend is an imposture, and is full of lying wonders. They show John Baptist's forehead for a relic in Spain, yet his whole head they affirm to be seen in St. Sylvester's in Rome. They show Peter's shadow at Rome. We read of St Peter's shadow in Acts v 15; but it is strange how the

Papists could catch it, and keep it by them so long. Instead of hallowing God's name, they dishonour it, by baptizing sin with the name of virtue. Breach of oaths is with the Papists a virtue. If a man has bound his soul to God by an oath, to violate it is virtuous, if it may propagate the Catholic cause. Killing those who are of a different religion, is not only venial, but a virtue among Catholics. Destroying two hundred thousand of the Albigenses, who were Protestants, was commended as a glorious action, honoured with a triumph at Rome, and crowned with his holiness's blessing. Is not this a high dishonour to God, to gild over the foulest crimes with the name of virtue and piety? Instead of hallowing God's name they dishonour it, by their damnable assertions. The Papists affirm that the Pope is above Scripture; that he may dispense with it, and that his canon binds more than the Word of God. They teach merit by good works; but if a debtor cannot pay his creditor, how can he merit at his hands? They affirm that the Scripture is not a perfect rule of faith and manners; and therefore eke it out with their traditions, which they hold to be of equal authority. They teach that an implicit faith is saving; though one may have an implicit faith, and yet be ignorant of all the articles of religion. They say, that the inward act of the mind is not required in God's worship. Diversion of the mind in duty, though one prays and never thinks of God, is no sin, as Angelus and Sylvester, and other Papists say. They make habitual love to God unnecessary. 'It is not needful,' says Bellarmine, 'to perform any acts of religion out of love to God.' Stapleton and Cajetan affirm, that the precept of loving God with all our heart is not binding; by which they cut asunder the sinews and soul of all religion. Thus, instead of honouring God's name, the Papists dishonour it. Let us pray heartily, that this Romish religion may never again get footing in this nation. God grant that this poisonous weed of Popery may never be watered here; but that being a plant which our heavenly Father has not planted, it may be rooted up.

(5) God's name is dishonoured by Protestants. How is his name this day dishonoured in England! Christians, instead of hallowing God's name, reproach and dishonour it by their tongues. They speak irreverently of his name. God's name is sacred. 'That thou mayest fear this glorious and fearful name: THE LORD THY GOD.' Deut xxviii 58. The names of kings are not mentioned without giving them their titles of honour, high and mighty; but men speak irreverently of God, as if he were like one of them. Psa l 21. This is taking God's name in vain. They swear by his name. Many seldom mention God's name but in oaths. How is he dishonoured, when men rend and tear his name by oaths and imprecations! 'Because of swearing the land mourneth.' Jer xxiii 10. If God will reckon with men for idle words, shall not idle oaths be put into the account-book? *'Oh! but,'* says one, *'I cannot*

help it: it is a custom of swearing I have got, and I cannot help it. I hope God will forgive me.' Is the custom of swearing a good plea? It is no excuse, but an aggravation of sin; as if one who had been accused of killing a man should plead with the judge to spare him, because it was his custom to murder. That would be an aggravation of the offence; for would not the judge say, 'Thou shalt the rather die'? So it is here.

As men dishonour God by their tongues, so by their lives. What is it to say, 'Hallowed be thy name,' when in their lives they profane his name? They dishonour God by their atheism, Sabbath-breaking, uncleanness, perjury, intemperance, and injustice. Men hang out a flag of defiance against heaven. As the Thracians, when it thunders, shoot their arrows against heaven, so men shoot their sins as bearded arrows against heaven. Sinners are hardened in sin, they despise counsel, they laugh at reproof, they cast off the veil of modesty. Satan has taken such full possession of them, that when they sin, they glory in their shame. Phil iii 19. They brag how many new oaths they have invented, how often they have been drunk, how many they have defiled; they declare their sin as Sodom. Such horrid impieties are committed that a modest heathen would blush at. Men in this age sin at that rate, as if either they did not believe there were a hell, or as if they feared hell would be full ere they could get there! Was God's name ever so openly dishonoured? All our preaching will not make them leave their sins. What a black veil is drawn over the face of religion at this day? *Vivimus in temporum faecibus.* Seneca. 'We live in the dregs of time,' wherein the common sewer of wickedness runs. Physicians call it cachexia, when there is no part of the body free from distemper. England has such a disease. 'The whole head is sick, the whole heart is faint.' Isa i 5. As black vapours rising out of the earth cloud and darken the sun, so the sins of people in our age, like hellish vapours, cast a cloud upon God's glorious name. O that our eyes were rivers of water of holy tears, to see how God's name, instead of being hallowed, is polluted and profaned! May we not justly fear some heavy judgments on this account? Can God put up with our affronts any longer? Can he endure to have his name reproached? Will a king suffer his crown-jewels to be trampled in the dust? Do we not see the symptoms of God's anger? Do we not see his judgments hovering over us? Surely God is whetting his sword, he has bent his bow, and is preparing his arrows to shoot. *Qualis per arva Leo fulvam minaci fronte concutiens jubam* [Like the Lion with threatening brows shaking his tawny mane over the land]. Seneca. The body politic is in a paroxysm, or burning fit; and may not the Lord cause a sad phlebotomy? Seeing we will not leave our sins, he may make us lose our blood. May we not fear that the ark should remove, the vision cease, the stars in God's church be removed, and we follow the gospel to the grave? When God's name, which should be hallowed, is profaned by a nation, it is just with God to write that dismal epitaph upon its tomb, 'The glory is departed.' It were well if the profane party only were guilty; but may not many professors be called to the bar, and indicted for having dishonoured God's name? 'Are there not with you, even with you, sins against the Lord your God?' 2 Chron xxviii 10. Are these the spots of God's children? Deut xxxii 5. If you are diamonds, have you no flaws? Have you not your vanities? If your discourse be not profane, is it not vain? Have you not your self-seekings, rash censures, indecent dresses? If the wicked of the land swear, do not you sometimes slander? If they are drunk with wine, are not you sometimes drunk with passion? If their sin be blaspheming, is not your sin murmuring? 'Are there not with you, even with you, sins against the Lord?' The sins of God's children go nearer to his heart than the sins of others. 'When the Lord saw it, he abhorred them, because of the provoking of his sons and of his daughters.' Deut xxxii 19. The sins of the wicked anger God, the sins of his own people grieve him; he will be sure to punish them. 'You only have I known of all the families of the earth; therefore I will punish you for all your iniquities.' Amos iii 2. O that our head were waters, that we could make this place a Bochim, a place of weeping, that God's children might mix blushing with tears, that they have so little hallowed, and so much eclipsed, God's name! Truly his own people have sinned enough to justify him in all his severe actings against them.

Use 3. For exhortation. Let us hallow and sanctify God's name. Could we but see a glimpse of God's glory, as Moses did in the rock, it would draw adoration and praise from us. Could we 'see God face to face,' as the angels in heaven do, could we behold him sitting on his throne like a jasper-stone, at the sight of his glory we should do as the twenty-four elders, who 'worship him that liveth for ever, and cast their crowns before the throne, saying, Thou art worthy, O Lord, to receive glory and honour and power.' Rev iv 11. That we may be stirred up to this great duty of hallowing, adoring, and sanctifying God's name, let us consider:

(1) It is the very end of our being. Why did God give us life, but that by living we may hallow his name? Why did he give us souls, but to admire him? and tongues, but to praise him? The excellence of a thing is the end for which it was made; as of a star to give light, and of a plant to be fruitful. So the excellence of a Christian is to answer the end of his creation, which is to hallow God's name, and live to that God by whom he lives. He who lives, and of whom God has no honour, buries himself alive, and exposes himself to a curse. Christ cursed the barren fig-tree.

(2) God's name is so excellent that it deserves to be hallowed. 'How

excellent is thy name in all the earth!' Psa viii 9. 'Thou art clothed with honour and majesty.' Psa civ 1. As the sun has its brightness, whether we admire it or not, so God's name is illustrious and glorious, whether we hallow it or not. In him are all shining perfections, holiness, wisdom, and mercy. He is 'worthy to be praised.' 2 Sam xxii 4. God is *dignus honore*, worthy of honour, love, and adoration. We often bestow titles of honour upon those who do not deserve them; but God is worthy to be praised; his name deserves hallowing; he is above all the honour and praise which angels in heaven give him.

(3) We pray, 'hallowed be thy name'; that is, let thy name be honoured and magnified by us. If we do not magnify his name, we contradict our own prayers. To say, 'hallowed be thy name,' yet not to bring honour to God's name, is to take his name in vain.

(4) If men will not hallow God's name, and bring revenues of honour to him, he will get honour upon them. 'I will get me honour upon Pharaoh.' Exod xiv 17. Pharaoh would not hallow God's name; he said, 'Who is the Lord that I should obey him?' Well, says God, if Pharaoh will not honour me, I will get honour upon him. When God overthrew him and his chariots in the sea, he got honour upon him. God's power and justice were glorified in his destruction. There are some whom God has raised to great power and dignity, and they will not honour his name; they make use of their power to dishonour him; they cast reproach upon his name, and revile his servants. If they will not honour God, he will get honour upon them in their final ruin. Herod did not give glory to God, but God got glory upon him. 'The angel of the Lord smote him because he gave not God the glory, and he was eaten of worms.' Acts xii 23.

(5) It will be no small comfort to us when we come to die, that we have hallowed and sanctified God's name. Christ's comfort a little before his death was, 'I have glorified thee on the earth.' John xvii 4. His redeeming mankind was hallowing and glorifying God's name. Never was more honour brought to God's name than by this great undertaking of Christ. Here was his comfort before death, that he had hallowed God's name, and brought glory to him. So, what a cordial will it be to us at last, when our whole life has been a hallowing of God's name! We have loved him with our hearts, praised him with our lips, honoured him with our lives; we have been to the praise of his glory. Eph i 6. At the hour of death, all your earthly comforts will vanish; to think how rich you have been, or what pleasures you have enjoyed upon earth, will not give one drachm of comfort. What is one the better for an estate that is spent? But to have conscience witnessing that you have hallowed God's name, that your whole life has been glorifying him, what sweet peace and satisfaction will this give! How glad is that

servant who has been all day working in the vineyard, when evening comes, that he shall receive his pay! How sweet will death be when they who have spent their lives in honouring God, shall receive the recompense of reward! What comfort was it to Hezekiah, when on his sick bed, that he could appeal to God, 'Remember, Lord, how I have walked before thee with a perfect heart, and have done that which is good in thy sight.' Isa xxxviii 3. I have hallowed thy name, I have brought all the honour I could to thee, 'I have done that which is good in thy sight.'

(6) There is nothing lost by what we do for God. If we bring honour to his name, he will honour us. As Balak said to Balaam, 'Am not I able to promote thee to honour?' Num xxii 37. So if we hallow and sanctify God's name, is he not able to promote us to honour? He will honour us *in our life*. He will put honour upon our persons: he will number us among his jewels. Mal iii 17. He will make us a royal diadem in his hand. Isa lxii 3. He will lift us up in the eyes of others. 'They shall be as the stones of a crown lifted up, as an ensign of glory.' Zech ix 17. He will esteem us as the cream and flower of the creation. 'Since thou wast precious in my sight, thou hast been honourable.' Isa xliii 4. God will put honour upon our names. 'The memory of the just is blessed.' Prov x 7. How renowned have the saints been in all ages, who have hallowed God's name! How renowned was Abraham for his faith, Moses for his meekness, David for his zeal, Paul for his love to Christ! Their names as a precious ointment, send forth a sweet perfume in God's church to this day. God will honour us *at our death*. He will send his angels to carry us up with triumph into heaven. 'The beggar died, and was carried by the angels into Abraham's bosom.' Luke xvi 22. Amasis king of Egypt, had his chariot drawn by four kings, whom he had conquered in war; but what is this to the glory every believer shall have at his death? He shall be carried by the angels of God. God will put honour upon us *after death*. He will put glory upon our bodies. We shall be as the angels, not for substance, but quality; our bodies shall be agile and nimble. Now they are as a weight, then they shall be as a wing, moving swiftly from place to place; they shall be full of clarity and brightness, like Christ's glorious body. Phil iii 21. The bodies of the saints shall be as cloth dyed into a scarlet colour, made more illustrious; they shall be so clear and transparent, that the soul shall sparkle through them, as the wine through the glass. God will put glory upon our souls. If the cabinet of the body shall be so illustrious, of what orient brightness shall the jewel be! Then will be the great coronation day, when the saints shall wear the robe of immortality, and the crown of righteousness which fades not away. Oh, how glorious will that garland be which is made of the flowers of paradise! Who then would not hallow and glorify his name, and spread his renown in the world,

who will put such immortal honour upon his people, 'as eye hath not seen, nor ear heard, nor hath entered into the heart of man to conceive'?

(7) If men do not hallow, but profane and dishonour God's name, he will pour contempt upon them. Though they be ever so great, and though clothed in purple and scarlet, they shall be abhorred of God, and their name shall rot. Though the name of Judas be in the Bible, and the name of Pontius Pilate be in the Creed, yet their names stand there for infamy, as traitors to the crown of heaven. 'I will make thy grave, for thou art vile.' Nahum i 14. It is said of Antiochus Epiphanes, though he was a king, and his name signifies illustrious, yet God esteemed him vile. To show how base the wicked are in God's esteem, he compares them to things most vile; to chaff (Psa i 4); to dross (Psa cxix 119); to the filth that foams out of the sea (Isa lvii 20). As God vilely esteems such as do not hallow his name, so he sends them to a vile place at last. Vagrants are sent to the house of correction; and hell is the house of correction to which the wicked are sent when they die. Let all this prevail with us to hallow and sanctify God's name.

What should we do to honour and sanctify God's name?

Let us get: (1) A sound knowledge of God. Take a view of his superlative excellencies; his holiness, his incomprehensible goodness. The angels know God better than we, therefore they sanctify his name, and sing hallelujahs to him. Let us labour to know him to be our God. 'This God is our God.' Psa xlviii 14. We may dread him as a judge, but we cannot honour him as a father, till we know he is our God.

(2) Get a sincere love to God; a love of appreciation, and a love of complacency to delight in him. 'Lord, thou knowest I love thee.' John xxi 15. He can never honour his master who does not love him. The reason God's name is no more hallowed, is because his name is no more loved.

So much for the first petition.

The Second Petition in the Lord's Prayer

'Thy kingdom come.' Matt vi 10

A SOUL truly devoted to God, joins heartily in this petition, *adveniat regnum tuum*, 'thy kingdom come.' In these words it is implied that God is a king, for he who has a kingdom, can be no less than a king. 'God is the King of all the earth.' Psa xlvii 7. He is a King upon his throne. 'God sitteth upon the throne of his holiness.' Psa xlvii 8. He has a regal title, high and mighty. 'Thus saith the high and lofty One.' Isa lvii 15. He has the ensigns of royalty. He has his sword. 'If I whet my glittering sword.' Deut xxxii 41. He has his sceptre. 'A sceptre of righteousness is the sceptre of thy kingdom.' Heb i 8. He has his crown royal. 'On his head were many crowns.' Rev xix 12. He has his *jura regalia*, his kingly prerogatives. He has power to make laws, to seal pardons, which are the flowers and jewels belonging to his crown. Thus the Lord is King.

Further, he is a great King. 'A great King above all gods.' Psa xcv 3. He is great in and of himself; and not like other kings, who are made great by their subjects. That he is so great a King appears by the immensity of his being. 'Do not I fill heaven and earth? saith the Lord.' Jer xxiii 24. His centre is everywhere; he is nowhere included, yet nowhere excluded; he is so immensely great, that 'the heaven of heavens cannot contain him'. 1 Kings viii 27. His greatness appears by the effects of his power. He 'made heaven and earth,' and can unmake it. Psa cxxiv 8. With a breath he can crumble us to dust; with a word he can unpin the world, and break the axle-tree of it in pieces. 'He poureth contempt upon princes.' Job xii 21. 'He shall cut off the spirit of princes.' Psa lxxvi 12. He is Lord paramount, who does whatever he will. Psa cxv 3. He weigheth 'the mountains in scales, and the hills in a balance.' Isa xl 12.

God is a glorious King. 'Who is this King of glory? The Lord of hosts, he is the King of glory.' Psa xxiv 10. He has internal glory. 'The Lord reigneth, he is clothed with majesty.' Psa xciii 1. Other kings have royal and sumptuous apparel to make them appear glorious to beholders, but all their magnificence is borrowed; God is clothed with his own majesty; his own glorious essence is instead of royal robes, and 'he hath girded himself with strength.' Kings have their guard about them to defend their person, because they are not able to defend themselves; but God needs no guard or assistance from others. 'He hath girded himself with strength.' His own power is his lifeguard. 'Who in the heaven can be compared unto the Lord? Who among the sons of the mighty can be likened unto the Lord?' Psa lxxxix 6. He has a pre-eminence above all other kings for majesty. 'He hath on his vesture a name written, *Rex Regum*, KING OF KINGS.' Rev xix 16. He has the highest throne, the richest crown, the largest dominions, and the longest possession. 'The Lord sitteth King for ever.' Psa xxix 10. Though he has many heirs, yet no successors. He sets up his throne where no other king does; he rules the will and affections; his power binds the conscience. Angels serve him, all the kings of the earth hold their crowns and diadems by immediate tenure from this great King. 'By me kings reign,' Prov viii 15. To this Lord Jehovah all kings must give account, and from his tribunal there is no appeal.

Use 1. For instruction (1) If God be so great a King, and sits King for ever, it is no disparagement for us to serve him, *Deo servire est regnare* [to serve God is to reign]; it is an honour to serve a king. If the angels fly swiftly upon the King of heaven's message, then well may we look upon it as a favour to be taken into his royal service. Dan ix 21. Theodosius thought it a greater honour to be God's servant, than to be an emperor. It is more honour to serve God than to have kings serve us. Every subject of this King is crowned with regal honour. He 'hath made us kings.' Rev i 6 .Therefore, as the queen of Sheba, having seen the glory of Solomon's kingdom, said, 'Happy are these thy servants which stand continually before thee.' 1 Kings x 8. So happy are those saints who stand before the King of heaven, and wait on his throne.

(2) If God be such a glorious King, crowned with wisdom, armed with power, bespangled with riches, it shows us what prudence it is to have this King to be ours; to say, 'My King, and my God.' Psa v 2. It is counted great policy to be on the strongest side. If we belong to the King of heaven, we are sure to be on the strongest side. The King of glory can with ease destroy his adversaries; he can pull down their pride, befool their policy and restrain their malice. That stone cut out of the mountain without hands, which smote the image (Dan ii 34), was an emblem, says Augustine, of Christ's monarchical power, conquering and triumphing over his enemies. If we are on God's side, we are on the strongest side; he can with a word destroy his enemies. 'Then shall he speak unto them in his wrath.' Psa ii 5. Nay, with a look he can destroy them. 'Look upon every one that is proud and bring him low.' Job xl 12. It needs cost God no more to confound those who rise up against him, than a look, a cast of his eye. 'In the morning watch, the Lord looked unto the host of the Egyptians, through the pillar of fire, and troubled the host of the Egyptians, and took off their

chariot-wheels.' Exod xiv 24. What wisdom is it then to have this King to be ours! Then we are on the strongest side.

Use 2. For exhortation (1) If God be so glorious a King, full of power and majesty, let us trust in him. 'They that know thy name will put their trust in thee.' Psa ix 10. Trust him with your soul; you cannot put this jewel in safer hands. And trust him with church and state affairs; he is King. 'The Lord is a man of war.' Exod xv 3. He can make bare his holy arm in the eyes of all the nations. If means fail, he is never at a loss; there are no impossibilities with him; he can make the dry bones live. Ezek xxxvii 10. As a King he can command, and as a God he can create salvation. 'I create Jerusalem a rejoicing.' Isa lxv 18. Let us trust all our affairs with this great King. Either God can remove mountains or can leap over them. Cant ii 8.

(2) If God be so great a King, let us fear him. 'Fear ye not me? saith the Lord: will ye not tremble at my presence?' Jer v 22. We have enough of fear of men. Fear makes danger appear greater, and sin less; but let us fear the King of kings, who has power to cast body and soul into hell. Luke xii 5. As one wedge drives out another, so the fear of God would drive out all base carnal fear. Let us fear that God whose throne is set above all kings; they may be mighty, but he is almighty. Kings have no power, but what God has given them; their power is limited, his is infinite. Let us fear this King, whose eyes are 'as a flame of fire.' Rev i 14. 'The mountains quake at him; and the rocks are thrown down by him.' Nahum i 5, 6. If he stamps with his foot, all the creatures are presently up in a battalion to fight for him. Oh, tremble and fear before this God. Fear is *janitor animae*, the doorkeeper of the soul. It keeps sin from entering. 'How can I do this great wickedness, and sin against God?' Gen xxxix 9.

(3) If God be so glorious a King, he has *jus vitae et necis*, he has the power of life and death in his hand. Let all the potentates of the earth take heed how they employ their power against the King of heaven. They employ their power against God, who with their sceptres beat down his truth, which is the most orient pearl of his crown; who crush and persecute his people, who are the apple of his eye (Zech ii 8); who trample upon his laws, and royal edicts, which he has set forth (Psa ii 3). What is a king without his laws? Let all that are invested with worldly power and grandeur take heed how they oppose the King of glory. The Lord will be too hard for all that come against him. 'Hast thou an arm like God?' Job xl 9. Wilt thou measure arms with the Almighty? Shall a little child fight with an archangel? 'Can thy heart endure, or can thy hands be strong in the days that I shall deal with thee?' Ezek xxii 14. Christ will put all his enemies at last under his feet. Psa cx 1. All the multitude of the wicked, who set themselves against God,

shall be but as so many clusters of ripe grapes, to be cast into the winepress of the wrath of God, to be trodden by him till their blood come forth. The King of glory will come off victor at last. Men may set up their standard, but God always sets up his trophies of victory. The Lord has a golden sceptre, and an iron rod. Psa ii 9. Those who will not bow to the one, shall be broken by the other.

(4) Is God so great a king, having all power in heaven and earth in his hand! let us learn subjection to him. You who have gone on in sin, and by your impieties hung out a flag of defiance against the King of heaven, O come in quickly, and make your peace, submit to God. 'Kiss the Son, lest he be angry.' Psa ii 12. Kiss Christ with a kiss of love, and a kiss of obedience. Obey the King of heaven, when he speaks to you by his ministers and ambassadors. 2 Cor v 20. When God bids you flee from sin, and espouse holiness, obey him: to obey is better than sacrifice. 'To obey God,' says Luther, 'is better than to work miracles.' Obey God willingly. Isa i 19. That is the best obedience that is cheerful, as that is the sweetest honey which drops out of the comb. Obey God swiftly. 'Then lifted I up mine eyes, and, behold, two women, and the wind was in their wings.' Zech v 9. Wings are swift, but wind in the wings denotes great swiftness; such should our obedience to God be. Obey the King of glory.

Use 3. For consolation. Here is comfort to those who are the subjects of the King of heaven. God will put forth all the royal power for their succour and comfort. (1) The King of heaven will plead their cause. 'I will plead thy cause, and take vengeance for thee.' Jer li 36. (2) He will protect his people. He sets an invisible guard about them. 'I will be unto her a wall of fire round about.' Zech ii 5. A wall, that is defensive; a wall of fire, that is offensive. (3) When it may be for the good of his people, he will raise up deliverance to them. 'The Lord saved them by a great deliverance.' 1 Chron xi 14. God reigning as a king, can save any way; even by contemptible means, as the blowing of the trumpets, and blazing of lamps. Judges vii 20. By contrary means; as when he made the sea a wall to Israel, and the waters were a means to keep them from drowning. The fish's belly was a ship in which Jonah sailed safe to shore. God will never want ways of saving his people; rather than fail, their very enemies shall do his work. 2 Chron xx 23. He sets Ammon and Mount Seir one against another. As God will deliver his people from temporal danger, so from spiritual danger, as from sin, and from hell. 'Jesus which delivered us from the wrath to come.' 1 Thess i 10.

Use 4. For intimidation. If God be king, he will set his utmost strength against those who are the enemies of his kingdom. 'A fire goeth before him, and burneth up his enemies round about.' Psa xcvii 3. (1) He will set himself against his enemies. He will set his attributes against them, his power and justice; and 'who knoweth the power of thine anger?' Psa xc 11. (2) He will set the creatures against them. 'The stars in their courses fought against Sisera.' Judges v 20. Tertullian observes, that when the Persians fought against the Christians, a mighty wind arose, which made the Persians' arrows to fly back in their own faces. Every creature has a quarrel with a sinner; the stone out of the wall, the hail and the frost. Hab ii 11. 'He destroyed their vines with hail, and their sycomore-trees with frost.' Psa lxxviii 47. (3) God will set men against themselves. He will set conscience against them. How terrible is this rod when turned into a serpent! Melanchthon calls it *Erinnys conscientiae*, a hellish fury; it is called *vermis conscientiae*, the worm of conscience. Mark ix 44. What a worm did Spira feel in his conscience! He was a terror to himself. The worst civil wars are between a man and his conscience. (4) God will set the diseases of men's bodies against them. 'The Lord smote [Jehoram] in his bowels with an incurable disease.' 2 Chron xxi 18. God can raise an army against a man out of his own bowels; he can set one humour of the body against another; the heat to dry up the moisture, and the moisture to drown the heat. The Lord needs not go far for instruments to punish the sinner; he can make the joints of the same body to smite one against another. Dan v 6. (5) God will set men's friends against them. Where they used to have honey, they shall have nothing but aloes and wormwood. 'When a man's ways please the Lord, he maketh even his enemies to be at peace with him.' Prov xvi 7. When he opposes God, he makes his friends to be his enemies. The wife of Commodus, the emperor, gave him poison in perfumed wine. Sennacherib's two sons were the death of him. 2 Kings xix 37. (6) God will set Satan against them. 'Let Satan stand at his right hand.' Psa cix 6. What does Satan at the sinner's elbows? He helps him to contrive sin. He tempts him to commit sin. He terrifies him for sin. He that has Satan standing at his right hand, is sure to be set at God's left hand. Here is the misery of such as oppose God's royal sceptre, that he will set everything in the world against them. If there be either justice in heaven or fire in hell, sinners shall not be unpunished.

Use 5. For encouragement. If God be such an absolute monarch, and crowned with such glory and majesty, let us all engage in his service, and stand up for his truth and worship. Dare to own God in the worst time. He is King of kings, and is able to reward all his servants. We may be losers for him, we shall never be losers by him. We are ready to say, as Amaziah, 'What shall I do for the hundred talents?' 2 Chron xxv 9. If I appear for God, I may lose my estate, my life. I say with the prophet, God is able to give you much more than this; he can give you for the present inward peace, and for the future a crown of glory which fadeth not away.

What kingdom is meant when Christ says, 'Thy kingdom come'?

Let us show first what he does not mean. (1) He does not mean a political or earthly kingdom. The apostles indeed did desire Christ's temporal reign. 'Wilt thou at this time restore the kingdom again to Israel?' Acts i 6. But Christ said his kingdom was not of this world. John xviii 36. So that, when Christ taught his disciples to pray, 'Thy kingdom come,' he did not mean it of any earthly kingdom, that he should reign here in outward pomp and splendour. (2) It is not meant of God's providential kingdom. 'His kingdom ruleth over all;' that is, the kingdom of his providence. Psa ciii 19. This kingdom we do not pray for when we say, 'Thy kingdom come;' for this kingdom is already come. God exercises the kingdom of his providence in the world. 'He putteth down one and setteth up another.' Psa lxxv 7. Nothing stirs in the world but God has a hand in it; he sets every wheel at work; he humbles the proud, and raises the poor out of the dust to set them among princes. 1 Sam ii 8. The kingdom of God's providence rules over all; kings do nothing but what his providence permits and orders. Acts iv 27, 28. This kingdom of God's providence we do not pray should come, for it is already come.

What kingdom then is meant when we say, 'Thy kingdom come'? Positively a twofold kingdom is meant. (1) The kingdom of grace, which God exercises in the consciences of his people. This is *regnum Dei mikron*. God's lesser kingdom. When we pray, 'Thy kingdom come,' we pray that the kingdom of grace may be set up in our hearts and increased. (2) We pray also, that the kingdom of glory may hasten, and that we may, in God's good time be translated into it. These two kingdoms of grace and glory, differ not specifically, but gradually; they differ not in nature, but in degree only. The kingdom of grace is nothing but the beginning of the kingdom of glory. The kingdom of grace is glory in the seed, and the kingdom of glory is grace in the flower. The kingdom of grace is glory in the daybreak, and the kingdom of glory is grace in the full meridian. The kingdom of grace is glory militant, and the kingdom of glory is grace triumphant. There is such an inseparable connexion between these two kingdoms, grace and glory, that there is no passing into the one but by the other. At Athens there were two temples, a temple of virtue and a temple of honour; and there was no going into the temple of honour, but through the temple of virtue; so the kingdoms of grace and glory are so closely joined together, that we cannot go into the kingdom of glory but through the kingdom of grace. Many people aspire after the kingdom of glory, but never look after grace;

E

but these two, which God hath joined together, may not be put asunder. The kingdom of grace leads to the kingdom of glory.

I. *The first thing implied in this petition, 'Thy kingdom come,' is that we are in the kingdom of darkness.* We pray that we may be brought out of the kingdom of darkness. The state of nature is a kingdom of darkness, where sin is said to reign. Rom vi 12. It is called, 'the power of darkness.' Col i 13. Man, before the fall, was illuminated with perfect knowledge, but this light is now eclipsed, and he is fallen into the kingdom of darkness.

How many ways is a natural man in the kingdom of darkness?

(1) He is under the darkness of ignorance. 'Having the understanding darkened.' Eph iv 18. Ignorance is a black veil drawn over the mind. Men by nature may have a deep reach in the things of the world, and yet be ignorant of the things of God. Nahash the Ammonite would make a covenant with Israel to thrust out their right eyes. 1 Sam xi 2. Since the fall, our left eye remains, a deep insight into worldly matters; but our right eye is thrust out, we have no saving knowledge of God. Something we know by nature, but nothing as we ought to know. 1 Cor viii 2. Ignorance draws the curtains round about the soul. 1 Cor ii 14.

(2) A natural man is under the darkness of pollution. Hence sinful actions are called 'works of darkness.' Rom xiii 12. Pride and lust darken the glory of the soul. A sinner's heart is a dark conclave that looks blacker than hell.

(3) A natural man is under the darkness of misery; he is exposed to divine vengeance; and the sadness of this darkness is, that men are not sensible of it. They are blind, yet they think they see. The darkness of Egypt was such thick darkness as 'might be felt.' Exod x 21. Men by nature are in thick darkness; but here is the misery, the darkness cannot be felt; they will not believe they are in the dark till they are past recovery.

Use 1. See what the state of nature is. It is a 'kingdom of darkness,' and it is a bewitching darkness. 'Men loved darkness rather than light;' as the Athlantes in Ethiopia curse the sun. John iii 19. Darkness of sin leads to 'chains under darkness.' Jude 6. What comfort can such take in earthly things? The Egyptians might have food, gold, silver; but they could take but little comfort in them, while they were in such darkness as might be felt; so the natural man may have riches and friends to delight in, yet he is in the kingdom of darkness, and how dead are all these comforts! Thou who art in the kingdom of darkness, knowest not whither thou goest. As the ox is driven to the shambles, but knows not whither he goes, so the devil is driving thee before him to hell, but thou knowest not whither thou goest.

Shouldest thou die in thy natural estate, while thou art in the kingdom of darkness, blackness of darkness is reserved for thee. 'To whom is reserved the blackness of darkness for ever.' Jude 13.

Use 2. Let us pray that God will bring us out of this kingdom of darkness. God's kingdom of grace cannot come into our hearts till we are brought out of the kingdom of darkness. Col i 13. Why should not we strive to get out of this kingdom of darkness? Who would desire to stay in a dark dungeon? O fear the chains of darkness. Jude 6. These chains are God's power, binding men as in chains under wrath for ever. O pray that God would deliver you out of the kingdom of darkness! (1) Be sensible of thy dark, damned estate, that thou hast not one spark of fire to give thee light! (2) Go to Christ to enlighten thee! 'Christ shall give thee light;' he will not only bring thy light to thee, but open thine eyes to see it. Eph v 14. That is the first thing implied, 'Thy kingdom come;' we pray that we may be brought out of the kingdom of darkness.

II. *The second thing implied in 'Thy kingdom come,' is that we pray against the devil's kingdom;* that his kingdom may be demolished in the world. His kingdom stands in opposition to Christ's kingdom; and when we pray, 'Thy kingdom come,' we pray against Satan's kingdom. He has a kingdom: he got it by conquest: he conquered mankind in paradise. He has his throne. 'Thou dwellest where Satan's seat is.' Rev ii 13. His throne is set up in the hearts of men; he does not care for their purses, but their hearts. He is served upon the knee. Eph ii 2. 'They worshipped the dragon,' that is, the devil. Rev xiii 4. Satan's empire is very large. Most kingdoms in the world pay tribute to him. His kingdom has two qualifications or characters: [1] It is *regnum nequitiae:* a kingdom of impiety. [2] It is *regnum servitutis:* a kingdom of slavery.

[1] The kingdom of Satan is a kingdom of impiety. Nothing but sin goes on in his kingdom. Murder and heresy, lust and treachery, oppression and division, are the constant trade driven in his dominions. He is called 'the unclean spirit.' Luke xi 24. What else is propagated in his kingdom but a mystery of iniquity?

[2] Satan's kingdom is a kingdom of slavery. He makes all his subjects slaves. *Peccati reus dura daemonis tyrannide tenetur* [The sinner is held captive under the grim tyranny of the devil]. Satan is a usurper and a tyrant; he is a worse tyrant than any other. (1) Other tyrants do but rule over the body, but Satan's kingdom rules over the soul. He rides some men as we do upon horses. (2) Other tyrants have some pity on their slaves. Though they make them work in the galleys, yet they give them meat, and let them have their

hours for rest; but Satan is a merciless tyrant, who gives his slaves poison instead of meat, and hurtful lusts to feed on. 1 Tim vi 9. Nor will he let his slaves have any rest: he hires them out to do his drudgery. 'They weary themselves to commit iniquity.' Jer ix 5. When the devil had entered into Judas, he sent him to the high priests, and from thence to the garden, and never let him rest till he had betrayed Christ and hanged himself. Thus he is the worst of tyrants. When men have served him to their utmost strength, he welcomes them to hell with fire and brimstone.

Use. Let us pray that Satan's kingdom, set up in the world, may be overthrown. It is sad to think that, though the devil's kingdom be so bad, yet that it should have so many to support it. He has more to stand up for his kingdom than Christ has for his. What a large harvest of souls has Satan! and God only a few gleanings. The Pope and the Turk give the power to Satan. If in God's visible church the devil has so many loyal subjects that serve him with their lives and souls, how do his subjects swarm in places of idolatry and paganism, where there is none to oppose him, but all vote on the devil's side! Men are willing slaves to Satan; they will fight and die for him; therefore he is not only called 'the prince of this world,' but 'the god of this world' (John xii 31; 2 Cor iv 4), to show what power he has over men's souls. O let us pray that God would break the sceptre of the devil's kingdom; that Michael may destroy the dragon; that, by the help of a religious magistracy and ministry, the hellish kingdom of the prince of darkness may be beaten down! Satan's kingdom must be thrown down before Christ's kingdom can flourish in its power and majesty.

When we pray, 'Thy kingdom come,' something is positively intended.

III. *We pray that the kingdom of grace may be set up in our hearts.*

When we pray, 'Thy kingdom come,' we pray that the kingdom of grace may come into our hearts. This is *regnum Dei mikron*, God's lesser kingdom. 'The kingdom of God is righteousness.' Rom xiv 17. 'The kingdom of God is within you.' Luke xvii 21.

Why is grace called a kingdom?

Because, when grace comes, there is a kingly government set up in the soul. Grace rules the will and affections, and brings the whole man in subjection to Christ; it kings it in the soul, sways the sceptre, subdues mutinous lusts, and keeps the soul in a spiritual decorum.

Why is there such need to pray that this kingdom of grace may come into our hearts?

(1) Because, till the kingdom of grace come, we have no right to the

covenant of grace. The covenant of grace is sweetened with love, be-spangled with promises; it is our *Magna Charta*, by virtue of which God passes himself over to us to be our God. Who are heirs of the covenant of grace? Only such as have the kingdom of grace in their hearts. 'A new heart will I give you, and a new spirit will I put within you.' Ezek xxxvi 26. Here the kingdom of grace is set up in the soul; it then follows, 'I will be your God', v 28. The covenant of grace is to an ungracious person a sealed fountain; it is kept as a paradise with a flaming sword, that the sinner may not touch it. Without grace, you have no more right to it than a farmer to the city-charter.

(2) Unless the kingdom of grace be set up in our hearts, our purest offerings are defiled. They may be good as to the matter, but not as to the manner; they want that which should meliorate and sweeten them. Under the law, if a man who was unclean by a dead body, carried a piece of holy flesh in his skirt, the holy flesh could not cleanse him, but he polluted it. Hag ii 12. Till the kingdom of grace be in our hearts, ordinances do not purify us, but we pollute them. Even the prayer of an ungracious person becomes sin. Prov xv 8. In what a sad condition is a man before God's kingdom of grace is set up in his heart! Whether he comes or comes not to the ordinance, he sins. If he does not come to the ordinance, he is a contemner of it; if he does come, he is a polluter of it. A sinner's works are *opera mortua*, dead works; and those works which are dead, cannot please God. A dead flower has no sweetness. Heb xi 6.

(3) We had need pray that the kingdom of grace may come, because until this kingdom come into our hearts, we are loathsome in God's eyes. 'My soul lothed them.' Zech xi 8. *Quanta est foeditas vitiosae mentis* [How great is the foulness of a corrupt mind]. A heart void of grace looks blacker than hell. Sin transforms man into a devil. 'Have I not chosen you twelve, and one of you is a devil?' John vi 70. Envy is the devil's eye, hypocrisy is his cloven foot. Thus it is before the kingdom of grace come. So deformed is a graceless person, that when once he sees his own filth and leprosy, the first thing he does is to loathe himself. 'Ye shall lothe yourself in your own sight for all your evils.' Ezek xx 43. I have read of a woman who always used flattering glasses, and who, by chance, seeing her face in a true glass, *in insaniam delapsa est*, she ran mad. When once God gives those who now dress themselves by the flattering glass of presumption, a sight of their own filthiness, they will abhor themselves. 'Ye shall lothe yourselves in your own sight for all your evils.'

(4) Before the kingdom of grace comes unto us we are spiritually illegitimate, of the bastard brood of the old serpent. John viii 44. To be illegitimate is the greatest infamy. 'A bastard shall not enter into the con-

gregation of the Lord even to his tenth generation.' Deut xxiii 2. He was to be kept out of the holy assemblies of Israel as an infamous creature. A bastard by law cannot inherit. Before the kingdom of grace comes into the heart, a person is to God as illegitimate, and so continuing he cannot enter into the kingdom of heaven.

(5) Before the kingdom of grace be set up in men's hearts, the kingdom of Satan is set up in them. They are said to be under 'the power of Satan.' Acts xxvi 18. Satan commands the will; though he cannot force the will, by his subtle temptations he can draw it. He is said to take men captive 'at his will.' 2 Tim ii 26. The Greek word signifies to take them alive as the fowler does the bird in the snare. The sinner's heart is the devil's mansion-house. 'I will return into my house.' Matt xii 44. It is *officina diaboli*, Satan's shop, where he works. 'The prince of the air that now worketh in the children of disobedience.' Eph ii 2. The members of the body are the tools with which Satan works. He possesses men. In Christ's time many had their bodies possessed, but it is far worse to have the souls possessed. One is possessed with an unclean devil, another with a revengeful devil. No wonder the ship goes full sail when the wind blows; no wonder men go full sail in sin when the devil, the prince of the air, blows them. Thus, till the kingdom of grace come, men are under the power of Satan, who, like Draco, writes all his laws in blood.

(6) Till the kingdom of grace comes, a man is exposed to the wrath of God. 'Who knoweth the power of thine anger?' Psa xc 11. If when but a spark of God's wrath flies into a man's conscience in this life it is so terrible, what will it be when God stirs up all his anger? So inconceivably torturing is God's wrath, that the wicked call to the rocks and mountains to fall on them and hide them from it. Rev vi 16. The hellish torments are compared to a fiery lake. Rev xx 15. Other fire is but painted in comparison of this; and this lake of fire burns for ever. Mark ix 44. God's breath kindles this fire. Isa xxx 33. Where shall we find engines or buckets to quench it? Time will not finish it; tears will not quench it. To this fiery lake are men exposed till the kingdom of grace be set up in them.

(7) Till the kingdom of grace comes, men cannot die with comfort. He only who takes Christ in the arms of his faith can look death in the face with joy. It is sad to have the king of terrors in the body and not the kingdom of grace in the soul. It is a wonder every graceless person does not die distracted. What will a grace-despiser do when death comes to him with a writ of *habeas corpus*? Hell follows death. 'Behold, a pale horse, and his name that sat on him was death, and hell followed with him.' Rev vi 8. Thus you see what need we have to pray that the kingdom of grace may come. Of him that dies without Christ I may say, 'It had been good for that man if he had

not been born.' Matt xxvi 24. Few believe the necessity of having the kingdom of grace set up in their hearts, as appears by this, that they are well content to live without it. Does that man believe the necessity of pardon who is content to be without it? Most people, if they may have trading, and may sit quietly under their vine and fig-trees, are in their kingdom, though they have not the kingdom of God within them. If the candle of prosperity shine upon their head, they care not whether the grace of God shine in their hearts. Do these men believe the necessity of grace? Were they convinced how needful it is to have the kingdom of God within them, they would cry out as the jailor, 'What must I do to be saved?' Acts xvi 30.

How may we know that the kingdom of grace is set up in our hearts?

It concerns us to examine this, for our salvation depends upon it; and we had need be cautious in the search, because there is something that looks like grace, which is not. 'If a man think himself to be something, when he is nothing, he deceiveth himself.' Gal vi 3. Many think they have the kingdom of grace come into their heart, and it is only a chimera, a golden dream. *Quam multi cum vana spe descendunt ad inferos!* [How many with vain hope go down to hell!] Augustine. Zeuxis painted grapes so lively that he deceived the living birds. There are many deceits about grace.

(1) Men think they have the kingdom of grace in their hearts because they have the means of grace. They live where the silver trumpet of the gospel sounds, they are lifted up to heaven with ordinances. 'I have a Levite to my priest,' surely I shall go to heaven. Judges xvii 13. The Jews cried, 'The temple of the Lord, the temple of the Lord are [we].' Jer vii 4. We are apt to glory in this, that the oracles of God are committed to us, that we have the word and sacrament. Alas! this is a fallacy; we may have the means of grace, and yet the kingdom of grace may not be set up in our hearts. We may have the kingdom of God come nigh us, but not into us; the sound of the word in our ears, but not the savour of it in our hearts. Luke xi 20. Many of the Jews, who had Christ for their preacher, were not the better for it. Hot clothes will not put warmth into a dead man. Thou mayest have hot clothes, warm and lively preaching, and yet be spiritually dead. 'The children of the kingdom shall be cast out.' Matt viii 12.

(2) Men think they have the kingdom of grace set up in their hearts, because they have some common works of the Spirit.

[1] They have great enlightenings of mind, profound knowledge, and almost speak like angels dropped from heaven; but the apostle supposes a case in which, after men have been enlightened, they may fall away. Heb. vi 4, 5, 6.

[65]

But wherein does this illumination come short?

The illumination of hypocrites is not virtual, it does not leave an impression of holiness behind; it is like weak physic that will not work. The mind is enlightened, but the heart is not renewed. A Christian that is all head, but no feet, does not walk in the ways of God.

[2] Men have had convictions and stirrings of conscience for sin, they have seen the evil of their ways, and now hope the kingdom of grace is come; but though convictions are a step towards grace, they are not grace. Had not Pharaoh and Judas convictions? Exod x 16.

What makes convictions prove abortive? Wherein do they fail?

They are not deep enough. A sinner never saw himself lost without Christ. The seed that wanted depth of earth withered. Matt xiii 5. These convictions are like blossoms blown off before they come to maturity. They are also involuntary. The sinner does what he can to stifle them; he drowns them in wine and mirth; he labours to get rid of them. As the deer when shot runs and shakes out the arrow, so does he the arrow of conviction; or as the prisoner files off his fetters, and breaks loose, so he breaks loose from convictions. His corruptions are stronger than his convictions.

[3] Men have had some kind of humiliation, and have shed tears for their sins, and therefore hope the kingdom of grace is come into their hearts. But this is no infallible sign of grace. Saul wept, and Ahab humbled himself.

Why is not humiliation grace? Wherein does it come short of it?

Tears in the wicked do not spring from love to God, but are forced by affliction, as water that drops from distillation is forced by the fire. Gen iv 13. The tears of sinners are forced by God's fiery judgments. They are deceitful tears; *lacrimae mentiri doctae* [tears taught to lie]. Men weep, yet go on in sin; they do not drown their sins in their tears.

[4] Men have begun some reformation, therefore surely now they think the kingdom of grace is come; but there may be deceit in this. A man may leave his oaths and drunkenness, and still be in love with sin. He may leave his sin, out of fear of hell, or because it brings shame and penury, but still his heart goes after it, 'They set their heart on their iniquity' (Hos iv 8); as Lot's wife left Sodom, but still her heart was in Sodom. Hypocrites are like the snake which casts her coat, but keeps her poison. They keep the love of sin as one that has been long suitor to another; though his friends break off the match, yet still he has a hankering love to her. It may be a partial reformation. He may leave off one sin and live in another; he may refrain

drunkenness and live in covetousness; he may refrain swearing and live in the sin of slandering; one devil may be cast out and another as bad may come in his room. A man may forsake gross sins, but have no reluctance against heart sins; *motus primo primi* [the very earliest motions of sin], as proud, lustful thoughts. Though he dams up the stream, he lets alone the fountain. Oh, therefore, if there be so many deceits, and men may think the kingdom of heaven is come into their hearts when it is not, how curious and critical had we need be in our search whether we have it really in our hearts! If a man be deceived in the title of his land, it is but the loss of his estate; but if he be deceived about his grace, it is the loss of his soul.

How may we know positively that the kingdom of grace is set up in us?

In general, by having a metamorphosis or change wrought in the soul, which is called the 'new creature.' 2 Cor v 17. The faculties are not new, but there is a new nature; as the strings of a lute are the same, but the tune is altered. When the kingdom of grace is set up, there is light in the mind, order in the affections, pliableness in the will, tenderness in the conscience. They who can find no change of heart, are the same as they were; as vain, as earthly, as unclean as ever; there is no sign of God's kingdom of grace in them.

More particularly we may know the kingdom of grace is set up in our hearts. (1) By having unfeigned desires after God, which is the smoking flax that Christ will not quench. A true desire of grace is grace: by the beating of this pulse we conclude there is life. 'O Lord, let thine ear be attentive to the prayer of thy servants who desire to fear thy name.' Neh i 11. But may not a hypocrite have good desires? 'Let me die the death of the righteous.' Num xxiii 10. Unfeigned desires evidence the kingdom of God within a man.

How may these unfeigned desires be known?

An unfeigned desire is ingenuous. We desire God *propter se*, for himself, for his intrinsic excellencies. The savour of the ointment of Christ's graces draws the virgins' desires after him. Cant i 3. A true saint desires him not only for what he has, but for what he is; not only for his rewards, but for his holiness. No hypocrite can thus desire God; he may desire him for his jewels, but not for his beauty.

An unfeigned desire is insatiable. It cannot be satisfied without God; let the world heap her honours and riches, they will not satisfy. No flowers or music will content him who is thirsty; so nothing will quench the soul's thirst but the blood of Christ. He faints away, his heart breaks with longing for God. Psa lxxxiv 2; Psa cxix 20.

An unfeigned desire is active; it flourishes into endeavour. 'With my soul have I desired thee in the night; yea, with my spirit within me will I seek thee early.' Isa xxvi 9. A soul that desires aright says, 'I must have Christ; I must have grace; I will have heaven, though I take it by storm.' He who desires water will let down the bucket into the well to draw it up.

An unfeigned desire is supreme. We desire Christ, not only more than the world, but more than heaven. 'Whom have I in heaven but thee?' Psa lxxiii 25. Heaven itself would not satisfy without Christ. He is the diamond in the ring of glory. If God should say to the soul, I will put thee into heaven, but I will hide my face from thee, I will draw a curtain between, that thou shalt not behold my glory, the soul would not be satisfied, but say, as Absalom, 'Now therefore let me see the king's face.' 2 Sam xiv 32.

An unfeigned desire is gradual. It increases as the sun in the horizon. A little of God will not satisfy, but the pious soul desires still more. A drop of water is not enough for the thirsty traveller. Though a Christian is thankful for the least degree of grace, yet he is not satisfied with the greatest; he still thirsts for more of Christ, and his Spirit. Desire is a holy dropsy. A saint would have more knowledge, more sanctity, more of Christ's presence. A glimpse of Christ through the lattice of an ordinance is sweet; and the soul will never leave longing till it sees him face to face. It desires to have grace perfected in glory. *Dulcissimo Deo totus immergi cupit et inviscerari* [it desires to be wholly plunged and embowelled in the sweetness of God]. We would be swallowed up in God, and be ever bathing ourselves in those perfumed waters of pleasure which run at his right hand for ever. Surely this unfeigned desire after God is a blessed sign that the kingdom of grace is come into our hearts. The beating of this pulse shows life. *Est a Deo ut bene velimus* [Good desires are from God]. Augustine. If iron move upwards contrary to its nature, it is a sign some loadstone has been there drawing it; if the soul move towards God in an unfeigned desire, it is a sign the loadstone of the Spirit has been drawing it.

(2) We may know the kingdom of grace has come into our hearts by having the princely grace of faith. *Fides est sanctissima humani pectoris* [Faith is the most sacred jewel of the human heart] *Gemma.* Faith cuts us from the wild olive of nature, and ingrafts us into Christ. It is the vital artery of the soul. 'The just shall live by faith.' Heb x 38. Faith makes a holy adventure on Christ's merits. As a princely grace it reigns in the soul, when the kingdom of God is come unto us. The Hebrew word for faith comes from *radix*, which signifies to nourish; faith nourisheth the soul, and is the nurse of all the graces. But, who will not say he is a believer? Simon Magus believed, yet was in the gall of bitterness. Acts viii 13, 23. The hypocrite can put on faith's mantle, as the devil did Samuel's.

How shall we know therefore that our faith is sound, that it is the faith of the operation of God, and that the kingdom of God is within us?

True faith is wrought by the ministry of the word. 'Faith cometh by hearing.' Rom x 17. Peter let down the net of his ministry, and at one draught caught three thousand souls. Let us examine how our faith was wrought. Did God in the ministry of the word humble us? Did he break up the fallow ground of our heart, and then cast in the seed of faith? A good sign; but, if you know not how you came by your faith, suspect yourselves; as we suspect men to have stolen goods, when they know not how they came by them.

True faith is at first small, like a grain of mustard-seed; it is full of doubts and fears; it is smoking flax: it smokes with desire, but does not flame with comfort. It is so small that a Christian can hardly discern whether he has faith or not.

True faith is long in working, *non fit in instanti* [it does not come about in a moment]. It costs many searchings of heart, many prayers and tears; there is a spiritual combat. The soul suffers many sore pangs of humiliation before the child of faith is born. To those whose faith is *per saltum* [at a leap], who leap out of sin into a confidence that Christ is theirs, we may say, as Isaac concerning his son's venison, 'How is it that thou hast found it so quickly?' Gen xxvii 20. How is it that thou camest by thy faith so soon? The seed in the parable which sprung up suddenly withered. Mark iv 5, 6. *Solent praecocia subito flaccescere* [Things that are too forward have a way of suddenly wilting].

True faith is joined with sanctity. As a little bezoar is strong in operation, and a little musk sweetens, so a little faith purifies. 'Holding the mystery of the faith in a pure conscience.' 1 Tim iii 9. Though faith does but touch Christ, it fetches a healing virtue from him. Justifying faith does that in a spiritual sense which miraculous faith does; it removes the mountains of sin, and casts them into the sea of Christ's blood.

True faith will trust God without a pawn. Though a Christian be cut short in provisions – the fig-tree does not blossom – yet he will trust in God. *Fides famem non formidat*. Faith fears not famine. God has given us his promise as his bond. 'Verily thou shalt be fed.' Psa xxxvii 3. Faith puts this bond in suit, that God will rather work a miracle than his promise shall fail. He has cause to suspect his faith, who says, he trusts God for the greater, but dares not trust him for the less: he trusts God for salvation, but dares not trust him for a livelihood.

True faith is prolific. It brings forth fruit; it has Rachel's beauty and Leah's fruitfulness. *Fides pinguescit operibus*. Luther. Faith is full of good works. It believes as if it did not work, and it works as if it did not believe. It is the spouse-like grace which marries Christ, and good works are the children which it bears. By having such faith we may know the kingdom of God is within us; that grace is certainly in our hearts.

(3) We may know the kingdom of grace is come into our hearts by having the grace of love. Faith and love are the two poles on which all religion turns. 'The upright love thee.' Cant i 4. True love is to love God out of choice. It turns the soul into a seraphim; it makes it burn in a flame of affection; it is the truest touchstone of sincerity; it is the queen of the graces; it commands the whole soul. 2 Cor v 14. If our love to God be genuine, we let him have the supremacy; we set him in the highest room of our soul; we give him the purest of our love. 'I would cause thee to drink of spiced wine of the juice of my pomegranate.' Cant viii 2. If the spouse had anything better than another, a cup more juicy and spiced, Christ should drink of that. We give the creature the milk of our love, but God the cream. In short, if we love God aright, we love his laws; we love his picture drawn in the saints by the pencil of the Holy Ghost; we love his presence in his ordinances. Sleidan says, that the Protestants in France had a church which they call paradise; as if they thought themselves in paradise while they had God's presence in his sanctuary. The soul that loves God, loves his appearing. 2 Tim iv 8. It will be a glorious appearing to the saints when their union with Christ shall be complete; then their joy shall be full. The bride longs for the marriage day. 'The Spirit and the bride say, Come: even so, come, Lord Jesus.' Rev xxii 17, 20. By this sacred love we may know the kingdom of God is within us.

(4) We may know the kingdom of grace is come into our hearts by spiritualizing the duties of religion. 'Ye are an holy priesthood to offer up spiritual sacrifices.' 1 Pet ii 5. Spiritualizing duty consists in three things:

[1] Fixedness of mind. We spiritualize duty when our minds are fixed on God. 'That you may attend on the Lord without distraction.' 1 Cor vii 35. Though impertinent thoughts sometimes come into the heart in duty, they are not allowed. Psa cxix 113. They come as unwelcome guests, which are no sooner spied but they are turned out.

[2] Fervency of devotion. 'Fervent in spirit, serving the Lord.' Rom xii 11. The allusion is to water that seethes and boils over; so the affections boil over, the eyes melt in tears, and the heart flows in holy ejaculations. We not only bring our offering to God, but our hearts.

[3] Uprightness of aim. A man whose heart is upright has three ends in duty. First, that he may grow more like God. Moses on the mount had some of God's glory reflected on him: 'his face shined.' Secondly, that he may have more communion with God. 'Our fellowship is with the Father.'

1 John i 3. Thirdly, that he may bring more glory to God. 1 Pet iv 11. 'That Christ shall be magnified.' Phil i 20. Sincerity aims at God in all things. Though we shoot short, yet we take a right aim, which is a sure evidence of grace. The spirits of wine are best, so is the spiritual part of duty. A little spiritualness in duty is better than all the gildings of the temple, or outward pompous worship which dazzles carnal eyes.

(5) We may know the kingdom of grace is come into us by antipathy and opposition against every known sin. 'I hate every false way.' Psa cxix 104. Hatred is against the whole kind; hatred is implacable: anger may be reconciled, hatred cannot. A gracious soul not only forsakes sin (as a man forsakes his country, never to return to it more), but hates sin. As there is an antipathy between the crocodile and the scorpion, so, if the kingdom of God be within us, we not only hate sin for hell, but we hate it as hell, as being contrary to God's holiness and happiness.

(6) We may know the kingdom of grace is come into us when we have given up ourselves to God by obedience. As a servant gives up himself to his master, as a wife gives up herself to her husband, so we give up ourselves to God by obedience. This obedience is free, as that is the sweetest honey which drops from the comb; and uniform. We obey God in one thing as well as another. 'Then shall I not be ashamed;' or, as it is in the Hebrew, I shall not blush 'when I have respect unto all thy commandments.' Psa cxix 6. As a pair of compasses has one foot upon the centre and the other goes round the circle, so a Christian, by faith, stands on God the centre, and by obedience goes round the circle of his commandments. It is a sign the kingdom of grace is not come into the heart, when it does not reign there by universal obedience. Hypocrites would have Christ to be their Saviour, but they pluck the government from his shoulders, and will not have him rule; but he who has the kingdom of God within him, submits cheerfully to every command of God; he will do what God will have him do; he will be what God will have him be; he puts a blank paper into God's hand, and says, 'Lord, write what thou wilt, I will subscribe.' Blessed is he that can find all these things in his soul. He is 'all glorious within.' Psa xlv 13. He carries a kingdom about him, and this kingdom of grace will certainly bring to a kingdom of glory.

I shall now answer some doubts and objections that a Christian may make against himself.

I fear the kingdom of grace is not yet come into my heart.

When a Christian is under temptation, or grace lies dormant, he is not fit to be his own judge; but must take the witness of others who have the spirit of discerning. But let us hear a Christian's objections against himself, why he thinks the kingdom of grace is not yet come into his heart.

I cannot discern grace.

A child of God may have the kingdom of grace in his heart, and yet not know it. The cup was in Benjamin's sack, though he did not know it was there; so thou mayest have faith in thy heart, the cup may be in thy sack, though thou knowest it not. Old Jacob wept for his son Joseph when Joseph was alive; so thou mayest weep for want of grace, when grace may be alive in thy heart. The seed may be in the ground, when we do not see it spring up; so the seed of God may be sown in thy heart, though thou dost not perceive it springing up. Think not grace is lost because it is hid.

Before the kingdom of grace come into the heart, there must be some preparation for it; the fallow ground must be broken up: I fear the plough of the law has not gone deep enough: I have not been humbled enough: therefore I have no grace.

God does not prescribe an exact proportion of sorrow and humiliation; Scripture mentions the truth of sorrow, but not the measure. Some are more flagitious sinners than others, and must have a greater degree of humiliation. A knotty piece of timber requires more wedges to be driven into it. Some stomachs are fouler than others, therefore need stronger physic. But wouldest thou know when thou hast been humbled enough for sin? When thou art willing to let go thy sins. The gold has lain long enough in the furnace when the dross is purged out; so, when the love of sin is purged out, a soul is humbled enough for divine acceptation, though not for divine satisfaction. Now, if thou art humbled enough, what needs more? If a needle will let out the imposthume, what needs a lance? Be not more cruel to thyself than God would have thee.

If the kingdom of God were within me, it would be a kingdom of power; it would enable me to serve God with vigour of soul. But I have a spirit of infirmity upon me, I am weak and impotent, and untuned to every holy action.

There is a great difference between the weakness of grace and the want of grace. A man may have life, though he be sick and weak. Weak grace is not to be despised, but cherished. Christ will not break the bruised reed. Do not argue from the weakness of grace to the nullity. (1) Weak grace will give us a title to Christ as well as strong. A weak hand of faith will receive the alms of Christ's merits. (2) Weak faith is capable of growth. The seed springs up by degrees, first the blade, and then the ear, and then the full corn in the ear. The faith that is strongest was once in its infancy. Grace is like the waters of the sanctuary, which rose higher and higher. Be not discouraged at thy weak faith; though it be but blossoming, it will by degrees come to more maturity. (3) The weakest grace shall persevere as well as the strongest. A child was as safe in the ark as Noah. An infant believer that is but newly laid to the breast of the promise, is as safe in Christ as the most eminent heroic saint.

I fear the kingdom of grace is not yet come, because I find the kingdom of sin so strong in me. Had I faith, it would purify my heart; but I find much pride, worldliness, and passion.

The best of saints have remainders of corruption. 'They had their dominion taken away, yet their lives were prolonged for a season.' Dan vii 12. So in the regenerate, though the dominion of sin be taken away, yet the life of it is prolonged for a season. What pride was there in Christ's own disciples, when they strove which should be greatest! The issue of sin will not be quite stopped till death. The Lord is pleased to let the in-being of sin continue, to humble his people, and make them prize Christ more. Because you find corruptions stirring, do not therefore presently unsaint yourselves, and deny the kingdom of grace to be come into your souls. That you feel sin is an evidence of spiritual life; that you mourn for it is a fruit of love to God; that you have a combat with sin, argues antipathy against it. Those sins which you once wore as a crown on your head, are now as fetters on the leg. Is not all this from the Spirit of grace in you? Sin is in you, as poison in the body, which you are sick of, and use all Scripture antidotes to expel. Should we condemn all those who have indwelling sin, nay, who have had sin sometimes prevailing, we should blot some of the best saints out of the Bible.

Where the kingdom of grace comes, it softens the heart; but I find my heart frozen and congealed into hardness; I can hardly squeeze out one tear. Do flowers grow on a rock? Can there be any grace in such a rocky heart?

There may be grief where there are no tears. The best sorrow is rational. In your judgment you esteem sin the most hyperbolical evil, you have a disgust against it which is a rational sorrow, and such as God will accept. A Christian may have some hardness in his heart, and yet not have a hard heart. A field may have tares in it, and we call it a field of wheat; so in the best heart there may be a mixture of hardness, yet because there is some softness and melting, God looks upon it as a soft heart. Therefore, Christian, dispute not against thyself, if thou canst find but this one thing, that the frame and temper of thy soul be holy. Art thou still breathing after God, delighting in him? Is the complexion of thy soul heavenly? Canst thou say, as David, 'When I awake, I am still with thee'? Psa cxxxix 18. As colours laid in oil, or a statue carved in gold abide, so does a holy complexion; the soul is still pointing towards God. If it be thus with thee, assure thyself the kingdom of grace is come into the soul. Be not unkind to God, to deny any work of his Spirit, which he has wrought in thee.

Use 1. For exhortation. Labour to find that this kingdom of grace is set up in your hearts. While others aspire after earthly kingdoms, labour to have the kingdom of God within you. Luke xvii 21. The kingdom of grace must come into us before we can go into the kingdom of glory. The motives to this are:

(1) The kingdom of God within is our spiritual beauty. The kingdom of grace adorns a person, and sets him off in the eyes of God and of angels. It makes the king's daughter all glorious within. Psa xlv 13. Grace sheds a glory and lustre upon the soul. As the diamond to the ring, so is grace to the soul. A heart beautified with grace has the King of heaven's picture hung in it.

(2) The kingdom of grace set up in the heart is our spiritual defence. Grace is called 'the armour of light.' Rom xiii 12. It is light for beauty, and armour for defence. He who has the kingdom of grace within him, is 'strengthened with all might according to [God's] glorious power.' Col i 11. He has the shield of faith, the helmet of hope, and the breastplate of righteousness. His armour can never be shot through. He is fortified against the assaults of temptation, and the terrors of hell.

(3) The kingdom of grace set up in the heart brings peace with it. 'The kingdom of God is righteousness and peace.' Rom xiv 17. There is a secret peace proceeding from holiness. Peace is the best blessing of a kingdom. *Pax una triumphis innumeris melior* [One peace is better than countless victories]. The kingdom of grace is a kingdom of peace. Grace is the root, peace is the flower that grows out of it. It is *pax in procella* [peace in a storm], such peace that no worldly affliction can shake. The doors of Solomon's temple were made of olive tree, carved with open flowers; so in a gracious heart is the olive of peace, and the open flowers of joy. 1 Kings vi 32.

(4) The kingdom of grace enriches the soul. A kingdom has its riches. A believer is said to be rich in faith. James ii 5. How rich is he who has God for his God, who is heir to all the promises! Heb vi 17. A man may be rich in bills and bonds, but a believer may say as Peter, 'Silver and gold have I none (Acts iii 6); yet I am rich in bills and bonds, an heir to all God's promises;' and to be heir to the promises, is better than to be heir to the crown.

(5) When the kingdom of grace comes, it fixes and establishes the heart. 'O God, my heart is fixed.' Psa lvii 7. Before the kingdom of grace comes,

the heart is very unfixed and unsettled; like a ship without ballast, like quicksilver that cannot be made to fix: but when the kingdom of grace comes, it doth *stabilire animum*, fixes the heart on God; and when the heart is fixed, it rests quiet as in its centre.

(6) This kingdom of grace is distinguishing. It is a sure pledge of God's love. God may give kingdoms in anger; but wherever the kingdom of grace is set up, it is in love. He cannot give grace in anger. The crown always goes with the kingdom; let us therefore be ambitious of this kingdom of grace.

What must we do to obtain this kingdom?

(1) In general, take pains for it. We cannot have the world without labour, and do we think to have grace? 'If thou seekest her as silver.' Prov ii 4. A man may as well expect a crop without sowing, as grace without labour. We must not think to have grace as Israel had manna; who did not plough nor sow, but it was rained down from heaven upon them. No, we must *operam dare*, take pains for grace. Our salvation cost Christ blood, and will cost us sweat.

(2) Let us go to God to set up this kingdom of grace in our hearts. He is called the 'God of all grace.' 1 Pet v 10. Say, Lord, I want this kingdom of grace, I want a humble, believing heart. O enrich me with grace; let thy kingdom come. Be importunate suitors. As Achsah said to her father Caleb, 'Thou hast given me a south land, give me also springs of water;' so, Lord, thou hast given me enough of the world, here is a south land; but Lord, give me the upper springs of grace; let thy kingdom come. Josh xv 19. What is the venison thou hast given me, without the blessing? When we are importunate with God, and will take no denial, he will set up his kingdom within us.

(3) Keep close to the word preached. The word preached, is *virga virtutis*, the rod of God's strength; it is the great engine he uses for setting up the kingdom of grace in the heart. 'Faith cometh by hearing.' Rom x 17. Though God could work grace immediately by his Spirit, or by the ministry of angels from heaven, yet he chooses to work by the word preached. This is the usual mean, by which he sets up the kingdom of grace in the heart; and the reason is, because he has put his divine sanction upon it; he has appointed it for the means of working grace, and he will honour his own ordinance. 1 Cor i 21. What reason could be given why the waters of Damascus should not have as sovereign virtue to heal Naaman's leprosy, as the waters of Jordan, but this, that God appointed and sanctified the waters of Jordan to heal, and not the others? Let us keep the word preached, because the power of God goes along with it.

Use 2. For thanksgiving. What will you be thankful for, if not for a kingdom? Grace is the best blessing, it is the result and product of God's electing love. In setting up his kingdom of grace, God has done more for you than if he had made you kings and queens; for you are born of God, and of the blood-royal of heaven. Oh! admire and exalt free grace. 'Make [God's] praise glorious.' Psa lxvi 2. The apostle seldom mentions the work of grace, but he joins praise. 'Giving thanks unto the Father, which hath made us meet to be partakers of the inheritance of the saints in light.' Col i 12. If God has crowned you with the kingdom of grace, do you crown him with your praises.

IV. *We pray that the kingdom of grace may increase, that it may come more into us:* and this may answer a question.

Why do we pray, 'Thy kingdom come,' when the kingdom of grace is already come into the soul?

Though the kingdom of grace be already come into us, yet still we must pray, 'Thy kingdom come,' that grace may be increased, and that this kingdom may flourish still more in our souls. Till we come to live among the angels, we shall need to pray this prayer, 'Thy kingdom come.' Lord, let thy kingdom of grace come in more power into my soul; let grace be more augmented and increased.

When does the kingdom of grace increase in the soul? When is it a flourishing kingdom?

When a Christian has further degrees of grace, there is more oil in the lamp, his knowledge is clear, his love is more inflamed. Grace is capable of degrees, and may rise higher as the sun in the horizon. It is not with us as it was with Christ, who received the Spirit without measure. John iii 34. He could not be more holy than he was; but our grace is receptive of further degrees; we may have more sanctity, we may add more cubits to our spiritual stature.

The kingdom of grace increases when a Christian has got more strength than he had. 'He that hath clean hands, shall be stronger and stronger.' Job xvii 9. 'He shall add to his strength.' Heb. A Christian has strength to resist temptation, to forgive his enemies, to suffer affliction. It is not easy to suffer; a man must deny himself before he can take up the cross. The way to heaven is like the way which Jonathan and his armour bearer had in climbing up a steep place. 'There was a sharp rock on the one side, and a sharp rock on the other.' 1 Sam xiv 4. It requires much strength to climb up this rocky way. That grace which will carry us through prosperity, will not carry us through sufferings. The ship needs stronger tackling to carry it through a storm than a calm. Now, when we are so strong in grace, that we can bear up under affliction without murmuring or fainting, the kingdom of grace is increased. What mighty strength of grace had he, who told the emperor Valentinian, You may take away my life, but you cannot take away my love to the truth!

The kingdom of grace increases when a Christian has most conflict with spiritual corruptions; when he not only abstains from gross evils, but has a combat with inward, hidden, close corruptions; as pride, envy, hypocrisy, vain thoughts, carnal confidence, which are spiritual wickedness, and both defile and disturb. 'Let us cleanse ourselves from all filthiness of the flesh and spirit.' 2 Cor vii 1. There are two sorts of corruptions, one of the flesh, the other of the spirit. When we grieve for and combat with spiritual sin, which is the root of all gross sins, then the kingdom of grace increases, and spreads its territories in the soul.

The kingdom of grace flourishes when a Christian has learned to live by faith. 'I live by the faith of the Son of God.' Gal ii 20. There is the habit of faith, and the drawing of this habit into exercise. For a Christian to graft his hope of salvation, only upon the stock of Christ's righteousness, and make Christ all in justification; to live on the promises, as a bee on the flower, and suck out the sweetness of them; to trust God where we cannot trace him; to believe his love through a frown; to persuade ourselves, when he has the face of an enemy, that he has the heart of a Father—when we are arrived at this, the kingdom of grace is flourishing in our souls.

It flourishes when a Christian is full of holy zeal. Numb xxv 13. Phinehas was zealous for his God. Zeal is the flame of the affections, it turns a saint into a seraphim. A zealous Christian is impatient when God is dishonoured. Rev ii 2. He will wrestle with difficulties, he will swim to Christ through a sea of blood. Acts xxi 13. Zeal loves truth when it is despised and opposed. 'They have made void thy law, therefore I love thy commandments.' Psa cxix 126, 127. Zeal resembles the Holy Ghost. 'There appeared cloven tongues like as of fire, and it sat upon each of them.' Acts ii 3. Tongues of fire were an emblem of that fire of zeal which the Spirit poured on them.

The kingdom of grace increases when a Christian is as diligent in his particular calling, as he is devout in his general calling. He is the wise Christian that carries things equally; that so lives by faith that he lives in a calling. Therefore it is worthy of notice, that when the apostle had exhorted the Thessalonians to increase in grace, he presently adds, 'And that you do your own business, and work with your own hands.' 1 Thess iv 10, 11. It is a sign grace is increasing, when Christians go cheerfully about their calling. Indeed, to be all the day in the mount with God, and to have the mind fixed on glory, is more sweet to a man's self, and is a heaven upon earth; but to be conversant in our callings, is more profitable to others. Paul says, 'To be with Christ is far better: nevertheless to abide in the flesh is more needful for you.' Phil 1 23, 24. So, to converse with God in prayer and sweet meditation all the week long, is more for the comfort of a man's own person; but to be sometimes employed in the business of a calling, is more profitable for the family to which he belongs. It is not good to be as the lilies, which toil not, neither do they spin. It shows the increase of grace when a Christian keeps a due decorum. He joins piety and industry, when zeal runs forth in religion, and diligence is put forth in a calling.

The kingdom of grace increases when a Christian is established in the belief and love of the truth. The heart by nature is as a ship without ballast, that wavers and fluctuates. Beza writes of one Bolezius, that his religion changed as the moon and planet Mercury. Such as are wandering stars will be falling stars; but when a soul is built on the rock Christ, and no winds of temptation can blow it away, the kingdom of grace flourishes. One calls Athanasius, *Adamas Ecclesiae*, an invincible adamant, in respect of his stability in the truth. 'Rooted and built up in him.' Col ii 7. The rooting of a tree evidences growth.

The kingdom of grace increases in a man's own heart when he labours to be instrumental to set up this kingdom in others. Though it is the greatest benefit to have grace wrought in ourselves, it is the greatest honour to be instrumental to work it in others. 'Of whom I travail in birth again until Christ be formed in you.' Gal iv 19. Such as are masters of a family should endeavour to see the kingdom of grace set up in their servants; such as are godly parents should not let God alone by prayer, till they see grace in their children. What a comfort to be both the natural and spiritual fathers of your children! Augustine says his mother Monica travailed with greater care and pain for his new birth, than his natural. It shows the increase of grace when we labour to see the kingdom of grace set up in others. As water abounds in the river, when it overflows and runs into the meadows, so grace increases in the soul when it has influence upon others, and we seek their salvation.

What need is there that the kingdom of grace should be increased?

God's design in keeping up a standing ministry in the church is to increase the kingdom of grace in men's hearts. 'He gave gifts unto men;' that is, ministerial gifts. Why so? 'For the edifying of the body of Christ.' Eph iv 8, 12. Not only for conversion, but for augmentation; therefore the word preached is compared not only to seed, but to milk; because God designs our growth in grace.

We need have the kingdom of grace increase, as we have a great deal of work to do, and a little grace will hardly carry us through. A Christian's life is laborious: there are many temptations to resist, many promises to believe, many precepts to obey, so that it will require a great deal of grace. A Christian must not only pray, but 'be zealous, and repent' (Rev iii 19); not only love, but be sick of love. Cant ii 5. What need, therefore, to have the kingdom of grace enlarged in his soul? As his work increases upon him, so his grace need increase.

If the kingdom of grace does not increase, it will decay. 'Thou hast left thy first love.' Rev ii 4. Grace, for want of increasing, is sometimes like a winter plant in which all the sap runs to the root, and it looks as if it were dead. 'Strengthen the things which remain, that are ready to die.' Rev iii 2. Though grace cannot expire, it may wither; and a withering Christian loses much of his beauty and fragrance. What great need have we to pray, 'Thy kingdom come,' that this kingdom of grace may be increased! If grace be not improved, it will soon be impaired. A Christian, for want of increasing his grace, loses his strength; he is like a sick man that cannot either walk or work; his prayers are sick and weak; he is as if he had no life in him; his faith can hardly fetch breath, and you can scarcely feel the pulse of his love to beat.

To have grace increasing is suitable to Christianity. Christians are called trees of righteousness. Isa lxi 3. The saints are not only jewels for sparkling lustre, but trees for growth. They are called the lights of the world. Phil ii 15. Light is still increasing. First there is the *crepusculum*, or daybreak, and so it shines brighter to the meridian. They who are the lights of the world must increase till they come to the meridian of glory. Not to grow is suspicious; painted things do not grow.

As the kingdom of grace increases, so a Christian's comforts increase. Comfort belongs to the *bene esse*, or well-being of a Christian; like sweetmeat, it is delicious to the taste. Psa xciv 19. The more grace, the more joy; as the more sap in the root, the more wine in the grape. Who more increased in grace than David? And who more in consolation? 'Thou hast put gladness in my heart.' Psa iv 7. Grace turns to joy as milk to cream.

How may they be comforted who bewail their want of growth, and weep that they cannot find the kingdom of grace increase?

To see and bewail our decay in grace, argues not only the life of grace, but growth. It is a sign that a man recovers and gets strength when he feels his weakness. It is a step forward in grace to see our imperfections. The more the Spirit shines in the heart, the more evil it discovers. A Christian thinks it worse with him than it was, whereas his grace may not grow less, but his light greater.

If a Christian does not increase in one grace, he may in another; if not in knowledge he may in humility. If a tree does not grow so much in the branches, it may in the root: and to grow downwards in the root, is good growth.

A Christian may grow less in affection when he grows more in judgment. As the fingers of a musician, when he is old, are stiff, and not so nimble at the lute as they were, but he plays with more art and judgment than before; so a Christian may not have so much affection in duty as at the first conversion, but he is more solid in religion, and more settled in his judgment than he was before.

A Christian may think he does not increase in grace because he does not increase in gifts; whereas there may be a decay of natural parts, the memory and other faculties, when there is not a decay of grace. Parts may be impaired when grace is improved. Be not discouraged, it is better to decay in parts, and be enlarged in grace, than to be enlarged in parts, and to decay in grace.

A Christian may increase in grace, and not be sensible of it. As seed may grow in the earth, when we do not perceive it to spring up, so grace may grow in time of desertion, and not be perceived.

V. *We pray that the kingdom of glory may hasten, and that God would in his due time translate us into it.* Under this we have now to consider [1] What this kingdom of glory is? [2] What are the properties of it? [3] Wherein it exceeds all other kingdoms? [4] When this kingdom comes? [5] Wherein appears the certainty of it? [6] Why we should pray for its coming?

[1] By this kingdom is meant, that glorious estate which the saints shall enjoy when they shall reign with God and angels for ever. If a man stand upon the sea-shore, he cannot see all the dimensions of the sea, its length, breadth, and depth, yet he may see it is of vast extension; so, though the kingdom of heaven be of that incomparable excellence, that neither tongue of man or angels can express, yet we may conceive of it to be an exceeding glorious thing, such as the eye hath not seen.

Concerning the kingdom of heaven I shall show what it implies, and what it imports.

First, it implies a blessed freedom from all evil.

(1) It implies a freedom from the necessities of nature. We are in this life subject to many necessities; we need food to nourish us, clothes to cover us, armour to defend us, sleep to refresh us; but in the kingdom of heaven there will be no need of these things; and it is better not to need them than to have them; as it is better not to need crutches than to have them. What need will there be of food when our bodies shall be made spiritual? 1 Cor xv 44.

Though not spiritual for substance, yet for qualities. What need will there be of clothing when our bodies shall be like Christ's glorious body? What need will there be of armour when there is no enemy? What need will there be of sleep when there is no night? Rev xxii 5. The saints shall be freed, in the heavenly kingdom, from these necessities of nature to which they are now exposed.

(2) In the kingdom of heaven we shall be freed from the imperfections of nature. Since the fall, our knowledge has suffered an eclipse.

Our natural knowledge is imperfect, it is chequered with ignorance. There are many hard knots in nature which we cannot easily untie. He who sees clearest, has a mist before his eyes. Socrates said on his death-bed, that there were many things he had yet to learn. Our ignorance is more than our knowledge.

Our divine knowledge is imperfect. We know but in part, said Paul, though he had many revelations, and was rapt up in the third heaven. 1 Cor xiii 9. We have but dark conceptions of the Trinity, 'Canst thou by searching find out God?' Job xi 7. Our narrow capacities would no more contain the Trinity, than a little glass vial would hold all the water in the sea. We cannot unriddle the mystery of the incarnation, the human nature assumed into the person of the Son of God; the human nature not God, yet united with God. We see now in *aenigmate*, in a glass darkly; but in the kingdom of heaven the veil shall be taken off, all imperfection of nature shall be done away. When the sunlight of glory shall begin to shine in the heavenly horizon, all dark shadows of ignorance shall fly away, our lamp of knowledge shall burn brightly, we shall have a full knowledge of God, though we shall not know him fully.

(3) In the kingdom of heaven we shall be freed from the toilsome labours of this life. God enacted a law in paradise, 'in the sweat of thy face shalt thou eat bread.' Gen iii 19. There is the labour of the hand in manufacture and the labour of the mind in study. 'All things are full of labour' (Eccl i 8); but in the kingdom of heaven we shall be freed from our labours.

There needs no labour when a man has got to the haven, he has no more need of sailing. In heaven there needs no labour, because the saints shall have the glory which they laboured for.

There shall be no labour. 'They rest from their labours.' Rev xiv 13. As when God had finished the work of creation, he rested from his labours, so, when his saints have finished the work of sanctification, they rest from theirs. Where should there be rest, but in the heavenly centre? Not that this sweet rest in the kingdom of heaven excludes all motion, for spirits cannot be idle; but the glorified saints shall rest from all wearisome employment. It will be a labour full of ease, a motion full of delight. The saints in heaven shall love

God, and what labour is that? Is it any labour to love beauty? They shall praise God, and that surely is delightful. When the bird sings, it is not so much a labour as a pleasure.

(4) In the kingdom of heaven, we shall be freed from original corruption, which is *causa causati*, the root of all actual sin. There would be no actual sin if there were no original; there would be no water in the stream if there were none in the fountain. Original sin is incorporated into our nature; it is as if the whole mass of blood were corrupted. Thus, to offend the God whom he loves, makes a Christian weary of his life. What would he give to have his chains taken off, to be rid of vain thoughts? How did Paul, that bird of paradise, bemoan himself for his sins! Rom vii 24. We cannot exercise either our duties or our graces without sin. The soul that is most refined and clarified by grace, is not without some dregs of corruption; but in the kingdom of heaven the fountain of original sin shall be quite dried up. What a blessed time will that be, never to grieve God's Spirit more! In heaven are virgin souls; their beauty is not stained with lust: nothing enters there that defiles. Rev xxi 27.

(5) In the kingdom of heaven we shall be freed from all sorrows. 'There shall be no more sorrow.' Rev xxi 4. Our life here is interwoven with trouble. Psa xxxi 10. Either losses grieve, or law-suits vex, or unkindness breaks the heart. We may as well separate moisture from air, or weight from lead, as troubles from man's life. *Quid est diu vivere, nisi diu torqueri?* [What is long life but long torment?] Augustine. But, in the kingdom of heaven, sorrow and sighing shall fly away. Here the saints sit by the rivers weeping, but one smile from Christ's face will make them forget all their sufferings. Their water shall then be turned into wine, their mourning into singing.

(6) In the kingdom of heaven we shall be beyond the reach of temptation. Satan is not yet fully cast into prison; like a prisoner under bail, he walks about tempting, and labouring, to draw us into sin. He is either laying snares, or shooting darts. *Stat in procinctu diabolus* [The devil stands girded for battle]. He laid a train of temptation to blow up the castle of Job's faith. It is as great a grief to a believer to be followed with temptations to sin, as for a virgin to have her chastity assaulted. But in the kingdom of heaven the saints shall be freed from the red dragon, who is cast out of paradise, and shall be for ever locked up in chains. Jude 6.

(7) In the kingdom of heaven we shall be freed from all vexing cares. The Greek word for care comes from a primitive which signifies to cut the heart in pieces. Care tortures the mind, wastes the spirits, and eats out the comfort of life. Care to prevent future dangers, and preserve present comforts, is an evil spirit that haunts us. All care is full of fear, and fear is full of

torment. 1 John iv 18. God threatens it as a judgment. 'They shall eat their bread with carefulness.' Ezek xii 19. Every comfort has its care, as every rose has its thorns; but in the kingdom of heaven we shall shake off the viper of care. What needs a glorified saint to take any anxious care, who has all things provided to his hand? There is the tree of life, bearing all sorts of fruit. When the heart shall be freed from sin, the head shall be freed from care.

(8) In the kingdom of heaven we shall be freed from all doubts and scruples. In this life the best saint has his doubtings, as the brightest star has his twinkling. If there were no doubtings, there would be no unbelief. Assurance itself does not exclude all doubting. 'Thy lovingkindness is before mine eyes.' Psa xxvi 3. At another time, 'Lord, where are thy former lovingkindnesses?' Psa lxxxix 49. A Christian is like a ship at anchor, which, though safe, may sometimes be tossed upon the water. Sometimes a Christian questions his interest in Christ, and his title to the promise. As these doubtings eclipse a Christian's comfort, so they bear false witness against the Spirit. But, when the saints shall come into the kingdom of heaven, there shall be no more doubtings; the Christian shall then say, as Peter, 'Now I know of a surety that the Lord hath sent his angel and hath delivered me.' Acts xii 11. Now I know that I am passed from death to life, and I am got beyond all rocks, I have shot the gulf, now I am in my Saviour's embraces for ever.

(9) In the kingdom of heaven we shall be freed from all society with the wicked. Here we are sometimes forced to be in their company. 'Woe is me, that I sojourn in Mesech, that I dwell in the tents of Kedar.' Psa cxx 5. Kedar was Ishmael's son, whose children dwelt in Arabia, a profane, barbarous people. Here the wicked are still raising persecutions against the godly, and crucifying their ears with their oaths and curses. Christ's lily is among thorns; but in the heavenly kingdom there shall be no more any pricking brier. 'The Son of man shall send forth his angels, and they shall gather out of his kingdom all things that offend.' Matt xiii 41. As Moses said, 'Stand still, and see the salvation of the Lord: for the Egyptians whom ye have seen to-day, ye shall see them again no more for ever;' so will God say, Stand still, and see the salvation of God; these your enemies, that vex and molest you, you shall see them again no more for ever. Exod xiv 13. At that day, God will separate the precious from the vile; Christ will thoroughly purge his floor; he will gather the wheat into the garner; and the wicked, which are the chaff, shall be blown into hell.

(10) In the kingdom of heaven we shall be freed from all signs of God's displeasure. Here he may be angry with his people. Though he has the heart of a father, he may have the look of an enemy; and this is sad. As when the

sun is gone, the dew falls; so when the light of God's face is gone, tears drop from the saints' eyes. But in the kingdom of heaven, there shall be no spiritual eclipses, there shall never appear any tokens of God's displeasure; the saints shall have a constant aspect of love from him, they shall never complain any more, 'My beloved had withdrawn himself.' Cant v 6.

(11) In the kingdom of heaven we shall be freed from all divisions. The saddest thing in the world is to see divisions among them that are good. It is sad that such as have one faith, should not be of one heart. Ephraim envies Judah, and Judah vexeth Ephraim. It is matter of tears, to see those who are united to Christ, divided one from another. The soldier's spear pierced Christ's side, but the divisions of saints wound his heart. But in the kingdom of heaven there shall be no vilifying one another, or censuring. Those who before could hardly pray together, shall praise God together. There shall not be one jarring string in the saints' music.

(12) In the kingdom of heaven we shall be freed from vanity and dissatisfaction. What Job says of wisdom, in chap. xxviii 14; 'The depth saith, It is not in me; and the sea saith, It is not with me;' I may say concerning satisfaction; every creature says, 'It is not in me.' Take things most pleasing, and from which we promise ourselves most content, still, of the spirit and essence of them all we shall say, 'Behold, all was vanity.' Eccl ii 11. God never did, nor will, put a satisfying virtue into any creature. In the sweetest music the world makes, either some string is wanting, or out of tune. Who would have thought that Haman, who was so great in the king's favour, that he 'set his seat above all the princes' of the provinces, for want of the bowing of a knee, would be dissatisfied? Est iii 1. But in the kingdom of heaven, we shall be freed from these dissatisfactions. The world is like a landscape painting, in which you may see gardens with fruit trees, curiously drawn, but you cannot enter them; but into the joys of heaven you may enter. 'Enter thou into the joy of thy Lord.' The soul shall be satisfied while it bathes in those rivers of pleasure at God's right hand. 'I shall be satisfied when I awake with thy likeness.' Psa xvii 15.

(13) In the kingdom of heaven we shall be freed from the torments of hell. 'Jesus which delivered us from the wrath to come.' 1 Thess i 10. Consider the multiplicity of those torments. In this life the body is usually exercised but with one pain, the stone or headache, at one time; but in hell there is a diversity of torments; there is darkness to affright, fire to burn, a lake of sulphur to choke, chains to bind, and the worm to gnaw. The torments of hell will seize upon every part of the body and soul. The eye shall be tortured with the sight of devils, and the tongue that has sworn so many oaths shall be tortured. 'Send Lazarus, that he may dip the tip of his finger in water, and cool my tongue.' Luke xvi 24. The memory will be

tormented to remember the mercies that have been abused, and seasons of grace neglected. The conscience will be tormented with self-accusations.

In the pains of hell there is no mitigation, no mixture of mercy. In this life God in anger remembers mercy. Hab iii 2. But in hell there is no alleviation or lessening of the pains. As in the sacrifice of jealousy, God would have no oil or frankincense put into it, so, in hell, there is no oil of mercy to lenify the sufferings of the damned, no incense of prayer to appease his wrath. Numb v 15. In the pains of hell there is no intermission. The poets feign of Endymion, that he got leave of Jupiter always to sleep. What would the damned in hell give for one hour's sleep! 'They have no rest day nor night.' Rev xiv 11. They are perpetually on the rack. In the pains of hell there is no expiration; they must always lie scorching in flames of wrath. 'The smoke of their torment ascended up for ever and ever;' but in the heavenly kingdom, the elect shall be freed from all infernal torments. 'Jesus delivered us from the wrath to come.' A prison is not made for the king's children. Christ drank that bitter cup of God's wrath that the saints might never drink it.

A second thing in the kingdom of heaven is, a glorious fruition of all good. Had I as many tongues as hairs on my head, I could not fully describe this. It is a place where there is no want of anything. Judges xviii 10. It is called 'the excellent glory.' 2 Pet i 17. I might as well span the firmament, or drain the ocean, as set forth the glory of this kingdom. *Coelum non habet hyperbolum;* the kingdom of heaven is above all hyperbole. Were the sun ten thousand times brighter than it is, it could not parallel the lustre of this kingdom. Apelles' pencil would blotch, angels' tongues would lessen it. I can but give you the *skiagraphia*, or dark shadow of it; expect not to see it in all its orient colours till you are mounted above the stars. But let us not stand afar off, as Moses, to behold this Canaan, but enter into it, and taste the honey. The privileges of this heavenly kingdom are:

(1) We shall have an immediate communion with God himself, who is the inexhaustible sea of all happiness. This divines call 'the beatific vision.' The psalmist triumphed in the enjoyment he had of God in this life. 'Whom have I in heaven but thee?' Psa lxxiii 25. If God, enjoyed by faith, gives so much comfort to the soul, how much more when he is enjoyed by immediate vision! Here we see God darkly through the glass of ordinances; but in the kingdom of heaven we shall see him 'face to face.' 1 Cor xiii 12. We shall have an intellectual sight of him; we shall see him with the eyes of our mind; we shall know him as much as the angels in heaven do. Matt xviii 10; we shall know as we are known. 1 Cor xiii 12. We shall have a full knowledge of God, though not know him fully; as a vessel in the sea is full of the sea, though it holds not all the sea. To see and enjoy God will be most

delicious; in him are beams of majesty, and bowels of mercy. God has all excellencies concentred in him, *bonum in quo omnia bona* [the good in which are all good things]. If one flower should have the sweetness of all flowers, how sweet would that flower be! All the beauty and sweetness which lies scattered in the creature is infinitely to be found in God. To see and enjoy him, therefore, will ravish the soul with delight. We shall see God so as to love him, and be made sensible of his love; and when we shall have this sweet communion with him he shall be 'all in all;' light to the eye, manna to the taste, and music to the ear. 1 Cor xv 28.

(2) In the kingdom of heaven, we shall with these eyes see the glorified body of Jesus Christ. The Saviour makes it a great part of the glory of heaven to view the glory of his human nature. 'That they may behold my glory.' John xvii 24. When Christ was transfigured upon earth, it is said, that 'his face did shine as the sun, and his raiment was white as the light.' Matt xvii 2. If the glory of his transfiguration was so great, what will the glory of his exaltation be! Much of the glory of God shines in Christ, by virtue of the hypostatic union. 'In him dwelleth all the fulness of the Godhead bodily.' Col ii 9. Through Christ's humanity, as through a bright mirror, we may see some beams of the divine majesty shine forth. Put a back of steel to a glass and you may see a face in it. Christ's human nature is as a back of steel put to the divine nature, through which we may see God, and then our capacities are enlarged to a wonderful degree, to receive this glorious object; and we not only see God's glory, but some of his glory shall be put upon us. *Non tantum aderit gloria sed inerit* [Glory will be not only present, but within]. Bernard. A beggar may behold the glory of a king and not be the happier; but Christ's glory shall be ours, 'We shall be like him.' 1 John iii 2. We shall shine by his beams.

(3) In the kingdom of heaven we shall enjoy the society of 'an innumerable company of angels.' Heb xii 22.

But is there not enough in God to fill the soul with delight? Can the sight of angels add to its happiness? What need is there of the light of torches, when the sun shines?

Besides the divine essence, the sight of angels is desirable. Much of God's curious workmanship shines in the angels; they are beautiful, glorious creatures; and as the several strings in a lute make the harmony sweeter, and the several stars make the firmament brighter, so the society with angels will make the delight of heaven the greater; and we shall not only see them with the glorified eye of our understanding, but converse with them.

(4) In the kingdom of heaven, we shall have sweet society with glorified saints. Oh! what a blessed time will it be when those who have prayed,

wept, and suffered together, shall rejoice together! We shall see the saints, in their white linen of purity, and see them as so many crowned kings: in beholding the glorified saints, we shall behold a heaven full of suns. Some have asked whether we shall know one another in heaven? Surely, our knowledge will not be diminished, but increased. The judgment of Luther and Anselm, and many other divines is, that we shall know one another; yea, the saints of all ages, whose faces we never saw; and, when we shall see the saints in glory without their infirmities of pride and passion, it will be a glorious sight. We see how Peter was transported when he saw but two prophets in the transfiguration; but what a blessed sight will it be when we shall see the whole glorious company of prophets, and martyrs, and holy men of God! Matt xvii 3. How sweet will the music be when all shall sing together in concert in the heavenly choir! And though, in this great assembly of saints and angels, 'one star may differ from another in glory,' yet no such weed as envy shall ever grow in the paradise of God; there shall be perfect love, which, as it casts out fear, so also envy. Though one vessel of glory may hold more than another, every vessel will be full.

(5) In the kingdom of heaven there shall be incomprehensible joy. Aristotle says, 'Joy proceeds from union.' When the saints' union with Christ is perfected in heaven, their joy shall be full. All the birds of the heavenly paradise sing for joy. What joy, when the saints shall see the great gulf shot, and know that they are passed from death to life! What joy, when they are as holy as they would be, and as God would have them to be! What joy to hear the music of angels; to see the golden banner of Christ's love displayed over the soul; to be drinking that water of life which is sweeter than all nectar and ambrosia! What joy, when the saints shall see Christ clothed in their flesh, sitting in glory above the angels! Then they shall enter into the joy of their Lord. Matt xxv 21. Here joy enters into the saints; in heaven 'they enter into joy.' O thou saint of God, who now hangest thy harp upon the willows, and minglest thy drink with weeping, in the kingdom of heaven thy water shall be turned into wine; thou shalt have so much felicity that thy soul cannot wish for more. The sea is not so full of water as the heart of a glorified saint is of joy. There can be no more sorrow in heaven than there is joy in hell.

(6) In heaven honour and dignity are put upon the saints. A kingdom implies honour. All that come into heaven are kings. They have, 1. A crown. Rev ii 10. 'I will give thee a crown of life.' *Corona est insigne regiae potestatis* [A crown is the sign of royal power] This crown is not lined with thorns, but hung with jewels; it is a never-fading crown. 1 Pet v 4. 2. The saints in heaven have their robes. They exchange their sackcloth for white robes. 'I beheld a great multitude, which no man could number, clothed

with white robes.' Rev vii 9. Robes signify their glory, white their sanctity. And, 3. They sit with Christ upon the throne. Rev iii 21. We read in 1 Kings vi 32, the doors of the holy of holies were made of palm-trees, and open flowers covered with gold – an emblem of that victory, and that garland of glory, which the saints shall wear in the kingdom of heaven. When all the titles and ensigns of worldly honour shall lie in the dust, the mace, the silver star, the garter, the saints' honour shall remain.

(7) In the kingdom of heaven we shall have a blessed rest. Rest is the end of motion; heaven is *centrum quietativum animae*, the blessed centre where the soul acquiesces and rests. In this life we are subject to unquiet motions and fluctuations. 'We were troubled on every side' (2 Cor vii 5): like a ship on the sea having the waves beating on both sides; but in the kingdom of heaven there is rest. Heb iv 9. How welcome is rest to a weary traveller! When death cuts asunder the string of the body, the soul, as a dove, flies away, and is at rest. This rest is when the saints shall lie on Christ's bosom, that hive of sweetness, that bed of perfume.

(8) The saints in the kingdom of heaven shall have their bodies richly bespangled with glory. They shall be full of brightness and beauty. As Moses' face shined, that Israel were not able to behold the glory (Exod xxxiv 30), so the bodies of the saints shall shine seven times brighter than the sun, as Chrysostom says; they shall have such a resplendence of beauty on them, that the angels shall fall in love with them; and no wonder, for they shall be made like Christ's glorious body. Phil iii 21. The bodies of saints glorified need no jewels, when they shall shine like Christ's body.

(9) In the heavenly kingdom is eternity. It is an eternal fruition, they shall never be put out of the throne. 'They shall reign for ever and ever.' Rev xxii 5. It is called 'the everlasting kingdom' (2 Pet i 11), and an 'eternal weight of glory.' 2 Cor iv 17. The flowers of paradise, of which the saints' garland is made, never wither. If there could be a cessation of heaven's glory, or the saints had but the least fear or suspicion of losing their felicity, it would infinitely abate and cool their joy; but their kingdom is for ever, the rivers of paradise cannot be dried up. 'At thy right hand there are pleasures for evermore.' Psa xvi 11. The kingdom of heaven was typified by the temple, which was built with stone, covered with cedar overlaid with gold, to show that the fixed permanent state of glory abides for ever. Well may we pray, 'Thy kingdom come.'

[2] The properties or qualifications of the kingdom of heaven.

(1) The glory of this kingdom is solid and substantial. The Hebrew word for glory signifies a weight, to show how solid and weighty the glory of the celestial kingdom is. The glory of the worldly kingdom is airy and

imaginary, like a blazing comet, or fancy. Agrippa and Bernice came with a great pomp, with a great fancy. Acts xxv 23. The earth hangs like a ball in the air, without anything to uphold it. Job xxvi 7. The glory of the heavenly kingdom is substantial, it hath twelve foundations. Rev xxi 14. That which God and angels count glory, is true glory.

(2) The glory of this kingdom is satisfying. 'With thee is the fountain of life.' Psa xxxvi 9. How can they choose but be full who are at the fountain-head? 'When I awake, I shall be satisfied with thy likeness,' *i.e.*, when I awake in the morning of the resurrection, having some of the beams of thy glory shining in me, I shall be satisfied. Psa xvii 15. The creature says, concerning satisfaction, 'It is not in me.' Job xxviii 14. If we go for happiness to the creature, we go to the wrong box: heaven's glory only is commensurate to the vast desires of an immortal soul. A Christian bathing himself in these rivers of pleasures, cries out in divine ecstasy, I have enough. The soul is never satisfied till it has God for its portion, and heaven for its haven. Dissatisfaction arises from some defect, but God is an infinite good, and there can be no defect in that which is infinite.

(3) The glory of heaven's kingdom is pure and unmixed. The streams of paradise are not muddied, *omnia clara, omnia jucunda* [all are clear, all are delightful]. There gold has no alloy. There is no bitter ingredient in that glory: it is pure as the honey that drops from the comb. There the rose of Sharon grows without thorns. There is ease without pain, honour without disgrace, life without death.

(4) The glory of this kingdom is constantly exhilarating and refreshing; there is fulness, but no surfeit. Worldly comforts, though sweet, yet in time grow stale. A down-bed pleases awhile, but soon we are weary and would rise. Too much pleasure is a pain; but the glory of heaven never surfeits or nauseates; because, as there are all rarities imaginable, so every moment fresh delights spring from God into the glorified soul.

(5) The glory of this kingdom is distributed to every individual saint. In an earthly kingdom the crown goes but to one, a crown will fit but one head; but in that kingdom above, the crown goes to all. Rev i 6. All the elect are kings. The land is settled chiefly upon the heir, and the rest are ill provided for; but in the kingdom of heaven all the saints are heirs. 'Heirs of God, and co-heirs with Christ.' Rom viii 17. God has land enough to give to all his heirs.

(6) Lucid and transparent. This kingdom of heaven is adorned and bespangled with light. 1 Tim vi 16. Light is the glory of the creation. 'The light is sweet.' Eccl. xi 7. Hell is a dark dungeon; fire, but no light. Matt xxii 13. The kingdom of heaven is a *diaphanum* [transparency], all embroidered with light, clear as crystal. How can there be want of light, where

Christ the Sun of Righteousness displays his golden beams? 'The glory of God did lighten it, and the Lamb is the light thereof.' Rev xxi 23.

(7) The glory of this kingdom is adequate and proportionable to the desire of the soul. In creature fruitions, that which commends them, and sets them off to us, is suitableness. The content of marriage lies not in beauty or portion, but in suitableness of disposition. The excellence of a feast is, when the meat is suited to the palate. One ingredient in the glory of heaven is, that it exactly suits the desires of the glorified saints. We shall not say in heaven, 'Here is a dish I do not love!' There shall be music to suit the ear in the anthems of angels; and food that suits the glorified palate in the hidden manna of God's love.

(8) The glory of this kingdom will be seasonable. The seasonableness of a mercy adds to its beauty and sweetness, like apples of gold to pictures of silver. After a hard winter in this cold climate, is it not seasonable to have the spring flowers of glory appear, and the singing of the birds of paradise come? When we have been wearied, and tired out in battle with sin and Satan, will not a crown be seasonable?

[3] The kingdom of heaven infinitely excels all the kingdoms of the earth.

(1) It excels in its Architect. Other kingdoms have men to raise their structures, but God himself laid the first stone in this kingdom. Heb xi 10. This kingdom is of the greatest antiquity. God was the first King and founder of it; no angel was worthy to lay a stone in this building.

(2) This heavenly kingdom excels in altitude. It is higher than any kingdom. The higher anything is the more excellent it is. Fire being the most sublime element, is most noble. The kingdom of heaven is seated above all the visible orbs. There is, 1. The airy heaven, which is the space from the earth to the sphere of the moon. 2. The starry heaven, the place where the planets are, of a higher elevation, as Saturn, Jupiter, and Mars. 3. The *coelum empyraeum*, the empyrean heaven, which Paul calls the third heaven; where Christ is, there the kingdom of glory is situated. This kingdom is so high that no scaling ladders of enemies can reach it; so high that the old serpent cannot shoot up his fiery darts to it. If wicked men could build their nests among the stars, the least believer would shortly be above them.

(3) The kingdom of heaven excels all others in splendour and riches. It is described by precious stones. Rev xxi 19. What are all the rarities of the earth to this kingdom – coasts of pearl, rocks of diamonds, islands of spices? What are the wonders of the world to it – the Egyptian pyramids, the temple of Diana, the pillar of the sun offered to Jupiter? What a rich kingdom is that where God will lay out all his cost! Those who are poor in the

world, soon as they come into this kingdom, grow rich, as rich as the angels. Other kingdoms are enriched with gold, this is enriched with the Deity.

(4) The kingdom of heaven excels all other kingdoms in holiness. Kingdoms on earth are for the most part unholy; there is a common sore of luxury and uncleanness running in them. Kingdoms are stages for sin to be acted on. 'All tables are full of vomit' (Isa xxviii 8); but the kingdom of heaven is so holy that it will not mix with any corruption. There shall enter into it nothing that defileth. Rev xxi 27. It is so pure a soil, that no serpent of sin will breed there. There beauty is not stained with lust, and honour is not swelled with pride. Holiness is the brightest jewel of the crown of heaven.

(5) The kingdom of heaven excels all other kingdoms in its pacific nature. It is *regnum pacis,* a kingdom of peace. Peace is the glory of a kingdom; *pax una triumphis innumeris melior* [one peace is better than countless victories]. A king's crown is more adorned with the white lily of peace, than when beset with the red roses of a bloody war. But where shall we find an uninterrupted peace upon earth? Either there are home-bred divisions or foreign invasions. 'There was no peace to him that went out, nor to him that came in.' 2 Chron xv 5. But the kingdom of heaven is a kingdom of peace; there are no enemies to conflict with; for all Christ's enemies shall be under his feet. Psa cx 1. The gates of that kingdom always stand open: 'The gates shall not be shut at all;' to show that there is no fear of an assault of an enemy. Rev xxi 25. When the saints die they are said to enter into peace. Isa lvii 2. There is no beating of drums or roaring of cannons; but the voice of harpers harping, in token of peace. Rev xiv 2. In heaven, 'righteousness and peace kiss each other.'

(6) The kingdom of heaven excels in magnitude; it is of vast dimensions. Though the gate of the kingdom be strait, and we must pass into it through the strait gate of mortification, yet, when once we are in it, it is very large. Though there be an innumerable company of saints and angels, yet there is room enough for them all. The kingdom of heaven may be called by the name of that well in Gen xxvi 22: Isaac 'called the name of it Rehoboth; and he said, For now the Lord hath made room for us.' Thou who art now confined to a small cottage, when thou comest into the celestial kingdom, shalt not be straitened for room. As every star has a large orb to move in, so it shall be with the saints, when they shall shine as stars in the kingdom of heaven.

(7) The kingdom of heaven excels in unity. All the inhabitants agree together in love. Love will be the perfume and music of heaven; as love to God will be intense, so to the saints. As perfect love casts out fear, so it casts

out envy and discord. Those Christians who could not live quietly together on earth (which was the blemish of their profession) in the heaven shall be all love; the fire of strife shall cease; there shall be no vilifying, or censuring one another, or raking into one another's sores, but all shall be tied together with the heart-strings of love. There Luther and Zwingli are agreed. Satan cannot put in his cloven foot there to make divisions. There shall be perfect harmony and concord, and not one jarring string in the saints' music. It were worth dying to be in that kingdom.

(8) This kingdom exceeds all earthly kingdoms in joy and pleasure, and is therefore called paradise. 2 Cor xii 4. For delight, there are all things to cause pleasure; there is the water of life clear as crystal; there is the honeycomb of God's love dropping. It is called 'entering into the joy of our Lord.' Matt xxv 23. There are two things which cause joy.

[1] Separation from sin shall be complete, and then joy follows. There can be no more sorrow in heaven than there is joy in hell.

[2] Perfect union with Christ. Joy, as Aristotle says, flows from union with the object. When our union with Christ shall be perfect our joy shall be full. If the joy of faith be so great, what will the joy of sight be? 1 Pet 1 8. Joseph gave his brethren provision for the way, but the full sacks of corn were kept till they came to their father's house. God gives the saints a taste of joy here, but the full sacks are kept till they come to heaven. Not only the organic parts, the outward senses, the eye, ear, taste, but the heart of a glorified saint shall be filled with joy. The understanding, will, and affections, are such a triangle as none can fill but the Trinity. There must needs be infinite joy, where nothing is seen but beauty; nothing is tasted but love.

(9) This kingdom of heaven excels all earthly kingdoms in self-perfection. Other kingdoms are defective, they have not all provision within themselves, but are fain to traffic abroad to supply their wants at home, as King Solomon sent to Ophir for gold. 2 Chron viii 18. But there is no defect in the kingdom of heaven; it has all commodities of its own growth. Rev xxii 2. There is the pearl of price, the morning star, the mountains of spices, the bed of love; there are those sacred rarities, wherewith God and angels are delighted.

(10) This kingdom of heaven excels all others in honour and nobility. It not only equals them in the ensigns of royalty, the throne and white robes, but it far transcends them. Other kings are of the blood-royal, but they in this heavenly kingdom are born of God. Other kings converse with nobles: the saints glorified are fellow commoners with angels; they have a more noble crown; it is made of the flowers of paradise, and is a crown that

fadeth not away. 1 Pet v 4. They sit on a better throne. King Solomon sat on a throne of ivory overlaid with gold (1 Kings x 18); but the saints in heaven are higher advanced, they sit with Christ upon his throne. Rev iii 21. They shall judge the princes and great ones of the earth. 1 Cor vi 2. This honour have all the glorified saints.

(11) This kingdom of heaven excels all others in healthfulness. Death is a worm that is ever feeding at the root of our gourd: kingdoms are often hospitals of sick persons; but the kingdom of heaven is a most healthful climate. Physicians there are out of date: no distemper there, no passing bell, or bill of mortality. 'Neither can they die any more.' Luke xx 36. In the heavenly climate are no ill vapours to breed diseases, but a sweet, aromatic smell coming from Christ; all his garments smell of myrrh, aloes, and cassia.

(12) This kingdom of heaven excels in duration, it abides for ever. Suppose earthly kingdoms to be more glorious than they are, their foundations of gold, their walls of pearl, their windows of sapphire; yet they are corruptible and fading. 'I will cause to cease the kingdom.' Hos i 4. Troy and Athens now lie buried in their ruins; *jam seges est ubi Troja fuit* [corn now grows where Troy once stood]. Mortality is the disgrace of all earthly kingdoms; but the kingdom of heaven has eternity written upon it, it is an everlasting kingdom. 2 Pet i 11. It is founded upon the strong basis of God's omnipotence. The saints shall never be turned out of this kingdom, or be deposed from their throne, as some kings have been, as Henry VI., &c. but shall reign for ever and ever. Rev xxii 5.

How should all this affect our hearts! What should we mind but this kingdom of heaven, which more outshines all the kingdoms of the earth than the sun outshines the light of a taper!

[4] This glory in the kingdom of heaven shall be begun at death, but not perfected till the resurrection.

(1) The saints shall enter upon the kingdom of glory immediately after death.

Before their bodies are buried, their souls shall be crowned. 'Having a desire to depart, and to be with Christ.' Phil i 23. From this connexion, departing, and being with Christ, we see clearly that there is a *subitus transitus*, speedy passage from death to glory; no sooner is the soul of a believer divorced from the body, but it presently goes to Christ. 'Absent from the body, present with the Lord.' 2 Cor v 8. It were better for believers to stay here, if immediately after death they were not with Christ in glory; for here the saints are daily increasing their grace; here they may have many *praelibamina* [foretastes], sweet tastes of God's love: so that it were better to stay here, if their soul should sleep in their body, and they should not have a speedy sight of God in glory; but the consolation of believers is that they shall not stay long from their kingdom; it is but winking and they shall see God. It will not only be a blessed change to a believer, from a desert to a paradise, from a bloody battle to a victorious crown, but a sudden change. No sooner did Lazarus die, but he had a convoy of angels to conduct his soul to the kingdom of glory. You who now are full of bodily diseases, scarce a day well, saying, 'My life is spent with grief' (Psa xxxi 10); be of good comfort, you may be happy before you are aware; before another week or month be over, you may be in the kingdom of glory, and then all tears shall be wiped away.

(2) The glory in the kingdom of heaven will be fully perfected at the resurrection and general day of judgment. Then the bodies and souls of believers will be reunited. What joy will there be at the reunion and meeting together of the soul and body of a saint! Oh, what a welcome will the soul give to the body! 'O my dear body, thou didst often join with me in prayer, and now thou shalt join with me in praise; thou wert willing to suffer with me, and now thou shalt reign with me; thou wert sown a vile body, but now thou art made like Christ's glorious body; we were once for a time divorced, but now we are married, and crowned together in a kingdom, and shall mutually congratulate each other's felicity.'

[5] The certainty and infallibility of this kingdom of glory.

That this blessed kingdom shall be bestowed on the saints, is beyond all dispute.

(1) God has promised it. 'It is your Father's good pleasure to give you the kingdom.' Luke xii 32. 'I appoint unto you a kingdom.' Luke xxii 29. 'I bequeath it as my last will and testament.' Has God promised a kingdom, and will he not make it good? God's promise is better than any bond. 'In hope of eternal life which God, that cannot lie, promised.' Tit i 2. The whole earth hangs upon the word of God's power; and cannot our faith hang upon the word of his promise?

(2) There is a price laid down for this kingdom. Heaven is not only a kingdom which God has promised, but which Christ has purchased; it is called a purchased possession. Eph i 14. Though this kingdom is given us freely, yet Christ bought it with the price of his blood; which is a heaven-procuring blood. 'Having boldness to enter into the holiest (*i.e.*, into heaven) by the blood of Jesus.' Heb x 19. *Crux Christi clavis paradisi* [The cross of Christ is the key of paradise], Christ's blood is the key that opens the gates of heaven. Should not the saints have this kingdom, then Christ should lose his purchase. Christ on the cross was in hard travail. Isa liii 11.

He travailed to bring forth salvation to the elect: should not they possess the kingdom when they die, Christ would lose his travail; all his pangs and agonies of soul upon the cross would be in vain.

(3) Christ prays that the saints may have this kingdom settled upon them. 'Father, I will that they also whom thou hast given me, be with me where I am.' *i.e.*, in heaven. John xvii 24. This is Christ's prayer, that the saints may be with him in his kingdom, and be bespangled with some of the beams of his glory. Now, if they should not go into this heavenly kingdom, then Christ's prayer would be frustrated; but that cannot be, for he is God's favourite. 'I knew that thou hearest me always;' and besides, what Christ prays for, he has power to give. John xi 42. Observe the manner of Christ's prayer, 'Father, I will;' *Father*, there he prays as man; '*I will*,' there he gives as God.

(4) The saints must have this blessed kingdom by virtue of Christ's ascension. 'I ascend unto my Father and your Father, to my God and your God.' John xx 17. Where lies the comfort of this? Jesus Christ ascended to take possession of heaven for all believers. As a husband takes up land in another country in behalf of his wife, so Christ went to take possession of heaven in behalf of all believers. 'I go to prepare a place for you.' John xiv 2. My ascension is to make all things ready against your coming: I go to prepare the heavenly mansions for you. The flesh that Christ has taken into heaven, is a sure pledge that our flesh and bodies shall be where he is ere long. Christ did not ascend to heaven as a private person, but as a public person, for the good of all believers; his ascension was a certain forerunner of the saints ascending into heaven.

(5) The elect must have this blessed kingdom, in regard of the previous work of the Spirit in their hearts. They have the beginning of the kingdom of heaven in them here: grace is heaven begun in the soul; besides, God gives them *primitias Spiritus*, the first-fruits of the Spirit. Rom viii 23. The first-fruits are the comforts of the Spirit. These first-fruits under the law were a certain sign to the Jews of the full crop of vintage which they should after receive. The first-fruits of the Spirit, consisting of joy and peace, assure the saints of the full vintage of glory they shall be ever reaping in the kingdom of God. The saints in this life are said to have the earnest of the Spirit in their hearts. 2 Cor v 5. As an earnest is part of payment, and an assurance of payment in full to be made in due time, so God's Spirit in the hearts of believers, giving them his comforts, bestows on them an earnest, or taste of glory, which further assures them of that full reward which they shall have in the kingdom of heaven. 'Believing, ye rejoice;' there is the earnest of heaven. 1 Pet i 8. 'Receiving the end of your faith,' salvation; there is the full payment; ver 9.

(6) The elect must have this blessed kingdom by virtue of their coalition and union with Jesus Christ, they are members of Christ, therefore they must be where their head is. Indeed, the Arminians hold, that a justified person may fall from grace, and so his union with Christ may be dissolved, and the kingdom lost; but I demand of them, can Christ lose a member of his body? Then he is not perfect; and if Christ may lose one member of his body, why not as well all, by the same reason? He will then be a head without a body; but be assured a believer's union with Christ cannot be broken, and so long he cannot be hindered of the kingdom. John xvii 12. What was said of Christ's natural body, is as true of his mystical. 'A bone of him shall not be broken.' John xix 36. Look how every bone and limb of Christ's natural body was raised up out of the grave, and carried into heaven; so shall every member of his mystical body be carried up into glory.

(7) We read of some who have been translated into this kingdom. Paul had a sight of it, for he was caught up into the third heaven. 2 Cor xii 2. And the converted thief on the cross was translated into glory. 'Today shalt thou be with me in paradise.' Luke xxiii 43. By all that has been said, it is most evident that believers have a glorious kingdom laid up for them in reversion, and that they shall go to this kingdom when they die. None doubt the certainty of the heavenly kingdom but such as doubt the verity of Scripture.

[6] We should pray earnestly, 'Thy kingdom come.'

(1) Because it is a kingdom worth praying for. It exceeds the glory of all earthly kingdoms, it has gates of pearl. Rev xxi 21. We have heard of a cabinet of pearl, but when did we hear of gates of pearl? In that kingdom is the bed of love, the mountains of spices; there are the cherubims, not to keep us out, but to welcome us into the kingdom. Heaven is a kingdom worth praying for; nothing is wanting in that kingdom which may complete the saints' happiness; for, wherein does happiness consist? Is it in knowledge? We 'shall know as we are known.' Is it in dainty fare? We shall be at the 'marriage supper of the Lamb.' Is it in rich apparel? We shall be 'clothed in long white robes.' Is it in delicious music? We shall hear the choir of angels singing. Is it in dominion? We shall reign as kings, and judge angels. Is it in pleasure? We shall enter into the joy of our Lord. Surely then this kingdom is worth praying for! 'Thy kingdom come.' Would God give us a vision of heaven awhile, as he did Stephen, who saw 'the heavens opened' (Acts vii 56), we should fall into a trance; and being a little recovered out of it, how importunately would we put up this petition, 'Thy kingdom come!'

(2) We must pray for this kingdom of glory, because God will not

bestow it on any without prayer. 'To them who seek for glory and immortality' (Rom ii 7); and how do we seek but by prayer? God has promised a kingdom, and we must by prayer put the bond in suit. God is not so lavish as to throw away a kingdom on those who do not ask it. And certainly, if Christ himself, who had merited glory, did pray, 'Now, O Father, glorify me with thine own self' (John xvii 5), how much more ought we to pray for the excellent glory who have this kingdom granted as a charter of God's mere grace and favour!

(3) We must pray that the kingdom of glory may come, that by going into it we may make an end of sinning. I think sometimes, what a blessed time it will be, never to have a sinful thought more! though we must not pray, 'Thy kingdom come,' out of discontent, because we would be rid of the troubles and crosses of this life. This was Jonah's fault; he would die in a pet, because God took away his gourd; 'Lord,' says he, 'take my life from me.' Jonah iv 3. But we must pray, 'Thy kingdom come,' out of a holy design that the fetters of corruption may be pulled off, and we may be as the angels, those virgin spirits, who never sin. This made the church pray in Rev xxii 20, *Veni, Domine Jesu* [Come, Lord Jesus].

(4) Because that all Christ's enemies shall be put under his feet. The devil shall have no more power to tempt, nor wicked men to persecute; the antichristian hierarchy shall be pulled down, and Zion's glory shall shine as a lamp, and the Turkish strength shall be broken.

(5) We must pray earnestly that the kingdom of glory may come, that we may see God 'face to face,' and have an uninterrupted and eternal communion with him in the empyrean heaven. Moses desired but a glimpse of God's glory. Exod xxxiii 18. How then should we pray to see him in all his embroidered robes of glory, when he shall shine ten thousand times brighter than the sun in its meridian splendour! Here, in this life, we rather desire God than enjoy him; how earnestly therefore should we pray, 'Thy kingdom of glory come!' The beholding and enjoying God will be the diamond in the ring, the very quintessence of glory. And must we pray, 'Thy kingdom come'? How then are they ever like to come to heaven who never pray for it? Though God gives some profane persons 'daily bread' who never pray for it, yet he will not give them a kingdom who never pray for it. God may feed them, but he will never crown them.

Use 1. For information.

(1) From all this, you see that nothing within the whole sphere of religion is imposed upon unreasonable terms. When God bids us serve him, it is no unreasonable request; out of free grace he will enthrone us in a kingdom. When we hear of repentance, steeping our souls in brinish tears for sin; or

of mortification, beheading our king-sin, we are ready to grumble, and think this is hard and unreasonable. 'But, do we serve God for nought?' Is it not infinite bounty to reward us with a kingdom? This kingdom is as far above our thoughts, as it is beyond our deserts. No man can say, without wrong to God, that he is a hard master; for though he sets us about hard work, yet he is no hard master. God gives double pay; he gives great perquisites in his service, sweet joy and peace; and a great reward after, 'an eternal weight of glory.' God gives the spring-flowers, and a crop; he settles upon us such a kingdom as exceeds our faith. *Praemium quod fide non attingitur* [The reward which is not attained by faith]. Augustine. Such as mortal eye hath not seen, nor can it enter into the heart of man to conceive. 1 Cor ii 9. Alas, what an infinite difference is there between duty enjoined, and the kingdom prepared! What is the shedding of a tear to a crown! So that God's 'commandments are not grievous.' 1 John v 3. Our service cannot be so hard as a kingdom is sweet.

(2) See hence the royal bounty of God to his children, that he has prepared a kingdom for them, a kingdom bespangled with glory; infinitely above the model we can draw of it in our thoughts. The painter going to draw the picture of Helena, as not being able to draw her beauty to the life, drew her face covered with a vail; so, when we speak of the kingdom of heaven, we must draw a vail, we cannot set it forth in all its orient beauty and magnificence; gold and pearl do but faintly shadow it out. Rev xxi 21. The glory of this kingdom is better felt than expressed.

They who inherit this kingdom are *amicti stolis albis*, 'clothed with white robes.' Rev vii 9. White robes denote three things: [1] Their dignity. The Persians were arrayed in white, in token of honour. [2] Their purity. The magistrates among the Romans were clothed in white, therefore called *candidati*, to show their integrity. Thus the queen, the Lamb's wife, is arrayed in fine linen, pure and white, which is 'the righteousness of the saints.' Rev xix 8. [3] Their joy. White is an emblem of joy. 'Eat thy bread with joy, let thy garments be always white.' Eccl ix 7, 8.

The dwellers in this kingdom have 'palms in their hands,' in token of victory. Rev vii 9. They are conquerors over the world: and, being victors, they have now palm-branches. They sit upon the throne with Christ. Rev iii 21. When Caesar returned from conquering his enemies, there was set for him a chair of state in the senate, and a throne in the theatre. Thus the saints in glory, after their heroic victories, shall sit upon a throne with Christ. It is royal bounty in God, to bestow such an illustrious kingdom upon the saints. It is a mercy to be pardoned, but what is it to be crowned? It is a mercy to be delivered from wrath to come, but what is it to be invested with a kingdom? 'Behold, what manner of love is this?' Earthly princes may bestow great gifts and donations upon their subjects, but they keep the kingdom to themselves. Though king Pharaoh advanced Joseph to honour, and took the ring off his finger and gave it to him, yet he would keep the kingdom to himself. Gen xli 40. But God enthrones the saints in a kingdom. He thinks nothing too good for his children. We are ready to think much of a tear, a prayer, or to sacrifice a sin for him; but he does not think much to bestow a kingdom upon us.

(3) See hence, that religion is no ignominious disgraceful thing. Satan labours to cast all the odium and reproach upon it that he can; that it is devout frenzy, ingrain folly. Acts xxviii 22. 'As concerning this sect, we know that everywhere it is spoken against.' But wise men measure things by the end. What is the end of a religious life? It ends in a kingdom. Would a prince regard the slightings of a few frantics, when he is going to be crowned? You who are beginners, bind their reproaches as a crown about your head; despise their censures as much as their praise: a kingdom is coming.

(4) See what contrary ways the godly and the wicked go at death. The godly go to a kingdom, the wicked to a prison: the devil is the jailor, and they are bound with the chains of darkness. Jude 6. But what are these chains? Not iron chains, but worse; the chain of God's decree, decreeing them to torment; and the chain of God's power, whereby he binds them fast under wrath. The deplorable condition of impenitent sinners, is that they do not go to a kingdom when they die, but to a prison. Oh, think what horror and despair will possess the wicked, when they see themselves in-gulfed in misery, and their condition hopeless, helpless, endless! They are in a fiery prison, and there is no possibility of getting out. A servant under the law, who had a hard master, at every seventh year might go free; but in hell there is no year of release when the damned shall go free; the fire, the worm, the prison are eternal. If the whole world, from earth to heaven, were filled with grains of sand, and once in a thousand years an angel should come and fetch one grain, how many millions of ages would pass before that vast heap of sand would be quite spent! Yet, if after all this time the sinner might come out of hell, there would be some hope: but this word *ever* breaks the heart with despair.

(5) See that which may make us in love with holy duties; that every duty spiritually performed brings us a step nearer to the kingdom. *Finis dat amabilitatem mediis* [The end makes the means lovable]. He whose heart is set on riches, counts trading pleasant, because it brings him riches. If our hearts are set upon heaven, we shall love duty, because it brings us by degrees to the kingdom; we are going to heaven in the way of duty. Holy duties increase grace; and as grace ripens, so glory hastens. The duties of

religion are irksome to flesh and blood, but we should look upon them as spiritual chariots to carry us apace to the heavenly kingdom. The Protestants in France call their church paradise; and well they might, because the ordinances led them to the paradise of God. As every flower has its sweetness, so would every duty, if we would look upon it as giving us a lift nearer heaven.

(6) It shows us what little cause the children of God have to envy the prosperity of the wicked. *Quis aerario quis plenis loculis indiget* [Who needs a full purse when he owns a treasury]? Seneca. The wicked have the 'waters of a full cup wrung out to them.' Psa lxxiii 10. As if they had a monopoly of happiness: they have all they can desire; nay, they have 'more than heart can wish.' Psa lxxiii 7. They steep themselves in pleasure. 'They take the timbrel and harp, and rejoice at the sound of the organ.' Job xxi 12. The wicked are high when God's people are low in the world: the goats clamber up the mountains of preferment, when Christ's sheep are below in the valley of tears. The wicked are clothed in purple, while the godly are in sackcloth. The prosperity of the wicked is a great stumbling-block. This made Averroes deny a providence, and made Asaph say, 'Verily I have cleansed my heart in vain.' Psa lxxiii 13. But there is no cause of envy at their prosperity, if we consider two things. First, this is all they have. 'Son, remember that thou in thy lifetime receivedst thy good things:' thou hadst all thy heaven here. Luke xvi 25. Luther calls the Turkish empire a bone which God casts to dogs. Secondly, that God has laid up better things for his children. He has prepared a kingdom of glory for them. They shall have the beatific vision: they shall hear the angels sing in concert; they shall be crowned with the pleasures of paradise for ever. Oh, then, envy not the flourishing prosperity of the wicked! they go through fair way to execution, and the godly go through foul way to coronation.

(7) Is there a kingdom of glory coming? See how happy all the saints are at death! They go to a kingdom; they shall see God's face, which shines ten thousand times brighter than the sun in its meridian glory. The godly at death shall be installed into their honour, and have the crown royal set upon their head. They have in the kingdom of heaven the quintessence of all delights; they have the water of life clear as crystal; they have all aromatic perfumes; they feed not on the dew of Hermon, but the manna of angels; they lie in Christ's bosom, that bed of spices. There is such a pleasant variety in the happiness of heaven, that after millions of years it will be as fresh and desirable as the first hour's enjoyment. In the kingdom of heaven, the saints are crowned with all those perfections which human nature is capable of. The desires of the glorified saints are infinitely satisfied; there is nothing absent that they could wish might be enjoyed; there is nothing present that

they could wish might be removed. They who are got into this kingdom would be loath to come back to the earth again, for it would be much to their loss. They would not leave the fatness and the sweetness of the olive, to court the bramble; the things which tempt us, they would scorn. What are golden bags to the golden beams of the Sun of Righteousness? In the kingdom of heaven there is glory in its highest elevation; in that kingdom is knowledge without ignorance, holiness without sin, beauty without blemish, strength without weakness, light without darkness, riches without poverty, ease without pain, liberty without restraint, rest without labour, joy without sorrow, love without hatred, plenty without surfeit, honour without disgrace, health without sickness, peace without war, contentment without cessation. Oh, the happiness of those that die in the Lord! They go into this blessed kingdom. And if they are so happy when they die, then let me make two inferences.

[1] What little cause have the saints to fear death! Are any afraid of going to a kingdom? What is there in this world that should make us desirous to stay here? Do we not see God dishonoured, and how can we bear it? Is not this world 'a valley of tears,' and do we weep to leave it? Are we not in a wilderness among fiery serpents, and are we afraid to go from these serpents? Our best friends live above. God is ever displaying the banner of his love in heaven, and is there any love like his? Are there any sweeter smiles, or softer embraces than his? What news so welcome as leaving the world and going to a kingdom? Christian, thy dying day will be thy wedding day, and dost thou fear it? Is a slave afraid to be redeemed? Is a virgin afraid to be matched into the crown? Death may take away a few worldly comforts, but it gives that which is better; it takes away a flower and gives a jewel; it takes away a short lease and gives land of inheritance. If the saints possess a kingdom when they die, they have no cause to fear death. A prince would not be afraid to cross the sea, though tempestuous, if he were sure to be crowned as soon as he came to shore.

[2] If the godly are so happy when they die, that they go to a kingdom, what cause have we to mourn immoderately for the death of godly friends? Shall we mourn for their preferment? Why should we shed tears immoderately for them who have all tears wiped from their eyes? Why should we be swallowed up of grief for them who are swallowed up of joy? They are gone to their kingdom; they are not lost, but gone a little before; not perished, but translated. *Non amissi sed praemissi.* Cyprian. They are removed for their advantage; as if one should be removed out of a smoky cottage to a palace. Elijah was removed in a fiery chariot to heaven. Shall Elisha weep inordinately because he enjoys not the company of Elijah?

Shall Jacob weep when he knows his son Joseph is preferred and made chief ruler in Egypt? We should not be excessive in grief when we know our godly friends are advanced to a kingdom. I confess when any of our relations die in their impenitence, there is just cause of mourning, but not when our friends take their flight to glory. David lost two sons: Absalom, a wicked son, he mourned for him bitterly; he lost the child he had by Bathsheba: he mourned not when the child was departed. Ambrose gives this reason, that David had a good hope, nay, assurance that the child was translated into heaven, but he doubted of Absalom; he died in his sins; therefore David wept for him, 'O Absalom, my son, my son.' But though we are to weep to think any of our flesh should burn in hell, yet let us not be cast down for them who are so highly preferred at death as to a kingdom. Our godly friends who die in the Lord, are in that blessed estate, and are crowned with such infinite delights, that if we could hear them speak to us out of heaven, they would say, 'Weep not for us, but weep for yourselves.' Luke xxiii 28. We are in our kingdom, weep not for our preferment, 'but weep for yourselves,' who are in a sinful sorrowful world. You are tossing on the troublesome waves, but we are got to the haven: you are fighting with temptations, while we are wearing a victorious crown, 'Weep not for us, but weep for yourselves.'

(8) See the wisdom of the godly. They have the serpent's eye in the dove's head; they are 'wise virgins.' Matt xxv 2. Their wisdom appears in their choice. They choose that which will bring them to a kingdom; they choose grace, and what is grace but the seed of glory? They choose Christ with his cross, but this cross leads to a crown. Moses chose 'rather to suffer affliction with the people of God.' Heb xi 25. It was a wise, rational choice, for he knew if he suffered he should reign. At the day of judgment, those whom the world accounted foolish, will appear to be wise. They made a prudent choice – they chose holiness; and what is happiness but the quintessence of holiness? They chose affliction with the people of God; but, through this purgatory of affliction they pass to paradise. God will proclaim the saints' wisdom before men and angels.

(9) See the folly of those who, for vain pleasures and profits, will lose such a glorious kingdom; like that cardinal of France who said, 'He would lose his part in paradise, if he might keep his cardinalship in Paris.' I may say (as Eccl ix 3), 'Madness is in their heart.' Lysimachus, for a draught of water, lost his empire; so, for a draught of sinful pleasure, these will lose heaven. We too much resemble our grandfather, Adam, who for an apple lost paradise. Many for trifles, to get a shilling more in the shop or bushel, will venture the loss of heaven. It will be an aggravation of the sinner's torment, to think how foolishly he was undone; for a flash of impure joy he lost an

eternal weight of glory. Would it not vex one who is the lord of a manor to think he should part with his stately inheritance for a fit of music. Such are they who let heaven go for a song. This will make the devil insult at the last day, to think how he hath gulled men, and made them lose their souls and their happiness for 'lying vanities.' If Satan could make good his brag, in giving all the glory and kingdoms of the world, it could not countervail the loss of the celestial kingdom. All the tears in hell are not sufficient to lament the loss of heaven.

Use 2. For reproof.

(1) It reproves such as do not look after this kingdom of glory, and live as if all we say about heaven were but a romance. That they mind it not appears, because they do not labour to have the kingdom of grace set up in their hearts. If they have some thoughts of this kingdom, yet it is in a dull, careless manner; they serve God as if they served him not; they do not *vires exercere*, put forth their strength for the heavenly kingdom. How industrious were the saints of old for this kingdom! 'Reaching forth unto those things which are before;' the Greek word is *epekteinomenos*, 'stretching out the neck,' a metaphor from racers, that strain every limb, and reach forward to lay hold on the prize. Phil iii 13. Luther spent three hours a day in prayer. Anna, the prophetess, 'departed not from the temple, but served God with fasting and prayers night and day.' Luke ii 37. How zealous and industrious were the martyrs to get into this heavenly kingdom! They wore their fetters as ornaments, snatched up torments as crowns, and embraced the flames as cheerfully as Elijah did the fiery chariot which came to fetch him to heaven; and do we not think this kingdom worth our labour? The great pains which the heathens took in their Olympic races, when they ran but for a crown made of olive intermixed with gold, will rise up in judgment against such as take little or no pains in seeking after the kingdom of glory. The dulness of many in seeking after heaven is such as if they did not believe there was such a kingdom; or as if it would not countervail their labour; or as if they thought it were indifferent whether they obtained it or not, which is as much as to say, whether they were saved or not; whether they were crowned in glory, or chained as galley slaves in hell for ever.

(2) It reproves those who spend their sweat more in getting the world than the kingdom of heaven. 'Who mind earthly things.' Phil iii 19. The world is the great Diana they cry up, as if they would fetch happiness out of the earth which God has cursed; they labour for honour and riches. Like Korah and Dathan, 'The earth swallowed them up.' Numb xvi 32. It swallows up their time and thoughts. If they are not pagans, they are infidels; they do

not believe there is such a kingdom: they go for Christians, yet question that great article in their faith, life everlasting. Like the serpent, they lick the dust. Oh, what is there in the world that we should so idolize it, and Christ and heaven are to be disregarded? What has Christ done for you? Died for your sins. What will the world do for you? Can it pacify an angry conscience? Can it procure God's favour? Can it fly death? Can it bribe the judge? Can it purchase for you a place in the kingdom of heaven? Oh, how are men bewitched with worldly profits and honours, that for these things they will let go paradise! It was a good prayer of Bernard, *Sic possideamus mundana, ut non perdamus aeterna*. Let us so possess things temporal, that we do not lose things eternal.

(3) It reproves such who delay and put off seeking this kingdom till it be too late; like the foolish virgins who came when the door was shut. *Mora trahit periculum* [Delay brings danger]. People let the lamp of life blaze out, and when the symptoms of death are upon them, and they know not what else to do, will look up to the kingdom of heaven. Christ bids them seek God's kingdom first, and they will seek it last; they put off the kingdom of heaven to a death-bed, as if it were as easy to make their peace as to make their will. How many have lost the heavenly kingdom through delays and procrastinations! Plutarch reports of Archias, the Lacedemonian, that when, being among his cups, one delivered him a letter and desired him to read it presently, being of serious business, he replied, '*Seria cras*, I will mind serious things to-morrow;' and that night he was slain. Thou that sayest, thou wilt look after the kingdom of heaven to-morrow, knowest not but that thou mayest be in hell before to-morrow. Sometimes death comes suddenly: it strikes without giving warning. What folly is it to put off seeking the kingdom of heaven till the day of grace expire; till the radical moisture be spent. As if a man should begin to run a race when a fit of the gout takes him.

(4) It reproves such as were once great zealots in religion, and seemed to be touched with a coal from God's altar, but have since cooled in their devotion, and left off pursuing the celestial kingdom. 'Israel hath cast off the thing that is good:' there is no face of religion to be seen: they have left off the house of prayer, and gone to play-houses; they have left off pursuing the heavenly kingdom. Hos viii 3.

Whence is this?

[1] For want of a supernatural principle of grace. That branch must needs die which has no root to grow upon. That which moves from a principle of life lasts, as the beating of the pulse; but that which moves from an artificial spring only, when the spring is down, the motion ceases. The hypocrite's

religion is artificial, not vital; he acts from the outward spring of applause or gain, and if that be down, his motion towards heaven ceases.

[2] From unbelief. 'An evil heart of unbelief in departing from the living God.' Heb iii 12. 'They believed not in God.' Psa lxxviii 22. 'They turned back;' v 41. Sinners have hard thoughts of God: they think they may pray and hear; yet be never the better. Mal iii 14. They question whether God will give them the kingdom at last; then they turn back, and throw away Christ's colours; they distrust God's love, and no wonder they desert his service. Infidelity is the root of apostasy.

[3] Men leave off pursuing the heavenly kingdom, from some secret lust nourished in the soul, perhaps a wanton or a covetous lust. Demas, for love of the world, forsook his religion, and afterwards turned priest in an idol temple. One of Christ's own apostles was caught with a silver bait. Covetousness will make men betray a good cause, and make shipwreck of a good conscience. If there be any lust unmortified in the soul, it will bring forth the bitter fruit either of scandal or apostasy.

[4] Men leave off pursuing the kingdom of heaven out of timidity. If they persist in religion, they may lose their places of profit, perhaps their lives. The reason, says Aristotle, why the chameleon turns into so many colours is through excessive fear. When carnal fear prevails, it makes men change their religion as fast as the chameleon does its colours. When many of the Jews, who were great followers of Christ, saw the swords and staves, they deserted him. What Solomon said of the sluggard, is as true of the coward: he says, 'There is a lion without.' Prov xxii 13. He sees dangers before him; he would go on in the way to the kingdom of heaven, but there is a lion in the way. This is dismal. 'If any man draw back (in the Greek, if he steals, as a soldier, from his colours), my soul shall have no pleasure in him.' Heb x 38.

Use 3. For trial.
Let us examine whether we shall go to this kingdom when we die. Heaven is called a 'kingdom prepared.' Matt xxv 34.

How shall we know this kingdom is prepared for us?

If we are prepared for the kingdom.

How may that be known?

By being heavenly persons. An earthly heart is no more fit for heaven, than a clod of dust is fit to be a star; there is nothing of Christ or grace in such a heart. It were a miracle to find a pearl in a gold mine; and it is as great a miracle to find Christ, the pearl of price, in an earthly heart. Would we go to the kingdom of heaven? Are we heavenly?

(1) Are we heavenly in our contemplations? Do our thoughts run upon this kingdom? Do we get sometimes upon Mount Pisgah, and take a prospect of glory? Thoughts are as travellers: most of David's thoughts travelled heaven's road. Psa cxxxix 17. Are our minds heavenlized? 'Walk about Zion, tell the towers thereof, mark ye well her bulwarks,' Psa lxviii 12, 13. Do we walk into the heavenly mount, and see what a glorious situation it is? Do we tell the towers of that kingdom? While a Christian fixes his thoughts on God and glory, he does as it were tread upon the borders of the heavenly kingdom, and peep within the veil. As Moses had a sight of Canaan, though he did not enter into it, so the heavenly Christian has a sight of heaven, though he be not yet entered into it.

(2) Are we heavenly in our affections? Do we set our affections on the kingdom of heaven? Col iii 2. If we are heavenly, we despise all things below in comparison of the kingdom of God; we look upon the world but as a beautiful prison; and we cannot be much in love with our fetters, though they are made of gold: our hearts are in heaven. A stranger may be in a foreign land to gather up debts owing him, but he desires to be in his own kingdom and nation: so we are here awhile as in a strange land, but our desire is chiefly after the kingdom of heaven, where we shall be for ever. The world is the place of a saint's abode, not his delight. Is it thus with us? Do we, like the patriarchs of old, desire a better country? Heb xi 16. This is the temper of a true saint, his affections are set on the kingdom of God: his anchor is cast in heaven, and he is carried thither with the sails of desire.

(3) Are we heavenly in our speeches? Christ, after his resurrection, spoke of the things pertaining to the kingdom of God. Acts i 3. Are your tongues turned to the language of the heavenly Canaan? 'Then they that feared the Lord, spake often one to another.' Mal iii 16. Do you in your visits season your discourses with heaven? There are many say, they hope they shall be saved, but you shall never hear them speak of the kingdom of heaven; perhaps of their wares and drugs, or of some rich purchase they have got, but nothing of the kingdom. Can men travel together in a journey, and not speak a word of the place they are travelling to? Are you travellers for heaven, and never speak a word of the kingdom you are travelling to? Herein many discover they do not belong to heaven, for you shall never hear a good word come from them. *Verba sunt speculum mentis.* Bernard. The words are the looking-glass of the mind, they show what the heart is.

(4) Are we heavenly in our trading? Is our traffic and merchandise in heaven? Do we trade in the heavenly kingdom by faith? A man may live in one place, and trade in another; he may live in Ireland, and trade in the

West Indies; so we trade in the heavenly kingdom. They who do not trade in heaven while they live, shall never go to heaven when they die. Do we send up to heaven volleys of sighs and groans? Do we send forth the ship of prayer thither, which fetches in returns of mercy? Is our communion with the Father and his Son Jesus? 1 John i 3. Phil iii 20.

(5) Are our lives heavenly? Do we live as if we had seen the Lord with bodily eyes? Do we emulate and imitate the angels in sanctity? Do we labour to copy out Christ's life in ours? 1 John ii 6. It was a custom among the Macedonians, on Alexander's birth-day, to wear his picture about their necks set with pearl and diamond. Do we carry Christ's picture about us, and resemble him in the heavenliness of our conversation? If we are thus heavenly, we shall go to the kingdom of heaven when we die; and truly there is a great deal of reason why we should be thus heavenly in our thoughts, affections, and conversation, if we consider that the main end why God has given us our souls, is, that we may mind the kingdom of heaven. Our souls are of noble extraction, they are akin to angels, a glass of the Trinity, as Plato speaks. Now, is it rational to imagine that God would have breathed into us such noble souls only to look after sensual objects? Were such bright stars made only to shoot into the earth? Were these immortal souls made only to seek after dying comforts? Had this been the only end of our creation, to eat and drink, and converse with earthly objects, worse souls would have served us: sensitive souls had been good enough for us. What need our souls to be rational and divine, to do that work only which a beast may do?

Great reason we should be heavenly in our thoughts, affections, conversation, if we consider what a blessed kingdom heaven is. It is beyond all hyperbole. Earthly kingdoms scarce deserve the names of cottages compared with it. We read of an angel coming down from heaven, who set his right foot upon the sea, and his left foot on the earth. Rev x 2. Had we but once been in the heavenly kingdom, and viewed the superlative glory of it, how might we, in holy scorn, trample with one foot on the earth, and with the other foot upon the sea? There are rivers of pleasure, gates of pearl, sparkling crowns, white robes; and should not this make our hearts heavenly? It is a heavenly kingdom, and such only go into it who are heavenly.

Use 4. For exhortation to all in general.

(1) If there be such a glorious kingdom, believe this great truth. Socinians deny it. The Rabbis say, the great dispute between Cain and Abel was about the world to come; Abel affirmed it, Cain denied it. It should be engraven upon our hearts as with the point of a diamond, that there is a blessed king-

dom in reversion. 'Verily, there is a reward for the righteous.' Psa lviii 11. Let us not hesitate through unbelief. Doubting principles is the next way to denying them. Unbelief, like Samson, would pull down the pillars of religion. Be confirmed in this, there is a kingdom of glory to come; whoever denies this, cuts asunder the main article of the creed, 'life everlasting.'

(2) If there be such a blessed kingdom of glory to come, let us take heed lest we miss this kingdom; let us fear lest we lose heaven by short shooting. Trembling in the body, is a malady; in the soul, a grace. This fear is not a fear of diffidence or distrust, such as discourages the soul, for such fear frights from religion, it cuts the sinews of endeavour; but holy fear lest we miss the kingdom of heaven, is a fear of diligence; it quickens us in the use of means, and puts us forward, that we may not fail of our hope. 'Noah, moved with fear, prepared an ark.' Heb xi 7. Fear is a watch-bell to awaken sleepy Christians; it guards against security; it is a spur to a sluggish heart. He who fears he shall come short of his journey, rides the faster. And indeed this exhortation to fear lest we miss this kingdom, is most necessary, if we consider two things:

[1] There are many who have gone many steps in the way to heaven, and yet have fallen short of it. 'Thou art not far from the kingdom of God;' yet he was not near enough. Mark xii 34.

How many steps may a man take in the way to the kingdom of God, and yet miss it?

He may be adorned with civility; he may be morally righteous; he may be prudent, just, temperate; he may be free from penal statutes; all which is good, but not enough to bring a man to heaven.

He may hang out the flag of a glorious profession, and yet fall short of the kingdom. The Scribes and Pharisees went far; they sat in Moses' chair, were expounders of the law; they prayed, gave alms, were strict in the observation of the Sabbath; if one had got a thorn in his foot, he would not pull it out on the Sabbath-day, for fear of breaking the Sabbath. They were so externally devout in God's worship, that the Jews thought, that if but two in all the world went to heaven, the one would be a Scribe, and the other a Pharisee; but the mantle of their profession was not lined with sincerity; they did all for the applause of men, and therefore missed heaven. 'Except your righteousness shall exceed the righteousness of the Scribes and Pharisees, ye shall in no case enter into the kingdom of heaven.' Matt v 20.

A man may be a frequenter of ordinances, and yet miss the kingdom. It is a good sight to see people flock as doves to the windows of God's house;

it is good to lie in the way where Christ passes by; yet, be not offended, if I say, one may be a hearer of the word, and fall short of glory. Herod heard John the Baptist gladly, yet beheaded John instead of beheading his sin. The prophet Ezekiel's hearers came with as much delight to his preaching, as one would do to a piece of music. 'Thou art to them as a very lovely song of one that hath a pleasant voice, and can play well on an instrument; for they hear thy words, but they do them not.' Ezek xxxiii 32. What is it to hear one's duty, and not do it? It is as if a physician prescribed a good recipe, but the patient would not take it.

A man may have some trouble for sin, and weep for it, and yet miss the heavenly kingdom.

Whence is this? A sinner's tears are forced by God's judgments; as water which comes out of a distillery is forced by the fire. Trouble for sin is transient, it is quickly over again. As some that go to sea are sea-sick, but when they come to land are well again; so hypocrites may be sermon-sick, but this trouble does not last, the sick-fit is soon over. A sinner weeps, but goes on in sin; his sins are not drowned in his tears.

A man may have good desires, and yet miss the kingdom. 'Let me die the death of the righteous.' Numb xxiii 10.

Wherein do these desires come short? They are sluggish. A man would have heaven, but will take no pains. As if one should say, he desires water, but will not let down the bucket into the well. 'The desire of the slothful killeth him, for his hands refuse to labour.' Prov xxi 25. The sinner desires mercy, but not grace; he desires Christ as a Saviour, but not as he is the Holy One; he desires Christ only as a bridge to lead him over to heaven. Such desires as these may be found among the damned.

A man may forsake his sins, oaths, drunkenness, uncleanness, and yet come short of the kingdom. He may forsake gross sins, and yet have no reluctance to heart-sins, pride, unbelief, and the first risings of malice and concupiscence. Though he dams up the stream, he lets alone the fountain; though he lop and prune the branches, he does not strike at the root of it. Though he leaves sin for fear of hell, or because it brings shame and penury, yet he still loves sin; as if a snake should cast her coat, and yet retain her poison. 'They set their heart on their iniquity.' Hos iv 8. It is but a partial forsaking of sin; though he leaves one sin, he lives in some other. Herod reformed very much. 'He did many things;' but he lived in incest. Mark vi 20. Some leave drunkenness, and live in covetousness; they forbear swearing, and live in slandering. It is but a partial reformation, and so they miss of the kingdom of glory. Thus you see there are some who have gone many steps in the way to heaven, and yet have come short. Some have gone so far in profession, that they have been confident their estate has been good.

and that they should go to the kingdom of heaven, and yet have missed it. 'When once the master of the house is risen up, and hath shut to the door, and ye begin to stand without, and to knock, saying, Lord, Lord, open unto us.' Luke xiii 25. How confident were these of salvation! They did not beseech, but knock, as if they did not doubt but to be let into heaven; yet to these Christ says, 'I know you not whence ye are; depart from me, all ye workers of iniquity.' Therefore fear and tremble, lest any miss of this kingdom of heaven.

[2] This fear is necessary, if we consider what a loss it is to lose the heavenly kingdom. All the tears in hell are not sufficient to lament the loss of heaven. They who lose the heavenly kingdom, lose God's sweet presence, the ravishing views and smiles of his glorious face. God's presence is the diamond in the ring of glory. 'In thy presence is fulness of joy.' Psa xvi 11. If God be the fountain of all bliss, then, to be separated from him, is the fountain of all misery. They who lose the heavenly kingdom, lose the society of angels; and, what sweeter music than to hear them praise God in concert? They lose all their treasure, their white robes, their sparkling crowns; they lose their hopes. 'Whose hope shall be cut off.' Job viii 14. Their hope is not an anchor, but a spider's web. If hope deferred makes the heart sick, what is hope disappointed? Prov xiii 12. They lose the end of their being. Why were they created, but to be enthroned in glory? Now, to lose this, is to lose the end of their being, as if an angel should be turned to a worm. There are many aggravations of the loss of this heavenly kingdom.

The eyes of the wicked shall be opened to see their loss; now they care not for the loss of God's favour, because they know not the worth of it. A man that loses a rich diamond, and took it but for an ordinary stone, is not much troubled at the loss of it; but when he comes to know what a jewel he lost, he laments. He whose heart would never break at the sight of his sins, breaks at the sight of his loss. When the wife of Phinehas heard the ark was lost, she cried out, 'The glory is departed.' 1 Sam iv 21. When the sinner sees what he has lost, that he has lost the beatific vision, he has lost the kingdom of heaven, he will cry out in horror and despair, 'The glory, the everlasting glory, is departed.'

A second aggravation of the loss of this kingdom will be, that sinners shall be upbraided by their own conscience. This is the worm that never dies, a self-accusing mind. Mark ix 44. When sinners shall consider that they were in a fair way to the kingdom; that they had a possibility of salvation; that though the door of heaven was strait, yet it was open; that they had the means of grace; that the jubilee of the gospel was proclaimed in their ears; that God called, but they refused; that Jesus Christ offered them a plaister of his own blood to heal them, but they trampled it under foot; that the Holy Spirit stood at the door of their heart, knocking and crying to them to receive Christ and heaven, but they repulsed the Spirit, and sent away this dove; and that now, through their own folly and wilfulness, they have lost the kingdom of heaven; a self-accusing conscience will be terrible, it will will be like a venomous worm gnawing at the heart.

A third aggravation of the loss of heaven will be, to look upon others that have gained the kingdom. The happiness of the blessed will be an eyesore. 'There shall be weeping and gnashing of teeth, when ye shall see Abraham, and Isaac, and Jacob, and all the prophets in the kingdom of God, and you yourselves thrust out.' Luke xiii 28. When the wicked shall see those whom they hated and scorned exalted to a kingdom, and shine with robes of glory, and they themselves miss the kingdom, it will be a dagger at the heart, and make them gnash their teeth for envy.

A fourth aggravation is, that this loss of the kingdom of heaven is accompanied with the punishment of sense. He who leaps short of the bank, falls into the river: such as come short of heaven, fall into the river of fire and brimstone. 'The wicked shall be turned into hell;' and how dreadful is that! Psa ix 17. If to have but a spark of God's anger light upon the conscience be so torturing here, what will it be to have mountains of God's wrath thrown upon the soul? 'Who knoweth the power of thine anger?' Psa xc 11. The angel never poured out his vial, but some woe followed. Rev xvi 3. When the bitter vials of God's wrath are poured out, damnation follows. Dives cries out, 'I am tormented in this flame.' Luke xvi 24. In hell there is not a drop of mercy. There was no oil nor frankincense used in the sacrifice of jealousy. Numb v 15. In hell there is no oil of mercy to lenify the sufferings of the damned, nor incense of prayer to appease God's wrath.

A fifth aggravation of the loss of this kingdom will be to consider on what easy and reasonable terms men might have had this kingdom. If indeed God had commanded impossibilities, to have satisfied justice in their own persons, it had been another matter; but what God did demand was reasonable, and was for their good, which was to accept of Christ for their Lord and Husband, and to part with that which would ruin them. These were the fair terms on which they might have enjoyed the heavenly kingdom. Now, to lose heaven, which might have been had upon such easy terms, will be a cutting aggravation. It will rend a sinner's heart with rage and grief, to think how easily he might have prevented the loss of the heavenly kingdom.

It will be an aggravation of the loss of heaven for sinners to think how active they were in doing that which lost them the kingdom. It was *felo de se*. What pains they took to resist the Spirit and to stifle conscience! They sinned until they were out of breath. 'They weary themselves to commit iniquity.' Jer ix 5. What difficulties men went through! How much they endured for their sins! How much shame and pain! How sick was the drunkard with his cups! How sore in his body was the adulterer! What marks of sin he carried about him! What dangers men adventure upon for their lusts! They adventure God's wrath, and adventure the laws of the land. Oh, how will this aggravate the loss of heaven! How will it make men curse themselves to think what pains they were at to lose happiness! How will it sting men's consciences to think that had they but taken as much pains for heaven as they did for hell, they had not lost it!

It will be an aggravation of the loss of this kingdom, that it will be irreparable: heaven once lost can never be recovered. Worldly losses may be made up again. If a man lose his health he may have it repaired by physic; if he be driven out of his kingdom he may be restored to it again as king Nebuchadnezzar was, 'Mine honour returned unto me, and I was established in my kingdom.' Dan iv 36. King Henry VI was deposed from his throne, and restored to it again. But they who once lose heaven can never be restored to it again. After millions of years they are as far from obtaining glory as at first. Thus you see how needful this exhortation is, that we should fear lest we fall short of this kingdom of heaven.

What shall we do that we may not miss this kingdom of glory?

Take heed of those things which will make you miss heaven. (1) Take heed of spiritual sloth. Many Christians are settled upon their lees; they are loath to put themselves to too much pains. It is said of Israel, 'They despised the pleasant land.' Psa cvi 24. Canaan was a paradise of delights, a type of heaven; ay, but some of the Jews thought it would cost them a great deal of trouble and hazard in the getting, and they would rather go without it. 'They despised the pleasant land.' I have read of certain Spaniards that live where there is a great store of fish, but are so lazy that they will not be at the pains to catch them, but buy of their neighbours. Such sinful sloth is upon the most, that though the kingdom of heaven be offered them, yet they will not put themselves to any labour for it. They have some faint wishes and desires. O that I had this kingdom! They are like a man that wishes for venison, but will not hunt for it. 'The soul of the sluggard desireth, and hath nothing.' Prov xiii 4. Men could be content to have the kingdom of heaven if it would drop as a ripe fig into their mouths, but they are loath to fight for it. O take heed of spiritual sloth! God never made heaven to be a hive for drones. We cannot have the world without labour, and do we think to have the kingdom of heaven? Heathens will rise up in judgment against many Christians. What pains did they take in their Olympic races when they ran but for a crown of olive or myrtle intermixed with gold; and do we stand still when we are running for a kingdom? 'Slothfulness casteth into a deep sleep.' Prov xix 15. Sloth is the soul's sleep. Adam lost his rib when he was asleep. Many a man loses the kingdom of heaven when he is in this deep sleep of sloth.

(2) Take heed of unbelief. Unbelief kept Israel out of Canaan. 'So we see that they could not enter in because of unbelief.' Heb iii 19. And it keeps many out of heaven. Unbelief is an enemy to salvation, it is a damning sin; it whispers thus, To what purpose is all this pains for the heavenly kingdom? I had as good sit still; I may come near to heaven, yet come short of heaven. 'And they said, There is no hope.' Jer xviii 12. Unbelief destroys hope; and if you cut this sinew, a Christian goes but lamely in religion, if he goes at all. Unbelief raises jealous thoughts of God; it represents him as a severe judge; it discourages many a soul, and takes it off from duty. Beware of unbelief: believe the promises. 'The Lord is good to the soul that seeketh him:' seek him earnestly and he will open both heart and heaven to you. Lam iii 25. *Deus volentibus non deest* [God does not fail those who desire him]. Do what you are able, and God will help you. While you spread the sails of your endeavour, God's Spirit will blow upon these sails, and carry you swiftly to the kingdom of glory.

(3) If you would not miss the heavenly kingdom, take heed of mistake by imagining the way to be easier than it is; as though it were but a sigh, or, Lord have mercy. There is no going to heaven *per saltum* [at a leap]; one cannot leap out of Delilah's lap into Abraham's bosom. The sinner is 'dead in trespasses.' Eph ii 1. Is it easy for a dead man to restore himself to life? Is regeneration easy? Are there no pangs in the new birth? Does not the Scripture call Christianity a warfare and a race? And do you fancy this easy? The way to the kingdom is not easy, but a mistake about the way is easy.

(4) If you would not miss the heavenly kingdom, take heed of delays and procrastinations. *Mora trahit periculum* [Delay brings danger]. It is a usual delusion, I will mind the kingdom of heaven, but not yet; when I have gotten an estate, and grown old, then I will look after heaven; but on a sudden, death surprises men, and they fall short of heaven. Delay strengthens sin, hardens the heart, and gives the devil fuller possession of a man. Take heed of adjourning and putting off seeking the kingdom of heaven till it be too late. Caesar, deferring to read a letter put into his hand, was killed in the senate-house. Consider how short your life is; it is a taper soon blown out. *Animantis cujusque vita in fuga est* [The life of everyone living is fleeing away]. The body is like a vessel tunned with breath: sickness broaches it, death draws it out. Delay not the business of salvation a day longer; sometimes death strikes, and gives no warning.

(5) If you would not come short of the kingdom of heaven, take heed of prejudice. Many take a prejudice at religion, and on this rock dash their souls. They are prejudiced at Christ's person, his truths, his followers, his ways.

They are prejudiced at his person. 'And they were offended in him.' Matt xiii 57. What is there in Christ that men should be offended at him? He is the 'pearl of great price.' Matt xiii 46. Are men offended at pearls and diamonds? Christ is the wonder of beauty. 'Fairer than the children of men.' Psa xlv 2. Is there anything in beauty to offend? He is the mirror of mercy. Heb ii 17. Why should mercy offend any? He is a Redeemer. Why should a captive slave be offended at him who comes with a sum of money to ransom him? The prejudice men take at Christ is from the inbred depravity of their hearts. The eye that is sore cannot endure the light of the sun: the fault is not in the sun, but in the sore eye. There are two things in Christ against which men are prejudiced: [1] His meanness. The Jews expected a monarch for their Messiah; but Christ came not with outward pomp and splendour. His kingdom was not of this world. The stars which are seated in the brightest orbs are least seen. Christ, who is the bright morning-star, was not much seen; his divinity was hid in the dark lantern of his humanity; all who saw the man did not see the Messiah. The Jews stumbled at the meanness of his person. [2] Men are prejudiced at Christ's strictness. They look upon him as austere, and his laws as too severe. 'Let us break their bands, and cast away their cords from us.' Psa ii 3. Though to a saint, Christ's laws are no more burdensome than wings to a bird, yet to the wicked his laws are a yoke; and they love not to come under restraint, therefore they hate Christ. Though they pretend to love him as a Saviour, they hate him as he is the Holy One.

Men are prejudiced at the truths of Christ. [1] Self-denial. A man must deny his righteousness. Phil iii 9. He will graft the hope of salvation upon the stock of his own righteousness. [2] He must deny his unrighteousness. The Scripture seals no patents to sin; it teacheth us to deny all 'ungodliness and worldly lusts.' Tit ii 12. We must divorce those sins which bring in pleasures and profit. [3] Forgiveness of injuries. Mark xi 25. These truths men are prejudiced at; they can rather want forgiveness from God, than they can forgive others.

Men are prejudiced at the followers of Christ. [1] Their paucity. There are but few, in comparison, that embrace Christ; but why should this offend? Men are not offended at pearls and precious stones, because they are few. [2] Their poverty. Many that wear Christ's livery are low in the world; but why should this give offence? Christ has better things than these to bestow upon his followers; as the holy anointing, the white stone, the hidden manna, and the crown of glory. All Christ's followers are not humbled with poverty. Abraham was rich with gold and silver, as well as rich in faith. Though not many noble are called, yet some noble are. 'Honourable women which were Greeks' believed. Acts xvii 12. Constantine and Theodosius were godly emperors. So that this stumbling-block is removed. [3] Their scandals. Some of Christ's followers, under a mask of piety, commit sin, which begets a prejudice against religion; but does Christ or his gospel teach any such thing? The rules he prescribes are holy. Why should the master be thought the worse of, because some of his servants prove bad?

Men are prejudiced at the ways of Christ. They expose them to sufferings. 'Let him take up his cross and follow me.' Matt xvi 24. Many stumble at the cross. There are, as Tertullian says, *delicatuli*, silken Christians, who love their ease; they will follow Christ to mount Tabor, to see him transfigured, but not to mount Golgotha, to suffer with him. But, alas! what is affliction to the glory that follows! The weight of glory makes affliction light. *Adimant caput, non coronam* [Let them take the head, but not the crown]. O take heed of prejudice, which has been a stumbling-stone in men's way to heaven, and has made them fall short of the kingdom!

(6) If you would not miss the kingdom of heaven, take heed of presumption. Men presume all is well, and take it as a principle not to be disputed, that they shall go to heaven. The devil has given them opium, to cast them into a deep sleep of security. The presumptuous sinner is like the leviathan, made 'without fear;' he lives as bad as the worst, yet hopes he shall be saved as well as the best; he blesses himself and saith, he shall have peace, though he goes on in sin. Deut xxix 19. As if a man should drink poison, yet not fear but he will have his health. But whence does this presumptuous hope arise? Surely from a conceit that God is made up of all mercy. It is true that God is merciful, but he is just too. 'Keeping mercy for thousands, and that will by no means clear the guilty.' Exod xxxiv 7. If a king proclaimed that those only should be pardoned who came in and submitted, ought any still persisting in rebellion, to claim the benefit of the pardon? Dost thou hope for mercy who wilt not lay down thy weapons, but stand out in rebellion against heaven? None might touch the ark but the priests: none may touch this ark of God's mercy, but holy, consecrated persons. Presumption is *heluo animarum*, the great devourer of souls. A thousand have missed heaven by putting on the broad spectacles of presumption.

(7) If you would not miss the heavenly kingdom, take heed of the delights and pleasures of the flesh. Soft pleasures harden the heart; many people cannot endure a serious thought, but are for comedies and romances;

they play away their salvation. *Homines capiuntur voluptate, ut pisces hamo* [Men are caught by pleasure, as fish by the hook]. Cicero. Pleasure is the sugared bait men bite at, but there is a hook under it. 'They take the timbrel and harp; and rejoice at the sound of the organ.' Job xxi 12. 'That lie upon beds of ivory, that chant to the sound of the viol, that drink wine in bowls, and anoint themselves with the chief ointments.' Amos vi 4, 5, 6. The pleasures of the world keep many from the pleasures of paradise. What a shame is it, that the soul, that princely thing, which sways the sceptre of reason, and is akin to angels, should be enslaved by sinful pleasure! Beard, in his *Theatre*, speaks of one who had a room richly hung with fair pictures, he had most delicious music, he had the rarest beauties, he had all the candies, and curious preserves of the confectioner, to gratify his senses with pleasure, and swore he would live one week as a god, though he were sure to be damned in hell the next day. Diodorus Siculus observes, that the dogs of Sicily while hunting among the sweet flowers, lose the scent of the hare; so, many while hunting after the sweet pleasures of the world, lose the kingdom of heaven. It is, says Theophylact, one of the worst sights to see a sinner go laughing to hell.

(8) If you would not fall short of the kingdom of heaven, take heed of worldly-mindedness. A covetous spirit is a dunghill spirit, it chokes good affections, as the earth puts out the fire. The world hindered the young man from following Christ; *abiit tristis*, he went away sorrowful, which extorted these words from our Saviour: 'How hardly shall they that have riches enter into the kingdom of God!' Luke xviii 23, 24. *Divitiae saeculi sunt laquei diaboli* [The riches of the world are the snares of the devil]. Bernard. Riches are golden snares. If a man were to climb up a steep rock, and had weights tied to his legs, it would hinder him in his ascent; so too many golden weights will hinder us from climbing up the steep rock which leads to heaven. 'They are entangled in the land, the wilderness hath shut them in.' Exod xiv 3. So it may be said of many, they are entangled in earthly affairs, the world has shut them in. The world is no friend to grace. The more the child sucks, the weaker the nurse is; and the more the world sucks and draws from us, the weaker our grace is. 'Love not the world.' 1 John ii 15. Had a man a monopoly of all the wealth of the world; were he able to empty the western parts of gold, and the eastern of spices; could he heap up riches to the starry heaven, yet his heart would not be filled. Covetousness is a dry dropsy. Joshua could stop the course of the sun, but could not stop Achan in his covetous pursuit of the wedge of gold. He whose heart is locked up in his chest, will be locked out of heaven. Some ships that have escaped the rocks, have been cast away upon the sands; so, many who have escaped gross sins, have been cast away upon the world's golden sands.

(9) If you would not come short of the kingdom of heaven, take heed of indulging any sin. One millstone will drown, as well as more; and one sin lived in will damn, as well as more. *Ubi regnat peccatum, non potest regnare Dei regnum.* Jerome. If any one sin reign, it will keep you from reigning in the kingdom of heaven. Especially keep from sins of presumption, which waste conscience, *vastare conscientiam* (Tertullian); and the sin of your natural constitution; the *peccatum in deliciis* (Augustine); thy darling sin; 'I kept myself from mine iniquity,' that sin which my heart would soonest decoy and flatter me into. Psa xviii 23. As in the hive there is one master-bee, so in the heart one master-sin: Oh, take heed of this!

How may this sin be known?

That sin for which a man cannot endure the arrow of a reproof is the bosom-sin. Herod could not brook to have his incest meddled with, that was a *noli me tangere* [touch me not]. Men can be content to have other sins declaimed against; but if a minister put his finger upon the sore, and touches upon one special sin, then *igne micant oculi* [their eyes flash with fire], they are enraged, and spit the venom of malice.

That sin which a man's heart runs out most to, and he is most easily captivated by, is the *Delilah* in the bosom. One man is overcome with wantonness, another by worldliness. It is a sad thing for a man to be so bewitched by a beloved sin, that if it ask him to part with not only one half the kingdom, but the whole kingdom of heaven, he must part with it to gratify that lust.

That sin which most troubles a man and flies in his face in an hour of sickness and distress, is the sin he has allowed himself in, and is his complexion-sin. When Joseph's brethren were distressed, their sin in selling their brother came into their remembrance. 'We are verily guilty concerning our brother,' &c. Gen xlii 21. So, when a man is upon his sick-bed, and conscience shall say, Thou hast been guilty of such a sin, the sin of slandering or uncleanness, conscience reads a man a sad lecture, and affrights him most for one sin; that is the complexion-sin.

That sin which a man is least inclined to part with, is the endeared sin. Of all his sons Jacob could most hardly part with Benjamin. 'Will ye take Benjamin away.' Gen xlii 35. So says the sinner, this and that sin I have left, but must Benjamin go too? Must I part with this delightful sin? That goes to the heart. As with a castle that has several forts about it, the first and second forts of which are yielded, when it comes to the main castle, the governor will rather fight and die than yield it; so a man may suffer many of his sins to be demolished; but when it comes to one, that is like the taking of a castle, he will never yield to part with that; surely that is the master-sin.

Take heed especially of this sin; the strength of sin lies in the beloved sin, which, like a humour striking to the heart, brings death. I have read of a monarch, who being pursued by the enemy, threw away the crown of gold on his head, that he might run the faster; so the sin which thou didst wear as a crown of gold must be thrown away, that thou mayest run the faster to the kingdom of heaven. Oh, if you would not lose glory, mortify the beloved sin; set it, as Uriah, in the forefront of the battle to be slain. By plucking out this right eye you will see the better to go to heaven.

(10) If you would not fall short of the kingdom of heaven, take heed of inordinate passion. Many a ship has been lost in the storm; and many a soul has been lost in a storm of unruly passions. Every member of the body is infected with sin, as every branch of wormwood is bitter; but 'the tongue is full of deadly poison.' James iii 8. Some care not what they say in their passion; they will censure, slander, and wish evil to others. How can Christ be in the heart, when the devil has taken possession of the tongue? Passion disturbs reason, it is *brevis insania*, a short frenzy. Jonah in a passion flies out against God. 'I do well to be angry, even unto death.' Jon iv 9. What! to be angry with God, and to justify it? 'I do well to be angry;' the man was not well in his wits. Passion unfits for prayer. 'I will, therefore, that men pray, lifting up holy hands, without wrath.' 1 Tim ii 8. He that prays in wrath may lift up his hands in prayer, but he does not lift up holy hands. Water, when hot, soon boils over; so, when the heart is heated with anger, it soon boils over in fiery passionate speeches. Some curse others in their passion. Let those whose tongues are set on fire, take heed that they do not one day in hell desire a drop of water to cool them. Oh, if you would not miss the heavenly kingdom, beware of giving way to unbridled passions. Some say, words are but wind; but they are such a wind as may blow them to hell.

(11) If you would not fall short of the heavenly kingdom, beware of too much indulging the sensual appetite. 'Make not provision for the flesh.' Rom xiii 14. The Greek word, *pronoian poiein*, to make provision, signifies to be caterers for the flesh. 'Whose god is their belly.' Phil iii 19. The throat is a slippery place. Judas received the devil in the sop; and often the devil slides down in the liquor; excess in meat and drink clouds the mind, chokes good affections, and provokes lust. Many a man digs his own grave with his teeth. The heathen could say, *Magnus sum et ad majora natus quam ut sim corporis mei mancipium* [I am great and born to greater things than to be a slave to my body]. Seneca. He was higher born than to be a slave to his body. To pamper the body, and neglect the soul, is to feed the slave and to starve the wife. Take such a proportion of food as may recruit nature, but do not surfeit it. Excess in things lawful has lost many the kingdom of heaven. A bee may suck a little honey from the leaf, but put it in a barrel of

honey, and it is drowned. To suck temperately from the creature, God allows; but excess ingulfs men in perdition.

(12) If you would not fall short of the kingdom of heaven, take heed of injustice in your dealings. Defrauding lies in two things, 1. Mixing commodities, as if anyone should mix bad wheat with good, and sell it for pure wheat, which is to defraud. 'Thy wine mixed with water.' Isa i 22. 2. Giving scant measure. 'Making the ephah small.' Amos viii 5. The ephah was a measure which the Jews used in selling: they made the ephah small; they gave not full measure. I wish this were not the sin of many. 'He is a merchant, the balances of deceit are in his hand.' Hos xii 7. Can they be holy which are not just? 'Shall I count them pure with the wicked balances?' Micah vi 11. Is his heart sincere who has false weights? Many cannot reach heaven because of their over-reaching.

(13) If you would not miss the kingdom of heaven, take heed of evil company. There is a necessary commerce with men in buying and selling, or, as the apostle says, we must go out of the world, but do not voluntarily choose the company of the wicked. 1 Cor v 10. 'I have written unto you not to keep company.' 1 Cor v 11. Do not incorporate into the society of the wicked, or be too much familiar with them. The wicked are God-haters; and 'Shouldest thou love them that hate the Lord?' 2 Chron xix 2. A Christian is bound, by virtue of his oath of allegiance to God in baptism, not to have intimate converse with such as are God's sworn enemies: it is a thing of bad report. What do Christ's doves among birds of prey? What do virgins among harlots? The company of the wicked is very defiling, it is like going among them that have the plague. 'They were mingled among the heathen, and learned their works.' Psa cvi 35. If you mingle bright armour with rusty, the bright armour will not brighten the rusty, but the rusty armour will spoil the bright. Such as have had religious education, and have some inclinations to good, by mixing with the wicked, are apt to receive hurt. The bad will sooner corrupt the good, than the good will convert the bad. Pharaoh taught Joseph to swear, but Joseph did not teach Pharaoh to pray. There is a strange attractive power in ill company to corrupt and poison the best dispositions; they damp good affections. Throw a fire-ball into the snow, and it is soon quenched. Among the wicked, the heat of zealous affections is lost. By holding familiar correspondence with the wicked, they will dissuade us from strict godliness, and debar us our liberty and pleasure. 'This sect everywhere is spoken against.' Acts xxviii 22.

Hereupon he, who before looked towards heaven, begins to be discouraged, and gradually declines from goodness. There steals upon him a dislike of his former religious course of life; he thinks he was righteous over much, stricter than needed. There is instilled into his heart a secret delight of evil. He begins to like foolish scurrilous discourse; he can hear religion spoken against, and be silent, nay, well pleased; he loves vanity, and makes sport of sin. He is by degrees so metamorphosed, and made like the company he converses with, that he now grows into disgust and hatred of his former sober ways. He is ill-affected towards good men, transformed into scoffing Ishmael, a breathing devil; and becomes at last as much the child of hell as any of that graceless damned crew he conversed with. And what is the end of all? A blot in the name, a moth in the estate, a worm in the conscience. Oh, if you would not miss the kingdom of heaven, beware of evil company! Bad company is the bane and poison of the youth of this age. Such as were once soberly inclined, by coming among the profane, grow familiar, till at last they keep one another company in hell.

(14) If you would not miss the kingdom of heaven, take heed of parleying with the fleshly part. The flesh is a bosom traitor. When an enemy is gotten within the walls of a castle, it is in great danger of being taken. The flesh is an enemy within: it is a bad counsellor; it says, There is a lion in the way; it discourages from religious strictness; it says as Peter did to Christ, 'Spare thyself;' it says as Judas, 'What needs all this waste?' What needs this praying? Why do you waste your strength and spirits in religion? What needs all this waste? The flesh cries out for ease and pleasure. How many, by consulting with the flesh, have lost the kingdom of heaven!

(15) If you would not fall short of heaven, take heed of carnal relations. Our carnal friends are often bars and locks in our way to heaven; they will say, Religion is preciseness and singularity. A wife in the bosom may be a tempter. Job's wife was so. 'Dost thou still retain thine integrity? Curse God, and die.' Job ii 9. What! still pray? What dost thou get by serving God? Job, where are thy earnings? What canst thou show thou hast had in God's service, but boils and ulcers? And dost thou still retain thy integrity? Throw off God's livery, renounce religion. Here was a temptation handed over to him by his wife. The woman was made of the rib, the devil turned this rib into an arrow, and would have shot Job to the heart, but his faith quenched his fiery dart. Beware of carnal relations. We read that some of Christ's kindred laid hold on him, and would have hindered him when he was going to preach. 'They said, He is beside himself.' Mark iii 21. Our kindred sometimes would stand in our way to heaven, and, judging all zeal rashness, would hinder us from being saved. Such carnal relations Spira had; for having advised with them whether he should remain constant in his orthodox opinion, they persuaded him to recant; and so, abjuring his former faith, he fell into horror and despondency of mind. Galeacius, Marquis of Vico, found his carnal relations a great block in his way; and

what ado had he to break through their temptations! Take heed of a snare in your bosom. It is a brave saying of Jerome, *si mater mihi ubera ostendat,* &c. 'If my parent should persuade me to deny Christ, if my mother should show me her breast that gave me suck, if my wife should go to charm me with her embraces, I would forsake all, and fly to Christ.'

(16) If you would not fall short of the kingdom of heaven, take heed of falling off. Beware of apostasy. He misses the prize who does not hold out in the race; he who makes shipwreck of the faith cannot come to the haven of glory. We live in the fall of the leaf; men fall from that goodness they seemed to have; some are turned to error, others to vice; some to drinking and dicing, and others to whoring; the very mantle of their profession is fallen off. It is dreadful for men to fall off from hopeful beginnings. The apostate, says Tertullian, seems to put God and Satan in the balance, and having weighed both their services, prefers the devil's service, and proclaims him to be the best master; in which respect he is said to put Christ to open shame. Heb vi 6. This is sad at last. Heb x 38. If you would not miss the glory, take heed of apostasy. Those who fall away, must needs fall short of the kingdom.

What, then, must we do?

(1) If we would not come short of this heavenly kingdom, let us be much in the exercise of self-denial. 'If any man will come after me, let him deny himself.' Matt xvi 24. He who would go to heaven must deny self-righteousness. *Cavendum est a propria justitia* [We must beware of our own righteousness]. 'That I may be found in him, not having mine own righteousness.' Phil iii 9. The spider weaves a web out of her own bowels; so a hypocrite would spin a web of salvation out of his own righteousness. We must deny our civility in point of justification. Civility is a good staff to walk with among men, but it is a bad ladder to climb up to heaven. We must deny our holy things in point of justification. Alas! how are our duties chequered with sin! Put gold in the fire, and there comes out dross; so our most golden services are mixed with unbelief. Deny self-righteousness; use duty, but trust to Christ. Noah's dove made use of her wings to fly, but trusted to the ark for safety! Let duties have your diligence, but not your confidence. Self-denial is *via ad regnum* [the way to the kingdom]. There is no getting into heaven but through this strait gate of self-denial.

(2) The second means for obtaining the kingdom is serious consideration. Most men fall short of heaven for want of consideration.

We should often consider what a kingdom heaven is. It is called *regnum paratum*, a kingdom prepared, which implies something that is rare and excellent. Matt xxv 34. God has prepared in his kingdom such things as 'eye hath not seen nor ear heard.' 1 Cor ii 9. Heaven is beyond hyperbole. In particular in this celestial kingdom are two things. A stately palace, and a royal feast. The stately palace is large and has several storeys. The dimensions of it are twelve thousand furlongs, or, as it is in some Greek copies, twelve times twelve thousand furlongs, a finite number put for an infinite; no arithmetician can number these furlongs. Rev xxi 15. Though there be an innumerable company of saints and angels in heaven, yet there is infinitely enough room to receive them. The palace of this kingdom is lucid and transparent; it is adorned with light, and the light is sweet. Hell is a dark dungeon, but the palace above is bespangled with light. Col i 12. Such illustrious beams of glory shine from God, as shed a brightness and splendour upon the empyrean heaven. This palace of the kingdom is well situated for good air and a pleasant prospect. There is the best air, which is perfumed with the odours of Christ's ointments; and a most pleasant prospect of the bright morning-star. The palace is rich and sumptuous. It has gates of pearl. Rev xxi 21. It is enriched with white robes and crowns of glory; it never falls to decay, and the dwellers in it never die. 'They shall reign for ever and ever.' Rev xxii 5.

There is also a royal feast. It is called 'the marriage-supper of the Lamb.' Rev xix 9. Bullinger and Gregory the Great understood this of the magnificent supper prepared in the kingdom of heaven. A glorious feast it will be in respect of the founder. The glorified saints shall feast their eyes with God's beauty, and their hearts with his love. A delicious feast it will be in respect of the festivity and holy mirth. What joy shall there be in the anthems and triumphs of glorified spirits! Saints and angels shall twist together in an inseparable union of love, and lie in each others' sweet embrace. A royal banquet it will be, where there is no surfeit, because a fresh course is continually served in. The serious consideration of what a kingdom of heaven is, would be a means to quicken our endeavours in the pursuit after it. What causes men to make voyages to the Indies but the consideration of the gold and spices which are to be had there? Did we survey and contemplate the glory of heaven, we should soon take a voyage, and never leave till we had arrived at the celestial kingdom.

How it will trouble you if you should perish to think you came short of heaven for want of a little more pains! The prophet Elisha bid the king of Israel smite the ground six times, and he smote but thrice, and stayed. 2 Kings xiii 19. He lost many victories by it; so when a man shall think thus, I did something in religion, but did not do enough; I prayed, but it was coldly; I did not put coals to the incense; I heard the word, but did not meditate on it; I did not chew the cud; I smote but thrice, when I should have smote six times; had I taken a little more pains I had been happy, but I have lost the kingdom of heaven by short-shooting. The consideration, how terrible the thought will be of losing heaven for want of a little more pains, should be a means to spur on our sluggish hearts, and make us more diligent to get the kingdom.

(3) The third means for obtaining this kingdom is to keep up daily prayer. 'I give myself unto prayer.' Psa cix 4. Prayer inflames the affections, and oils the wheels of endeavour; it prevails with God, unlocks his bowels, and then he unlocks heaven. All that have got to heaven have crept thither upon their knees. The saints now in heaven have been men of prayer. Daniel prayed three times a day, Jacob wrestled with God in prayer, and as a prince, prevailed. Prayer must be fervent, else it is *thuribulum sine prunis*, as Luther says, a golden censer without fire. O follow God with prayers and tears; say as Jacob to the angel, 'I will not let thee go, except thou bless me.' Gen xxxii 26. Prayer *vincit invincibilem*; as Luther says, it conquers the Omnipotent. Elijah by prayer opened heaven: by ardent and constant prayer heaven is opened to us.

(4) If you would obtain the heavenly kingdom, get a love to heaven. Love puts a man upon the use of all means to enjoy the thing loved. He who loves the world, how active is he! He will break his sleep and peace for it. He that loves honour, what hazards will he run! He will swim to the throne in blood. Jacob loved Rachel, and what would he not do, though it were serving two seven-years' apprenticeships for obtaining her! Love carries a man out violently to the object loved. Love like wings to the bird, like sails to the ship, carries a Christian full sail to heaven. Heaven is a place of rest and joy, it is paradise, and will you not love it? Love heaven, and you cannot miss it. Love breaks through all opposition; it takes heaven by storm. Though it labour, it is never weary. It is like the rod of myrtle in the traveller's hand, which makes him fresh and lively in his travel, and keeps him from being weary.

(5) If you would obtain the kingdom of heaven, make religion your business. What a man looks upon as a *parergon*, a thing by the by, he does not much mind. If ever we would have heaven, we must look upon it as our main concern; other things do but concern our livelihood, this concerns our salvation. We make religion our business when we wholly devote ourselves to God's service. Psa cxxxix 18. We count those the best hours which are spent with God; we give God the cream of our affections, the flower of our time and strength; we traffic in heaven every day, we are merchants for the 'pearl of price.' He will not get an estate who does not mind his trade; he will never get heaven who does not make religion his main business.

(6) If you would obtain the kingdom of heaven, bind your hearts to God

by sacred vows. Vow to the Lord that, by his grace, you will be more intent upon heaven than ever. 'Thy vows are upon me, O God.' Psa lvi 12. A vow binds the votary to duty; he looks upon himself as obliged by his vow to cleave to God. When bees fly in a great wind, they ballast themselves with little stones, that they may not be carried away; so we must fortify ourselves with strong vows, that we may not be carried away from God with the violent wind of temptation. No question, a Christian may make such a vow, because the ground of it is morally good; he vows nothing but what he is bound to do by virtue of his baptismal vow, namely, to walk with God more closely, and to pursue heaven more vigorously.

(7) If you would obtain the kingdom, embrace all seasons and opportunities for your soul's welfare. 'Redeeming the time.' Eph v 16. Opportunity is the cream of time; improving seasons of grace is as much as our salvation is worth. The mariner, by taking the present season while the wind blows, gets to the haven; by taking the season, while we have the means of grace, and the wind of the Spirit blows, we may arrive at the kingdom of heaven. We know not how long we shall enjoy the gospel. The seasons of grace, like Noah's dove, come with an olive branch in their mouth, but they soon take wings and fly. Though they are sweet, yet they are swift. God may remove the golden candlestick from us, as he did from the churches of Asia. We have many sad symptoms, 'Grey hairs are here and there upon him.' Hos vii 9. Therefore let us lay hold upon the present seasons. They that sleep in seedtime, will beg in harvest.

(8) If you would go to the kingdom of heaven, you must *excubias agere*, keep a daily watch. 'I say unto all, watch.' Mark xiii 37. Many have lost heaven for want of watchfulness. Our hearts are ready to decoy us into sin, and the devil lies in ambush by his temptations; we must every day set a spy, and keep sentinel in our souls. 'I will stand upon my watch.' Hab ii 1.

We must watch our eye. . 'I made a covenant with mine eyes.' Job xxxi 1. Much sin comes in by the eye. When Eve saw the tree was good for food, and pleasant to the eyes, then she took. Gen iii 6. First she looked, and then she lusted; the eye, by beholding an impure object, sets the heart on fire; the devil often creeps in at the window of the eye. Watch your eyes.

Watch your ear. Much poison is conveyed through the ear. Let your ear be open to God, and shut to sin.

Watch your hearts. We watch suspicious persons. 'The heart is deceitful.' Jer xvii 9. Watch your heart, [1] When you are about holy things, it will be stealing out to vanity. When I am at prayer, says Jerome, *aut per porticum deambulo aut de foenore computo*; either I am walking through galleries or casting up accounts. [2] Watch your hearts when you are in company. The basilisk poisons the herbs he breathes on; so the breath of the wicked is infectious. Nay, watch your hearts when you are in good company. Such as have some good in them may be some grains too light, and have much levity of discourse; so that, if no scum boils up, yet there may be too much froth. The devil is subtle, and he can as well creep into the dove as he did once into the serpent. Satan tempted Christ by an apostle. [3] Watch your hearts in prosperity. Now you are in danger of pride. The higher the water of the Thames rises, the higher the boat is lifted up: the higher men's estates rise, the higher their hearts are lifted up in pride. In prosperity, you are in danger not only to forget God, but to lift up the heel against him. 'Jeshurun waxed fat, and kicked.' Deut xxxii 15. It is hard to carry a full cup without spilling, and to carry a full, prosperous estate without sinning. *Turpi fregerunt saecula luxu divitiae molles* [Soft riches have ruined the age by disgraceful luxury]. Seneca. As Samson fell asleep in Delilah's lap, so many have fallen so fast asleep in the lap of prosperity, that they have never awaked till they have been in hell. [4] Watch your hearts after holy duties. When Christ had been praying and fasting, the devil tempted him. Matt iv 3. After combating with Satan in prayer, we are apt to grow secure and put our spiritual armour off, and then the devil falls on and wounds us. Oh, if you would get to heaven, be always upon your watch-tower, set a spy, keep close sentinel in your souls. Who would not watch when it is for a kingdom!

(9) If you would arrive at the heavenly kingdom, get these three graces, which will undoubtedly bring your thither.

[1] Divine knowledge. There is no going to heaven blindfold. In the creation, light was the first thing that was made; so it is in the new creation. Knowledge is the pillar of fire that goes before us, and lights us into the heavenly kingdom. It is light that must bring us to the 'inheritance in light.' Col i 12.

[2] Faith. Faith ends in salvation. 'Receiving the end of your faith, salvation.' 1 Pet i 9. He who believes, is as sure to go to heaven as if he were in heaven already. Acts xvi 31. Faith touches Christ; and can he miss of heaven who touches Christ? Faith unites to Christ; and shall not the members be where the head is? All have not the same degree of faith; we must distinguish between the direct act of faith and the reflex act of affiance and assurance; yet the least seed and spark of faith gives an undoubted title to the heavenly kingdom. I am justified because I believe, not because I know I believe.

[3] Love to God. Heaven is prepared for those that love God. 1 Cor ii 9. Love is the soul of obedience, the touchstone of sincerity; by our loving

God, we may know he loves us. 1 John iv 19. And those whom God loves, he will lay in his bosom. Ambrose, in his funeral oration for Theodosius, brings in the angels hovering about his departing soul, and ready to carry it to heaven, who ask him, 'What that grace was he had practised most on earth?' Theodosius replied, *Dilexi, Dilexi*, 'I have loved, I have loved;' and straightway, by a convoy of angels, he was translated to glory. Love is a sacred fire kindled in the breast; in the flames of which the devout soul ascends to heaven.

(10) If we would obtain this heavenly kingdom, let us labour for sincerity. 'Whoso walketh uprightly, shall be saved.' Prov xxviii 18. The sincere Christian may fall short of some degrees of grace, but he never falls short of the kingdom. God will pass by many failings where the heart is right. Numb xxiii 21. True gold, though it be light, has grains of alloy. 'Thou desirest truth in the inward parts.' Psa li 6. Sincerity is the sauce which seasons all our actions, and makes them savoury; it is an ingredient in every grace; it is called 'unfeigned faith,' and 'love in sincerity.' 2 Tim i 5; Eph vi 24. Coin will not go current that wants the king's stamp; and grace is not current if it be not stamped with sincerity. Glorious duties soured with hypocrisy are rejected, when great infirmities sweetened with sincerity are accepted. If any thing in the world will bring us to heaven, it is sincerity. Sincerity signifies plainness of heart. 'In whose spirit there is no guile,' Psa xxxii 2. The plainer the diamond is, the richer.

Sincerity is when we serve God with our heart; when we do not worship him only, but love him. Cain brought his sacrifice, but not his heart. God's delight is a sacrifice flaming upon the altar of the heart. A sincere Christian, though he has a double principle in him, flesh and spirit, has not a double heart, his heart is for God.

Sincerity is when we aim purely at God in all we do. The glory of God is more worth than the salvation of all men's souls. Though a sincere Christian comes short in duty, he takes a right aim. As the herb, heliotropium, turns about according to the motion of the sun, so a godly man's actions all move towards the glory of God.

(11) If we would obtain the heavenly kingdom, let us keep up fervency in duty. What is a dead form without the power? 'Because thou art luke-warm, and neither cold nor hot, I will spue thee out of my mouth.' Rev iii 16. Fervency puts life into duty. 'Fervent in spirit, serving God;' Gr. *Zeontes*, 'boiling over.' Rom xii 11. Christ prayed 'more earnestly.' Luke xxii 44. When the fire on the golden censer was ready to go out, Aaron was to put more coals to the incense; so praying with devotion is putting more coals to the incense. It is not formality, but fervency, that will bring us to heaven. The formalist is like Ephraim, a cake not turned, hot on one side,

and dough on the other. In the external part of God's worship, he seems to be hot; but as for the spiritual part of God's worship, he is cold. Oh! if you would have the kingdom of heaven, keep up heart and fervour in duty. Elijah was carried up to heaven in a fiery chariot: if you would go to heaven, you must be carried thither in the fiery chariot of zeal. It is violence that takes the kingdom of heaven.

(12) If we would arrive at the heavenly kingdom, let us cherish the motions of God's Spirit in our hearts. The mariner may spread his sails, but the ship cannot get to the haven without a gale of wind; so we may spread the sails of our endeavour, but we cannot get to the haven of glory without the north and south wind of God's Spirit. How nearly therefore does it concern us to make much of the motions of the Spirit – motions to prayer, motions to repentance. 'When thou hearest the sound of a going in the tops of the mulberry trees, then thou shalt bestir thyself, for then shall the Lord go out before thee.' 2 Sam v 24. So, when we hear a voice within us, a secret inspiration stirring us up to good duties, we should bestir ourselves. While the Spirit works in us, we should work with the Spirit. Many men have God's Spirit striving with them, he puts good motions in their hearts and holy purposes; but they neglect to prosecute these good motions, and the Spirit is grieved, and, being grieved, withdraws his assistance, and that assistance being gone, there is no getting to heaven. Oh! make much of the motion of the Spirit; it is as much as your salvation is worth. The Spirit of God is compared to fire. Acts ii 3. If we are careful to blow the spark, we may have fire to inflame our affections, and to light our feet into the way of peace. If we quench the Spirit by neglecting and resisting its motions, we cut ourselves off from salvation. The Spirit of God has a drawing power. Cant i 4. The blessed Spirit draws by attraction, as the loadstone the iron. In the preaching of the word, the Spirit draws the heart up to heaven in holy longings and ejaculations. Now, when the Spirit is about thus to draw us, let us take heed of drawing back, lest it be to perdition. Heb x 39. Do as Noah, who, when the dove came flying to the ark, put forth his hand, and took it into the ark; so when the sweet dove of God's Spirit comes flying to your hearts, and brings a gracious impulse as an olive-branch of peace in its mouth, O take this dove into the ark; entertain the Spirit in your hearts, and it will bring you to heaven.

How shall we know the motions of the Spirit from a delusion?

The motions of the Spirit are always agreeable to the word. If the word be for holiness, so is the Spirit. The Spirit persuades to nothing but what the word directs. Which way the tide of the word runs, that way the wind of the Spirit blows.

(13) We obtain the kingdom of heaven by uniform and cheerful obedience. Obedience is the road through which we travel to heaven. Many say they love God, but refuse to obey him. Does he love the prince's person who slights his commands?

Obedience must be uniform. 'Then shall I not be ashamed' (Heb. I shall not blush) 'when I have respect unto all thy commandments.' Psa cxix 6. As the sun goes through all the signs of the zodiac, so we must go through all the duties of religion. If a man has to go a hundred miles, and he goes ninety-nine, and there stops, he comes short of the place he is to travel to. If, with Herod, we do many things that God commands, yet, if we die in the total neglect of any duty, we come short of the kingdom of heaven. For instance, if a man seem to make conscience of duties of the first table, and not the duties of the second; if he seem to be religious, but is not just, he is a transgressor, and is in danger of losing heaven. As the needle which points the way which the loadstone draws, so a good heart moves the way which the word draws.

Obedience must be cheerful. 'I delight to do thy will, O my God, yea, thy law is within my heart.' Psa xl 8. That is the sweetest obedience which is cheerful, as that is the sweetest honey which drops from the comb freely. God sometimes accepts willingness without the work, but never of the work without willingness. 'There came out two women, and the wind was in their wings.' Zech v 9. Wings are swift, but wind in the wings denotes great swiftness; and is an emblem of the swiftness and cheerfulness which should be in obedience. We go to heaven in the way of obedience.

(14) If we would obtain this kingdom we must be much in the communion of saints. One coal of juniper will warm and inflame another; so, when the heart is dead and frozen, the communion of saints will help to warm it. 'They that feared the Lord spake often one to another.' Mal iii 16. 'Christians should never meet,' says Mr Bolton, 'without speaking of their meeting together in heaven.' One Christian may be very helpful by prayer and conference to another, and give him a lift towards heaven. Old Latimer was much strengthened and comforted by hearing Mr Bilney's confession of faith. We read that when Moses' hands were heavy, and he was ready to let them fall, Aaron and Hur stayed them up. Exod xvii 12. A Christian who is ready to faint under temptation, and lets down the hands of his faith, by conversing with other Christians is strengthened, and his hands are held up. A great benefit of holy conference is counsel and advice. 'If a man,' says Chrysostom, 'who has but one head to advise him, could make that head a hundred, he would be very wise; but a single Christian has this benefit by the communion of saints, that they are as so many heads to advise him what to do in such a case or exigency.' By Christian conference the saints can say,

'Did not our hearts burn within us?' Communion of saints we have in our creed, but it is too little in our practice. Men usually travel fastest in company; so we travel fastest to heaven in the communion of saints.

(15) If we would attain to this kingdom of heaven, let us be willing to come up to Christ's terms. Many will cheapen, and bid something for the kingdom of heaven; they will avoid gross sin, and will come to church, and say their prayers; and yet all this while they are not willing to come up to God's price, that is, they will not resist the idol of self-righteousness, flying only to Christ as the horns of the altar; they will not sacrifice their bosom-sin; they will not give God spirit-worship, serving him with zeal and intenseness of soul. John iv 24. They will not forgive their enemies; they will not part with their carnal profits for Christ; they would have the kingdom of heaven, but they will not come up to the price. If you would have this kingdom, do not article and bargain with Christ, but accept of his terms; say, 'Lord, I am willing to have the kingdom of heaven, whatever it cost me; I am willing to pluck out my right eye, to part with all for the kingdom; here is a blank paper I put into thy hand, Lord, write thy own articles, I will subscribe to them.'

(16) If we would obtain the heavenly kingdom, let us attend to the holy ordinances, by which God brings souls to heaven. 'Except these abide in the ship, ye cannot be saved.' Acts xxvii 31. Some people would leap out of the ship of ordinances, and then God knows whither they leap; but except ye abide in the ship of ordinances, ye cannot be saved. Especially, if you would get to heaven, attend to the word preached. It was by the ear, by our first parents listening to the serpent, that we lost paradise; and it is by the ear, by hearing of the word, that we get to heaven. 'Hear, and your soul shall live.' Isa lv 3. God sometimes in the preaching of the word drops the holy oil into the ear, which softens and sanctifies the heart. The word preached is called the 'ministration of the Spirit,' because the Spirit of God makes use of the engine to convert souls. 2 Cor iii 8. If the word preached does not work upon men, nothing will; not judgment, nor miracles; no, not though one should rise from the dead. Luke xvi 31. If a glorified saint should come out of heaven, and assume a body, and tell you of all the glory of heaven, and the joys of the blessed, and persuade you to believe; if the preaching of the word will not bring you to heaven, neither would his rhetoric do it who rose from the dead. In heaven there will be no need of ordinances, but while we live here there is. The lamp needs oil, but the star needs none. While the saints have their lamp of grace burning here, they need the oil of ordinances to be continually dropping upon them; but there will be no need of this oil when they are stars in heaven. If you intend to get to heaven, be swift to hear: for faith comes by hearing. Rom x 14, 17. Peter let down the net of his

ministry, and at one draught caught three thousand souls. If you would have heaven's door opened to you, wait at the posts of wisdom's door.

(17) If you would arrive at heaven, have this kingdom ever in your eye. Our blessed Lord looked at the joy that was set before him; and Moses had an 'eye to the recompence of the reward.' Heb xi 26. Let the kingdom be much in your thoughts; meditation is the means to help us to heaven.

How does it help?

As it is a means to prevent sin. No sword like this to cut asunder the sinews of temptation. It is almost impossible to sin presumptuously with lively thoughts and hopes of heaven. It was when Moses was out of sight that Israel set up a calf, and worshipped it; so when the kingdom of heaven is out of sight, out of men's thoughts, they set up their lusts and idolize them. The meditation of heaven banishes sin; he who thinks of the weight of glory, throws away the weight of sin.

To meditate on the kingdom of heaven would excite and quicken obedience. We should think we could never pray enough, never love God enough, who has prepared such a kingdom for us. *Immensum gloria calcar habet* [Glory possesses an immeasurable stimulus]. Paul had heaven in his eye, he was once caught up thither; and how active was he for God! 1 Cor xvi 10. This oils the wheels of obedience.

It would make us strive after holiness, because none but such are admitted into this kingdom; only the pure in heart shall see God. Matt v 8. Holiness is the language of heaven, it is the only coin that will pass current there. This consideration should make us 'cleanse ourselves from all filthiness of the flesh and spirit, perfecting holiness in the fear of God.' 2 Cor vii 1.

(18) The last means for obtaining the heavenly kingdom is perseverance in holiness. 'Be thou faithful unto death, and I will give thee a crown of life.' Rev ii 10. In Christians *non initia sed fines laudantur* [it is not the beginning but the end which wins praise]. Jerome.

Is there such a thing as persevering till we come to heaven?

That any one holds out to the kingdom, is a wonder, if you consider, (1) What a world of corruption is mingled with grace. Grace is apt to be stifled, as the coal to be choked with its own ashes. Like a spark in the sea, it is a wonder it is not quenched. It is a wonder that sin does not overlay grace, as the nurse sometimes does the child, that it dies.

(2) The implacable malice of Satan. He envies that we should have a kingdom, when he himself is cast out. It cuts him to the heart to see a piece of dust and clay made a bright star in glory, and he himself an angel of darkness. He will *Acheronta movere*, move all the powers of hell to hinder us from

the kingdom; he spits his venom, shoots his fiery darts, raises a storm of persecution; yea, and prevails against some. 'There appeared a great red dragon, and his tail drew the third part of the stars of heaven, and did cast them to the earth.' Rev xii 3, 4. By the red dragon is meant the heathenish empire; now, when his tail cast so many to the earth, it is a wonder that any of the stars keep fixed in their orb.

(3) The blandishments of riches. The young man in the gospel went very far, but he had rich possessions, and these golden weights hindered him from the kingdom. Luke xviii 23. Jonathan pursued the battle till he came at the honeycomb, and then he stood still. 1 Sam xiv 27. Many are forward for heaven, till they taste the sweetness of the world; but when they come at the honeycomb, they stand still, and go no further. *Faenus pecuniae funus animae* [The gain of money is the ruin of the soul]. Those who have escaped the rocks of gross sins, have been cast away upon the golden sands. What a wonder therefore that any holds on till he come to the kingdom!

(4) It is a wonder that any hold out in grace, and do not tire in their march to heaven, if you consider the difficulty of the Christian's work. He has no time to lie fallow, he is either watching or fighting; nay, he is to do those duties which to the eye of sense and reason seem inconsistent. While he does one duty, he seems to cross another. He must come with holy boldness to God in prayer, yet must serve him with fear; he must mourn for sin, yet rejoice; he must be contented, yet covet (1 Cor xii 31); contemn men's impieties, and yet reverence their authority. What difficult work is this! It is a wonder that any saint arrives at the heavenly kingdom. To this I might add, the evil examples abroad, which are so attractive, that we may say the devils are come among us in the likeness of men. What a wonder is it that any soul perseveres till he come to the kingdom of heaven! But great as the wonder is, there is such a thing as perseverance. A saint's perseverance is built upon three immutable pillars.

Upon God's eternal love. We are inconstant in our love to God; but he is not so in his love to us. 'I have loved thee with an everlasting love;' with a love of eternity. Jer xxxi 3. God's love to the elect is not like a king's love to his favourite, which when it is at the highest spring-tide, soonest ebbs; but God's love is eternized. He may desert, not disinherit; he may change his love into a frown, not into hatred; he may alter his providence, not his decree. When once the sunshine of God's electing love is risen upon the soul, it never sets finally.

A saint's perseverance is built upon the covenant of grace. It is a firm, impregnable covenant; as you read in the words of the sweet singer of Israel. 'God hath made with me an everlasting covenant, ordered in all things and sure.' 2 Sam xxiii 5. It is a sweet covenant, that God will be our God; the marrow and quintessence of all blessing; and it is a sure covenant, that he will put his fear in our heart, and we shall never depart from him. Jer xxxii 40. This covenant is inviolable, it cannot be broken; indeed, sin may break the peace of the covenant, but it cannot break the bond of the covenant.

The third pillar upon which perseverance is built is the mystic union. Believers are incorporated into Christ, they are knit to him as members to the head, by the nerve and ligament of faith, so that they cannot be broken off. Eph v 23. What was once said of Christ's natural body is as true of his mystic body. 'A bone of him shall not be broken.' John xix 36. As it is impossible to sever the leaven and the dough when they are once mingled, so it is impossible when Christ and believers are once united, ever by the power of death or hell to be separated. How can Christ lose any member of his body and be perfect? You see upon what strong pillars the saints' perseverance is built.

How does a Christian hold on till he comes to the kingdom? How does he persevere?

(1) *Auxilio Spiritus* [By the help of the Spirit]. God carries on a Christian to perseverance by the energy and vigorous working of his Spirit. The Spirit maintains the essence and seed of grace; it blows up the sparks of grace into a holy flame. *Spiritus est Vicarius Christi* [The Spirit is the Vicar of Christ]. Tertullian. It is Christ's deputy and proxy; it is every day at work in a believer's heart, exerting grace into exercise, and ripening it into perseverance. The Spirit carves and polishes the vessels of mercy, and makes them fit for glory.

(2) Christ causes perseverance, and carries on a saint till he comes to the heavenly kingdom, *vi orationis*, by his intercession. He is an advocate as well as a surety; he prays that the saints may arrive safe at the kingdom. 'Wherefore he is able to save them to the uttermost (*i.e.* perfectly), seeing he ever liveth to make intercession for them.' Heb vii 25. That prayer he made for Peter on earth, he prays now in heaven for the saints, that their faith fail not, and that they may be with him where he is. Luke xxii 32. John xvii 24. And surely if he pray that they may be with him in his kingdom, they cannot perish by the way. Christ's prayer is efficacious. If the saints' prayers have so much force and prevalence in them, as Jacob, who had power with God, and as a prince prevailed, and Elijah by prayer unlocked heaven; if the prayers of the saints have so much power with God, what has Christ's prayer? How can the children of such prayers miscarry? How can they fall short of the kingdom who have him praying for them, who is not only a Priest, but a Son? Besides, what he prays for as he is man, he has power to give as he is God.

But methinks I hear some Christian say, if only perseverance obtains the kingdom, they fear they shall not come thither; they fear they shall faint by the way, and the weak legs of their grace will never carry them to the kingdom of heaven.

Wert thou indeed to stand in thy own strength, thou mightest fall away. The branch withers and dies that has no root to grow upon. Thou growest upon the root Christ, who will be daily sending forth vital influence to strengthen thee; though thou art imbecile and weak in grace, yet fear not falling short of heaven: For,

(1) God has made a promise to weak believers. What is a bruised reed but an emblem of a weak faith? yet it has a promise made to it. 'A bruised reed shall he not break.' Matt xii 20. God has promised to supply the weak Christian with as much grace as he shall need, until he comes to heaven. Beside the two pence which the good Samaritan left to pay for the cure of the poor wounded man, he passed his word for all that he should need beside. Luke x 35. So, Christ does not only give a little grace in hand, but his bond for more, that he will give as much grace as a saint should need till he comes to heaven. 'The Lord will give grace and glory:' that is, a fresh supply of grace, till we be perfected in glory. Psa lxxxiv 11.

(2) God has most care of his weak saints, who fear they shall never hold out till they come to the kingdom. Does not the mother tend the weak child most? 'He shall gather the lambs with his arm, and carry them in his bosom.' Isa xl 11. If thou thinkest that thou art so weak that thou shalt never hold out till thou comest to heaven, thou shalt be carried in the arms of the Almighty. He gathers the lambs in his arms. Christ, the Lion of the tribe of Judah, marches before his people, and his power is their rereward, so that none of them faint or die in their march to heaven.

What are the encouragements to make Christians hold on till they come to the kingdom of heaven?

(1) It is a great credit to a Christian, not only to hold forth the truth, but to hold fast the truth till he comes to heaven. When grace flourishes into perseverance, and with the church of Thyatira, our last works are more than our first, it is *insigne honoris*, a star of honour. Rev ii 19. It is matter of renown to see grey hairs shine with golden virtues. The excellency of a thing lies in the finishing of it. Where is the excellence of a building? Not when the first stone is laid, but when it is finished. So the beauty and excellence of a Christian is, when he has finished his faith, having done his work, and is landed safe in heaven.

(2) You that have made a progress in religion, have not many miles to go before you come at the kingdom of heaven. 'Now is our salvation nearer than when we believed.' Rom xiii 11. You who have hoary hairs, your green tree is turned into an almond tree; you are near to heaven, it is but going a little further and you will set your feet within heaven's gates. Oh! therefore now be encouraged to hold out, your salvation is nearer than when you first began to believe. Our diligence should be greater when our salvation is nearer. When a man is almost at the end of the race, will he now tire and faint? Will he not put forth all his strength, and strain every limb, that he may lay hold upon the prize? Our salvation is now nearer; the kingdom is as it were within sight; how should we now put forth all our strength, that we may lay hold upon the garland of glory! Doctor Taylor, when going to his martyrdom, said, 'I have but two stiles to go over, and I shall be at my Father's house.' Though the way to heaven be up-hill, you must climb the steep rock of mortification; and though there be thorns in the way, you have gone the greatest part of it, and are within a few days' march of the kingdom, and will not you persevere? Christian, pluck up thy courage, fight the good fight of faith, pursue holiness. Ere long you will put off your armour, and end all your weary marches, and receive a victorious crown; your salvation is nearer, you are within a little of the kingdom, therefore now persevere, you are ready to commence and take your degree of glory.

(3) The blessed promise annexed to perseverance is an encouragement. The promise is a crown of life. Rev ii 10. Death is a worm that feeds in the crowns of princes, but behold here a living crown, and a never-fading crown. 1 Pet v 4. 'He that overcometh, and keepeth my works to the end, I will give him *stellam matutinam*, the morning-star.' Rev ii 28. The morning-star is brighter than the rest. This morning-star is meant of Christ; as if Christ had said, I will give to him that perseveres some of my beauty; I will put some of my illustrious rays upon him; he shall have the next degree of glory to me, as the morning-star is next the sun. Will not this animate and make us hold out? We shall have a kingdom, and that which is better than a kingdom, a bright morning-star.

What are the means which conduce to perseverance, or, what shall we do that we may hold out to the kingdom?

(1) Take up religion upon good grounds, not in a fit or humour, or out of worldly design; but be deliberate, weigh things well in the balance. 'Which of you intending to build a tower, sitteth not down first and counteth the cost?' Luke xiv 28. Think with yourselves what religion must cost you; it must cost you the parting with your sins; and may cost you the

parting with your lives. Consider if a kingdom will not countervail your sufferings. Weigh things well, and then make your choice. 'I have chosen the way of truth.' Psa cxix 30. Why do many apostatize, and fall away, but because they never sit down and count the cost?

(2) If we would hold out to the kingdom, let us cherish the grace of faith. 'By faith ye stand.' 2 Cor i 24. Faith, like Hercules' club, beats down all opposition before it; it is a conquering grace.

How comes faith to be so strong?

Faith fetches Christ's strength into the soul. Phil iv 13. A captain may give his soldier armour, but not strength. Faith partakes of Christ's strength, and gets strength from the promise; as the child by sucking the breast gets strength, so faith by sucking the breast of the promise; hence faith is such a wonder-working grace, and enables a Christian to persevere.

(3) If you would hold out to the kingdom, set before your eyes the examples of those noble heroic saints who have persevered to the kingdom. *Vivitur exemplis* [Life is lived by examples], examples have more influence upon us than precepts. 'My foot hath held his steps.' Job xxiii 11. Though the way of religion hath flints and thorns in it, yet my foot hath held its steps; I have not fainted in the way, nor turned out of the way. Daniel held on his religion, and would not intermit prayer, though he knew the writing was signed against him, and a prayer might cost him his life. Dan vi 10. The blessed martyrs persevered to the kingdom through sufferings. Saunders, that holy man, said, 'Welcome the cross of Christ; my Saviour began to me in a bitter cup, and shall I not pledge him?' Another martyr, kissing the stake, said, 'I shall not lose my life, but change it for a better; instead of coals I shall have pearls.' What a spirit of gallantry was in these saints! Let us learn constancy from their courage. A soldier, seeing his general fight valiantly, is animated by his example, and has new spirits put into him.

(4) Let us add fervent prayer to God, that he would enable us to hold out to the heavenly kingdom. 'Hold thou me up, and I shall be safe.' Psa cxix 117. Let us not presume on our own strength. When Peter cried to Christ on the water, 'Lord save me,' then Christ took him by the hand. Matt xiv 30. When he grew confident of his own strength, Christ let him fall. Oh, pray to God for auxiliary grace. The child is safe when held in the nurse's arms; so are we in Christ's arms. Let us pray that God will put his fear in our hearts, that we do not depart from him; and that prayer of Cyprian, *Domine, quod coepisti perfice, ne in portu naufragium accidat*. Lord, perfect that which thou hast begun in me, that I may not suffer shipwreck when I am almost at the haven.

Use 5. Here let me lay down some powerful persuasives, or divine arguments to make you put to all your strength for obtaining this blessed kingdom.

(1) The great errand for which God sent us into the world is to prepare for this heavenly kingdom. 'Seek ye first the kingdom of God.' Matt vi 33. First in time, before all things; and first in affection, above all things. Great care is taken for securing worldly things. Matt vi 25. To see people labouring for the earth, as ants about a molehill, would make one think it were the only errand they came about. But, alas! what is all this to the kingdom of heaven? I have read of a devout pilgrim travelling to Jerusalem, who passing through several cities, where he saw many stately edifices, wares and monuments, would say, 'I must not stay here, this is not Jerusalem;' so when we enjoy worldly things, peace and plenty, and have our presses burst out with new wine, we should say to ourselves, this is not the kingdom we are to look after, this is not heaven. It is wisdom to remember our errand. It will be but sad upon a death-bed for a man to find he has busied himself about trifles, played with a feather, and neglected the main thing he came into the world about.

(2) Seeking the heavenly kingdom will be judged most prudent by all men at last. Those who are most regardless of their souls now, will wish before they die that they had minded eternity more. When conscience is awakened, and men begin to come to themselves, what would they give for the kingdom of heaven? How happy would it be if men were of the same mind now, as they will be at death! Death will alter men's opinions. They who most slighted and disparaged the ways of religion, will wish their time and thoughts had been taken up about the excellent glory. At death men's eyes will be opened, and they will see their folly when it is too late. All men, even the worst, will wish at last that they had minded the kingdom of heaven. Why should not we do now what all will wish they had done when they come to die?

(3) This kingdom of heaven deserves our utmost pains and diligence. It is glorious, beyond hyperbole. Suppose earthly kingdoms more magnificent than they are, their foundations of gold, their walls of pearl, their windows of sapphire, they are not comparable to the heavenly kingdom. If the pavement of it be bespangled with so many bright shining lights and glorious stars, what is the kingdom itself? 'It doth not yet appear what we shall be.' 1 John iii 2. This kingdom exceeds our faith. How sublime and wonderful is that place where the blessed Deity shines forth in his immense glory, infinitely beyond the comprehension of angels!

The kingdom of heaven is a place of honour. There are glorious triumphs and sparkling crowns. In other kingdoms there is but one king, but in heaven all are kings. Rev i 6. Every glorified saint partakes of the same glory as Christ does. 'The glory which thou gavest me, I have given them.' John xvii 22.

This kingdom is a place of joy. 'Enter thou into the joy of thy Lord.' Matt xxv 21. To have a continual aspect of love in God's face, to be crowned with immortality, to be as the angels of God, to drink of the rivers of pleasure for ever, this will cause raptures of joy. Surely it deserves our utmost pains to pursue and to secure this kingdom. Julius Caesar coming towards Rome with his army, and hearing the senate and people had fled from it, said, 'They that will not fight for this city, what city will they fight for?' If we will not take pains for the kingdom of heaven, what kingdom will we take pains for? It was the speech of the spies to their brethren, 'We have seen the land, and behold, it is very good; and are ye still? Be not slothful to go, and to enter to possess the land.' Judg xviii 9. We have had a lively description of the glory of heaven, we find the kingdom is very good; why then do we sit still? Why do we not *operam navare*, put forth our utmost zeal and industry for this kingdom? The diligence of others in seeking after earthly kingdoms, shames our coldness and indifference in pursuing after the kingdom of heaven.

(4) The time we have to make sure of the heavenly kingdom is very short and uncertain. Take heed it does not slip away before you have prepared for the kingdom. Time passes on apace, *cito pede preterita vita:* it will not be long before the silver cord be loosed, and the golden bowl broken. Eccl xii 6. The skull wherein the brains are inclosed is a bowl that will soon be broken. Our soul is in the body as the bird in the shell, which soon breaks, and the bird flies out; the shell of the body broken, the soul flies into eternity. We know not whether we shall live to another Sabbath. Before we hear another sermon-bell go, our passing-bell may go. Our life runs as a swift stream into the ocean of eternity. Brethren, if our time be so minute and transient, if the taper of life be so soon wasted, or perhaps blown out by violent death, how should we put to all our strength, and call in help from heaven that we may obtain the kingdom of glory! If time be so short, why do we waste it about things of less moment, and neglect the 'one thing needful,' which is the kingdom of heaven? A man that has a great work to be done, and but one day for doing it, needs to work hard. We have a great work to do, we are striving for a kingdom, and alas! we are not certain of one day to work in; therefore what need have we to bestir ourselves, and what we do for heaven, to do it with all our might!

(5) To excite our diligence, let us consider how inexcusable we shall be if we miss the kingdom of heaven. Who have had such helps for heaven as we have had? Indians who have mines of gold, have not such advantages for

glory as we. They have the light of the sun, moon, and stars, and the light of reason, but this is not enough to light them to heaven. We have had the light of the gospel shining in our horizon; we have been lifted up to heaven with ordinances; we have had the word in season and out of season. The ordinances are the pipes of the sanctuary, which empty the golden oil of grace into the soul; they are *scala paradisi*, the ladder by which we ascend to the kingdom of heaven. 'What nation is there so great who hath God so nigh unto them, as the Lord our God is in all things that we call upon him for?' Deut iv 7. We have had heaven and hell set before us; we have had counsels of friends, warnings, examples, the motions and inspirations of the Holy Ghost; how should all these spurs quicken us in our pace to heaven? Should not that ship sail apace to the haven which has the tide of ordinances, and the wind of the Spirit to carry it? Surely if we, through negligence, miss the kingdom of heaven, we shall have nothing to say for ourselves; we shall be as far from excuse as from happiness.

(6) You cannot do too much for the kingdom of heaven. You cannot pray too much, sanctify the Sabbath too much, nor love God too much. In secular things a man may labour too hard, he may kill himself with work; but there is no fear of working too hard for heaven. *In virtute non est verendum ne quid nimium sit* [In righteousness there is no need to fear excess]. Seneca. The world is apt to censure the godly, as if they were too zealous, and overstrained themselves in religion. Indeed, a man may follow the world too much, he may make too much haste to be rich. The ferry-man may take too many passengers into his boat, so as to sink it; so a man may heap up so much gold and silver as to sink himself in perdition. I Tim vi 9. We cannot be too earnest and zealous for the kingdom of heaven; there is no fear of excess here; when we do all we can, we come short of the golden rule set us, and of Christ's golden pattern. When our faith is highest, like the sun in the meridian, still there is something lacking in our faith, so that all our labour for the kingdom is little enough. I Thess iii 1. When a Christian has done his best, still he has sins, and wants to bewail.

(7) You may judge of the state of your souls, whether you have grace or not, by your earnest pursuit after the heavenly kingdom. Grace infuses a spirit of activity into a person; it does not lie dormant in the soul; it is not a sleepy habit, but it makes a Christian like the seraphim, swift and winged in his heavenly motion; like fire, it makes him burn in love to God; and the more he loves him, the more he presses forward to heaven, where he may fully enjoy him. Hope is an active grace, it is called 'a lively hope.' I Pet i 3. It is like the spring in the watch, which sets all the wheels of the soul running. Hope of a crop makes the husbandman sow his seed; hope of victory makes the soldier fight; and a true hope of glory makes a Christian

vigorously pursue it. Here is a spiritual touchstone by which to try our grace. If we have the anointing of the Spirit, it will oil the wheels of our endeavour, and make us lively in our pursuit of the heavenly kingdom. No sooner had Paul grace infused, but it is said, 'Behold, he prayeth.' Acts ix 11. The affections are by divines called 'the feet of the soul;' if these feet move not towards heaven, it is because there is no life in them.

(8) Your labour for heaven is not lost. Perhaps you may think that you have served God in vain; but know that your pains are not lost. The seed is cast into the earth, and it dies, yet at last it brings forth a plentiful crop; so your labours seem to be fruitless, but at last they bring you to a kingdom. Who would not work hard for one hour, when, for that hour's work, he should be a king as long as he lived? And let me tell you, the more labour you have put forth for the kingdom of heaven, the more degrees of glory you shall have. As there are degrees of torment in hell, so of glory in heaven. Matt xxiii 14. As one star differeth from another in glory, so shall one saint. 1 Cor xv 41. Though every vessel of mercy shall be full, yet one may hold more than another. Such as have done more work for God, shall have more glory in the heavenly kingdom. Could we hear departed saints speaking to us from heaven, surely they would speak after this manner: 'Were we to leave heaven awhile, and live on the earth again, we would do God a thousand times more service than ever we did; we would pray with more life, act with more zeal; for now we see, the more has been our labour, the greater is our reward in heaven.'

(9) While we are labouring for the kingdom, God will help us. 'I will put my Spirit within you, and cause you to walk in my statutes.' Ezek xxxvi 27. The promise encourages us, and God's Spirit enables us. A master gives his servant work to do, but he cannot give him strength to work; but God both cuts us out work and gives us strength. 'Give thy strength unto thy servant.' Psa lxxxvi 16. God not only gives us a crown when we have done running, but gives us legs to run; he gives exciting, assisting grace; *lex jubet, gratia juvat* [law commands, grace assists]; the Spirit helping us in our work for heaven, makes it easy. If the loadstone draw the iron, it is not hard for the iron to move; so, if God's Spirit draws the heart, it moves towards heaven with facility and alacrity.

(10) The more pains we have taken for heaven, the sweeter heaven will be when we come there. As when a husbandman has been grafting trees, or setting flowers in his garden, it is pleasant to review and look over his labours: so, when in heaven, we shall remember our former zeal and earnestness for the kingdom, which will sweeten heaven, and add to the joy of it. For a Christian to think, such a day I spent in examining my heart; such a day I was weeping for sin; when others were at their sport, I was at

K

prayer; and now, have I lost any thing by my devotion? My tears are wiped away, and the wine of paradise cheers my heart. I now enjoy him whom my soul loves, I am possessed of a kingdom; my labour is over, but joy remains.

(11) If you do not take pains for the kingdom of heaven now, there will be nothing to be done for your souls after death. This is the only fit season for working; and if this season be lost, the kingdom is forfeited. 'Whatsoever thy hand findeth to do, do it with thy might, for there is no work, nor device, nor wisdom in the grave whither thou goest.' Eccl ix 10. It was a saying of Charles V, 'I have spent my treasure, but that I may recover again; I have lost my health, but that I may have again; but I have lost a great many brave soldiers, but them I can never have again.' So other temporal blessings may be lost and recovered again; but if the term of life, wherein you should work for heaven, be once lost, it is past all recovery, you can never have another season again for your souls.

(12) There is nothing else but this kingdom of heaven of which we can make sure. We cannot make sure of life. *Quis scit an adjiciant hodiernae crastina vitae tempora di superi?* [Who knows whether the gods above will add a tomorrow to the life of today?]. Horace. When our breath goes out, we know not whether we shall draw it in again. How many are taken away suddenly! We cannot make riches sure; it is uncertain whether we shall get them. The world is like a lottery, in which every one is not sure to draw a prize. If we get riches, we are not sure to keep them. 'Riches make themselves wings, they fly away.' Prov xxiii 5. Experience seals the truth of this. Many who have had plentiful estates, by fire, or losses at sea, have been squeezed as sponges, and all their estates exhausted; but if men should keep their estates awhile, death strips them of all. When death's gun goes off, away flies the estate. 'It is certain we can carry nothing out' of the world. 1 Tim vi 7. So that there is no making sure of anything here below, but we may make sure of the kingdom of heaven. 'To him that soweth righteousness shall be a sure reward.' Prov xi 18. He who has grace is sure of heaven, for he has heaven begun in him. A believer has an evidence of heaven. 'Faith is the evidence of things not seen.' Heb xi 1. He has an earnest of glory. 'Who hath given us the earnest of the Spirit.' 2 Cor i 22. An earnest is part of the whole sum. He has a sure hope. 'Which hope we have as an anchor.' Heb vi 19. This anchor is cast upon God's promise. 'In hope of eternal life, which God that cannot lie promised.' Tit i 2. So that here is great encouragement to take pains for heaven, that we may make sure of this kingdom.

(13) The kingdom of heaven cannot be obtained without labour. *Non est ad astra mollis e terris via* [The way from earth to heaven is not easy]. A boat

may as well get to land without oars, as we to heaven without labour. We cannot have the world without labour, and do we think to have heaven? If a man digs for gravel, much more for gold. 'I press toward the mark.' Phil iii 14. Heaven's gate is not like that iron gate which opened to Peter of its own accord. Acts xii 10. Heaven is not like those ripe figs which fall into the mouth of the eater. Nah iii 12. No, there must be taking pains. Two things are requisite for a Christian, a watchful eye and a working hand. We must, as Hannibal to Rome, force a way to the heavenly kingdom through difficulties. We must win the garland of glory by labour, before we wear it with triumph. God has enacted this law, 'That no man shall eat of the tree of paradise but in the sweat of his brows.' How, then, dare any censure Christian diligence? How dare they say you take more pains for heaven than need? God says, 'Strive as in an agony: fight the good fight of faith;' and they say, 'You are too strict:' but whom shall we believe, a holy God who bids us strive, or a profane atheist who says we strive too much?

(14) Much of our time being already mis-spent, we had need work the harder for the kingdom of heaven. He who has lost his time at school, and often played truant, had need ply it the harder, that he may gain a stock of learning; and he who has slept and loitered in the beginning of his journey, had need ride the faster in the evening, lest he fall short of the place to which he is travelling. Some are in their youth, others in the flower of their age, others have grey hairs, the almond tree blossoms, and yet perhaps have been very regardless of their souls and heaven. Time spent unprofitably is not time lived, but time lost. If there be any such here who have mis-spent their golden hours, they have not only been slothful, but wasteful servants. They had need now to redeem the time, and press forward with might and main to the heavenly kingdom. 'The time past of our life may suffice us to have wrought the will of the Gentiles.' 1 Pet iv 3. It may suffice us that we have lost so much time already, let us now work the harder. They who have crept as snails, had need now fly as eagles to the paradise of God. If, in the former part of your life, you have been as willows, barren in goodness, in the latter part, be as 'an orchard of pomegranates, with pleasant fruits.' Cant iv 13. Recompense former remissness with future diligence.

(15) How uncomely and sordid a slothful temper of soul is! 'I will punish the men who are settled on their lees;' (Heb 'Curdled on their lees.') Zeph i 12. Settling on the lees is an emblem of a dull, inactive soul. The snail, by reason of its slow motion, was reckoned among the unclean. Lev xi 30. 'A slothful man hideth his hand in his bosom:' he is loath to pull it out, though it be to lay hold on a crown. Prov xix 24. *Non capit porta illa caelestis torpore languidos* [That gate of heaven does not receive those who are dull with sloth]. Brugensis. The devil himself cannot be charged with idleness. He

[141]

'walketh about.' 1 Pet v 8. An idle soul stands in the world for a cipher, and God writes down no ciphers in the book of life. Heaven is no hive for drones. An idle person is fit for a temptation. When the bird sits still upon the bough, it is in danger of the gun: when one sits still in sloth, the devil shoots him with a temptation. Standing water putrifies. Heathens will rise up in judgment against supine Christians. What pains did they take in the Olympic games! They ran but for a garland of flowers, or olive; and do we sit still who run for a kingdom? How can he expect a reward who never works, or a crown who never fights? *Inertia animae somnus.* Sloth is the soul's sleep. Adam, when asleep, lost his rib; and when a person is in the deep sleep of sloth, he loses salvation.

(16) Holy activity and industry ennoble a Christian. *Labor splendore decoratur* [Work is adorned with honour]. Cicero. The more excellent anything is, the more active. The sun is a glorious creature, it is ever in motion, going its circuit. Fire is the purest element, and the most active, it is ever sparkling and flaming; the angels are the most noble creatures, they are represented by the cherubims, with wings displayed. The more active for heaven, the more illustrious, and the more do we resemble the angels. The phœnix flies with a coronet on its head; so the industrious soul has his coronet, his labour is his ensign of honour.

(17) It is a mercy that there is a possibility of happiness, and that upon our painstaking we may have a kingdom. By our fall in Adam we forfeited heaven. Why might not God have dealt with us as with the lapsed angels? They had no sooner sinned than they were expelled from heaven, never to come thither more. We may say, as the apostle, 'Behold the goodness and severity of God.' Rom xi 22. The apostate angels behold the severity of God, that he should throw them down to hell for ever; we behold the goodness of God in that he has put us into a possibility of mercy; so that if we do but take pains, a kingdom stands ready for us. How should this whet and sharpen our industry, that we are in a capacity of salvation; and that if we do but what we are able, we shall receive an eternal weight of glory!

(18) Our labour for the kingdom of heaven is minute and transient. It is not to endure long; it expires with our life. It is but awhile, and we shall leave off working; for a little labour we shall have an eternal rest. Who would think much to wade through a little water, if he were sure to be crowned as soon as he came on shore? Christians, let this encourage you, you have but a little more pains to take, a few tears more to shed, a few more Sabbaths to keep, and, behold an eternal recompense of reward. What are a few tears to a crown, a few minutes of time to an eternity of glory?

(19) What striving is there for earthly kingdoms, which are corruptible, and subject to change! With what vigour and alacrity did Hannibal's

soldiers continue their march over the Alps, and craggy rocks, and Caesar's soldiers fight with hunger and cold! Men will break through laws and oaths, they will swim to a crown in blood. Will they venture thus for earthly promotions, and shall not we strive more for a heavenly kingdom? This is 'a kingdom which cannot be moved' (Heb xii 28); a kingdom where there is unparalleled beauty, unstained honour, unmixed joy; a kingdom where there shall be nothing present which we could wish were removed, and nothing absent which we could wish were enjoyed. Surely if there be any spark of grace, or true generosity in our breasts, we shall not suffer ourselves to be out-striven by others; we shall not let them take more pains for earthly honours, than we do for that excellent glory which will crown all our desires.

(20) What pains some men take to go to hell, and shall not we take more pains to go to heaven? 'They weary themselves to commit iniquity.' Jer ix 5. Sinners hackney themselves out in the devil's service. What pains some men take to satisfy their unclean lusts! They waste their estates, wear the shameful marks of their sin about them, and visit the harlot's house, though it stands the next door to hell. 'Her house is the way to hell.' Prov vii 27. What pains do others take in persecuting! Holiness is the mark they shoot at. It is said of Antiochus Epiphanes, that he undertook more tedious journeys, and went upon greater hazards, to vex and oppose the Jews, than any of his predecessors had done in getting victories. The devil blows the horn, and men ride post to hell, as if they feared hell would be full ere they should get thither. When Satan had entered into Judas, how active was he! He went to the high priests, from them to the band of soldiers, and with them back again to the garden, and never left till he had betrayed Christ! How industrious were the idolatrous Jews! So fiercely were they bent upon their sin, that they would sacrifice their sons and daughters to their idol-gods. Jer xxxii 35. Do men take all these pains for hell, and shall not we take pains for the kingdom of heaven? The wicked have nothing to encourage them in their sins, they have all the threatenings of God as a flaming sword against them. Oh, let it never be said that the devil's servants are more active than Christ's; that they serve him better who rewards them only with fire and brimstone, than we do God, who rewards with a kingdom!

(21) The labour we take for heaven is a labour full of pleasure. Prov iii 17. A man sweats at his recreation, tires himself with hunting, but there is a delight he takes in it which sweetens it. 'I delight in the law of God after the inward man.' (Gr. I take pleasure) Rom vii 22. Not only is the kingdom of heaven delightful, but the way thither. What a delight has a gracious soul in prayer! 'I will make them joyful in my house of prayer.' Isa lvi 7. While a

Christian weeps, joy drops with tears; while he is musing on God, he has such quickenings of the Spirit, and, as it were, such transfigurations of soul, that he thinks himself half in heaven. 'My soul shall be satisfied as with marrow and fatness, and my mouth shall praise thee with joyful lips, when I remember thee upon my bed,' &c. Psa lxiii 5, 6. A Christian's work for heaven is like a bridegroom's work on the morning of the marriage-day, he puts on his vesture and wedding-robes in which he shall be married to his bride; so, in all the duties of religion, we are putting on those wedding robes in which we shall be married to Christ in glory. Oh, what solace and inward peace is there in close walking with God! 'The work of righteousness shall be peace.' Isa xxxii 17. Serving God is like gathering spices or flowers, wherein there is some labour, but the labour is recompensed with delight. Working for heaven is like digging in a gold mine; the digging is labour, but getting the gold is pleasure! O, then, let us bestir ourselves for the kingdom of heaven; it is a labour of pleasure. A Christian would not part with his joy for the most delicious music; he would not exchange his anchor of hope for a crown of gold. Well might David say, 'In keeping [thy precepts] there is great reward,' not only after keeping thy precepts, but in keeping them. Psa xix 11. A Christian has both the spring-flowers and the crop; inward delight in serving God is the spring-flowers, in the kingdom of glory at last is the full crop.

(22) How industrious have the saints in former ages been! They thought they could never do enough for heaven; they could never serve God enough, love him enough. *Minus te amavi Domine.* Augustine. Lord, I have loved thee too little. What pains did Paul take for the heavenly kingdom. 'Reaching forth unto those things which are before.' Phil iii 13. The Greek word, to reach forth, signifies to stretch out the neck; a metaphor from racers, who strain every limb, and reach forward to lay hold on the prize. Anna, the prophetess, 'departed not from the temple, but served God with fastings and prayers night and day.' Luke ii 37. Basil the Great, by much labour and watching, exhausted his bodily strength. 'Let racks, pulleys, and all torments come upon me,' said Ignatius, 'so I may win Christ.' The industry and courage of former saints, who are now crowned with glory, should provoke our diligence, that so at last we may sit down with them in the kingdom of heaven.

(23) The more pains we take for heaven, the more welcome will death be to us. What is it that makes men so loath to die? They are like a tenant that will not go out of the house till the serjeant pull him out. They love not to hear of death. Why so? Because their conscience accuses them that they have taken little or no pains for heaven; they have been sleeping when they should have been working, and now they are afraid lest death should carry

them prisoners to hell; but he who has spent his time in serving God, can look death in the face with comfort; he was wholly taken up about heaven, and now he shall be taken up to heaven; he traded before in heaven, and now he shall go to live there. *Cupio dissolvi*, I desire to be dissolved, and to be with Christ. Phil i 23. Paul had wholly laid himself out for God, and now he knew there was a crown laid up for him, and he longed to take possession.

Thus I have given you twenty-three persuasives or arguments to exert and put forth your utmost diligence for obtaining the kingdom of heaven. O that they were written in all your hearts, as with the point of a diamond! Because delays in these cases are dangerous, let me desire you to set upon this work for heaven at once. 'I made haste, and delayed not to keep thy commandments.' Psa cxix 60. Many people are convinced of the necessity of looking after the kingdom of glory, but they say as those in Hag i 2, 'The time is not come.' They adjourn and put off till their time is slipped away, and so they lose the kingdom of heaven. Beware of this fallacy; delay strengthens sin, hardens the heart, and gives the devil fuller possession of a man. 'The king's business required haste;' so the business of salvation requires haste. 1 Sam xxi 8. Do not put off an hour longer. *Volat ambiguis mobilis alis hora* [The fleeting hour flies on fickle wings]. What assurance have you that you shall live another day? Have you any lease of life granted? Why then do you not presently arise out of the bed of sloth, and put forth all your strength and spirits, that you may be possessed of the kingdom of glory? Should not things of the highest importance be done first? Settling a man's estate, and clearing the title to his land, is not delayed, but done in the first place. What is there of such grand importance as the saving of your souls, and the gaining a kingdom? Therefore to-day hear God's voice; now mind eternity; now get your title to heaven cleared before the decree of death brings forth. What imprudence is it to lay the heaviest load upon the weakest horse! So it is to lay the heavy load of repentance on thyself when thou art enfeebled by sickness, the hands shake, the lips quiver, and the heart faints. O be wise in time; prepare now for the kingdom. If a man begins his voyage to heaven in the storm of death, it is a thousand to one if he does not suffer an eternal shipwreck.

Use 6. For exhortation to those who have any good hope through grace. You that are the heirs of this kingdom, let me exhort you to six things:

(1) Often take a prospect of this heavenly kingdom. Climb up the celestial mount; take a turn, as it were, in heaven every day by holy meditation. 'Walk about Zion, tell the towers thereof, mark ye well her bulwarks.' Psa xlviii 12, 13. See what a glorious kingdom heaven is; go tell the towers, view the palaces of the heavenly Jerusalem. Christian, show thy heart the

gates of pearl, the beds of spices, the clusters of grapes which grow in the paradise of God. Say, 'O my soul, all this glory is thine, it is thy Father's good pleasure to give thee this kingdom.' The thoughts of heaven are very delightful and ravishing. Can men of the world so delight in viewing their bags of gold, and fields of corn, and shall not the heirs of promise take more delight in contemplating the celestial kingdom? The serious meditation of the kingdom of glory would work these three effects:

It would put a damp and slur upon all worldly glory. To those who stand upon the top of the Alps, the great cities of Campania seem but small in their eye; so, could we look through the perspective glass of faith, and take a view of heaven's glory, how small and minute would all other things appear! Moses slighted the honours of Pharaoh's court, having an eye to the recompense of reward. Heb xi 26. When Paul had a vision of glory, and John was carried away in the Spirit, and saw the holy Jerusalem descending out of heaven, having the glory of God in it, how did the world after appear in an eclipse to them!

The meditation of the heavenly kingdom would much promote holiness in us. Heaven is a holy place: 'an inheritance undefiled.' 1 Pet i 4. It is described by transparent glass, to denote its purity. Rev xxi 21. Contemplating heaven would put us upon the study of holiness, because none but such are admitted to that kingdom. Heaven is not like Noah's ark, into which came clean beasts and unclean. Only the pure in heart shall see God. Matt v 8.

The meditation of the heavenly kingdom would be a spur to diligence. *Immensum gloria calcar habet* [Glory possesses an immeasurable stimulus]. 'Always abounding in the work of the Lord, forasmuch as ye know that your labour is not in vain in the Lord.' 1 Cor xv 58. When the mariner sees the haven, he plies harder with his oars; so when we have a sight and prospect of glory, we should be much in prayer, alms, and watching; it should add wings to duty, and make the lamp of our devotion burn brighter.

(2) If you have hopes of this kingdom, be content though you have but a little of the world! Contentment is a rare thing, it is a jewel that but few Christians wear; but if you have a grounded hope of heaven, it may work your heart to contentation. What though you have but little in possession, you have a kingdom in reversion! Were you to take an estimate of a man's estate, how would you value it? By what he has in his house, or by his land? Perhaps he has little money or jewels in his house, but he is a landed man – there lies his estate. A believer has but a little oil in the cruse, and meal in the barrel, but he is a landed man, he has a title to a kingdom, and may not this satisfy him? If a man who lived here in England, had a great estate befallen him beyond the seas, and perhaps had no more money at present but just to

pay for his voyage, he is content; he knows when he comes to his estate he shall have money enough; so, thou who art a believer hast a kingdom befallen thee; though thou hast but little in thy purse, yet if thou hast enough to pay for thy voyage, enough to bear thy charges to heaven, it is sufficient. God has given thee grace, which is the fore-crop, and will give thee glory, which is the after-crop; and may not this make thee content?

(3) If you have hope of this blessed kingdom, pray often for its coming; say, 'Thy kingdom come.' Only believers can pray heartily for the hastening of the kingdom of glory.

They cannot pray that Christ's kingdom of glory may come who never had the kingdom of grace set up in their hearts. Can the guilty prisoners pray that the assizes may come?

They cannot pray heartily that Christ's kingdom of glory may come who are lovers of the world. They have found paradise, they are in their kingdom already; this is their heaven, and they desire to hear of no other; they are of his mind who said, If he might keep his cardinalship in Paris, he would give up his part in paradise.

They cannot pray heartily that Christ's kingdom of glory may come who oppose his kingdom of grace, who break his laws, which are the sceptre of his kingdom, who shoot at those who bear Christ's name and carry his colours. Surely these cannot pray that Christ's kingdom of glory may come, for then Christ will judge them; and if they say this prayer, they are hypocrites, they mean not what they speak. But you who have the kingdom of grace set up in your hearts, pray much that the kingdom of glory may hasten; say, 'Thy kingdom come.' When this kingdom comes, then you shall behold Christ in all his embroidered robes of glory, shining ten thousand times brighter than the sun in all its meridian splendour. When Christ's kingdom comes, the bodies of the saints that sleep in the dust shall be raised in honour, and made like Christ's glorious body; then your souls like diamonds shall sparkle with holiness; you shall never have a sinful thought more, you shall be as holy as the angels; you shall be as holy as you would be, and as holy as God would have you to be; then you shall be in a better state than in innocence. Adam was created a glorious creature, but mutable; a bright star, but a falling star; but in the kingdom of heaven is a fixation of happiness. When Christ's kingdom of glory comes, you shall be rid of all your enemies; as Moses said, 'The Egyptians whom you have seen to day, you shall see them no more for ever.' Exod xiv 13. So those enemies who have ploughed on the backs of God's people, and made deep their furrows, when Christ shall come in his glory, you shall see no more. All Christ's enemies shall be 'put under his feet.' 1 Cor xv 25. Before the wicked be destroyed, the saints shall judge them. 'Do ye not know that the saints shall judge the world?' 1 Cor vi 2. It will cut the wicked to the heart that those whom they have formerly scorned and scourged, shall sit as judges upon them, and vote with Christ in his judicial proceedings. Oh, then, well may you pray for the hastening of the kingdom of glory, 'Thy kingdom come.'

(4) If you have any good hope of this blessed kingdom, let it make the colour come in your faces, be of a sanguine, cheerful temper. Have you a title to a kingdom, and are sad? 'We rejoice in hope of the glory of God.' Rom v 2. Christians, the trumpet is ready to sound, an eternal jubilee is at hand, when a freedom from sin shall be proclaimed; your coronation-day is coming. It is but putting off your clothes, and laying your head upon a pillow of dust, and you shall be enthroned in a kingdom, and invested with the embroidered robes of glory. Does not all this call for a cheerful spirit? Cheerfulness adorns religion. It is a temper of soul that Christ loves. 'If ye loved me, ye would rejoice.' John xiv 28. It makes many suspect heaven is not so pleasant, when they see those that walk thither sad. How does the heir rejoice in hope of the inheritance? Who should rejoice if not a believer, who is heir of the kingdom, and such a kingdom as eye hath not seen? When the flesh begins to droop, let faith lift up its head, and cause a holy jubilation and rejoicing in the soul.

(5) Let the saints long to be in that blessed kingdom. Does not a prince that travels in foreign parts long to be in his own nation, that he may be crowned? The bride desires the marriage day. 'The Spirit and the bride say, Come: even so, come, Lord Jesus.' Rev xxii 17, 20. Sure our unwillingness to go hence, shows either the weakness of our faith in the belief of the heavenly kingdom, or the strength of our doubts whether we have an interest in it. Were our title to heaven more clear, we should need patience to be content to stay here any longer.

Again, our unwillingness to go hence, declares we love the world too much, and Christ too little. Love, as Aristotle says, desires union. Did we love Christ as we should, we should desire to be united to him in glory, when we might take our fill of love. Be humbled that ye are so unwilling to go hence. Let us labour to arrive at that divine temper of soul which Paul had: *Cupio dissolvi*, 'Having a desire to depart and to be with Christ.' Phil i 23. We are compassed with a body of sin: should we not long to shake off this viper? We are in Mesech, and the tents of Kedar, in a place where we see God dishonoured. Should we not desire to have our pass to be gone? We are in a valley of tears. Is it not better to be in a kingdom? Here we are combating with Satan. Should we not desire to be called out of the bloody field, where the bullets of temptation fly so fast, that we may receive a victorious crown? O ye saints, breathe after the heavenly kingdom. Though we should be willing to stay to do service, yet we should ambitiously desire to be always sunning ourselves in the light of God's countenance. Think what it will be to be ever with the Lord! Are there any sweeter smiles or embraces than his? Is there any bed so soft as Christ's bosom? Is there any such joy as to have the golden banner of Christ's love displayed over us? Is there any such honour as to sit upon the throne with Christ? Rev iii 21. O, then, long for the celestial kingdom!

(6) Wait for this kingdom of glory. It is not incongruous or improper to long for heaven, yet wait for it. Long for it because it is a kingdom, yet wait your Father's good pleasure. God could bestow this kingdom at once, but he sees it good that we should wait awhile.

[1] Had we the kingdom of heaven as soon as ever grace is infused, then God would lose much of his glory. Where would be our living by faith, which is the grace that brings in the chief revenues of glory to God? Rom v 20. Where would be our suffering for God, which is a way of honouring him which the angels in heaven are not capable of? Where would be the active service we are to do for God? Would we have God give us a kingdom, and we do nothing for him before we come there? Would we have rest before labour, a crown before victory? This were disingenuous. Paul was content to stay out of heaven awhile that he might be a means of bringing others thither. Phil i 24.

[2] While we wait for the kingdom, our grace is increasing. Every duty religiously performed, adds a jewel to our crown. Do we desire to have our robes of glory shine brighter? Let us wait and work. The longer we stay for the principal, the greater will the interest be. As the husbandman waits till the seed spring up, wait for the harvest of glory. Some have their waiting weeks at court; this is your waiting time. Christ says, men ought to pray, and not to faint. Luke xviii 1. So, wait, and faint not. Be not weary, the kingdom of heaven will make amends for waiting. 'I have waited for thy salvation, O Lord,' said the dying patriarch. Gen xlix 18.

Use 7. For comfort to the people of God.

(1) In all their sufferings. The true saint, as Luther says, is *haeres crucis*, heir to the cross. Affliction is his diet-drink, but this keeps him from fainting, that his sufferings bring a kingdom. The hope of the kingdom of heaven, says Basil, should indulcerate and sweeten all our troubles. 'If we suffer, we shall also reign with him.' 2 Tim ii 12. It is but a short fight, but an eternal triumph. This light suffering produces an 'eternal weight of glory.' 2 Cor iv 17. The more weighty precious things are, the more they are worth, as the more weight in a crown of gold, the more it is worth. Did this glory last

for awhile only, it would much abate and embitter the joys of heaven; but it runs parallel with eternity. God will be a deep sea of blessedness, and the glorified saints shall for ever bathe themselves in the ocean. One day's wearing the crown will abundantly pay for all the saints' sufferings; how much more when 'they shall reign for ever and ever!' Rev xxii 5. O let this be our support under all the calamities and sufferings in this life. What a vast difference is there between a believer's sufferings and his reward! 'The sufferings of this present time are not worthy to be compared with the glory which shall be revealed in us.' Rom viii 18. For a few tears, rivers of pleasure; for mourning, white robes. This made the primitive Christians laugh at imprisonments, and snatch up torments as so many crowns. Though now we drink in a wormwood-cup, there is sugar in the bottom to sweeten it. 'It is your Father's good pleasure to give you the kingdom.'

(2) Comfort in death. That which takes away from God's children the terror of death, is that they are entering into the kingdom. No wonder if wicked men be appalled and terrified at the approach of death, for they die unpardoned. Death carries them to the jail, where they must lie for ever, without bail or deliverance; but why should any of God's children be scared and half dead with the thoughts of death? What hurt can death do to them, but lead them to a glorious kingdom? Faith gives a title to heaven, death a possession. Let this be a gospel antidote to expel the fear of death. Hilarion, that blessed man, cried out, *Egredere, anima, egredere, quid times?* Go forth, my soul, go forth, what fearest thou? Let them fear death who do not fear sin; but let not God's children be over much troubled at the grim face of that messenger, which brings them to the end of their sorrow, and the beginning of their joy. Death is yours, it is a part of the believer's inventory. 1 Cor iii 22. Is a prince afraid to cross a narrow sea, who shall be crowned when he comes to shore? Death to the saints shall be an usher to bring them into the presence of the King of glory. This thought puts lilies and roses into the ghastly face of death, and makes it look amiable. Death brings us to a crown of glory which fades not away. The day of death is better to a believer than the day of his birth. Death is *aditus ad gloriam*, an entrance into a blessed eternity. Fear not death, but rather let your hearts revive when you think these rattling wheels of death's chariot are but to carry you home to an everlasting kingdom.

The Third Petition in the Lord's Prayer

'Thy will be done in earth, as it is in heaven.' Matt vi 10

We come next to the third petition, 'Thy will be done in earth, as it is in heaven.'

This petition consists of two parts: the matter, 'Doing God's will;' and the manner, 'As it is in heaven.'

What is meant by the will of God?

There is a twofold will. (1) *Voluntas decreti*, God's secret will, or 'the will of his decree'. We pray not that God's secret will may be done by us. This secret will cannot be known, it is locked up in God's own breast, and neither man nor angel has a key to open it. (2) *Voluntas revelata*, God's 'revealed will.' This will is written in the book of Scripture, which is a declaration of God's will, and discovers what he would have us do in order to our salvation.

What do we pray for in these words, 'Thy will be done?'

We pray for two things; 1. For active obedience; that we may do God's will actively in what he commands. 2. For passive obedience; that we may submit to God's will patiently in what he inflicts.

I *We pray that we may do God's will actively*, subscribe to all his commands, believe in Jesus, which is the cardinal grace, and lead holy lives. So Augustine, upon this petition, *Nobis a Deo precamur obedientiam;* we pray that we may actively obey God's will. This is the sum of all religion, the two tables epitomized, the doing God's will. 'Thy will be done.' We must know his will before we can do it; knowledge is the eye which must direct the foot of obedience. At Athens there was an altar set up, 'To the unknown God.' Acts xvii 23. It is as bad to offer the blind to God as the dead. Knowledge is the pillar of fire to give light to practice; but though knowledge is requisite, yet the knowledge of God's will is not enough without doing it. If one had a system of divinity in his head; if he had 'all knowledge,' yet, if obedience were wanting, his knowledge were lame, and would not carry him to heaven. 1 Cor xiii 2. Knowing God's will may make a man admired, but it is doing it that makes him blessed. Knowing God's will without doing it, will not crown us with happiness.

[1] The bare knowledge of God's will is inefficacious, it does not better the heart. Knowledge alone is like a winter-sun, which has no heat or influence; it does not warm the affections, or purify the conscience. Judas was a great luminary, he knew God's will, but he was a traitor.

[2] Knowing without doing God's will, will make the case worse. It will heat hell the hotter. 'That servant which knew his Lord's will,' and did it not, 'shall be beaten with many stripes.' Luke xii 47. Many a man's knowledge is a torch to light him to hell. Thou who hast knowledge of God's will but dost not do it, wherein dost thou excel a hypocrite? Nay, wherein dost thou excel the devil, who transforms himself into an angel of light? It is improper to call such Christians, who are knowers of God's will but not doers of it. It is improper to call him a tradesman who never wrought in his trade; so to call him a Christian, who never wrought in the trade of religion. Let us not rest in knowing God's will. Let it not be said of us, as Plutarch speaks of the Grecians, 'They knew what was just, but did it not.' Let us set upon the doing God's will. 'Thy will be done.'

Why is the doing God's will requisite?

(1) Out of equity. God may justly claim a right to our obedience. He is our founder, and we have our being from him; and it is but just that we should do his will at whose word we were created. God is our benefactor. It is but just that, if he gives us our allowance, we should give him our allegiance.

(2) The great design of God in the word is to make us doers of his will. [1] All God's royal edicts and precepts are to bring us to be doers of his will. What needed God to have been at the pains to give us the copy of his law, and write it out with his own finger but for this end? The word of God is not only a rule of knowledge, but of duty. 'This day the Lord thy God hath commanded thee to do these statutes; thou shalt therefore keep and do them.' Deut xxvi 16. If you tell your children what is your mind, it is not only that they may know your will, but do it. God gives us his word, as a master gives his scholar a copy, to write after it; he gives it as his will and testament, that we should be the executors to see it performed. [2] The end of all God's promises is to draw us to do his will. The promises are loadstones to obedience. 'A blessing if ye obey;' as a father gives his son money to bribe him to obedience. Deut xi 27. 'If thou shalt hearken unto the voice of the Lord thy God, to do all his commandments, the Lord thy God will set thee

on high above all the nations of the earth; blessed shalt thou be in the city and in the field.' Deut xxviii 1, 3. The promises are a royal charter settled upon obedience. [3] The minatory part of the word, the threatenings of God, stand as the angel with a flaming sword to deter us from sin, and make us doers of God's will. 'A curse if ye will not obey.' Deut xi 28. 'God shall wound the hairy scalp of such an one as goeth on still in his trespasses.' Psa lxviii 21. These threatenings often take hold of men in this life; they are made examples, and hung up in chains to scare others from disobedience. [4] All God's providences are to make us doers of his will. As he makes use of all the seasons of the year for harvest, so all his various providences are to bring on the harvest of obedience. [5] Afflictions are said to be sent us to make us do God's will. 'When he [Manasseh] was in affliction, he besought the Lord, and humbled himself greatly.' 2 Chron xxxiii 12. The rod has this voice, 'Be doers of God's will.' Affliction is called a furnace. The furnace melts the metal, and then it is cast into a new mould. God's furnace is to melt us and mould us into obedience. [6] God's mercies are to make us do his will. 'I beseech you by the mercies of God, that ye present your bodies a living sacrifice.' Rom xii 1. Body is by synecdoche put for the whole man; if the soul should not be presented to God as well as the body, it could not be a reasonable service; therefore the apostle says, 'I beseech you by the mercies of God, that ye present your bodies a living sacrifice.' Mercies are the strongest obligations to duty. 'I drew them with cords of a man;' that is, with golden cords of my mercy. Hos xi 4. In a word, all that is written in the law or gospel tends to this, that we should be doers of God's will. 'Thy will be done.'

(3) By doing the will of God, we evidence sincerity. As Christ said in another sense, 'The works that I do, bear witness of me.' John x 25. It is not all our golden words, if we could speak like angels, but our works, our doing of God's will which bears witness of our sincerity. We judge not the health of a man's body by his high colour, but by the pulse of the arm, where the blood chiefly stirs; so a Christian's soundness is not to be judged by his profession; but the estimate of a Christian is to be taken by his obediential acting, his doing the will of God. This is the best certificate and testimonial to show for heaven.

(4) Doing God's will propagates the gospel. It is the diamond that sparkles in religion. Others cannot see what faith is in the heart; but when they see we do God's will on earth, it makes them have a venerable opinion of religion, and become proselytes to it. Julian, in one of his epistles, writing to Arsatius, says, 'that the Christian religion did much flourish, by the sanctity and obedience of them that professed it.'

(5) By doing God's will, we show our love to Christ. 'He that hath my

commandments, and keepeth them, he it is that loveth me.' John xiv 21. What greater love to Christ than to do his will, though it cross our own? Every one would be thought to love Christ; but, how shall it be known but by this? – Do you do his will on earth? *Neque principem veneramur, si odio ejus leges habemus* [We do not honour the ruler if we hate his laws]. Isidore. It is a vain thing for a man to say he loves Christ's person, when he slights his commands. Not to do God's will on earth is a great evil.

It is sinful. We go against our prayers; we pray, *fiat voluntas tua*, thy will be done, and yet we do not obey his will; we confute our own prayer. We go against our vow in baptism; we have vowed to fight under the Lord's banner, to obey his sceptre, and this vow we have often renewed in the Lord's supper; if we do not God's will on earth, we are forsworn, and God will indict us for perjury.

Not to do God's will on earth is foolish; because there is no standing out against God. If we do not obey him, we cannot resist him. 'Are we stronger than he?' 1 Cor x 22. 'Hast thou an arm like God?' Job xl 9. Canst thou measure arms with him? To oppose God, is as if a child should fight with an archangel; as if a heap of briers should put themselves into a battalion against the flame. Not to do God's will is foolish; because, if we do it not, we do the devil's will. Is it not folly to gratify an enemy – to do his will who seeks our ruin?

But are any so wicked as to do the devil's will?

Yes! 'Ye are of your father the devil, and the lusts of your father ye will do.' John viii 44. When a man tells a lie, does he not do the devil's will? 'Ananias, why hath Satan filled thine heart to lie to the Holy Ghost?' Acts v 3.

Not to do God's will is dangerous. It brings a spiritual *Praemunire*. If God's will be not done by us, he will have his will upon us; if we obey not his will in commanding, we shall obey it in punishing. 'The Lord Jesus shall be revealed with his mighty angels, in flaming fire, taking vengeance on them that obey not the gospel.' 2 Thess 1 7, 8. Either we must do his will, or suffer it.

(6) To do God's will is for our benefit. It promotes our own self-interest. As if a king commands a subject to dig in a mine of gold, and gives him all the gold he had digged. God bids us do his will, and that is for our good. 'And now, Israel, what doth the Lord thy God require of thee, but to fear the Lord thy God, to keep the commandments of the Lord, which I command thee this day for thy good?' Deut x 13. It is God's will that we should repent, and this is for our good; for repentance ushers in remission. 'Repent, that your sins may be blotted out.' Acts iii 19. It is God's will that we should

believe; and why is it, but that we should be crowned with salvation? 'He that believeth, shall be saved.' Mark xvi 16. What God wills, is not so much our duty, as our privilege; he bids us obey his voice, and it is greatly for our good. 'Obey my voice, and I will be your God.' Jer vii 23. I will not only give you my angels to be your guard, but myself to be your portion; my spirit shall be yours to sanctify you; my love shall be yours to comfort you; my mercy shall be yours to save you; 'I will be your God.'

(7) To do God's will is our honour. A person thinks it an honour to have a king speak to him to do a thing. The angels count it their highest honour in heaven to do God's will. *Servire Deo regnare est,* to serve God is to reign. *Non onerant nos, sed ornant* [They do not burden us but adorn us]. Salvian. How cheerfully did the rowers row the barge that carried Caesar! To be employed in this barge was an honour: to be employed in doing God's will is *insigne honoris,* the highest ensign of honour that a mortal creature is capable of. Christ's precepts do not burden us, but adorn us.

(8) To do God's will on earth makes us like Christ, and akin to him. It makes us like Christ. Is it not our prayer that we may be like Christ? Jesus Christ did his Father's will. 'I came down from heaven, not to do mine own will, but the will of him that sent me.' John vi 38. As God the Father and Christ have but one essence, so but one will. Christ's will was melted into his Father's. 'My meat is to do the will of him that sent me.' John iv 34. By doing God's will on earth, we resemble Christ, nay, we are akin to him, and are of the blood royal of heaven. Alexander called himself cousin to the gods; but what honour is it to be akin to Christ! 'Whosoever shall do the will of my Father which is in heaven, the same is my brother, and sister, and mother.' Matt xii 50. Did king Solomon rise off his throne to meet his mother and set her on a throne by him? 1 Kings ii 19. Such honour will Christ bestow on such as are doers of God's will; he will salute them as his kindred, and set them on a glorious throne in the amphitheatre of heaven.

(9) Doing God's will on earth brings peace in life and death. [1] In life. 'In keeping them [thy precepts] there is great reward,' not only after keeping them, but in keeping them. Psa xix 11. When we walk closely with God in obedience, there is a secret joy let into the soul; and how swiftly and cheerfully do the wheels of the soul move when they are oiled with the oil of gladness! [2] Peace in death. When Hezekiah thought he was about to die, what gave him comfort? That he had done the will of God. 'Remember, O Lord, I beseech thee, how I have walked before thee in truth, and have done that which is good in thy sight.' Isa xxxviii 3. It was Augustus's wish that he might have an easy death, without much pain. If anything make our pillow easy at death, it will be that we have endeavoured to do God's will on earth. Did you ever hear any cry out on their death-bed, that they have

L

done God's will too much? No! Has it not been, that they have done his will no more, that they came so short in their obedience? Doing God's will, will be both your comfort and your crown.

(10) If we are not doers of God's will, we shall be looked upon as contemners of his will. Let God say what he will, yet men will go on in sin, which is to contemn God. 'Wherefore doth the wicked contemn God?' Psa x 13. To contemn God is worse than to rebel. The tribes of Israel rebelled against Rehoboam, because he made their yoke heavier. 1 Kings xii 16. But to contemn God is worse: it is to slight him; it is to put a scorn upon him, and affront him to his face; and an affront will make him draw his sword.

In what manner are we to do God's will, that we may find acceptance?

The manner of doing God's will is the chief thing. The schoolmen say well, *Modus rei cadit sub precepto*, 'the manner of a thing is as well required as the thing itself.' If a man build a house, and the owner likes it not, and it be not according to his mind, he thinks all his charges lost; so if we do not God's will in the right manner, it is not accepted. We must not only do what he appoints, but as he appoints. Here lies the very life-blood of religion. It is a great question, therefore, 'In what manner are we to do God's will that we may find acceptance?'

(1) We do God's will acceptably when we do duties spiritually. 'We worship God in the spirit.' Phil iii 3. To serve God spiritually, is to do duties *ab interno principio*, from an inward principle. The Pharisees were very exact about the external part of God's worship. How zealous were they in the outward observation of the Sabbath, even charging Christ with the breach of it! But all this was outward obedience only: there was nothing of spirituality in it. We do God's will acceptably when we serve him from a renewed principle of grace. A crab tree may bear as well as a good apple tree, but it is not so good fruit as the other, because it does not come from so sweet a root; so an unregenerate person may do as much external obedience as a child of God: he may pray as much, hear as much, but his obedience is harsh and sour, because it does not come from the sweet and pleasant root of grace. The inward principle of obedience is faith; therefore it is called 'the obedience of faith.' Rom xvi 26. But why must this silver thread of faith run through the whole work of obedience? Because faith looks at Christ in every duty, it touches the hem of his garment; and through Christ, both the person and the offering are accepted. Eph i 6.

(2) We do God's will acceptably when we prefer his will before all others. If God wills one thing, and man wills the contrary, we are not to obey man's will, but God's. 'Whether it be right to hearken unto you more than unto God, judge ye.' Acts iv 19. God says, 'Thou shalt not make a graven image.'

King Nebuchadnezzar set up a golden image to be worshipped; but the three children, or rather champions, resolved God's will should prevail, and they would obey him, though with the loss of their lives. 'Be it known unto thee, O king, that we will not serve thy gods, nor worship the golden image which thou hast set up.' Dan iii 18.

(3) We do God's will acceptably when we do it as it is done in heaven, that is, as the angels do it. To do God's will as the angels *similitudinem notat, non aequalitatem* [marks our likeness to them, not our equality with them]. Brugensis. It denotes this much, that we are to resemble them, and make them our pattern. Though we cannot equal the angels in doing God's will, yet we must imitate them; a child cannot write so well as the copy, yet he imitates it.

[1] We do God's will as the angels in heaven when we do it regularly, *sine deflexu* [without wavering]; when we go according to the divine institutions, not decrees of councils, or traditions of men. Angels do nothing but what is commanded; they are not for ceremonies. As there are statute laws in the land which bind, so the Scripture is God's statute law, which we must exactly observe. As the watch is set by the dial, so our obedience is right when it goes by the sun-dial of the word. If obedience has not the word for its rule, it is not doing God's will, but our own; it is will-worship. The Lord would have Moses make the tabernacle according to the pattern. Exod xxv 40. If Moses had left out anything or added anything to it, it would have been very provoking. To mix anything of our own devising in God's worship, is to go beside, yea, contrary to the pattern. His worship is the apple of his eye, that which he is the most tender of; and there is nothing he has more showed his displeasure against than corrupting his worship. How severely did he punish Nadab and Abihu for offering up strange fire, that is, such fire as God has not sanctified on the altar! Lev x 2. Whatever is not divinely appointed, is offering up strange fire. There is in many a strange itch after superstition: they love a gaudy religion, and are more for the pomp of worship than the purity; which cannot be pleasing to God. As if God were not wise enough to appoint the manner how he will be served, man will be so bold as to prescribe for him. To thrust human inventions into sacred things, is doing our will, not God's; and he will say, *quis quaesivit haec?* 'Who hath required this at your hand?' Isa i 12. We do God's will as it is done in heaven when we do it regularly, when we reverence his institutions, and the mode of worship, which have the stamp of divine authority upon them.

[2] We do God's will as it is done by the angels in heaven when we do it entirely, *sine mutilatione* [with nothing cut away]; when we do all God's

will. The angels in heaven do all that God commands; they leave nothing of his will undone. 'Ye his angels that do his commandments.' Psa ciii 20. If God sends an angel to the virgin Mary, he goes on God's errand; if he gives his angels a charge to minister for the saints, they obey. Heb i 14. It cannot stand with angelic obedience, to leave the least *iota* of God's will unfulfilled. It is to do God's will as the angels when we do all his will, *quicquid propter Deum fit aequaliter fit* [whatever is done for God's sake is done uniformly]. This was God's charge to Israel. 'Remember and do all my commandments.' Numb xv 40. It is said of David, 'I have found David, a man after mine own heart, which shall fulfil all my will.' (Gr. all my wills.) Acts xiii 22. Every command has the same authority; and if we do God's will uprightly, we do it uniformly; we obey every part and branch of his will; we join first and second table. Surely we owe to God our Father, what the Papists say we owe to our mother, the church, unlimited obedience. We must incline to every command, as the needle moves the way which the loadstone draws.

Many do God's will by halves, they pick and choose in religion: in some they comply with God's will, but not in others; like a lame horse, which sets some of its feet on the ground, but favours one. He who is to play upon a lute, must strike upon every string, or he spoils all the music. God's commandments may be compared to a ten-stringed lute; we must obey his will in every command, strike upon every string, or we can make no good melody in religion. The badger has one foot shorter than the other; so hypocrites are shorter in some duties than others. Some will pray, but not give alms; some hear the word, but not forgive their enemies; others receive the sacrament, but not make restitution. How can they be holy who are not just? Hypocrites profess fair, but when it comes to sacrificing the Isaac, crucifying the beloved sin, or parting with some of their estate for Christ, they pause and say, as Naaman, 'In this thing, the Lord pardon thy servant.' 2 Kings v 18. This is far from doing God's will as the angels do. God likes not such as do his will by halves. If your servant should do some of your work which you set him about, but not all, how would you like it?

But who is able to do all God's will?

Though we cannot do all his will legally, we may evangelically; which is: (1) When we mourn that we can do God's will no better; when we fail we weep. Rom vii 24. (2) When it is the desire of our soul to do God's whole will, 'O that my ways were directed to keep thy precepts.' Psa cxix 5. What a child of God wants in strength, he makes up in desire, *in magnis voluisse sat est* [in great matters it is enough to have had the will]. (3) When we endeavour *quoad conatum* [as far as we are able] to do the whole will of

God. When a father bids his child lift a burden, and the child is not able, but tries, and does his best, the father accepts it as if he had done it; so to do our best, is to do God's will evangelically. He takes it in good part; though it be not to satisfaction, it is to acceptation.

[3] We do God's will as it is done in heaven by the angels when we do it sincerely, *sine fuco* [without pretence]. To do God's will sincerely lies in two things, first, to do God's will out of a pure respect to his command. Abraham's sacrificing Isaac was contrary to flesh and blood. To sacrifice the son of his love, the son of the promise, and by no other hand but the father's own, was hard service; but, because God commanded it, and out of pure respect to the command, Abraham obeyed. This is to do God's will aright, when though we feel no present joy or comfort in duty, yet, because God commands we obey. Not comfort, but the command is the ground of duty. Thus the angels do God's will in heaven. His command is the weight that sets the wheels of their obedience going. Secondly, to do God's will sincerely, is to do it with a pure eye to his glory. The Pharisees did the will of God giving alms; but that which was a dead fly in the ointment, was that they did not aim at his glory, but vain glory; they blew a trumpet. Jehu did the will of God in destroying the Baal-worshippers, and God commended him for it; but because he aimed more at setting himself in the kingdom, than at the glory of God, God looked upon it as no better than murder, and said he would avenge the blood of Jezreel upon the house of Jehu. Hos i 4. Let us look to our ends in obedience; though we shoot short, let us take a right aim. We may do God's will, and yet not with a perfect heart. 'Amaziah did that which was right in the sight of the Lord, but not with a perfect heart.' 2 Chron xxv 2. The action was right for the matter, but his aim was not right; and the action which wants good aim, wants a good issue. He does God's will rightly that does it uprightly, whose end is to honour God and lift up his name in the world. A gracious soul makes God his centre. As Joab, when he had taken Rabbah, sent for King David, that he might have the glory of the victory, so when a gracious soul has done any duty, it desires that the glory of all may be given to God. 2 Sam xii 27, 28. 'That God in all things may be glorified.' 1 Pet iv 11. It is to do God's will as the angels, when we not only advance his glory, but design his glory. The angels are said to cast their crowns before the throne. Rev iv 10. Crowns are signs of the greatest honour, but these the angels lay at the Lord's feet, to show they ascribe the glory of all they do to him.

[4] We do God's will as it is done in heaven by the angels when we do it willingly, *sine murmuratione* [without complaint]. The angels love to be employed in God's service. It is their heaven to serve God. They willingly

descend from heaven to earth, when they bring messages from God, and glad tidings to the church. Heaven being a place of much joy, the angels would not leave it a minute were it not that they take such infinite delight in doing God's will. We resemble the angels when we do God's will willingly. 'And thou Solomon, my son, serve [the Lord] with a willing mind.' 1 Chron xxviii 9. God's people are called a willing people (Heb. a people of willingnesses); they give God a freewill offering; though they cannot serve him perfectly, they serve him willingly. Psa cx 3. A hypocrite is able *facere bonum* [to do good], yet not *velle* [desire it], he has no delight in duty; he does it rather out of fear of hell than love to God. When he does God's will it is against his own. *Virtus nolentium nulla est* [There is no virtue in the unwilling]. Cain brought his sacrifice, but grudgingly; his worship was rather a task than an offering, rather penance than a sacrifice; he did God's will, but against his own. We must be carried upon the wings of delight in every duty. Israel were to blow the trumpets when they offered burnt offerings. Num x 10. This was to show their joy and cheerfulness in serving God. We must read and hear the word with delight. 'Thy words were found, and I did eat them, and thy word was unto me the joy and rejoicing of mine heart.' Jer xv 16. A pious soul goes to the word as to a feast, or as one would go with delight to hear music. Sleidan reports that the Protestants of France had a church which they called paradise, because, when they were in the house of God, they thought themselves in paradise. The saints flock as doves to the windows of God's house. 'Who are these that fly as the doves to their windows?' Isa lx 8. Not that a truly regenerate person is always in the same cheerful temper of obedience; he may sometimes find an indisposition and weariness of soul, but his weariness is his burden; he is weary of his weariness; he prays, weeps, uses all means to regain the alacrity and freedom in God's service that he was wont to have. To do God's will acceptably is to do it willingly. Delight in duty is better than duty itself. The musician is not commended for playing long, but well; it is not how much we do, but how much we love. 'O, how love I thy law!' Psa cxix 97. Love is as musk among linen, that perfumes it; it perfumes obedience, and makes it go up to heaven as incense. It is doing God's will as the angels in heaven do. They are ravished with delight while praising God; they are said to have harps in their hands, to signify their cheerfulness in God's service. Rev xv 2.

[5] We do God's will as the angels in heaven when we do it fervently, *sine remissione* [without slackness]. 'Fervent in spirit, serving the Lord;' a metaphor taken from water when it seethes and boils over; so our affections should boil over in zeal and fervour. Rom xii 11. The angels serve God with

such fervour and intenseness that they are called seraphims, from a Hebrew word which signifies to burn, to show they are all on fire; they burn in love and zeal in doing God's will. Psa civ 4. Grace turns a saint into a seraphim. Aaron must put burning coals to the incense. Lev xvi 12. Incense was a type of prayer, burning coals of zeal, to show that the fire of zeal must be put to the incense of prayer. Formality starves duty. Is it like the angels to serve God dully and coldly? Duty without fervour is as a sacrifice without fire. We should ascend to heaven in a fiery chariot of devotion.

[6] We do God's will as the angels in heaven when we give him the best in every service. 'Out of all your gifts, ye shall offer all the best thereof.' Numb xviii 29. 'In the holy place shalt thou cause the strong wine to be poured unto the Lord for a drink offering.' Numb xxviii 7. The Jews might not offer to the Lord wine that was small or mixed, but the strong wine, to imply that we must offer to God the best, the strongest of our affections. If the spouse had a cup more juicy and spiced, Christ should drink of that. 'I would cause thee to drink of spiced wine of the juice of my pomegranate.' Cant viii 2. Thus the angels in heaven do God's will; they serve him in the best manner; they give him their seraphic high-stringed praises; so he who loves God, gives him the cream of his obedience. God challenged the fat of all the sacrifice as his due. Lev iii 16. Hypocrites care not what services they bring to God; they think to put him off with anything; they put no cost in their duties. 'Cain brought of the fruit of the ground.' Gen iv 3. The Holy Ghost took notice of Abel's offering that it was costly. He 'brought of the firstlings of his flock, and of the fat thereof.' Gen iv 4. When he speaks of Cain's offering, he says only, 'He brought of the fruit of the ground.' We do God's will aright when we offer *pinguia* [fat things], dedicate to him the best. Domitian would not have his image carved in wood or iron, but in gold. God will have the best we have – golden services.

[7] We do God's will as the angels in heaven when we do it readily and swiftly. The angels do not dispute or reason the case, but soon as they have their charge and commission from God, they immediately obey. To show how ready they are to execute God's will, the cherubims, representing angels, are described with wings. 'The man Gabriel (that was an angel) being caused to fly swiftly.' Dan ix 21. Thus should we do God's will as the angels. Soon as ever God speaks the word we should be ambitious to obey. Alas! how long is it sometimes ere we can get leave of our hearts to go to a duty! Christ went more readily *ad crucem* [to the cross], than we to the throne of grace. How many disputes and excuses have we! Is this to do God's will as the angels in heaven do it? O let us shake off this backwardness to duty, as Paul shook off the viper. *Nescit tarda molimina Spiritus Sancti*

gratia [The grace of the Holy Spirit knows nothing of sluggish efforts]. 'Behold two women, and the wind was in their wings.' Zech v 9. Wings are swift, but wind in the wings is great swiftness; such readiness should be in our obedience. Soon as Christ commanded Peter to let down his net, he let it down, and you know what success he had. Luke v 4. It was prophesied of such as were brought home to Christ, 'As soon as they hear of me, they shall obey me.' Psa xviii 44.

[8] We do God's will as the angels in heaven when we do it constantly. The angels are never weary of doing God's will; they serve him day and night. Rev vii 15. Thus we should imitate them. 'Blessed [is] he that doeth righteousness at all times.' Psa cvi 3. Constancy crowns obedience. *Non coepisse, sed perfecisse, virtutis est* [The righteousness consists not in beginning but in completing the work]. Cyprian. Our obedience must be like the fire of the altar, which was continually kept burning. Lev vi 13. Hypocrites soon give over doing God's will. They are like chrysolite, which is of a golden colour in the morning, very bright to look upon, but towards evening grows dull and loses its splendour. We should continue doing God's will, because of the great loss that will befall us if we do it not. There will be a loss of honour. 'That no man take thy crown;' implying, if the church of Philadelphia left off her obedience, she would lose her crown – that is, her honour and reputation. Rev iii 11. Apostasy creates infamy. Judas came from an apostle to be a traitor, which was a dishonour. If we give over our obedience, it is a loss of all that has been already done; as if one should work in silver, and then pick out all the stitches. All a man's prayers are lost, all the Sabbaths he has kept are lost; he unravels all his good works. 'All his righteousness that he hath done shall not be mentioned.' Ezek xviii 24. He undoes all he has done; as if one drew a curious picture with the pencil, and then came with his sponge and wiped it out again. A loss of the soul and happiness. We were in a fair way for heaven, but left off doing God's will, missed the excellent glory, and are plunged deeper in damnation. 'It had been better not to have known the way of righteousness than, after they have known it, to turn from the holy commandment.' 2 Pet ii 21. Therefore let us continue in doing God's will. Constancy sets the crown upon the head of obedience.

Use 1. For instruction.

(1) See hence our impotence. We have no innate power to do God's will. What need to pray, 'Thy will be done,' if we have power of ourselves to do it? I wonder freewillers pray this petition.

(2) If we are to do God's will on earth as it is done by the angels in heaven, see the folly of those who go by a wrong pattern. They do as most of their

neighbours do: if they talk vain on the Sabbath, if now and then they swear an oath, it is the custom of their neighbours to do so; but we are to do God's will, as the angels in heaven. We must make the angels our patterns, and not our neighbours. If our neighbours do the devil's will, shall we do so too? If our neighbours go to hell, shall we go thither too for company?

(3) See here that which may make us long to be in heaven, where we shall do God's will perfectly, as the angels do. Alas! how defective are we in our obedience here! How far we fall short! We cannot write a copy of holiness without blotting. Our holy things are blemished like the moon, which, when it shines brightest, has a dark spot in it; but in heaven we shall do God's will perfectly, as the angels in glory.

Use 2. For reproof.

(1) It reproves such as do not God's will. They have a knowledge of God's will, but though they know it, they do it not. They know what God would have them avoid. They know they should not swear. 'Swear not at all.' Matt v 34. 'Because of swearing the land mourneth.' Jer xxiii 10. Yet, though they pray 'hallowed be thy name,' they profane it by shooting oaths like chain bullets against heaven. They know they should abstain from fornication and uncleanness, yet they cannot but bite at the devil's hook, if he bait it with flesh. Jude 7.

They know what God would have them practise, but they 'Leave undone those things which they ought to have done.' They know it is the will of God they should be true in their promises, just in their dealings, good in their relations; but they do it not. They know they should read the Scriptures, consult with God's oracles: but the Bible, like rusty armour, is hung up, and seldom used; they look oftener upon a pack of cards than upon a Bible. They know their houses should be *palestrae pietatis*, nurseries of piety, yet they have no religion in them; they do not perfume their houses with prayer. What hypocrites are they who kneel down in the church, and lift up their eyes to heaven and say, 'Thy will be done,' and yet have no care at all to do God's will! What is this but to hang out a flag of defiance against heaven! Rebellion is as the sin of witchcraft.

(2) It reproves those who do not God's will in a right acceptable manner. They do not God's will entirely. They will obey him in some things, but not in others; as if a servant should do some of your work you set him about, but not all. Jehu destroyed the idolatry of Baal, but let the golden calves of Jeroboam stand. 2 Kings x 28, 29. Some will observe the duties of the second table, but not the first. Others make a high profession, as if their tongues had been touched with a coal from God's altar, but live idly, and out of a calling; of whom the apostle thus complains: 'We hear there are

some which walk among you disorderly, working not at all.' 2 Thess iii 11. Living by faith, and living in a calling, must go together. It is an evil thing not to do all God's will.

They do not God's will ardently, nor cheerfully. They put not coals to the incense; they bring their sacrifice, but not their heart. This is far from doing God's will as the angels. How can God like us to serve him as if we served him not? How can he mind our duties, when we ourselves do not mind them?

Use 3. For examination.

Let us examine all our actions whether they are according to God's will. The will of God is the rule and standard: it is the sun-dial by which we must regulate all our actions. He is no good workman that does not work by rule; so he can be no Christian who goes not according to the rule of God's will. Let us examine our actions whether they do *quadrare* [square with], agree to the will of God. Are our speeches according to his will? Are our words savoury, being seasoned with grace? Is our apparel according to God's will? 'In like manner that women adorn themselves in modest apparel;' not wanton and garish, to invite comers. 1 Tim ii 9. Is our diet according to God's will? Do we hold the golden bridle of temperance, and only take so much as may rather satisfy nature than surfeit it? Too much oil chokes the lamp. Is our whole carriage and behaviour according to God's will? Are we patterns of prudence and piety? Do we keep up the credit of religion, and shine as lights in the world? We pray, 'Thy will be done as it is in heaven.' Are we like our pattern? Would the angels do this if they were on earth? Would Jesus Christ do this? It is to Christianise, this is to be saints of degrees; when we live our prayer, and our actions are the counterpart of God's will.

Use 4. For exhortation.

Let us be doers of the will of God, 'Thy will be done.' It is our wisdom to do God's will. 'Keep and do [these statutes], for this is your wisdom.' Deut iv 6. Further, it is our safety. Has not misery always attended the doing our own will, and happiness the doing of God's will?

(1) Misery has always attended the doing our own will. Our first parents left God's will to fulfil their own, in eating the forbidden fruit; and what came of it? The apple had a bitter core in it; they purchased a curse for themselves and all their posterity. King Saul left God's will to do his own; he spared Agag and the best of the sheep, and what was the issue, but the loss of his kingdom?

(2) Happiness has always attended the doing God's will. Joseph obeyed God's will, in refusing the embrace of his mistress; and was not this his

preferment? God raised him to be the second man in the kingdom. Daniel did God's will contrary to the king's decree; he bowed his knee in prayer to God, and did not God make all Persia bow their knees to Daniel?

(3) The way to have our will is to do God's will. Would we have a blessing in our estate? Let us do God's will. 'If thou shalt hearken to the voice of the Lord thy God, to do all his commandments, the Lord thy God will set thee on high above all nations of the earth: blessed shalt thou be in the city, and blessed shalt thou be in the field.' Deut xxviii 1, 3. This is the way to have a good harvest. Would we have a blessing in our souls? Let us do God's will. 'Obey my voice, and I will be your God:' I will entail myself upon you, as an everlasting portion; my grace shall be yours to sanctify you, my mercy shall be yours to save you. Jer vii 23. You see you lose nothing by doing God's will; it is the way to have your own will. Let God have his will in being obeyed, and you shall have your will in being saved.

How shall we do God's will aright?

(1) Get sound knowledge. We must know his will before we can do it; knowledge is the eye to direct the foot of obedience. The Papists make ignorance the mother of devotion; but Christ makes ignorance the mother of error. 'Ye do err, not knowing the Scriptures.' Matt xxii 29. We must know God's will before we can do it aright. Affection without knowledge, is like a horse full of mettle, but his eyes are out.

(2) If we would do God's will aright, let us labour for self denial. Unless we deny our own will, we shall never do God's will. His will and ours are like the wind and tide when they are contrary. He wills one thing, we will another; he calls us to be crucified to the world, by nature we love the world; he calls us to forgive our enemies, by nature we bear malice in our hearts. His will and ours are contrary, and till we can cross our own will, we shall never fulfil his.

(3) Let us get humble hearts. Pride is the spring of disobedience. 'Who is the Lord, that I should obey his voice?' Exod v 2. A proud man thinks it below him to stoop to God's will. Be humble. The humble soul says, 'Lord, what wilt thou have me to do?' He puts, as it were, a blank paper into God's hand; and bids him write what he will, and he will subscribe to it.

(4) Beg grace and strength of God to do his will. 'Teach me to do thy will:' as if David had said, Lord, I need not be taught to do my own will, I can do it fast enough, but teach me to do thy will. Psa cxliii 10. And that which may add wings to prayer, is God's gracious promise, 'I will put my Spirit within you, and cause you to walk in my statutes.' Ezek xxxvi 27. If the loadstone draw the iron, it is not hard for the iron to move: if God's Spirit enable, it will not be hard, but rather delightful to do God's will.

II. *We pray that we may have grace to submit to God's will patiently in what he inflicts.* The text is to be understood as well of suffering God's will as of doing it; so Maldonet, and the most judicious interpreters. A good Christian, when under any disastrous providence, should lie quietly at God's feet, and say, 'Thy will be done.'

What is patient submission to God's will not?

There is something that looks like patience which is not: as when a man bears a thing because he cannot help it; he takes affliction as his fate and destiny, therefore he endures quietly what he cannot avoid: this is necessity rather than patience.

What accompanies patient submission to God's will?

(1) A Christian may be deeply sensible of affliction, and yet patiently submit to God's will. We ought not to be Stoics, insensible and un-concerned with God's dealings; like the sons of Deucalion, who, as the poets say, were begotten of a stone. Christ was sensible when he sweat great drops of blood, but there was submission to God's will. 'Nevertheless, not as I will, but as thou wilt.' Matt xxvi 39. We are bid to humble ourselves under God's hand, which we cannot do unless we are sensible of it. 1 Pet v 6.

(2) A Christian may weep under an affliction, and yet patiently submit to God's will. God allows tears: it is a sin to be 'without natural affection.' Rom i 31. Grace makes the heart tender; *strangulat inclusus dolor* [grief which is held in chokes the heart]; weeping gives vent to sorrow; *expletur lacrimis dolor* [grief is poured out in tears]. Joseph wept over his dead father; Job, when he had much ill news brought him at once, rent his mantle, as an expression of grief, but did not tear his hair in anger. Worldly grief, how-ever, must not be immoderate; a vein may bleed too much; the water rises too high when it overflows the banks.

(3) A Christian may complain in his affliction, and yet be submissive to God's will. 'I cried unto the Lord with my voice, I poured out my complaint before him.' Psa cxlii 1, 2. We may, when under oppression, tell God how it is with us, and desire him to write down our injuries. Shall not the child complain to his father when he is wronged? Holy complaint may agree with patient submission to God's will; but though we may complain to God, we must not complain of God.

What is inconsistent with patient submission to God's will?

(1) Discontent with providence. Discontent has a mixture of grief and anger in it, and both these must needs raise a storm of passion in the soul.

When God has touched the apple of our eye, and smitten us in that we loved, we are touchy and sullen, and he has not a good look from us. 'Why art thou wroth?' like a sullen bird that is angry, and beats herself against the cage. Gen iv 6.

(2) Murmuring cannot stand with submission to God's will. Murmuring is the height of impatience, it is a kind of mutiny in the soul against God. 'The people spake against God.' Numb xxi 5. When a cloud of sorrow is gathered in the soul, and it not only drops in tears, but out of it come hailstones, murmuring words against God, this is far from patient submission to his will. When water is hot the scum boils up; when the heart is heated with anger against God, then murmuring boils up. Murmuring springs, [1] From pride. Men think they have deserved better at God's hand; and, when they begin to swell, they spit poison. [2] From distrust. Men believe not that God can make a treacle of poison, bring good out of all their troubles, therefore they murmur. 'They believed not his word, but murmured.' Psa cvi 24, 25. Men murmur at God's providences because they distrust his promises. God has much ado to bear this sin. Numb xiv 27. It is far from submission to God's will.

(3) Discomposedness of spirit cannot agree with quiet submission to God's will; as when a man says, I am so encompassed with trouble that I know not how to get out; head and heart are so taken up, that I am not fit to pray. When the strings of a lute are snarled, the lute can make no good music; so when a Christian's spirits are perplexed and disturbed, he cannot make melody in his heart to the Lord. To be under discomposure of mind, is as when an army is routed, one runs this way and another that, all is in disorder; so when a Christian is in a hurry of mind, his thoughts run up and down distracted, as if he were undone, which cannot consist with patient submission to God's will.

(4) Self apology cannot agree with submission to God's will, when, instead of being humbled under God's hand, a person justifies himself. A proud sinner stands upon his own defence, and is ready to accuse God of unrighteousness, which is, as if we should tax the sun with darkness. This is far from submission to God's will. God smote Jonah's gourd, and he stood upon his own vindication. 'I do well to be angry, even unto death.' Jonah iv 9. What! to be angry with God, and to justify this! 'I do well to be angry!' This was strange to come from a prophet, and was far from the prayer Christ taught us, 'Thy will be done.'

What is patient submission to God's will?

It is a gracious frame of soul, whereby a Christian is content to be at God's disposal, and acquiesces in his wisdom. 'It is the Lord, let him do what

seemeth him good.' 1 Sam iii 18. 'The will of the Lord be done.' Acts xxi 14.
That I may further illustrate this, I shall show you wherein this submission
to the will of God lies. It lies chiefly in three things:

(1) In acknowledging God's hand; seeing God in the affliction. 'Affliction
cometh not forth of the dust;' it comes not by chance. Job v 6. Job eyed
God in all that befell him. 'The Lord hath taken away.' Job i 21. He complains not of the Chaldeans, or the influence of the planets: he looks beyond
second causes, he sees God in the affliction. 'The Lord hath taken away.'
There can be no submission to God's will till there be an acknowledging of
God's hand.

(2) Patient submission to God's will lies in justifying God. 'O my God, I
cry but thou hearest not,' thou turnest a deaf ear to me in my affliction. Psa
xxii 2. 'But thou art holy;' ver 3. God is holy and just, not only when he
punishes the wicked, but when he afflicts the righteous. Though he put
wormwood in our cup, yet we vindicate him, and proclaim his righteousness. When Mauricius, the emperor, saw his son slain before his eyes, he
exclaimed, *Justus es, Domine*, 'Righteous art thou, O Lord, in all thy ways.'
We justify God, and confess he punishes us less than we deserve. Ezra ix 13.

(3) Patient submission to God's will lies in accepting the punishment.
'And they then accept of the punishment of their iniquity.' Lev xxvi 41.
Accepting the punishment, is taking all that God does in good part. He who
accepts of the punishment says, 'Good is the rod of the Lord;' he kisses the
rod, yea, blesses God that he would use such a merciful severity, and rather
afflict him than lose him.

Patient submission to God's will in affliction shows a great deal of wisdom
and piety. The skill of a pilot is most discerned in a storm, so a Christian's
grace in the storm of affliction. Submission to God's will is most requisite
for us while we live in this lower region. In heaven there will be no more
need of patience than there is need of the starlight when the sun shines. In
heaven there will be all joy, and what need of patience then? It requires no
patience to wear a crown of gold; but while we live here in a valley of tears,
patient submission to God's will is much needed. 'Ye have need of patience.'
Heb x 36.

The Lord sometimes lays heavy affliction upon us. 'Thy hand presseth
me sore.' Psa xxxviii 2. The word in the original for 'afflicted' signifies to
be 'melted.' God sometimes melts his people in a furnace. He sometimes
lays divers afflictions upon us. 'He multiplieth my wounds.' Job ix 17. God
shoots divers sorts of arrows.

(1) Sometimes God afflicts with poverty. The widow had nothing left
her save a pot of oil. 2 Kings iv 2. Poverty is a great temptation. To have an
estate reduced almost to nothing, is hard to flesh and blood. 'Call me not

Naomi, but Mara; I went out full, and the Lord hath brought me home again empty.' Ruth i 20, 21. This exposes to contempt. When the prodigal was poor, his brother was ashamed to own him. 'This thy son;' he said not, this my brother, but this thy son; he scorned to call him brother. Luke xv 30. When the deer is shot and bleeds, the rest of the herd push it away; so when God shoots the arrow of poverty at one, others are ready to push him away. When Terence was grown poor, his friend Scipio cast him off. The poets feign that the muses, Jupiter's daughters, had no suitors, because they wanted a dowry.

(2) God sometimes afflicts with reproach. Such as have the light of grace shining in them may be eclipsed in their name. The primitive Christians were reproached as if they were guilty of incest, says Tertullian. Luther was called a trumpeter of rebellion. David calls reproach heart-breaking. Psa lxix 20. God often lets his dear saints be exercised with this. Dirt may be cast upon a pearl, and those names may be blotted which are written in the book of life. Sincerity shields from hell, but not from slander.

(3) God sometimes afflicts with the loss of dear relations. 'Son of man, behold, I take away from thee the desire of thine eyes with a stroke.' Ezek xxiv 16. This is like pulling away a limb from the body. He takes away a holy child: Jacob's life was bound up in Benjamin. Gen xliv 30. That which is worse than the loss of children is, when they are continued as living crosses; where the parents expected honey, there to have wormwood. What greater cut to a godly parent than a child who disclaims his father's God? A corrosive applied to the body may do well, but a bad child is a corrosive to the heart. Such an undutiful son had David, who conspired treason, and would not only have taken away his father's crown, but his life.

(4) God sometimes afflicts with infirmity of body. Sickness takes away the comfort of life, and makes one in deaths oft.

God tries his people with various afflictions, so that there is need of patience to submit to his will. He who has divers bullets shot at him needs armour; so when divers afflictions assault, we need patience as proof armour. He sometimes lets the affliction continue long. Psa lxxiv 9. As with diseases, some are chronic, that linger and hang about the body several years together; so it is with affliction, the Lord is pleased to exercise many of his precious ones with chronic affliction, such as lies upon them a long time. In all these cases we need patience and submissiveness of spirit to God's will.

Use 1. For reproof. It reproves such as have not yet learned this part of the Lord's prayer: 'Thy will be done;' they have only said it, but not learned it. If things be not according to their mind, if the wind of Providence crosses the tide of their will, they are discontented and querulous. Where is now submission of will to God? To be displeased with God if things do not please us, is this to lie at God's feet, and acquiesce in his will? It is a very bad temper of spirit, and God may justly punish us by letting us have our will. Rachel cried, 'Give me children, or else I die.' Gen xxx 1. God let her have a child, but it cost her her life. Gen xxxv 18. Israel was not content with manna, but they must have quails, and God punished them by letting them have their will. 'There went forth a wind from the Lord and brought quails; and while the flesh was yet between their teeth, the wrath of the Lord was kindled against them, and the Lord smote the people with a very great plague.' Numb xi 31, 33. They had better been without their quails than had such sour sauce to them. Many have importunately desired the life of a child, and could not bring their will to God's to be content to part with it; and the Lord has punished them by letting them have their will; for the child has lived and been a burden to them. Seeing their wills crossed God, their child shall cross them.

Use 2. For exhortation. Let us be exhorted, whatever troubles God exercises us with, *aequo animo ferre* [to bear with a calm mind], to resign up our wills to him, and say, 'Thy will be done.' Which is fittest, that God should bring his will to ours, or we bring our wills to his? Say as Eli, 'It is the Lord, let him do what seemeth him good;' and as David, 'Behold, here am I; let him do to me as seemeth good unto him.' 1 Sam iii 18. 2 Sam xv 26. It was the saying of Harpulas, *Placet mihi quod Regi placet*, 'That pleases me which pleases the king;' so should we say, that which pleases God pleases us. 'Thy will be done.' Some have not yet learned this art of submission to God; and truly he who wants patience in affliction is like a soldier in battle who wants armour.

When do we not submit to God's will in affliction as we ought?

(1) When we have hard thoughts of him, and our hearts begin to swell against him.

(2) When we are so troubled at our present affliction that we are unfit for duty. We can mourn as doves, but not pray or praise God. We are so discomposed that we are not fit to hearken to any good counsel. 'They hearkened not unto Moses for anguish of spirit.' Exod vi 9. Israel was so full of grief under their burdens, that they minded not what Moses said, though he came with a message from God to them; 'They hearkened not unto Moses for anguish of spirit.'

(3) We do not submit as we ought to God's will when we labour to break loose from affliction by indirect means. Many, to rid themselves out of

trouble, run themselves into sin. When God has bound them with the cords of affliction, they go to the devil to loosen their bands. Better it is to stay in affliction than to sin ourselves out of it. O let us learn to stoop to God's will in all afflictive providences.

But how shall we bring ourselves, in all occurrences of providence, patiently to acquiesce in God's will, and say, 'Thy will be done'?

The means for a quiet resignation to God's will in affliction are:

[1] Judicious consideration. 'In the day of adversity consider.' Eccl vii 14. When any thing burdens us, or runs cross to our desires, did we but sit down and consider, and weigh things in the balance of judgment, it would much quiet our minds, and subject our wills to God. Consideration would be as David's harp, to charm down the evil spirit of frowardness and discontent.

But what should we consider?

That which should make us submit to God in affliction, and say, 'Thy will be done,' is:

(1) To consider that the present state of life is subject to afflictions, as a seaman's life is subject to storms; *ferre quam sortem omnes patiuntur nemo recusat* [no one escapes bearing the lot which all suffer]. 'Man is born unto trouble;' he is heir apparent to it; he comes into the world with a cry, and goes out with a groan. Job v 7. *Ea lege nati sumus* [On that condition are we born]. The world is a place where much wormwood grows. 'He hath filled me with bitterness (Heb with bitternesses); he hath made me drunken with wormwood.' Lam iii 15. Troubles arise like sparks out of a furnace. Afflictions are some of the thorns which the earth after the curse brings forth. We may as well think to stop the chariot of the sun when it is in its swift motion, as put a stop to trouble. The consideration of a life exposed to eclipses and sufferings should make us say with patience, 'Thy will be done.' Shall a mariner be angry that he meets with a storm at sea?

(2) Consider that God has a special hand in the disposal of all occurrences. Job eyed God in his affliction. 'The Lord hath taken away;' chap i 21. He did not complain of the Sabeans, or the influences of the planets; he looked beyond all second causes; he saw God in the affliction, and that made him cheerfully submit; he said, 'Blessed be the name of the Lord.' Christ looked beyond Judas and Pilate to God's determinate counsel in delivering him up to be crucified, which made him say, 'Father, not as I will, but as thou wilt.' Acts iv 27, 28, Matt xxvi 39. It is vain to quarrel with instruments: wicked men are but a rod in God's hand. 'O Assyrian, the rod of mine anger.' Isa x 5. Whoever brings an affliction, God sends it. The consideration of this should

make us say, 'Thy will be done;' for what God does he sees a reason for. We read of a wheel within a wheel. Ezek i 16. The outward wheel, which turns all, is providence; the wheel within this wheel is God's decree; this believed, would rock the heart quiet. Shall we mutiny at that which God does? We may as well quarrel with the works of creation as with the works of providence.

(3) Consider that there is a necessity for affliction. 'If need be, ye are in heaviness.' 1 Pet i 6. It is needful some things be kept in brine. Afflictions are needful upon several accounts.

[1] To keep us humble. Often there is no other way to have the heart low but by being brought low. When Manasseh 'was in affliction, he humbled himself greatly.' 2 Chron xxxiii 12. Corrections are corrosives to eat out the proud flesh. 'Remembering my misery, the wormwood and the gall, my soul is humbled in me.' Lam iii 19, 20.

[2] It is necessary that there should be affliction; for if God did not sometimes bring us into affliction, how could his power be seen in bringing us out? Had not Israel been in the Egyptian furnace, God had lost his glory in their deliverance.

[3] If there were no affliction, then many parts of Scripture could not be fulfilled. God has promised to help us to bear affliction. Psa xxxvii 24, 39. How could we experience his supporting us in trouble, if we did not sometimes meet with it? God has promised to give us joy in affliction. John xvi 20. How could we taste this honey of joy if we were not sometimes in affliction? Again, he has promised to wipe away tears from our eyes. Isa xxv 8. How could he wipe away our tears in heaven if we never shed any? So that, in several respects, there is an absolute necessity that we should meet with affliction; and shall not we quietly submit, and say, 'Lord, I see there is a necessity for it?' 'Thy will be done!'

(4) Consider that whatever we feel is what we have brought upon ourselves; we have put a rod into God's hand to chastise us. Christian, God lays thy cross on thee; but it is of thy own making. If a man's field be full of tares, it is what he has sown in it: if thou reapest a bitter crop of affliction, it is what thou thyself hast sown. The cords that pinch thee are of thy own twisting; *meme adsum qui feci* [it is I myself here who made them]. If children will eat green fruit, they may thank themselves if they are sick; and if we eat the forbidden fruit, no wonder we feel it gripe. Sin is the Trojan horse that lands an army of afflictions upon us. 'A voice publisheth affliction:' 'Thy way and thy doings have procured these things unto thee; this is thy wickedness.' Jer iv 15, 18. If we by sin run ourselves into arrears with God,

no wonder if he set affliction as a sergeant on our back to arrest us. This should make us patiently submit to God in affliction, and say, 'Thy will be done.' We have no cause to complain of God; it is nothing but what our sins have merited. 'Hast not thou procured this unto thyself?' Jer ii 17. The cross, though it be of God's laying, is of our making. Say, then, as Micah (chap vii 9), 'I will bear the indignation of the Lord, because I have sinned against him.'

(5) Consider that God is about to prove and try us. 'Thou, O God, hast tried us as silver is tried, thou laidst affliction upon our loins.' Psa lxvi 10, 11. If there were no affliction, how could God have an opportunity to try men? Hypocrites can serve in a pleasure boat: they can serve God in prosperity; but when we can keep close to him in times of danger, when we can trust him in darkness, and love him when we have no smile, and say, 'Thy will be done,' that is the trial of sincerity! God is only trying us; and what hurt is there in that? What is gold the worse for being tried?

(6) Consider that in all our crosses God has kindness for us. As there was no night so dark but Israel had a pillar of fire to give light, so there is no condition so cloudy but we may see that which gives light of comfort. David could sing of mercy and judgment. Psa ci 1. It should make our wills cheerfully submit to God's, to consider that in every path of providence we may see a footstep of kindness.

There is kindness in affliction when God seems most unkind.

[1] There is kindness in that there is love in it. God's rod and his love may stand together. 'Whom the Lord loveth he chasteneth.' Heb xii 6. As when Abraham lifted up his hand to sacrifice, Isaac loved him; so when God afflicts his people, and seems to sacrifice their outward comforts, he loves them. The husbandman loves his vine when he cuts it and makes it bleed; and shall not we submit to God? Shall we quarrel with that which has kindness in it, which comes in love? The surgeon binds the patient, and lances him, but no wise man will quarrel with him, because it is in order to a cure.

[2] There is kindness in affliction, in that God deals with us as children. 'If ye endure chastening, God dealeth with you as with sons.' Heb xii 7. God has one Son without sin, but no son without stripes. Affliction is a badge of adoption; it is *Dei sigillum*, says Tertullian, it is God's seal by which he marks us for his own. When Munster, that holy man, lay sick, his friends asked him how he did? He pointed to his sores, saying, *Hae sunt gemmae Dei*, these are the jewels with which God decks his children. Shall not we then say, 'Thy will be done'? Lord, there is kindness in the cross, thou usest us as children. The rod of discipline is to fit us for the inheritance.

[3] In kindness God in all our afflictions has left us a promise; so that in the most cloudy providences the promise appears as the rainbow in the cloud. Then we have God's promise to be with us. 'I will be with him in trouble.' Psa xci 15. It cannot be ill with that man with whom God is; I will be with him, to support, sanctify, and sweeten every affliction. I had rather be in prison and have God's presence, than be in a palace without it.

We have the promise that he will not lay more upon us than he will enable us to bear. 1 Cor x 13. He will not try us beyond our strength; either he will make the yoke lighter, or our faith stronger. Should not this make us submit our wills to his, when afflictions have so much kindness in them? In all our trials he has left us promises, which are like manna in the wilderness.

[4] It is great kindness that all troubles that befall us shall be for our profit. 'He for our profit.' Heb xii 10.

What profit is in affliction?

Afflictions are disciplinary, they teach us. They are, *Schola crucis, Schola lucis* [the school of the cross, the school of light]. Many psalms have the inscription, *Maschil*, a psalm giving instruction; so affliction has the inscription *Maschil* upon it, an affliction giving instruction. 'Hear ye the rod.' Micah vi 9. Luther says he could never rightly understand some of the psalms till he was in affliction. Gideon 'took thorns of the wilderness, and briers, and with them he taught the men of Succoth.' Judges viii 16. God by the thorns and briers of affliction teaches us.

Affliction shows us more of our own hearts. Water in a glass vial looks clear; but set it on the fire, and the scum boils up; so when God sets us upon the fire, corruption boils up which we did not discern before. Sharp afflictions are to the soul as a soaking rain to the houses; we know not that there are holes in the house till the shower comes, but then we see it drop down here and there; so we do not know what unmortified lusts are in the soul till the storm of affliction comes; then we find unbelief, impatience, carnal fear, dropping down in many places. Affliction is a sacred *collyrium* [eye-salve], it clears our eye-sight: the rod gives wisdom.

Affliction brings those sins to remembrance which we had buried in the grave of forgetfulness. Joseph's brethren, for twenty years together, were not at all troubled for their sin in selling their brother; but when they came into Egypt, and began to be in straits, their sin came to their remembrance, and their hearts smote them. 'They said one to another, we are verily guilty concerning our brother.' Gen xlii 21. When a man is in distress his sin comes fresh into his mind; conscience makes a rehearsal-sermon of all the evils which have passed in his life; his expense of precious time, his Sabbath-breaking, his slighting of the word, come to remembrance, and he goes out with Peter and weeps bitterly. Thus the rod gives wisdom, shows the hidden evil of the heart, and brings former sins to remembrance.

There is profit in affliction, as it quickens the spirit of prayer; *premuntur justi ut pressi clament* [the righteous are afflicted that in their affliction they may pray]. Jonah was asleep in the ship, but at prayer in the whale's belly. Perhaps in a time of health and prosperity we prayed in a cold and formal manner, we put no coals to the incense, we scarcely minded our own prayers, and how should God mind them? God sends some cross or other to make us stir up ourselves to take hold of him. When Jacob was in fear of his life by his brother, he wrestled with God, and wept in prayer, and would not leave him till he blessed him. Hos xii 4. It is with many of God's children as with those who formerly had the sweating sickness in this land, it was a sleepy disease, if they slept they died; therefore, to keep them waking, they were smitten with rosemary branches; so the Lord uses affliction as a rosemary branch to keep us from sleeping, and to awaken a spirit of prayer. 'They poured out a prayer, when thy chastening was upon them;' now their prayer pierced the heavens. Isa xxvi 16. In times of trouble we pray feelingly, and we never pray so fervently as when we pray feelingly; and is not this for our profit?

Affliction is for our profit, as it is a means to purge out our sins. 'By this therefore shall the iniquity of Jacob be purged.' Isa xxvii 9. Affliction is God's physic to expel the noxious humour, it cures the imposthume of pride, the fever of lust; and is not this for our profit? Affliction is God's file to fetch off our rust, his flail to thresh off our husks. The water of affliction is not to drown us, but to wash off our spots.

To be under the black rod is profitable, in that hereby we grow more serious, and are more careful to clear our evidences for heaven. In times of prosperity, when the rock poured out rivers of oil, we were careless in getting, at least clearing, our title to glory. Job xxix 6. Had many no better evidences for their land than they have for their salvation, they were in an ill case; but when an hour of trouble comes, we begin to look after our spiritual evidences, and see how things stand between God and our souls; and is it not for our profit to see our interest in Christ more clear than ever?

Affliction is for our profit, as it is a means to take us more off from the world. The world often proves not only a spider's web, but a cockatrice egg. Pernicious worldly things are great enchantments, they are *retinacula spei* [the tether of hope]. Tertullian. They hinder us in our passage to heaven. If a clock be overwound, it stands still; so, when the heart is wound up too much to the world, it stands still to heavenly things. Affliction sounds a retreat to call us off the immoderate pursuit of earthly things. When things are frozen and congealed together, the only way to separate them is by fire; so, when the heart and the world are congealed together, God has no better way to separate them than by the fire of affliction.

Affliction is for our profit, as it is a refiner. It works us up to further degrees of sanctity. 'He for our profit, that we might be partakers of his holiness.' Heb xii 10. The vessels of mercy are the brighter for scouring. As you pour water on your linen when you would whiten it, so God pours the waters of affliction upon us to whiten our souls. The leaves of the fig-tree and root are bitter, but the fruit is sweet; so afflictions are in themselves bitter, but they bring forth the sweet fruits of righteousness. Heb xii 11. This should make us submit to God and say, 'Thy will be done.'

[5] There is kindness in affliction, in that there is no condition so bad but it might be worse. When it is dusk, it might be darker. God does not make our cross so heavy as he might: he does not stir up all his anger. Psa lxxviii 38. He does not put so many nails in our yoke, so much wormwood in our cup, as he might. Does God chastise thy body? He might torture thy conscience. Does he cut thee short? He might cut thee off. The Lord might make our chains heavier. Is it a burning fever? It might have been the burning lake. Does God use the pruning knife to lop thee? He might bring his axe to hew thee down. 'The waters were up to the ankles.' Do the waters of affliction come up to the ankles? God might make them rise higher; nay, he might drown thee in the waters. God uses the rod when he might use the scorpion.

[6] There is kindness in affliction, in that your case is not so bad as others, who are always upon the rack, and spend their years with sighing. Psa xxxi 10. Have you a gentle fit of the ague? Others cry out of the stone and strangulation. Do you bear the wrath of men? Others bear the wrath of God. You have but a single trial: others have them twisted together. God shoots but one arrow at you, he shoots a shower of arrows at others. Is there not kindness in all this? We are apt to say, never any suffered as we! Was it not worse with Lazarus, who was so full of sores that the dogs took pity on him, and licked his sores? Nay, was it not worse with Christ, who lived poor and died cursed? May not this cause us to say, 'Thy will be done'? It is in kindness that God deals not so severely with us as with others.

[7] There is kindness in affliction, in that, if we belong to God, it is all the hell we shall have. Some have two hells: they suffer in their body and conscience, which is one hell, and another hell to come is unquenchable fire. Judas had two hells, but a child of God has but one. Lazarus had all his hell here; he was full of sores, but had a convoy of angels to carry him to

heaven when he died. Say, then, Lo! if this be the worst I shall have, if this be all my hell, I will patiently acquiesce: 'Thy will be done.'

[8] There is kindness in that God gives gracious supports in affliction. If he strikes with one hand, he supports with the other. 'Underneath are the everlasting arms.' Deut xxxiii 27. There is not the least trial, but if God would desert us, and not assist us with his grace, we should sink under it; as the frown of a great man, the fear of reproach. Peter was frighted at the voice of a maid. Matt xxvi 69. Oh, therefore, what mercy is it to have Christ strengthen us, and as it were, bear the heaviest part of the cross with us! One said, I have no ravishing joys in my sickness, but I bless God I have sweet supports; and should not this cause submission to God's will, and make us say, 'Lo! if thou art so kind as to bear us up in affliction, that we do not faint, put us into what winepress thou pleasest: 'Thy will be done'?

[9] There is kindness in affliction in that it is preventive. God, by this stroke of his, would prevent some sin. Paul's 'thorn in the flesh' was to prevent his being lifted up in pride. 2 Cor xii 7. Affliction is sometimes sent for the punishing of sin, at other times for its prevention. Prosperity exposes to much evil: it is hard to carry a full cup without spilling, and a full estate without sinning. God's people know not how much they are beholden to their affliction; they might have fallen into some scandal, had not God set a hedge of thorns in their way to stop them. What kindness is this! God lets us fall into sufferings to prevent falling into snares; say then, Lord, do as it seems good in thy sight, 'Thy will be done.'

God by affliction would prevent damnation. We are corrected in the world, 'that we should not be condemned with the world.' 1 Cor xi 32. A man, by falling into briers, is saved from falling into the river; so God lets us fall into the briers of affliction that we may not be drowned in perdition. It is a great favour when a less punishment is inflicted to prevent a greater. Is it not clemency in the judge, when he lays some light penalty on the prisoner, and saves his life? So it is when God lays upon us light affliction, and saves us from wrath to come. As Pilate said, 'I will chastise him, and let him go;' so God chastises his children and lets them go, frees them from eternal torment. Luke xxiii 16. What is the drop of sorrow the godly taste, to that sea of wrath the wicked shall be drinking to all eternity? Oh! what kindness is here! Should it not make us say, 'Thy will be done'?

[10] There is kindness in that God mixes his providences. In anger he remembers mercy. Hab iii 2. Not all pure gall, but some honey mixed with it. Asher's shoes were iron and brass, but his foot was dipped in oil. Deut xxxiii 24, 25. Affliction is the shoe of brass, but God causes the foot to be

dipped in oil. As the painter mixes with his dark shadows bright colours, so the wise God mingles the dark and bright colours, crosses and blessings. The body is afflicted, but within is peace of conscience. Joseph was sold into Egypt, and put into prison; there was the dark side of the cloud. Job lost all that ever he had, his skin was clothed with boils and ulcers; here was a sad providence. But God gave a testimony from heaven of Job's integrity, and afterwards doubled his estate. 'The Lord gave Job twice as much;' here was the goodness of God towards Job. Job xlii 10. God chequers his works of providence, and shall not we submit and say, Lord, if thou art so kind, mixing so many bright colours with my dark condition, 'Thy will be done.'

[11] There is kindness in affliction in that God moderates his stroke. 'I will correct thee in measure.' Jer xxx 11. God in the day of his east wind will stay his rough wind. Isa xxvii 8. The physician that understands the crisis and temper of the patient will not give too strong physic for the body, nor will he give one drachm or scruple too much: so God knows our frame, he will not over-afflict; he will not stretch the strings of the viol too hard, lest they break. And, is there no kindness in all this? Should not this work our hearts to submission? Lord, if thou usest so much gentleness, and correctest in measure, 'Thy will be done.'

[12] There is kindness in affliction in that God often sweetens it with divine consolation. 'Who comforteth us in all our tribulation.' 2 Cor i 4. After a bitter potion he gives a lump of sugar. God comforts in affliction. (1) Partly by his word. 'This is my comfort in my affliction, for thy word hath quickened me.' Psa cxix 50. The promises of the word are a shop of cordials. (2) God comforts by his Spirit. Philip, landgrave of Hesse, said that in his troubles, *Se divinas martyrum consolationes sensisse*, he felt the divine consolations of the martyrs. David had his pilgrimage-songs, and Paul his prison-songs. Psa cxix 54; Acts xvi 25. Thus God candies our worm-wood with sugar, and makes us gather grapes off thorns. Some of the saints have such ravishing joys in affliction, that they had rather endure their sufferings than want their comforts. Oh, how much kindness there is in the cross! In the belly of this lion is a honeycomb. Should it not make us cheerfully submit to God's will, when he lines the yoke with comfort, and gives us honey at the end of the rod?

[13] There is kindness in affliction in that God curtails and shortens it; he will not let it lie on too long. 'I will not contend for ever, for the spirit should fail before me.' Isa lvii 16. God will give his people a writ of ease, and proclaim a year of jubilee; the wicked may plough upon the backs of the saints, but God will cut their traces. Psa cxxix 3, 4. The goldsmith will

not let his gold lie any longer in the furnace than till it be purified. The wicked must drink a sea of wrath, but the godly have only a cup of affliction, and God will say, 'Let this cup pass away.' Isa li 17. Affliction may be compared to frost, that will break, and spring-flowers will come on. 'Sorrow and sighing shall flee away.' Isa xxxv 10. Affliction has a sting, but withal a wing: sorrow shall fly away. This land-flood shall be dried up. If there be so much kindness in the cross, and God will cause a cessation of trouble, say then, *fiat voluntas tua*, 'Thy will be done.'

[14] There is kindness in affliction in that it is a means to make us happy. 'Behold, happy is the man whom God correcteth.' Job v 17. It seems strange to flesh and blood that affliction should make us happy. When Moses saw the bush burning and not consumed, he said 'I will turn aside and see this great sight.' Exod iii 3. So here is a strange sight, a man afflicted, and yet happy. The world counts them happy who can escape affliction, but happy is the man whom God correcteth.

How do afflictions contribute to our happiness?

As they are a means of bringing us nearer to God. The loadstone of prosperity does not draw us so near to God as the cords of affliction. When the prodigal was pinched with want, he said, 'I will arise, and go to my father.' Luke xv 18. As the deluge brought the dove to the ark, the floods of sorrow make us hasten to Christ.

Afflictions make us happy, as they are safe guides to glory. The storm drives the ship into the harbour. Blessed storm that drives the soul into the heavenly harbour. Is it not better to go through affliction to glory, than through pleasure to misery? Not that afflictions merit glory, but they prepare us for it. No cross ever merited but that which Christ endured. Think, O Christian, what affliction leads to! it leads to paradise, where are rivers of pleasure always running. Should not this make us cheerfully submit to God's will, and say, Lord, if there be so much kindness in affliction, if all thou doest is to make us happy, 'Thy will be done.'

(7) Consider that it is God's ordinary course to keep his people to a bitter diet-drink, and exercise them with great trials. Affliction is the beaten road in which all the saints have gone. The lively stones in the spiritual building have been all hewn and polished. Christ's lily has grown among the thorns. 'All that will live godly in Christ Jesus, shall suffer persecution.' 2 Tim iii 12. It is too much for a Christian to have two heavens: it is more than Christ had. It has been ever the lot of saints to encounter sore trials. It was of the prophets, 'Take, my brethren, the prophets for an example of suffering affliction.' James v 10. It was of the apostles: for Peter was crucified with his

head downwards. James was beheaded by Herod, John was banished into the isle of Patmos, the apostle Thomas was thrust through with a spear, Matthias (who was chosen apostle in Judas's room) was stoned to death, and Luke, the evangelist, was hanged on an olive-tree. Those saints, of whom the world was not worthy, passed under the rod. Heb xi 38. Christ's kingdom is *regnum crucis* [the kingdom of the cross]. Those whom God intends to save from hell, he does not save from the cross. The consideration of this should quiet our minds in affliction, and make us say, 'Thy will be done.' Do we think God will alter his course of providence for us? Why should we look for exemption from trouble more than others? Why should we think to tread only upon roses and violets, when prophets and apostles have marched through briars to heaven?

(8) Consider that what God has already done for thee, Christian, should make thee content to suffer anything at his hand, and say, 'Thy will be done.'

[1] He has adopted thee for his child. David thought it no small honour to be the king's son-in-law. 1 Sam xviii 18. What an honour is it to derive thy pedigree from heaven, to be born of God! Why then art thou troubled, and murmurest at every slight cross? As Jonadab said to Amnon, 'Why art thou, being the king's son, lean?' 2 Sam xiii 4. Why art thou, who art son or daughter to the king of heaven, troubled at these petty things? What! the king's son, and look lean! Let it quiet thy spirit and bring thy will to God's, that he has dignified thee with honour, he has made thee his son and heir, and will entail a kingdom on thee.

[2] God has given thee Christ. Christ is *communis thesaurus*, a magazine or storehouse of all heavenly treasure; a pearl of price to enrich, a tree of life to quicken; he is the quintessence of all blessings. Why then art thou discontented at thy worldly crosses? They cannot be so bitter as Christ is sweet. As Seneca said once to Polybius, 'Why dost thou complain of hard fortune, *salvo Caesare* [while it is well with Caesar]? Is not Caesar thy friend?' So, is not Christ thy friend? He can never be poor who has a mine of gold in his field; nor he who has the unsearchable riches of Christ. Say then, 'Lord, Thy will be done;' though I have my cross, yet I have Christ with it. The cross may make me weep, but Christ wipes off all tears. Rev vii 17.

[3] God has given thee grace. Grace is the rich embroidery and workmanship of the Holy Ghost; it is the sacred unction. 1 John ii 27. The graces are a chain of pearl to adorn, and beds of spices which make a sweet odour to God. Grace is a distinguishing blessing; Christ gave Judas his purse, but not

his Spirit. May not this quiet the heart in affliction, and make it say, 'Thy will be done'? Lord, thou hast given me that jewel which thou bestowest only on the elect; grace is the seal of thy love, it is both food and cordial, it is an earnest of glory.

(9) Consider that when God intends the greatest mercy to any of his people, he brings them low in affliction. He seems to go quite cross to sense and reason, for when he intends to raise us highest, he brings us lowest. As Moses' hand, before it wrought miracles, was leprous; and Sarah's womb, before it brought forth the son of promise, was barren. God brings us low before he raiseth us, as water is at the lowest ebb before there is a spring-tide.

This is true in a temporal sense. When God would bring Israel to Canaan, a land flowing with milk and honey, he first led them through a sea and a wilderness. When he intended to advance Joseph to be the second man in the kingdom, he cast him first into prison, and the iron entered into his soul. Psa cv 18. He usually lets it be darkest before the morning-star of deliverance appears.

It is true in a spiritual sense. When God intends to raise a soul to spiritual comfort, he first lays it low in desertion. Isa xii 1. As the painter lays his dark colour first, and then lays his gold colour on it, so God first lays the soul in the dark of desertion, and then his golden colour of joy and consolation. Should not this make us cheerfully submit, and say, 'Thy will be done'? Perhaps now God afflicts me, he is about to raise me, he intends me a greater mercy than I am aware of.

(10) Consider the excellency of this frame of soul, to lie at God's feet and say, 'Thy will be done.'

A soul that is melted into God's will shows variety of grace. As the holy ointment was made up of several aromatic spices, myrrh, cinnamon, and cassia, so this sweet temper of soul, submission to God's will in affliction, has in it a mixture of several graces. Exod xxx 23. In particular, it is compounded of three graces, faith, love, humility. [1] Faith. Faith believes God does all in mercy, that affliction is to mortify some sin, or exercise some grace; that God corrects in love and faithfulness. Psa cxix 75. The belief of this causes submission of will to God. [2] Love. Love thinks no evil. 1 Cor xiii 5. It takes all God does in the best sense, it has good thoughts of God, and causes submission. Let the righteous God smite me, says love, it shall be a kindness; yea, it shall be an excellent oil, which shall not break my head. [3] Humility. The humble soul looks on its sins, and how much he has provoked God; he says not his afflictions are great, but his sins are great; he lies low at God's feet and says, 'I will bear the indignation of the Lord, because I have sinned against him.' Micah vii 9. Thus a submissive frame of heart is full of grace; it is compounded of several graces. God is pleased to see so many graces at once sweetly exercised; he says of such a Christian, as David of Goliath's sword, 'None like that, give it me.' 1 Sam xxi 9.

He who puts his *fiat et placet* [so be it; agreed] to God's will, and says, 'Thy will be done,' shows not only variety of grace, but strength of grace. It argues much strength in the body to be able to endure hard weather, yet not to be altered by it; so to endure hard trials, yet not faint or fret, shows more than ordinary strength of grace. You that can say you have brought your wills to God's – God's will and yours agree, as the copy and the original – let me assure you, you have outstripped many Christians who perhaps shine in a higher sphere of knowledge than you. To be content to be at God's disposal, to be anything that God will have us, shows a noble, heroic soul. It is reported of the eagle that it is not like other fowls, which, when they are hungry, make a noise, as the ravens cry for food, but it is never heard to make a noise, though it wants meat, because of the nobleness and greatness of its spirit; it is above other birds, and has a spirit suitable to its nature: so it is a proof of great magnitude of spirit, that whatsoever cross providences befall a Christian, he does not cry and whine as others, but is silent, and lies quietly at God's feet. There is much strength of grace in such a soul, nay, the height of grace. When grace is crowning, it is not so much to say, 'Lord, thy will be done;' but when grace is conflicting, and meets with crosses and trials, then to say, 'Thy will be done,' is a glorious thing indeed, and prepares for the garland of honour.

(11) Consider that persons are usually better in adversity than prosperity; therefore stoop to God's will. A prosperous condition is not always so safe. True it is more pleasing to the palate, and every one desires to get on the warm side of the hedge, where the sun of prosperity shines, but it is not always best; in a prosperous state there is more burden, *plus oneris*. Many look at the shining and glittering of prosperity, but not at the burden.

[1] There is the burden of care. Therefore God calls riches 'cares.' Luke viii 14. A rose has its prickles, so have riches. We think them happy that flourish in their silks and cloth of gold, but we see not the troubles and cares that attend them. A shoe may have silver lace on it, yet pinch the foot. Many a man that goes to his day-labour, lives a more contented life than he that has his thousands *per annum*. Disquieting care is the *malus genius*, the evil spirit that haunts the rich man. When his chests are full of gold, his heart is full of care how to increase, or how to secure what he has gotten. He is sometimes full of care to whom he shall leave it. A large estate, like a long, trailing garment, is often more troublesome than useful.

[2] In a prosperous estate there is the burden of account. Such as are in

high places, have a far greater account to give to God than others. 'Unto whomsoever much is given, of him shall be much required.' Luke xii 48. The more golden talents any are entrusted with, the more they have to answer for; the more their revenues, the more their reckonings. God will say, I gave you a great estate, what have you done with it? How have you employed it for my glory? I have read of Philip, king of Spain, that when he was about to die, said, 'O that I had never been a king! O that I had lived a private, solitary life! Here is all the fruit of my kingdom, it has made my accounts heavier!' So, then, may not this quiet our hearts in a low, adverse condition, and make us say, 'Lord, thy will be done!' as thou hast given me a less portion of worldly things, so I have a less burden of care, and a less burden of account.

[3] A prosperous condition has *plus periculi*, more danger in it. Such as are on the top of the pinnacle of honour, are in more danger of falling; they are subject to many temptations; their table is often a snare. Heliogabalus made ponds of sweet water to bathe in; millions are drowned in the sweet waters of pleasure. A great sail overturns the vessel: how many, by having too great sails of prosperity, have had their souls overturned! It must be a strong head that bears heady wine; he had need have much wisdom and grace that knows how to bear a high condition. It is hard to carry a full cup without spilling, and a full estate without sinning. Agur feared if he were full, he should deny God and say, 'Who is the Lord?' Prov xxx 9. Prosperity breeds pride. The children of Korah were in a higher estate than the rest of the Levites: they were employed in the tabernacle about the most holy things of all; they had the first lot; but as they were lifted up above others of the Levites in honour, so in pride. Numb iv 4; Josh xxi 10; Numb xvi 3. When the tide rises higher in the Thames, the boat rises higher; so, when the tide of an estate rises higher, many men's hearts rise higher in pride. Prosperity breeds security. Samson fell asleep in Delilah's lap, so do men in the lap of ease and plenty. The world's golden sands are quicksands. 'How hardly shall they that have riches enter into the kingdom of God!' Luke xviii 24. The consideration of this should make us submit to God in adversity, and say, 'Thy will be done.' God sees what is best for us. If we have less estate, we are in less danger; if we want the honours of others, so we want their temptations.

(12) Consider that, having our wills melted into God's is a good sign that the present affliction is sanctified. Affliction is sanctified when it attains the end for which it was sent. The end why God sends affliction, is to calm the spirit, to subdue the will, and bring it to God's will; when this is done, affliction has attained the end for which it came; it is sanctified, and it will

not be long ere it be removed. When the sore is healed, the smarting plaister is taken off.

(13) Consider how unworthy it is of a Christian to be froward and insubmissive, and not bring his will to God's.

[1] It is below the spirit of a Christian. The spirit of a Christian is dovelike, meek, and sedate, willing to be at God's disposal. 'Not my will, but thine be done.' Luke xxii 42. A Christian spirit is not fretful, but humble; not craving, but contented. See the picture of a Christian spirit in Paul. 'I know how to be abased, and how to abound.' Phil iv 12. He could be either higher or lower, as God saw good; he could sail with any wind of providence, either a prosperous or boisterous gale; his will was melted into God's. To be of a cross spirit that cannot submit to God, is unworthy of the spirit of a Christian; it is like the bird that, because it is pent up and cannot fly in the open air, beats itself against the cage.

[2] A froward insubmissive frame that cannot submit to God's will, is unworthy of a Christian's profession. He professes to live by faith, yet repines at his condition. Faith lives not by bread alone; it feeds on promises, it makes future glory present; it sees all in God. When the fig-tree does not blossom, faith can joy in the God of its salvation. Hab iii 17, 18. To be troubled at our present estate, because low and mean, shows weak faith. Surely that is a weak faith, or no faith, which must have crutches to support it. Oh, be ashamed to call thyself believer, if thou canst not trust God, and acquiesce in his will, in the deficiency of outward comforts.

[3] To be of a froward insubmissive spirit, that cannot surrender its will unto God, is unworthy of the high dignities God has put upon a Christian. He is a rich heir; he is exalted above all creatures that ever God made, except the angels; yea, in some sense, as his nature is joined in a hypostatic union to the divine nature, he is above the angels. Oh! then, how is he below his dignity, for want of a few earthly comforts, to be froward, and ready to quarrel with the Deity! Is it not unworthy of a king's son, because he may not pluck such a flower, to be discontented and rebel against his royal father? A Christian is espoused to Jesus Christ. What! to be married to Christ, yet froward and insubmissive! Hast not thou enough in him? as Elkanah said to Hannah, 'Am not I better than ten sons?' 1 Sam i 8. Is not Christ better than a thousand worldly comforts? *Omnia bona in summo bono* [All good things in the highest good]. It is a disparagement to Christ, that his spouse should be froward when she is matched to the crown of heaven.

[4] To be of a froward insubmissive spirit is unsuitable to the prayers of a

Christian. He prays, 'Thy will be done.' It is the will of God he should meet with such troubles, whether sickness, loss of estate, crosses in children, God has decreed and ordered it; why then is there not submission? Why are we discontented at that for which we pray? It is a saying of Latimer, speaking of Peter, who denied his Master, that he forgot the prayer, 'Hallowed be thy name.' So, we often forget our prayers, nay, contradict them, when we pray 'Thy will be done.' Now, if insubmissiveness to God be so unworthy of a Christian, should we not labour to bring our wills to God's, and say, Lord, let me not disparage religion, let me do nothing unworthy of a Christian?

(14) Consider that frowardness or insubmissiveness of will to God, is very sinful.

[1] It is sinful in its nature. To murmur when God crosses our will, shows much ungodliness. The apostle Jude speaks of ungodly ones; and that we may better know who these are, he sets a mark upon them: 'These are murmurers;' ver 15, 16. Some think they are not so ungodly as others, because they do not swear, nor get drunk, but they may be ungodly in murmuring. There are not only ungodly drunkards, but ungodly murmurers: nay, this is the height of ungodliness, it is rebellion. Korah and his company murmured against God, and see how the Lord interpreted it. 'Bring Aaron's rod to be kept for a token against the rebels.' Num xvii 10. To be a murmurer, and a rebel, is, in God's account, all one. 'This is the water of Meribah, because the children of Israel strove with the Lord.' Num xx 13. How did they strive with God? They murmured at his providence; ver 3. What! wilt thou be a rebel against God? It is a shame for a servant to strive with his master, but what is it for a creature to strive with its Maker.

[2] To quarrel with God's providence, and be insubmissive to his will, is sinful in the spring and cause; it arises from pride. It was Satan's temptation, 'ye shall be as gods.' Gen iii 5. A proud person makes a god of himself, he disdains to have his will crossed; he thinks himself better than others, therefore he finds fault with God's wisdom, that he is not above others.

[3] Quarrelsomeness or insubmissiveness to God's will, is sinful in the concomitants of it.

It is joined with sinful risings of the heart. Evil thoughts arise. We think hardly of God, as if he had done us wrong, or, as if we had deserved better at his hands. Passions begin to rise; the heart secretly frets against God. Jonah was crossed in his will, and passion began to boil in him. 'He was very angry.' Jonah iv 1. Jonah's spirit, as well as the sea, wrought and was tempestuous. Insubmissiveness of will is joined with unthankfulness.

Because in some one thing we are afflicted, we forget all the mercies we have. We deal with God just as the widow of Sarepta did with the prophet; the prophet Elijah had been a means to keep her alive in the famine, but as soon as her child died she quarrelled with the prophet, 'O thou man of God, art thou come to slay my son?' I Kings xvii 18. So, we can be content to receive blessings at the hand of God; but soon as in the least thing he crosses us in our will, we grow touchy, and are ready in a passion to fly out against him.

[4] Frowardness and insubmissiveness to God's will is evil in the effects. It unfits for duty. It is bad sailing in a storm, and it is ill praying when the heart is stormy and unquiet; it is well if such prayers do not suffer shipwreck. Insubmissiveness of spirit, sometimes unfits for the use of reason. Jonah was discontented because he had not his will; God withered the gourd, and his heart fretted against him; and in the midst of his passion, he spake no better than nonsense and blasphemy. 'I do well to be angry, even unto death.' Jonah iv 9. Surely he did not know well what he said. What! to be angry with God and die for anger! He speaks as if he had lost the use of his reason. Thus insubmissiveness of will is sinful in its nature, causes concomitants and effects. Should not this martyr our wills, and bring them to God in everything, making us say, 'Thy will be done?'

(15) Consider that insubmissiveness to God's will is very imprudent: we get nothing by it, it does not ease us of our burden, but rather makes it heavier. The more the child struggles with the parent, the more it is beaten; so, when we struggle with God, and will not submit to his will, we get nothing but more blows. Instead of having the cords of affliction loosened, we make God tie them tighter. Let us then submit, and say, 'Lord, thy will be done.' Why should I spin out my own trouble by impatience, and make my cross heavier? What got Israel by their frowardness? They were within eleven days' journey of Canaan, and fell into murmuring, and God led them a march of forty years longer in the wilderness.

(16) Consider that being insubmissive to God's will in affliction, lays a man open to many temptations. Where the heart frets against God by discontent, there is good fishing for Satan in those troubled waters. He usually puts discontented persons upon indirect means. Job's wife fretted (so far was she from holy submission) and she presently put her husband upon cursing God. 'Curse God, and die.' Job ii 9. What is the reason why some have turned witches, and given themselves to the devil, but out of envy and discontent, because they have not had their will! Others being under a temptation of poverty, and not having their wills in living at such a high rate as others, have laid violent hands upon themselves. Oh, the temptations

that men of discontented spirits are exposed to! Here, says Satan, is good fishing for me.

(17) Consider how far insubmissiveness of spirit is from that temper of soul which God requires in affliction! He would have us in patience possess our souls. Luke xxi 19. The Greek word for patience signifies to bear up under a burden without fainting or fretting; but is frowardness in affliction, and quarrelling with God's will, Christian patience? God would have us rejoice in affliction. 'Count it all joy when ye fall into divers temptations:' that is, afflictions; count it joy, be as birds that sing in winter. James i 2. 'Having received the word in much affliction, with joy.' 1 Thess i 6. Paul could leap in his fetters, and sing in the stocks. Acts xvi 25. How far is a discontented soul from this frame! He is far from rejoicing in affliction that has not learned to submit.

(18) Consider what is it that makes the difference between a godly man and an ungodly man in affliction, but this, that the godly man submits to God's will, the ungodly man will not submit. A wicked man frets and fumes, and is like a wild bull in a net. In affliction he blasphemes God. 'Men were scorched with great heat, and blasphemed the name of God.' Rev xvi 9. Put a stone in the fire, and it flies in your face; so stony hearts fly in God's face. The more a stuff that is rotten is rubbed, the more it frets and tears. When God afflicts the sinner, he tears himself in anger, but a godly man is sweetly submissive to his will. His language is, 'Shall not I drink the cup which my Father has given me?' Spices when bruised, send out a sweet fragrant smell; so, when God bruises his saints, they send out the sweet perfume of patience. Servulus, a holy man, was long afflicted with the palsy, yet his ordinary speech was *Laudatur Deus*, let God be praised. Oh, let us say, 'Thy will be done;' let us bear that patiently which God inflicts justly, or how do we show our grace? What difference is there between us and the wicked in affliction?

(19) Consider that not to submit to God's providential will, is highly provoking to him. Can we anger him more than by quarrelling with him, and not let him have his will? Kings do not love to have their wills opposed, though they may be unjust. How ill does God take it, when we will be disputing against his righteous will? It is a sin which he cannot bear. 'How long shall I bear with this evil congregation which murmur against me?' Numb xiv 27. May not God justly say, How long shall I bear with this wicked person, who, when anything falls out cross, murmurs against me? 'Say unto them, As truly as I live, saith the Lord, as ye have spoken in mine ears, so will I do to you;' ver 28. God swears against a murmurer, 'As I live;' and what will he do as he lives? 'Your carcases shall fall in this wilderness;' ver 29. You see how provoking a discontented quarrelsome spirit is to God; it

N

may cost men their lives, nay, their souls. God sent fiery serpents among the people for their murmuring. 1 Cor x 10. He may send worse than fiery serpents, he may send hell fire.

(20) Consider how much God bears at our hand, and shall not we be content to bear something at his hand? It would tire the patience of angels to bear with us one day. 'The Lord is longsuffering to us-ward.' 2 Pet iii 9. How often we offend in our eye by envious impure glances, and in our tongues by rash censuring, but God passes by many injuries, and bears with us! Should the Lord punish us every time we offend, he might draw his sword every day. Shall he bear so much at our hands, and can we bear with nothing at his hand? Shall he be patient with us, and we impatient with him? Shall he be meek, and we murmur? Shall he endure our sins, and shall not we endure his strokes? Oh, let us say, 'Thy will be done.' Lord, thou hast been the greatest sufferer, thou hast borne more from me than I can from thee.

(21) Consider that submitting our wills to God in affliction disappoints Satan of his hope, and quite spoils his design. The devil's end is in all our afflictions to make us sin. The reason why Satan smote Job in his body and estate was to perplex his mind, and put him into a passion; he hoped that Job would have been discontented, and in a fit of anger, not only have cursed his birthday, but cursed his God. But Job, lying at God's feet, and blessing him in affliction, disappointed Satan of his hope, and quite spoiled his plot. Had Job murmured, he had pleased Satan; had he fallen into a heat, and sparks of his anger had flown about, the devil had warmed himself at the fire of Job's passion; but Job quietly submitted, and blessed God. Thus Satan's design was frustrated, and he missed his intent. The devil has often deceived us; the best way to deceive him is by quiet submission to God in all things, saying, 'Thy will be done.'

(22) Consider that to the godly the nature of affliction is quite changed. To a wicked man it is a curse, the rod is turned into a serpent; affliction to him is but an effect of God's displeasure, the beginning of sorrow; but the nature of affliction is quite changed to a believer; it is by divine chemistry turned into a blessing; it is like poison corrected, which becomes a medicine; it is a love token, a badge of adoption, a preparation for glory. Should not this make us say, 'Thy will be done'? The poison of the affliction is gone; it is not hurtful, but healing. This has made the saints not only patient in affliction, but send forth thankfulness. When bells have been cast into the fire, they afterwards make a sweeter sound; so the godly, after they have been cast into the fire of affliction, sound forth God's praise. 'It is good for me that I have been afflicted.' Psa cxix 71. 'Blessed be the name of the Lord.' Job i 21.

(23) Consider how many good things we receive from God, and shall we not be content to receive some evil? 'Shall we receive good at the hand of God, and shall we not receive evil?' Job ii 10. In the Hebrew, shall we receive good from God, and not evil? This may make us say, 'Thy will be done.' How many blessings have we received at the hand of God's bounty? We have been bemiracled with mercy. What sparing, preventing, delivering mercy have we had! The honeycomb of mercy has continually dropped upon us. His mercies 'are new every morning.' Lam iii 23. Mercy comes in as constantly as the tide; nay, how many tides of mercies do we see in one day. We never feed, but mercy carves every bit to us; we never drink but in the golden cup of mercy; we never go abroad, but mercy sets a guard of angels about us; we never lie down in bed, but mercy draws the curtains of protection close about us. Shall we receive so many good things at the hand of God, and shall we not receive evil? Our mercies far outweigh our afflictions; for one affliction we have a thousand mercies. O then, let us submit to God, and say, 'Thy will be done.' The sea of God's mercy should swallow up a few drops of affliction.

(24) Consider that the conformity of our wills to God in affliction brings much honour to the gospel. An insubmissive Christian reproaches religion, as if it were not able to subdue an unruly spirit. It is weak physic which cannot purge out ill humours; and sure it is a weak gospel if it cannot master our discontent, and martyr our wills. Insubmissiveness is a reproach, but a cheerful resignation of our will to God sets a crown of honour upon the head of religion, it shows the power of the gospel, which can charm down the passions, and melt the will into God's will; therefore in Scripture, submissive patience is brought in as an adorning grace. 'Here is the patience of the saints.' Rev xiv 12.

(25) Consider the example of our Lord Jesus, how flexible and submissive was he to his Father! He who taught us this prayer, 'Thy will be done,' had learned it himself. Christ's will was perfectly tuned to his Father's will; it was the will of his Father that he should die for our sins, and he 'endured the cross.' Heb xii 2. It was a painful, shameful, cursed death; he suffered the very pains of hell equivalently, yet he willingly submitted. 'He opened not his mouth:' he opened his side when the blood ran out, but he opened not his mouth in repining; his will was resolved into the will of his Father. Isa liii 7. 'The cup which my Father hath given me shall I not drink it?' John xviii 11. Now, the more our wills are subject to God's will in affliction, the nearer we come to Christ our pattern. Is it not our prayer that we may be like Christ? By holy submission we imitate him; his will was melted into his Father's will.

(26) Consider that to submit our wills to God, is the way to have our own

will. Every one would be glad to have his will. The way to have our will is to resign it. God deals with us as we do with froward children; while we fret and quarrel, he will give us nothing, but when we are submissive, and say, 'Thy will be done,' he carves out mercy to us. The way to have our will is to submit to his. David brought his will to God's. 'Here am I, let him do to me as seemeth good unto him.' 2 Sam xv 26. After he resigned his will, he had his will. God brought him back to the ark and settled him again on his throne. 2 Sam xix. Many a parent who has had a dear child sick, when he could bring his will to part with it, has had his child restored. Nothing is lost by referring our will to God, the Lord takes it kindly from us, and it is the only way to have our will.

(27) Consider that we may the more cheerfully surrender our souls to God when we die, when we have surrendered our will to God while we live. Our blessed Saviour had all along submitted his will to God. There was but one will between God the Father and Christ. Christ in his lifetime having given up his will to his Father, at death cheerfully gave up his soul to him. 'Father, into thy hands I commend my spirit.' Luke xxiii 46. You that resign up your wills to God, may at the hour of death comfortably bequeath your souls to him.

[2] The second means to bring our will to God in affliction is, to study his will.

(1) It is a sovereign will. He has a supreme right and dominion over his creatures, to dispose of them as he pleases. A man may do with his own as he lists. 'Is it not lawful for me to do what I will with mine own?' Matt xx 15. A man may cut his own timber as he will. God's sovereignty may cause submission; he may do with us as he sees good. He is not accountable to any creature for what he does. 'He giveth not account of any of his matters.' Job xxxiii 13. Who shall call God to account? Who is higher than the highest? Eccl v 8. What man or angel dare summon God to his bar? 'He giveth not account of any of his matters.' God will take an account of our carriage towards him, but he will give no account of his carriage towards us. He has an absolute jurisdiction over us, the remembrance of which, as a sovereign will, to do with us what he pleases, may silence all discontents, and charm down all unruly passions. We are not to dispute, but to submit.

(2) God's will is wise. He knows what is conducive to the good of his people, therefore submit. 'The Lord is a God of judgment,' that is, he is able to judge what is best for us; therefore rest in his wisdom and acquiesce in his will. Isa xxx 18. We rest in the wisdom of a physician; we are content he should scarify and let blood, because he is judicious, and knows what is most conducive to our health. If the pilot be skilful, the passenger says, 'Let him

alone; he knows best how to steer the ship.' Shall we not rest in God's wisdom? Did we but study how wisely he steers all occurrences, and how he often brings us to heaven by a cross wind, it would much quiet our spirits, and make us say, 'Thy will be done.' God's will is guided by wisdom. Should he sometimes let us have our will, we should undo ourselves; did he let us carve for ourselves, we should choose the worst piece. Lot chose Sodom because it was well watered, and was as the garden of the Lord, but God rained fire upon it out of heaven. Gen xiii 10; Gen xix 24.

(3) God's will is just. 'Shall not the judge of all the earth do right?' Gen xviii 25. God's will is *regula et mensura* [rule and measure], it is the rule of justice. The wills of men are corrupt, therefore unfit to give law; but God's will is a holy and unerring will, which may cause submission. Psa xcvii 2. God may cross, but he cannot wrong us; severe he may be, not unjust; therefore we must strike sail, and say, 'Thy will be done.'

(4) God's will is good and gracious. It promotes our interest: if it be his will to afflict us, he shall make us say at last, it was good for us that we were afflicted. His flail shall only thresh off our husks. That which is against our will shall not be against our profit. Let us study what a good will God's is, and we shall say, *fiat voluntas*, 'Thy will be done.'

(5) God's will is irresistible. We may oppose it, but we cannot hinder it. The rising wave cannot stop the ship when it is in full sail, so the rising up of our will against God cannot stop the execution of his will. 'Who hath resisted his will?' Rom ix 19. Who can stay the chariot of the sun in its full career? Who can hinder the progress of God's will? Therefore it is in vain to contest with God; his will shall take place: there is no way to overcome him but by lying at his feet.

[3] The means of submission to God in affliction is, to get a gracious heart. All the rules and helps in the world will do but little good till grace is infused. The bowl must have a good bias, or it will not run according to our desire; so till God put a new bias of grace into the soul, which inclines the will, it never submits to him. Grace renews the will, and it must be renewed before it be subdued. Grace teaches self-denial, and we can never submit our will till we deny it.

[4] A fourth means is to labour to have our covenant interest cleared, to know that God is our God. 'This God is our God.' Psa xlviii 14. He whose faith flourishes in assurance, that can say God is his, will say, 'Thy will be done.' A wicked man may say, 'God has laid this affliction upon me, and I cannot help it;' but a believer says, 'My God has done it, and I will submit.' He who can call God his, knows God loves him as he loves Christ, and designs his salvation; therefore he will, with Paul, take pleasure in re-

proaches. 2 Cor xii 10. In every adverse providence yield to God, as the wax to the impression of the seal.

[5] Another means to submission to God in affliction is, to get a humble spirit. A proud man will never stoop to God; he will rather break than bend; but when the heart is humble, the will is pliable. What a vast difference was there between Pharaoh and Eli! Pharaoh cried out, 'Who is the Lord that I should obey his voice?' Exod v 2. But Eli said, 'It is the Lord, let him do what seemeth him good.' 1 Sam iii 18. See the difference between a heart that is swelled with pride, and that which is ballasted with humility! Pharaoh said, 'Who is the Lord?' Eli, 'It is the Lord.' A humble soul has a deep sense of sin, he sees how he has provoked God, he wonders he is not in hell; therefore, whatever God inflicts, he knows it is less than his iniquities deserve, which makes him say, 'Lord, thy will be done.' O, get into a humble posture. The will is never flexible till the heart is humble.

[6] Another means is to get your hearts loosened from things below. Be crucified to the world. Whence children's frowardness but when you take away their playthings? When we love the things of the world, and God takes them away us, we grow froward and insubmissive to his will. Jonah was exceedingly glad of the gourd; and when God smote it, he grew froward, and because God had killed his gourd, he said, Kill me too. Jonah iv 8. He who is a lover of the world, can never pray this prayer heartily: 'Thy will be done;' his heart boils with anger against God; and when the world is gone, his patience is gone too. Get mortified affections to these sublunary things.

[7] A further means for submission to God's will is to get some good persuasion that your sin is pardoned. *Feri, Domine, feri, quia peccata mea condonata sunt:* 'Smite, Lord, smite where thou wilt,' said Luther, 'because my sins are pardoned.' Pardon of sin is a crowning blessing. Has God forgiven my sin? I will bear anything; I will not murmur but admire; I will not complain of the burden of affliction, but bless God for removing the burden of sin. The pardoned soul says this prayer heartily, 'Thy will be done.' Lord, use thy pruning-knife, so long as thou wilt not come with thy bloody axe to hew me down.

[8] Another means is, if we would have our wills submit to God, not to look so much on the dark side of the cloud as the light side; that is, let us not look so much on the smart of affliction as the good. It is bad to pore all on the smart, as it is bad for sore eyes to look too much on the fire; but we should look on the good of affliction. Samson not only looked on the lion's carcase, but on the honeycomb within it. 'He turned aside to see the carcase

of the lion, and behold, there was honey in the carcase.' Judges xiv 8. Affliction is the frightful lion, but see what honey there is in it. It humbles, purifies, fills us with the consolations of God; there is honey in the belly of the lion. Could we but look upon the benefit of affliction, stubbornness would be turned into submissiveness, and we should say, 'Thy will be done.'

[9] As a further means, let us pray to God that he would calm our spirits and conquer our wills. It is no easy thing to submit to God in affliction. There will be risings of the heart; therefore let us pray that what God inflicts righteously, we may bear patiently. Prayer is the best spell or charm against impatience. It does to the heart what Christ did to the sea when it was tempestuous, he rebuked the wind, and there was a great calm. So, when passions are up, and the will is apt to mutiny against God, prayer makes a gracious calm in the soul. Prayer does to the heart what sponge does to the cannon: when hot, it cools it.

[10] Another means, if we would submit to God's will in affliction, is to put a good interpretation upon God's dealings, and take all he does in the best sense. We are apt to misconstrue God's dealings, and put a bad interpretation upon them, as Israel did. 'Why have ye brought up the congregation of the Lord into this wilderness, that we should die there?' Numb xx 4. God has brought affliction upon us, we say, because he hates us, and intends to destroy us; and such hard thoughts of God cause sullenness and stubbornness. Oh, let us make a fair and candid interpretation of providence. Does God afflict us? Say, perhaps he intends us mercy in this: he will try us whether we will love him in afflictions; he is about to mortify some sin, or exercise some grace; he smites the body that he may save the soul. Could we put such a good meaning upon God's dealings, we should say, 'Thy will be done.' 'Let the righteous smite me; it shall be a kindness; it shall be an excellent oil, which shall not break my head.' Psa cxli 5.

[11] The last means, if you would submit to God in affliction, is to believe that the present condition is best for you. We are not competent judges. We fancy it is best to have ease and plenty, and have the rock pour out rivers of oil; but God sees affliction to be best. He sees our souls thrive best upon the bare common. The fall of the leaf is the spring of our grace. Could we believe that condition to be best which God carves out to us, the quarrel would soon be at an end, and we should sit down satisfied with what he does, and say, 'Thy will be done.'

The Fourth Petition in the Lord's Prayer

'Give us this day our daily bread.' Matt vi 11

IN this petition there are two things observable – the order, and the matter.

I. *First, we pray, 'Hallowed be thy name, thy kingdom come, thy will be done,' before we pray, 'Give us this day our daily bread.'* God's glory ought to weigh down all before it; it must be preferred before our dearest concerns. Christ preferred his Father's glory before his own as he was man. 'I honour my Father, I seek not mine own glory.' John viii 49, 50. God's glory is that which is most dear to him; it is the apple of his eye; all his riches lie here. As Micah said, 'What have I more' (Judges xviii 24), so I may say of God's glory, what has he more? His glory is the most orient pearl of his crown, which he will not part with. 'My glory will I not give to another.' Isa xlii 8. God's glory is more worth than heaven, more worth than the salvation of all men's souls; better kingdoms be demolished, better men and angels be annihilated, than God lose any part of his glory. We are to prefer God's glory before our nearest concerns; but before we prefer God's glory to our private concerns, we must be born again. The natural man seeks his own secular interest before God's glory. He is 'of the earth, earthly.' John iii 31. Let him have peace and trading, let the rock pour out rivers of oil, and let God's glory go which way it will, he minds it not. A worm cannot fly and sing as a lark; so a natural man, whose heart creeps upon the earth, cannot admire God, or advance his glory, as a man elevated by grace does.

Use. For trial. Do we prefer God's glory before our private concerns? *Minus te amat qui aliquid tecum amat, quod non propter te amat* [He loves thee too little, who loves anything as well as thee which he does not love for thy sake]. Augustine. (1) Do we prefer God's glory before our own credit? *Fama pari passu ambulat cum vita* [Credit keeps pace with life]. Credit is a jewel highly valued; like precious ointment, it casts a fragrant smell; but God's glory must be dearer than credit or applause. We must be willing to have our credit trampled upon, that God's glory may be raised higher. The apostles rejoiced 'that they were counted worthy to suffer shame for his name;' that they were graced so far as to be disgraced for Christ. Acts v 41. (2) Do we prefer God's glory before our relations? Relations are dear, they are of our own flesh and bones; but God's glory must be dearer. 'If any man

come to me, and hate not his father and mother, he cannot be my disciple.'
Luke xiv 26. Here *odium in suos* [hatred towards one's own kin] is *pietas in
Deum* [devotion towards God]. 'If my friends,' says Jerome, 'should persuade me to deny Christ, if my wife should hang about my neck, if my
mother should show me her breasts that gave me suck, I would trample
upon all and flee to Christ.' (3) We must prefer God's glory before estate.
Gold is but shining dust: God's glory must weigh heavier. If it come to this,
I cannot keep my place of profit, but God's glory will be eclipsed, I must
rather suffer in my estate than God's glory should suffer. Heb x 34. (4) We
must prefer God's glory before our life. 'They loved not their lives unto the
death.' Rev xii 11. Ignatius called his fetters his spiritual jewels; he wore
them as a chain of pearl. Gordius the martyr, said, 'It is to my loss, if you
bate me anything of my sufferings. This argues grace to be growing and
elevated in a high degree. Who but a soul inflamed with love to God can
set God highest on the throne, and prefer him above all private concerns?

II. *The second thing in the petition is, the matter of it.* 'Give us this day our
daily bread.' The sum of this petition is, that God would give us such a
competency in outward things as he sees most excellent for us. It is much like
that prayer of Agur, 'Feed me with food convenient for me;' give me a
viaticum, a bait by the way, enough to bear my charges till I come to heaven,
and it suffices. Prov xxx 8. Let me explain the words, 'Give us this day our
daily bread.' The good things of this life are the gifts of God; he is the donor
of all our blessings. 'Give us.' Not faith only, but food is the gift of God; not
daily grace only is from God, but 'daily bread;' every good thing comes
from God. 'Every good gift is from above, and cometh down from the
Father of lights.' James i 17. Wisdom is the gift of God. 'His God doth
instruct him to discretion.' Isa xxviii 26. Riches are the gift of God. 'I will
give thee riches.' 2 Chron i 12. Peace is the gift of God. 'He maketh peace
in thy borders.' Psa cxlvii 14. Health, which is the cream of life, is the gift
of God. 'I will restore health unto thee.' Jer xxx 17. Rain is the gift of
God. 'Who giveth rain upon the earth.' Job v 10. All comes from God;
he makes the corn to grow, and the herbs to flourish.

(1) See our own poverty and indigence. We all live upon alms and upon
free gifts – 'Give us this day.' All we have is from the hand of God's royal
bounty; we have nothing but what he gives us out of his storehouse; we
cannot have one bit of bread but from God. The devil persuaded our first
parents, that by disobeying God, they should 'be as gods;' but we may now
see what goodly gods we are, that we have not a bit of bread to put in our
mouths unless God give it us. Gen iii 5. That is a humbling consideration.

(2) Is all a gift? Then we are to seek every mercy from God by prayer.

'Give us this day.' The tree of mercy will not drop its fruit unless shaken by the hand of prayer. Whatever we have, if it do not come in the way of prayer, it does not come in the way of love; it is given, as Israel's quails, in anger. If everything be a gift, we do not deserve it, we are not fit for this alms. And must we go to God for every mercy? How wicked are they, who, instead of going to God for food when they want, go to the devil, and make a compact with him; and if he will help them to a livelihood, they will give him their souls? Better starve than go to the devil for provender. I wish there were none in our age guilty of this, who, when they are in want, use indirect means for a livelihood; they consult with witches, who are the devil's oracles, whose end will be fearful, as that of Saul was, whom the Lord is said to have killed, because he asked counsel at a familiar spirit.

(3) If all be a gift, then it is not a debt, and we cannot say to God as that creditor who said, 'Pay me that thou owest.' Matt xviii 28. Who can make God a debtor, or do any act that is obliging and meritorious? Whatever we receive from God is a gift; we can give nothing to him but what he has given to us. 'All things come of thee, and of thine own have we given thee.' 1 Chron xxix 14. David and his people offered to the building of God's house gold and silver, but they offered nothing but what God had given them. 'Of thine own have we given thee.' If we love God, it is he that has given us a heart to love him; if we praise him, he both gives us the organ of tongue, and puts it in tune; if we give alms to others, he has given alms to us first, so that we may say, 'We offer, O Lord, of thine own to thee.' Is all of gift, how absurd, then, is the doctrine of merit? That was a proud speech of the friar, who said, *redde mihi Vitam Eternam quam debes*; give me, Lord, eternal life, which thou owest me. We cannot deserve a bit of bread, much less a crown of glory. If all be a gift, then merit is exploded, and shut out of doors.

(4) If all be a gift, then take notice of God's goodness. There is nothing in us that can deserve or requite God's kindness; yet such is the sweetness of his nature, that he gives us rich provision, and feeds us with the finest of the wheat. Pindar says it was an opinion of the people of Rhodes that Jupiter rained down gold upon the city. God has rained down golden mercies upon us; he is upon the giving hand. Observe three things in his giving:

[1] He is not weary of giving; the springs of mercy are ever running. He not only dispensed blessings in former ages, but he gives gifts to us; as the sun not only enriches the world with its morning light, but keeps light for the meridian. The honeycomb of God's bounty is still dropping.

[2] He delights in giving. 'He delighteth in mercy.' Mic vii 18. As the

mother delights to give the child the breast, God loves that we should have the breast of mercy in our mouth.

[3] God gives to his very enemies. Who will send in provisions to his enemies? Men spread nets for their enemies, God spreads a table. The dew drops on the thistle as well as the rose; the dew of God's bounty drops upon the worst. God puts bread in the mouths that are opened against him. Oh, the royal bounty of God! 'The goodness of God endureth continually.' Psa lii 1. He puts jewels upon swinish sinners, and feeds them every day.

(5) If all be a gift, see the odious ingratitude of men who sin against their giver! God feeds them, and they fight against him; he gives them bread, and they give him affronts. How unworthy is this! Should we not cry shame of him who had a friend always feeding him with money, and yet he should betray and injure him? Thus ungratefully do sinners deal with God; they not only forget his mercies, but abuse them. 'When I had fed them to the full, they then committed adultery.' Jer v 7. Oh, how horrid is it to sin against a bountiful God! – to strike the hands that relieve us! How many make a dart of God's mercies and shoot at him! He gives them wit, and they serve the devil with it; he gives them strength, and they waste it among harlots; he gives them bread to eat, and they lift up the heel against him. 'Jeshurun waxed fat and kicked.' Deut xxxii 15. They are like Absalom, who, as soon as David his father kissed him, plotted treason against him. 2 Sam xv 10. They are like the mule who kicks the dam after she has given it milk. Those who sin against their giver, and abuse God's royal favours, the mercies of God will come in as witnesses against them. What smoother than oil? But if it be heated, what more scalding? What sweeter than mercy? But if it be abused, what more dreadful? It turns to fury.

(6) If God gives us all, let his giving excite us to thanksgiving. He is the founder and donor of all our blessings, and should have all our acknowledgments. 'Unto the place from whence the rivers come, thither they return again.' Eccl i 7. All our gifts come from God, and to him must all our praises return. We are apt to burn incense to our own drag, to attribute all we have to our own second causes. Hab i 16.

[1] Our own skill and industry. God is the giver; he gives daily bread. Psa cxxxvi 25; he gives riches. 'It is he that giveth thee power to get wealth.' Deut viii 18.

Or [2], We often ascribe the praise to second causes and forget God. If friends have bestowed an estate, we look at them and admire them, but not God who is the great giver; as if one should be thankful to the steward, and never take notice of the master of the family that provides all. Oh, if God gives all, our eye-sight, our food, our clothing, let us sacrifice the chief praise to him; let not God be a loser by his mercies. Praise is a more illustrious part of God's worship. Our wants may send us to prayer, nature may make us beg daily bread; but it shows a heart full of ingenuity and grace to be rendering praises to God. In petition we act like men, in praise we act like angels. Does God sow seeds of mercy? Let thankfulness be the crop we bring forth. We are called the temples of God, and where should God's praises be sounded forth but in his temples? 1 Cor iii 16; 'While I live will I praise the Lord, I will sing praises unto my God while I have any being.' Psa cxlvi 2. God gives us daily bread, let us give him daily praise. Thankfulness to our donor is the best policy; there is nothing lost by it. To be thankful for one mercy is the way to have more. Musicians love to sound their trumpets where there is the best echo, and God loves to bestow his mercies where there is the best echo of praise. Offering the calves of our lips is not enough, but we must show our thankfulness by improving the gifts which God gives us, and as it were putting them out to use. God gives us an estate, and we honour the Lord with our substance. Prov iii 9. He gives us the staff of bread, and we lay out the strength we receive by it in his service; this is to be thankful; and that we may be thankful, let us be humble. Pride stops the current of gratitude. A proud man will never be thankful; he looks upon all he has either to be of his own procuring or deserving. Let us see all we have is God's gift, and how unworthy we are to receive the least favour; and this will make us much in doxology and gratitude; we shall be silver trumpets sounding forth God's praise.

[1] Thus we argue from the word *Give*, that the good things of this life are the gifts of God; he is the founder and donor; and that it is not unlawful to pray for temporal things. We may pray for daily bread. 'Feed me with food convenient for me.' Prov xxx 8. We may pray for health. 'O Lord, heal me; for my bones are vexed.' Psa vi 2. As these are in themselves good things, so they are useful for us; they are as needful for preserving the comfort of life as oil is needful for preserving the lamp from going out. Only let me insert two things:

(1) There is a great difference between praying for temporal things and spiritual. In praying for spiritual things we must be absolute. When we pray for pardon of sin, and the favour of God, and the sanctifying graces of the Spirit, which are indispensably necessary to salvation, we must take no denial; but when we pray for temporal things, our prayers must be limited; we must pray conditionally, so far as God sees them good for us. He sometimes sees cause to withhold temporal things from us: when they would be snares, and draw our hearts from him; therefore we should pray for these things with submission to God's will. It was Israel's sin that they would be

peremptory and absolute in their desire for temporal things; God's bill of fare did not please them, they must have dainties. 'Who shall give us flesh to eat?' Numb xi 18. God has given them manna, he fed them with a miracle from heaven, but their wanton palates craved more: they must have quails. God let them have their desire, but they had sour sauce to their quails. 'While their meat was yet in their mouths, the wrath of God came upon them and slew them.' Psa lxxviii 31. Rachel was importunate in her desires for a child. 'Give me children, or I die;' God let her have a child, but it was a *Ben-oni*, a son of my sorrow; it cost her her life in bringing forth. Gen xxx 1; Gen xxxv 18. We must pray for outward things with submission to God's will, else they come in anger.

(2) When we pray for things pertaining to this life, we must desire temporal things for spiritual ends; we must desire these things to be as helps in our journey to heaven. If we pray for health, it must be that we may improve this talent of health for God's glory, and may be fitter for his service; if we pray for a competency of estate, it must be for a holy end, that we may be kept from the temptations which poverty usually exposes to, and that we may be in a better capacity to sow the golden seeds of charity, and relieve such as are in want. Temporal things must be prayed for for spiritual ends. Hannah prayed for a child, but it was for this end, that her child might be devoted to God. 'O Lord, if thou wilt remember me, and wilt give unto thine handmaid a man child, then I will give him unto the Lord all the days of his life.' 1 Sam i 11. Many pray for outward things only to gratify their sensual appetites, as the ravens cry for food. Psa cxlvii 9. To pray for outward things only to satisfy nature, is to cry rather like ravens than Christians. We must have a higher end in our prayers; we must aim at heaven while we are praying for earth. Must we pray for temporal things for spiritual ends, that we may be fitter to serve God? Then how wicked are they who beg temporal mercies that they may be more enabled to sin against God! 'Ye ask that ye may consume it upon your lusts.' James iv 3. One man is sick, and he prays for health that he may be among his cups and harlots; another prays for an estate; he would not only have his belly filled, but his barns; and he would be rich that he may raise his name, or that, having more power in his hand, he may now take a fuller revenge on his enemies. It is impiety joined with impudence to pray to God to give us temporal things that we may be the better enabled to serve the devil.

If we are to pray for temporal things, how much more for spiritual? If we are to pray for bread, how much more for the bread of life? If for oil, how much more for the oil of gladness? If to have our hunger satisfied, much more should we pray to have our souls saved. Alas! what if God should hear our prayers, and grant us these temporal things and no more, what were we the better? What is it to have food and want grace? What is it to have the back clothed and the soul naked? To have a south land, and want the living springs in Christ's blood, what comfort could that be? O therefore let us be earnest for spiritual mercies! Lord, not only feed me, but sanctify me; give me rather a heart full of grace than a house full of gold. If we are to pray for daily bread, the things of this life, much more for the things of the life that is to come.

Some may say we have an estate already, and what need we pray, 'Give us daily bread'?

Supposing we have a plentiful estate, yet we need make the petition, 'Give us daily bread;' and that upon a double account.

(1) That we may have a blessing upon our food, and all that we enjoy. 'I will bless her provision.' Psa cxxxii 15. 'Man shall not live by bread alone, but by every word that proceedeth out of the mouth of God.' Matt iv 4. What is that but a word of blessing? Though the bread is in our hand, yet the blessing is in God's hand, and it must be fetched out of his hand by prayer. Well, therefore, may rich men pray, 'Give us our bread,' let it be seasoned with a blessing. If God should withhold a blessing, nothing we have would do us good; our clothes would not warm us, our food would not nourish us. 'He gave them their request, but sent leanness into their soul;' that is, they pined away, and their meat did not nourish them. Psa cvi 15. If God should withhold a blessing, what we eat would turn to bad humours, and hasten death. If God do not bless our riches, they will do us more hurt than good. 'Riches kept for the owners thereof to their hurt.' Eccl v 13. So that, granting we have plentiful estates, yet we had need pray, 'Give us our bread;' let us have a blessing of what we have.

(2) Though we have estates, yet we had need pray, *Give*, that we may hereby engage God to continue these comforts to us. How many casualties may fall out! How many have had corn in their barn, and a fire has come on a sudden and consumed all! How many have had losses at sea, and great estates boiled away to nothing! 'I went out full, and the Lord hath brought me home again empty.' Ruth i 21. Therefore, though we have estates, yet we had need pray, 'Give us;' Lord, give us a continuance of these comforts, that they may not, before we are aware, take wings and fly from us. So much for the first word in the petition, Give.

[2] Secondly, *us*. 'Give us.'

Why do we pray in the plural, 'Give us'? Why is it not said, give me?

To show that we are to have a public spirit in prayer. We must not only pray for ourselves, but others. Both the law of God and the law of love bind us to this, we must love our neighbour as ourselves; therefore we must pray for them as well as ourselves. Every good Christian has a fellow-feeling of the wants and miseries of others, and he prays God would extend his bounty to them; especially he prays for the saints. 'Praying always for all saints.' Eph vi 18. These are children of the family.

Use 1. Should we have a public spirit in prayer? It reproves narrow-spirited men who move within their own sphere only; who look only at themselves, and mind not the case of others; who leave others out of their prayers; if they have daily bread, they care not though others starve; if they are clothed, they care not though others go naked. Christ taught us to pray for others, to say, 'Give us;' but selfish persons are shut up within themselves, as the snail in the shell, and never speak a word in prayer for others. These have no commiseration or pity; they are like Judas, whose bowels fell out.

Use 2. Let us pray for others as well as for ourselves. *Vir bonus aliis prodest aeque ac sibi* [A good man benefits others as much as himself]. Spiders work only for themselves, but bees for the good of others. The more excellent anything is, the more it operates for the good of others. Springs refresh others with their crystal streams; the sun enlightens others with its golden beams: the more a Christian is ennobled with grace, the more he besieges heaven with his prayers for others. If we are members of the mystic body, we cannot but have a sympathy with others in their wants; and this sympathy would lead us to pray for them. David had a public spirit in prayer. 'Do good, O Lord, unto those that be good.' Psa cxxv 4. Though he begins the Psalm with prayer for himself, 'Have mercy upon me, O God,' yet he ends the Psalm with prayer for others. 'Do good in thy good pleasure unto Zion.' Psa li 1, 18.

Use 3. It is matter of comfort to the godly, who are but low in the world, that they have the prayers of God's people for them; who pray not only for the increase of their faith, but their food, that God will give them 'daily bread.' He is like to be rich who has several stocks going; so they are in a likely way to thrive who have the prayers of the saints going for them in several parts of the world.

[3] The third word in the petition is 'This day.' We pray not give us bread for a month or a year, but a day. 'Give us this day.'

Is it not lawful to lay up for the future? Does not the apostle say, that he who provides not for his family, 'is worse than an infidel'? 1 Tim v 8.

True, it is lawful to lay up for posterity; but our Saviour has taught us to pray, 'Give us this day our bread,' for two reasons:

(1) That we should not have anxious care for the future. We should not set our wits upon the tenter, or torment ourselves how to lay up great estates; if we do *vivere in diem* [live for the day], if we have but enough to supply for the present, it should suffice. 'Give us this day:' 'Take no thought for the morrow.' Matt vi 34. God fed Israel with manna in the wilderness, and he fed them from hand to mouth. Sometimes all their manna was spent; and if anyone had asked them where they would have their breakfast next morning, they would have said, 'Our care is only for the day: God will rain down what manna we need. If we have bread to-day, let us not distrust God's providence for the future.'

(2) Our Saviour will have us pray, 'Give us bread this day,' to teach us to live every day as if it were our last. We are not to pray, Give us bread to-morrow, because we do not know whether we shall live till to-morrow; but, 'Lord, Give us this day;' it may be the last day we shall live, and then we shall need no more.

If we pray for bread for a day only, then you who have great estates have cause to be thankful. You have more than you pray for; you pray but for bread for one day, and God has given you enough to suffice all your life. What a bountiful God do you serve! Two things should make rich men thankful. (1) God gives them more than they deserve. (2) He gives them more than they pray for.

[4] The fourth thing in the petition is, 'Our bread.'

Why is it called 'Our bread,' when it is not ours, but God's?

(1) We must understand it in a qualified sense; it is our bread, being gotten by honest industry. There are two sorts of bread that cannot properly be called our bread: the bread of idleness and the bread of violence.

The bread of idleness. 'She eateth not the bread of idleness.' Prov xxxi 27. An idle person lives at another body's cost. 'His hands refuse to labour.' Prov xxi 25. We must not be as the drones, which eat the honey that other bees have brought into the hive. If we eat the bread of idleness, it is not our own bread. 'There are some which walk disorderly, working not at all; such we command that they work, and eat their own bread.' 2 Thess iii 11, 12. The apostle gives this hint, that such as live idly do not eat their own bread.

The bread of violence. We cannot call that 'our bread' which is taken away from others; that which is gotten by stealth or fraud, or any manner of extortion, is not 'our bread,' it belongs to another. He who is a bird of prey, who takes away the bread of the widow and fatherless, eats the bread which is not his, nor can he pray for a blessing upon it. Can he pray God to bless that which he has gotten unjustly.

(2) It is called our bread by virtue of our title to it. There is a twofold title to bread. [1] A spiritual title. In and by Christ we have a right to the creature, and may call it 'our bread.' As we are believers we have the best title to earthly things, we hold all *in capite* [in chief]. 'All things are yours;' by what title? 'ye are Christ's.' 1 Cor iii 23. [2] A civil title, which the law confers on us. To deny men a civil right to their possessions, and make all common, opens the door to anarchy and confusion.

See the privilege of believers. They have both a spiritual and a civil right to what they possess. They who can say, 'our Father,' can say 'our bread.' Wicked men that have a legal right to what they possess, but not a covenant-right; they have it by providence, not by promise; with God's leave, not with his love. Wicked men are in God's eye no better than usurpers; all they have, their money and land, is like cloth taken up at the draper's, which is not paid for; but the sweet privilege of believers is, that they can say, 'our bread.' Christ being theirs, all is theirs. Oh, how sweet is every bit of bread dipped in Christ's blood! How well does that meat relish, which is a pledge and earnest of more! The meal in the barrel is an earnest of our angels' food in paradise. It is the privilege of saints to have a right to earth and heaven.

[5] The fifth and last thing in this petition is, the thing we pray for, 'daily bread.'

What is meant by bread?

Bread here, by a synecdoche, *species pro genere* [the particular for the whole class], is put for all the temporal blessings of this life, food, fuel, clothing, &c. *Quicquid nobis conducit ad bene esse* [Whatever serves for our well-being]. Augustine. Whatever may serve for necessity or sober delight.

Learn to be contented with the allowance God gives. If we have bread and a competence of outward things, let us rest satisfied. We pray but for bread, 'Give us our daily bread;' we do not pray for superfluities, nor for quails or venison, but for bread which may support life. Though we have not so much as others, so full a crop, so rich an estate, yet if we have the staff of bread to keep us from falling, let us be content. Most people are herein faulty. Though they pray that God would give them bread, as much as he sees expedient for them, yet they are not content with his allowance, but overgreedily covet more, and with the daughters of the horse-leech, cry, 'Give, give.' Prov xxx 15. This is a vice naturally ingrafted in us. Many pray Agur's first prayer, 'Give me not poverty,' but few pray his last prayer, 'Give me not riches.' Prov xxx 8. They are not content with 'daily bread,'

o

but have the dry dropsy of covetousness; they are still craving for more. 'Who enlargeth his desire as hell, and is as death, and cannot be satisfied.' Hab ii 5. There are, says Agur, four things that say it is not enough, the grave, the barren womb, the earth, the fire; and I may add a fifth thing, the heart of a covetous man. Prov xxx 15. Such as are not content with daily bread, but thirst insatiably after more, will break over the hedge of God's command; and to get riches will stick at no sin. *Cui nihil satis est, eidem nihil turpe* [The man for whom nothing is enough holds nothing shameful]. Tacitus. Therefore covetousness is called a radical vice. 'The root of all evil.' 1 Tim vi 10. *Quid non mortalia pectora cogis, auri sacra fames?* [Oh cursèd hunger for gold, to what dost thou not drive the hearts of men?] The Greek word for covetousness, *pleonexia*, signifies an inordinate desire of getting. Covetousness is not only in getting riches unjustly, but in loving them inordinately, which is a key that opens the door to all sin. It causes, (1) Theft. Achan's covetous humour made him steal the wedge of gold, which cleft asunder his soul from God. Josh vii 21. (2) It causes treason. What made Judas betray Christ? It was the thirty pieces of silver. Matt xxvi 15. (3) It produces murder. It was the inordinate love of the vineyard that made Ahab conspire Naboth's death. 1 Kings xxi 13. (4) It is the root of perjury. Men shall be covetous; and it follows, truce-breakers. 2 Tim iii 2, 3. Love of silver will make men take a false oath, and break a just oath. (5) It is the spring of apostasy. 'Demas hath forsaken me, having loved this present world.' 2 Tim iv 10. He not only forsook Paul's company, but his doctrine. Demas afterwards became a priest in an idol-temple, according to Dorotheus. (6) Covetousness will make men idolaters. 'Covetousness which is idolatry.' Col iii 5. Though the covetous man will not worship graven images in the church, yet he will worship the graven image in his coin. (7) Covetousness makes men give themselves to the devil. Pope Sylvester II sold his soul to the devil for a popedom. Covetous persons forget the prayer, 'Give us daily bread.' They are not content with that which may satisfy nature, but are insatiable in their desire. O let us take heed of this dry dropsy! 'Be content with such things as ye have.' Heb xiii 5. *Natura parvo dimittitur* [Nature is satisfied with little]. Seneca.

Use. That we may be content with 'daily bread,' that which God in his providence carves out to us, and not covet or murmur, take the following considerations:

(1) God can bless a little. 'He shall bless thy bread and thy water.' Exod. xxiii 25. A blessing puts sweetness into the least morsel of bread, it is like sugar in wine. 'I will bless her provision.' Psa cxxxii 15. Daniel, and the three children, ate pulse, which was a coarse fare, and yet they looked fairer

than those who ate of the king's meat. Dan i 12, 15. Whence was this? God infused a more than ordinary blessing into the pulse. His blessing was better than the king's venison. A piece of bread with God's love is angels' food.

(2) God, who gives us our allowance, knows what quantity of outward things is fittest for us. A smaller provision may be fitter for some; bread may be better than dainties. Everyone cannot bear a high condition, any more than a weak brain can bear heavy wine. Has any one a larger proportion of worldly things? God sees he can better manage such a condition; he can order his affairs with discretion, which perhaps another cannot. As he has a large estate, so he has a large heart to do good, which perhaps another has not. This should make us content with a shorter bill of fare. God's wisdom is what we must acquiesce in; he sees what is best for every one. That which is good for one, may be bad for another.

(3) In being content with daily bread, though less than others have, much grace is seen. All the graces act their part in a contented soul. As the holy ointment was made up of several spices, myrrh, cinnamon, and cassia, so contentment has in it a mixture of several graces. Exod xxx 23. There is faith. A Christian believes that God does all for the best. There is love, which thinks no evil, but takes all God does in good part. There is patience, submitting cheerfully to what God orders wisely. God is much pleased to see so many graces at once sweetly exercised, like so many bright stars shining in a constellation.

(4) To be content with daily bread, though but sparing, keeps us from many temptations which discontented persons fall into. When the devil sees a person just of Israel's humour, not content with manna, but must have quails, he says, Here is good fishing for me. Satan often tempts discontented ones to murmuring, and to unlawful means, cozening and defrauding; and he who increases an estate by indirect means, stuffs his pillow with thorns, so that his head will lie very uneasy when he comes to die. If you would be freed from the temptations which discontent exposes to, be content with such things as ye have, bless God for 'daily bread.'

(5) What a rare and admirable thing is it to be content with 'daily bread,' though it be coarse, and though there be but little of it! Though a Christian has but a *viaticum*, a little meal in the barrel, yet he has that which gives him content. What he has not in the cupboard, he has in the promise. That bit of bread he has is with the love of God, and that sauce makes it relish sweet. The little oil in the cruse is a pledge and earnest of the dainties he shall have in the kingdom of God, and this makes him content. What a rare and wonderful thing is this! It is no wonder to be content in heaven, when we

are at the fountain-head, and have all things we can desire; but to be content when God keeps us to short commons, and we have scarcely 'daily bread,' is a wonder indeed. When grace is crowning, it is no wonder to be content; but when grace is conflicting with straits, to be content is a glorious thing, and deserves the garland of praise.

(6) To make us content with 'daily bread,' though God straitens us in our allowance, think seriously of the danger there is in a high, prosperous condition. Some are not content with 'daily bread,' but desire to have their barns filled, and heap up silver as dust; which proves a snare to them. 'They that will be rich fall into a snare.' 1 Tim vi 9. Pride, idleness, wantonness, are three worms that usually breed of plenty. Prosperity often deafens the ear against God. 'I spake unto thee in thy prosperity, but thou saidst, I will not hear.' Jer xxii 21. Soft pleasures harden the heart. In the body, the more fat, the less blood in the veins, and the less spirits; so the more outward plenty, often the less piety. Prosperity has its honey, and also its sting; like the full of the moon, it makes many lunatic. The pastures of prosperity are rank and surfeiting. Anxious care is the *malus genius*, the evil spirit that haunts the rich man, and will not let him be quiet. When his chests are full of money, his heart is full of care, either how to manage or how to increase, or how to secure what he has gotten. Sunshine is pleasant, but sometimes it scorches. Should it not make us content with what allowance God gives, if we have daily bread, though not dainties? Think of the danger of prosperity! The spreading of a full table may be the spreading of a snare. Many have been sunk to hell with golden weights. The ferry-man takes in all passengers, that he may increase his fare, and sometimes to the sinking of his boat. 'They that will be rich fall into many hurtful lusts, which drown men in perdition.' 1 Tim vi 9. The world's golden sands are quicksands, which should make us take our daily bread, though it be but coarse, contentedly. What if we have less food, we have less snare; if less dignity, less danger. As we lack the rich provisions of the world, so we lack the temptations.

(7) If God keeps us to a spare diet, if he gives us less temporals, he has made it up in spirituals; he has given us the pearl of price, and the holy anointing. The pearl of price, the Lord Jesus, he is the quintessence of all good things. To give us Christ, is more than if God had given us all the world. He can make more worlds, but he has no more Christs to bestow; he is such a golden mine, that the angels cannot dig to the bottom. Eph iii 8. From Christ we may have justification, adoption, and coronation. The sea of God's mercy in giving us Christ, says Luther, should swallow up all our wants. God has anointed us with the graces, the holy unction of his Spirit. Grace is a seed of God, a blossom of eternity. The graces are the impressions of the divine nature, stars to enlighten us, spices to perfume us, diamonds to

enrich us; and if God has adorned the hidden man of the heart with these sacred jewels, it may well make us content, though we have but short commons, and that coarse too. God has given his people better things than corn and wine; he has given them that which he cannot give in anger, and which cannot stand with reprobation, and they may say as David, 'The lines are fallen unto me in pleasant places; yea, I have a goodly heritage.' Psa xvi 6. Didimus was a blind man, but very holy; Anthony asked him, if he was not troubled for the want of his eyes, and he told him he was; Anthony replied, 'Why are you troubled? You want that which flies and birds have, but you have that which angels have.' So I say to Christians, if God has not given you the purse, he has given you his Spirit. If you want that which rich men have, God has given you that which angels have, and are you not content?

(8) If you have but daily bread enough to suffice nature, be content. Consider it is not having abundance that always makes life comfortable; it is not a great cage that will make the bird sing. A competency may breed contentment, when having more may make one less content. A staff may help the traveller, but a bundle of staves will be a burden to him. A great estate may be like a long trailing garment, more burdensome than useful. Many that have great incomes and revenues have not so much comfort in their lives as some that go to hard labour.

(9) If you have less daily bread, you will have less account to give. The riches and honours of this world, like alchymy, make a great show, and, with their glistening, dazzle men's eyes; but they do not consider the great account they must give to God. 'Give an account of thy stewardship.' Luke xvi 2. What good hast thou done with thy estate? Hast thou, as a good steward, traded thy golden talents for God's glory? Hast thou honoured the Lord with thy substance? The greater revenues the greater reckonings. Let it quiet and content us, that if we have but little daily bread, our account will be less.

(10) You that have but a small competence in outward things, may be content to consider how much you look for hereafter. God keeps the best wine till last. What though now you have a small pittance, and are fed from hand to mouth? You look for an eternal reward, white robes, sparkling crowns, rivers of pleasure. A son is content though his father give him but now and then a little money, as long as he expects his father should settle all his land upon him at last; so if God give you but little at present, yet you look for that glory which eye hath not seen. The world is but a *diversorium*, a great inn. If God give you sufficient to pay for your charges in your inn, you may be content, you shall have enough when you come to your own country.

How may we be content, though God cut us short in these externals; though we have but little daily bread, and coarse?

(1) Think with yourselves that some have been much lower than you, who have been better than you. Jacob, a holy patriarch, went over Jordan with his staff, and lived in a mean condition a long time; he had the clouds for his canopy, and a stone for his pillow. Moses, who might have been rich, as some historians say, that Pharaoh's daughter adopted him for her son, because king Pharaoh had no heir, and so Moses was like to have come to the crown, yet leaving the honours of the court, in what a low, mean condition did he live in, when he went to Jethro, his father-in-law! Musculus, famous for learning and piety, was put to great straits, even to dig in a town ditch, and had scarcely daily bread, and yet was content! Nay, Christ, who was heir of all, for our sakes became poor. 2 Cor viii 9. Let all these examples make us content.

(2) Let us labour to have the interest cleared between God and our souls. He who can say, 'My God,' has enough to rock his heart quiet in the lowest condition. What can he want who has *El-Shaddai*, the all-sufficient God for his portion? Though the nether springs fail, yet he has the upper springs; though the bill of fare grow short, yet an interest in God is a pillar of support to us, and we may, with David, encourage ourselves in the Lord our God.

The Fifth Petition in the Lord's Prayer

'And forgive us our debts, as we forgive our debtors.' Matt vi 12

BEFORE I speak strictly to the words, I shall notice

[1] That in this prayer there is but one petition for the body, 'Give us our daily bread,' but two petitions for the soul, 'Forgive us our trespasses, lead us not into temptation, but deliver us from evil.' Observe hence, that we are to be more careful for our souls than for our bodies; more careful for grace than for daily bread; and more desirous to have our souls saved than our bodies fed. In the law, the weight of the sanctuary was twice as big as the common weight, to typify that spiritual things must be of far greater weight with us than earthly. The excellency of the soul may challenge our chief care about it.

(1) The soul is an immaterial substance; it is a heavenly spark, lighted by the breath of God. It is the more refined and spiritual part of man; it is of an angelic nature; it has some faint resemblance to God. The body is the more humble part, it is the cabinet only, though curiously wrought, but the soul is the jewel; it is near akin to angels; it is *capax beatitudinis*, capable of communion with God in glory.

(2) It is immortal; it never expires. It can act without the body. Though the body dissolve into dust, the soul lives. Luke xii 4. The essence of the soul is eternal; it has a beginning, but no end. Surely, then, if the soul be so ennobled and dignified, more care should be taken about it than the body. Hence, we make but one petition for the body, but two petitions for the soul.

Use 1. They are reproved who take more care for their bodies than their souls. The body is but the brutish part, yet they take more care, (1) About dressing their bodies than their souls. They put on the best clothes, are dressed in the richest garb; but care not how naked or undressed their souls are. They do not get the jewels of grace to adorn the inner man. (2) About feeding their bodies than their souls. They are caterers for the flesh, they make provision for the flesh, they have the best diet, but let their souls starve; as if one should feed his hawk, but let his child starve. The body must sit in the chair of state, but the soul, that princely thing, is made a lackey to run on the devil's errands.

Use 2. Let us be more careful for our souls. *Omnia si perdas, animam servare memento* [If you lose everything, remember to keep your soul]. If it be well with the soul, it shall be well with the body. If the soul be gracious, the body shall be glorious, for it shall shine like Christ's body. Therefore, it is wisdom to look chiefly to the soul, because in saving the soul we secure the happiness of the body. And we cannot show our care for our souls more than by improving all seasons for their good; as reading, praying, hearing, and meditating. Oh, look to the main chance; let the soul be chiefly tended! The loss of the soul would be fatal. Other losses may be made up again. If one loses his health, he may recover it again; if he loses his estate, he may make it up again; but if he lose his soul, the loss is irreparable. The merchant who ventures all he has in one ship, if that be lost, is quite ruined.

[2] As soon as Christ had said, 'Give us daily bread,' he adds, 'and forgive us.' He joins the petition of forgiveness of sin immediately to the other of daily bread, to show us that though we have daily bread, yet all is nothing without forgiveness. If our sins be not pardoned, we can take but little comfort in our food. As a man that is condemned takes little comfort from the meat you bring him in prison, without a pardon; so, though we have daily bread, yet it will do us no good unless sin be forgiven. What though we should have manna, which was called angels' food, though the rock should pour out rivers of oil, all is nothing unless sin be done away. When Christ had said, 'Give us our daily bread,' he presently added, and 'forgive us our trespasses.' Daily bread may satisfy the appetite, but forgiveness of sin satisfies the conscience.

Use 1. It condemns the folly of most people, who, if they have daily bread, the delicious things of this life, look no further; they are not solicitous for the pardon of sin. If they have that which feeds them, they look not after that which should crown them. Alas! you may have daily bread, and yet perish. The rich man in the gospel had daily bread, nay, he had dainties, he fared 'sumptuously every day;' but 'in hell he lift up his eyes.' Luke xvi 19, 23.

Use 2. Let us pray that God would not give us our portion in this life, that he would not put us off with daily bread, but that he would give forgiveness. This is the sauce that would make our bread relish the sweeter. A speech of Luther, *valde protestatus sum me nolle sic satiari ab illo.* I did solemnly protest that God should not put me off with outward things. Be not content with that which is common to the brute creatures, the dog or elephant, to have your hunger satisfied; but, besides daily bread, get pardon of sin. A drop of Christ's blood, or a dram of forgiving mercy, is infinitely more valuable than all the delights under the sun. Daily bread may make us live comfortably, but forgiveness of sins will make us die comfortably. I come now to the words of the petition, 'Forgive us our debts,' etc.

Here is a term given to sin, it is a debt; the confession of the debt, 'our debts;' a prayer, 'forgive us;' and a condition on which we desire forgiveness, 'as we forgive our debtors.'

I. *The first thing is the term given to sin; it is a debt.* That which is here called a debt is called sin. 'Forgive us our sins.' Luke xi 4. So, then, sin is a debt, and every sinner is a debtor. Sin is compared to a debt of ten thousand talents. Matt. xviii 24.

Why is sin called a debt?

Because it fitly resembles it. (1) A debt arises upon non-payment of money, or the not paying that which is one's due. We owe to God exact obedience, and not paying what is due, we are in debt. (2) In case of non-payment, the debtor goes to prison; so, by our sin, we become guilty, and are exposed to God's curse of damnation. Though he grants a sinner a reprieve for a time, yet he remains bound to eternal death if the debt be not forgiven.

In what sense is sin the worst debt?

(1) Because we have nothing to pay. If we could pay the debt, what need to pray, 'forgive us'? We cannot say, as he in the gospel, 'Have patience with me, and I will pay thee all;' we can pay neither principal nor interest. Adam made us all bankrupts. In innocence Adam had a stock of original righteousness to begin the world with, he could give God personal and perfect obedience; but, by his sin, he was quite broken, and beggared all his posterity. We have nothing to pay; all our duties are mixed with sin, and so we cannot pay God in current coin.

(2) Sin is the worst debt, because it is against an infinite majesty. An offence against the person of a king, is *crimen laesae majestatis* [the crime of high treason], it enhances and aggravates the crime. Sin wrongs God, and so is an infinite offence. The schoolmen say, *omne peccatum contra con-scientiam est quasi deicidium, i.e.*, every known sin strikes at the Godhead. The sinner would not only unthrone God, but ungod him, which makes the debt infinite.

(3) Sin is the worst debt, because it is not a single, but a multiplied debt. Forgive us 'our debts;' we have debt upon debt. 'Innumerable evils have compassed me about.' Psa xl 12. We may as well reckon all the drops in the sea, as reckon all our spiritual debts; we cannot tell how much we owe. A

man may know his other debts, but he cannot number his spiritual debts. Every vain thought is a sin. 'The thought of foolishness is sin.' Prov xxiv 9. And what swarms of vain thoughts have we! The first rising of corruption, though it never blossom into outward act, is a sin; then, 'who can understand his errors?' We do not know how much we owe to God.

(4) Sin is the worst debt; because it is an inexcusable debt in two respects; [1] There is no denying the debt. Other debts men may deny. If the money be not paid before witnesses, or if the creditor lose the bond, the debtor may say he owes him nothing; but there is no denying the debt of sin. If we say we have no sin, God can prove the debt. 'I will set [thy sins] in order before thine eyes.' Psa l 21. God writes down our debts in his book of remembrance, and his book, and the book of conscience exactly agree: so that the debt cannot be denied.

[2] There is no shifting off the debt. Other debts may be shifted off. We may get friends to pay them, but neither man nor angel can pay this debt for us. If all the angels in heaven should make a purse, they cannot pay one of our debts. In other debts men may get a protection, so that none can touch their persons, or sue them for it; but who shall give us a protection from God's justice? 'There is none that can deliver out of thine hand.' Job x 7. Indeed, the Pope pretends that his pardon shall be men's protection, and God's justice shall not sue them: but that is a forgery, and cannot be pleaded at God's tribunal. Other debts, if the debtor dies in prison, cannot be recovered: death frees him from debt; but if we die in debt to God, he knows how to recover it. As long as we have souls to distrain on, God will not lose his debt. Not the death of the debtor, but the death of the Surety, pays a sinner's debt. In other debts men may flee from their creditor, leave their country, and go into foreign parts, and the creditor cannot find them; but we cannot flee from God. He knows where to find all his debtors. 'Whither shall I flee from thy presence? If I take the wings of the morning, and dwell in the uttermost parts of the sea, even there thy right hand shall hold me.' Psa cxxxix 7, 9, 10.

(5) Sin is the worst debt, because it carries men, in case of non-payment, to a worse prison than any upon earth, even to a fiery prison; and the sinner is laid in worse chains, chains of darkness, where he is bound under wrath for ever.

Wherein have we the character of bad debtors?

(1) A bad debtor does not love to be called to account. There is a day coming when God will call his debtors to account. 'So then, every one shall give an account of himself to God.' Rom xiv 12. But we play away the time, and do not love to hear of the day of judgment; we love not that

ministers should put us in mind of our debts, or speak of the day of reckoning. What a confounding word will that be to a self-secure sinner, *redde rationem*, give an account of your stewardship!

(2) A bad debtor is unwilling to confess his debt, he will put it off, or make less of it; so we are more willing to excuse sin than confess it. How hardly was Saul brought to confession. 'I have obeyed the voice of the Lord, but the people took of the spoil.' 1 Sam xv 20, 21. He rather excuses his sin than confesses it.

(3) A bad debtor is apt to hate his creditor. Debtors wish their creditors dead; so wicked men naturally hate God, because they think he is a just judge, and will call them to account. In the Greek they are called God-haters. A debtor does not love to see his creditor.

Use 1. They are reproved who are loath to be in debt, but make no reckoning of sin, which is the greatest debt; they use no means to get out of it, but run further in debt to God. We should think it strange, if writs or warrants were out against a man, or a judgment granted to seize his body and estate, and yet he was wholly regardless and unconcerned. God has a writ out against a sinner, nay, many writs, for swearing, drunkenness, Sabbath-breaking, and yet the sinner eats and drinks, and is quiet, as if he were not in debt. What an opiate has Satan given men!

Use 2. If sin be a debt, let us be humbled. The name of debt, says Ambrose, is *grave vocabulum*, grievous. Men in debt are full of shame, they lie hid, and do not care to be seen. A debtor is ever in fear of arrest. *Canis latrat et cor palpitat* [A dog barks and his heart pounds]. Oh! let us blush and tremble, who are so deeply indebted to God. A Roman dying in debt, Augustus the emperor sent to buy his pillow, because, said he, I hope that will have some virtue to make me sleep, on which a man so much in debt could take his ease. We that have so many spiritual debts lying upon us, how can we be at rest till we have some hope that they are discharged?

II. *The second thing in this petition is confession.* Let us confess our debt. Let us acknowledge that we are in arrears with God, and deserve that he should enforce the law upon us, and throw us into hell-prison. By confession we give glory to God. 'My son, give glory to the God of Israel, and make confession unto him.' Josh vii 19. Say that God would be righteous if he should distrain upon all we have. If we confess the debt, God will forgive it. 'If we confess our sins, he is just to forgive.' 1 John i 9. Do but confess the debt, and God will cross it out from the book. 'I said, I will confess my transgressions unto the Lord, and thou forgavest the iniquity of my sin.' Psa xxxii 5.

Let us not confess merely, but labour to get our spiritual debts paid, by Christ the Surety. Say, 'Lord, have patience with me, and Christ shall pay thee all. He hath laid down an infinite price.' The covenant of works would not admit of a surety; it demanded personal obedience: but this privilege we have by the gospel, which is a court of chancery to relieve us. If we have nothing to pay, God will accept a surety. Believe in Christ's blood, and the debt is paid.

WE have next to consider in these words the petition, 'Forgive us our sins,' and the condition, 'For we also forgive everyone that is indebted to us.' Our forgiving others is not a cause of God's forgiving us, but it is a condition without which he will not forgive us.

III. *We shall now consider the petition, 'Forgive us our sins.'* This is a blessed petition. The ignorant would say, 'Who will show us any good?' (Psa iv 6) meaning a good lease, a good purchase; but the Saviour teaches us to pray for that which is more noble, and will stand us in more stead, which is the pardon of sin. Forgiveness of sins is a primary blessing, it is one of the first mercies God bestows. 'Then will I sprinkle clean water upon you;' that is, forgiveness. Ezek xxxvi 25. When God pardons, there is nothing he will stick at to do for the soul; he will adopt, sanctify, crown.

What is forgiveness of sin?

It is God's passing by sin, wiping off the score and giving us a discharge. Micah vii 18.

[1] The nature of forgiveness will more clearly appear, by opening some Scripture phrases; and by laying down some propositions.

(1) To forgive sin, is to take away iniquity. 'Why dost thou not take away mine iniquity?' Job vii 21. Hebrew, lift off. It is a metaphor taken from a man that carries a heavy burden which is ready to sink him, and another comes, and lifts it off; so when the heavy burden of sin is on us, God in pardoning, lifts it off from the conscience, and lays it upon Christ. 'He hath laid on him the iniquity of us all.' Isa liii 6.

(2) To forgive sin, is to cover it. 'Thou hast covered all their sin.' Psa lxxxv 2. This was typified by the mercy-seat covering the ark, to show God's covering of sin through Christ. God does not cover sin in the Antinomian sense, so as he sees it not, but he so covers it, that he will not impute it.

(3) To forgive sin, is to blot it out. 'I am he that blotteth out thy transgressions.' Isa xliii 25. The Hebrew word, to blot out, alludes to a creditor, who, when his debtor has paid him, blots out the debt, and gives him an

acquittance; so when God forgives sin, he blots out the debt, he draws the red lines of Christ's blood over it, and so crosses the debt-book.

(4) To forgive sin is for God to scatter our sins as a cloud. 'I have blotted out as a thick cloud thy transgressions.' Isa xliv 22. Sin is the cloud, an interposing cloud, which disperses, that the light of his countenance may break forth.

(5) To forgive sin, is for God to cast our sins into the depths of the sea, which implies burying them out of sight, that they shall not rise up in judgment against us. 'Thou wilt cast all their sins into the depths of the sea.' Micah vii 19. God will throw them in, not as cork that rises again, but as lead that sinks to the bottom.

[2] The nature of forgiveness will further appear by laying down some propositions respecting it.

(1) Every sin deserves death, and therefore needs forgiveness. The Papists distinguish between mortal sins and venial sins. Some are *ex surreptione* [surreptitious], they creep unawares into the mind, as vain thoughts, sudden motions of anger and revenge, which Bellarmine says, are in their own nature venial. It is true that the greatest sins are in one sense venial, that is, God is able to forgive them; but the least sin is not in its own nature venial, but deserves damnation. We read of the lusts of the flesh, and the works of the flesh. Rom xiii 14; Gal v 19. The lusts of the flesh are sinful, as well as the works of the flesh. That which is a transgression of the law merits damnation; but the first stirrings of corruption are a breach of the royal law, and therefore merit damnation. Rom vii 7; Prov xxiv 9. So that the least sin is mortal, and needs forgiveness.

(2) It is God only that forgives sin. To pardon sin is one of the *jura regalia* [royal prerogatives], the flowers of God's crown. 'Who can forgive sins but God only?' Mark ii 7. It is most proper for God to pardon sin; only the creditor can remit the debt. Sin is an infinite offence, and no finite power can discharge an infinite offence. No man can take away sin, unless he is able to infuse grace; for, as Aquinas says, with forgiveness is always infusion of grace; but no man can infuse grace, therefore no man can forgive sin. He only can forgive sin, who can remit the penalty, but it is God's prerogative only to forgive sin.

But a Christian is charged to forgive his brother. 'Forgiving one another.' Col iii 13.

In all second-table sins, there are two distinct things; disobedience against God, and injury to man. That which man is required to forgive, is the wrong done to himself, but the wrong done to God, he cannot forgive.

Man may remit a trespass against himself, but not a transgression against God.

The Scripture speaks of a power committed to ministers to forgive sin: 'Whosesoever sins ye remit, they are remitted unto them.' John xx 23.

Ministers cannot remit sin authoritatively and effectually, but only declaratively. They have a special office and authority to apply the promises of pardon to broken hearts. When a minister sees one humbled for sin, but afraid God has not pardoned him, and is ready to be swallowed up of sorrow; for the easing of this man's conscience, he may, in the name of Christ, declare to him, that he is pardoned. He does not forgive sin by his own authority, but as a herald, in Christ's name, pronounces a man's pardon. As under the law, God cleansed the leper, and the priest pronounced him clean, so God, by his prerogative, forgives sin, and the minister pronounces forgiveness to the penitent sinner. Power to forgive sin authoritatively in his own name, was never granted to any mortal man. A king may spare a man's life, but cannot pardon his sin. Popes' pardons are insignificant, like blanks in a lottery, good for nothing but to be torn.

(3) Forgiveness of sin is purely an act of God's free grace. There are some acts of God which declare his power, as making and governing the world; others that declare his justice, as punishing the guilty; others that declare his free-grace, as pardoning sinners. 'I am he that blotteth out thy transgressions for mine own sake.' Isa xliii 25. He forgives as when a creditor freely forgives a debtor. 'I obtained mercy.' 1 Tim 1 16. I was all over besprinkled with mercy. When God pardons a sin, he does not pay a debt, but gives a legacy. Forgiveness is spun out of the bowels of God's mercy; there is nothing we can do that can deserve it; not our prayers, or tears, or good deeds can purchase pardon. When Simon Magus would have bought the gift of the Holy Ghost with money, 'Thy money,' said Peter, 'perish with thee.' Acts viii 20. So if men think they can buy pardon of sin with their duties and alms, let their money perish with them. Forgiveness is an act of God's free grace, in which he displays the banner of love. This will raise trophies of God's glory, and cause the saints' triumph in heaven, that when there was no worthiness in them, when they lay in their blood, God took pity on them, and held forth the golden sceptre of love in forgiving. Forgiveness is a golden thread spun out of the bowels of free-grace.

(4) Forgiveness is through the blood of Christ. Free grace is the inward moving cause. Christ's blood is the outward cause of meriting pardon. 'In whom we have redemption through his blood.' Eph i 7. All pardons are sealed in Christ's blood. The guilt of sin was infinite, and nothing but that blood which was of infinite value could procure forgiveness.

But if Christ laid down his blood as the price of our pardon, how can we say God freely forgives sin? If it be by purchase, how is it by grace?

It was God's free grace that found out a way of redemption through a Mediator. Nay, God's love appeared more in letting Christ die for us, than if he had forgiven us without exacting any satisfaction. It was free grace that moved God to accept of the price paid for our sins. That God should accept a surety; that one should sin, and another suffer, was free grace. So that forgiveness of sin, though purchased by Christ's blood, is by free grace.

(5) In forgiveness of sin, God remits the guilt and penalty. *Remissa culpa, remittitur poena* [On remission of guilt, the punishment is also remitted]. Guilt is an obligation to punishment, it cries for justice. God in forgiving indulges the sinner as to the penalty. He seems to say to him, 'Though thou art fallen into the hands of my justice, and deservest to die, yet I will take off the penalty; whatever is charged upon thee shall be discharged.' When God pardons a soul, he will not reckon with him in a purely vindictive way; he stops the execution of justice.

(6) By virtue of this pardon God will no more call sin to remembrance. 'Their sins and iniquities will I remember no more.' Heb viii 12. He will pass an act of oblivion, he will not upbraid with former unkindnesses. When you fear that God will call your sins again to remembrance after pardon, look into this act of indemnity, 'Their iniquities will I remember no more.' God is said therefore to 'blot out our sin.' A man does not call for a debt when he has crossed the book. When God pardons a man, his former displeasure ceases. 'Mine anger is turned away.' Hos xiv 4.

But is God angry with his pardoned ones?

Though a child of God, after pardon, may incur his fatherly displeasure, yet his judicial wrath is removed. Though he may lay on the rod, yet he has taken away the curse. Correction may befall the saints, but not destruction. 'My lovingkindness will I not take from him.' Psa lxxxix 33.

(7) Sin is not forgiven till it be repented of. Therefore they are put together: 'Repentance and remission.' Luke xxiv 47. *Domine, da poenitentiam, et postea indulgentiam* [Grant repentance, Lord, and afterwards pardon]. Fulgentius. In repentance there are three main ingredients, all which must be before forgiveness. They are contrition, confession, and conversion.

Contrition, or brokenness of heart. 'They shall be like doves of the valleys, all of them mourning, every one for his iniquity.' Ezek vii 16. This contrition or rending of the heart, is expressed sometimes by smiting on the breast; Luke xviii 13; sometimes by plucking off the hair; Ezra ix 3; and sometimes by watering the couch; Psa vi 6. But all humiliation is not contrition; some have only pretended sorrow for sin, and so have missed forgiveness; as Ahab humbled himself, whose garments were rent, but not his heart.

What is that remorse and sorrow which goes before forgiveness of sin?

It is a holy sorrow, it is a grieving for sin, quatenus sin, as it is sin, and as it is dishonouring God, and defiling the soul. Though there were no sufferings to follow, yet the true penitent would grieve for sin. 'My sin is ever before me.' Psa li 3. This contrition goes before remission. 'I repented; I smote upon my thigh. Is Ephraim my dear son? my bowels are troubled for him. I will surely have mercy upon him.' Jer xxxi 19, 20. Ephraim was troubled for sinning, and God's bowels were troubled for Ephraim. The woman in the gospel stood at Jesus' feet weeping, and a pardon followed. 'Wherefore, I say, her sins which are many, are forgiven.' Luke vii 47. The seal is set upon the wax when it melts; God seals his pardon upon melting hearts.

The second ingredient in repentance is confession. 'Against thee, thee only, have I sinned.' Psa li 4. This is not auricular confession; which the Papists make a sacrament, and affirm that without confession of all sins in the ears of the priest, no man can receive forgiveness. The Scripture is ignorant of this, nor do we read that any general Council, till the Lateran Council, which was about twelve hundred years after Christ, ever decreed auricular confession.

But does not the Scripture say, 'Confess your faults one to another'? James v 16.

This is absurdly brought for auricular confession; for, by this, the priest must confess to the people, as well as the people to the priest. The sense of that place is that in case of public scandals, or private wrongs, confession is to be made to others; but chiefly, confession is to be made to God, who is the party offended. 'Against thee, thee only, have I sinned.' Confession gives vent to sorrow; it must be free without compulsion, ingenuous without reserve, cordial without hypocrisy; the heart must go along with it. This makes way for forgiveness. 'I said I will confess my transgressions, and thou forgavest.' Psa xxxii 5. When the publican and thief confessed, they had pardon. The publican smote upon his breast with contrition, and said, 'God be merciful to me a sinner,' there was confession; he went away justified, there was forgiveness. The thief said, 'We indeed suffer justly': there was confession; and Christ absolved him before he died: 'To day shalt thou be with me in paradise.' Luke xxiii 43. These words of Christ may have occasioned that saying of Augustine: Confession shuts the mouth of hell, and opens the gate of paradise.

The third ingredient in repentance is conversion, or turning from sin. 'We have sinned:' there was confession. 'They put away the strange gods:' there was conversion. Judges x 15, 16. It must be a universal turning from sin. 'Cast away from you all your transgressions.' Ezek xviii 31. You would be loath that God should forgive some of your sins only. Would you have him forgive all, and will you not forsake all? He that hides one rebel, is a traitor to the crown; he that lives in one known sin, is a traitorous hypocrite. There must not only be a turning from sin, but a turning to God. Therefore it is called 'Repentance toward God.' Acts xx 21. The heart points towards God as the needle to the north pole. The prodigal not only left his harlots, but arose and went to his father. Luke xv 18. This repentance is the ready way to pardon. 'Let the wicked forsake his way, and return unto the Lord, and he will abundantly pardon.' Isa lv 7. A king will not pardon a rebel whilst he continues in open hostility. Thus repentance goes before remission. They who never repented can have no ground to hope that their sins are pardoned.

Not that repentance merits the forgiveness of sin. To make repentance satisfy is Popish. By repentance we please God, but we do not satisfy him. 'Christ's blood must wash our tears.' Repentance is a condition, not a cause. God will not pardon for repentance, nor yet without it. He seals his pardons on melting hearts. Repentance makes us prize pardon the more. He who cries out of his broken bones, will the more prize the mercy of having them set again; so, when there is nothing in the soul but clouds of sorrow, and God brings pardon, which is setting a rainbow in the cloud to tell the soul the flood of God's wrath shall not overflow, oh! what joy is there at the sight of this rainbow! The soul burns in love to God.

(8) The greatest sins come within the compass of forgiveness. Incest, sodomy, adultery, theft, murder, which are sins of the first magnitude, are pardonable. Paul was a blasphemer, and so sinned against the first table; a persecutor, and so sinned against the second table; and yet he obtained mercy. 1 Tim i 13. Zacchæus, an extortioner, Mary Magdalene, an unchaste woman, out of whom seven devils were cast, Manasseh, who made the streets run with blood, had pardon. Some of the Jews, who had a hand in crucifying Christ, were forgiven. God blots out not only the cloud, but the thick cloud, enormities as well as infirmities. Isa xliv 22. The king, in the parable, forgave his debtor that owed him ten thousand talents. Matt xviii 27. A talent weighed three thousand shekels, ten thousand talents contained almost twelve tons of gold. This was an emblem of God's forgiving great sins. 'Though your sins be as scarlet, they shall be as white as snow.' Isa i 18. Scarlet, in the Greek, is called twice dipped, and the art of man cannot wash out the dye again. Though your sins are of a scarlet dye,

P

God's mercy can wash them way, as the sea covers great rocks as well as little sands. This I mention that sinners may not despair. God counts it a glory to him to forgive great sins: in which mercy and love ride in triumph. 'The grace of our Lord was exceeding abundant,' it was exuberant, it over-flowed, as the Nile. 1 Tim i 14. We must not measure God by ourselves. His mercy excels our sins as much as heaven does the earth. Isa lv 9. If great sins could not be forgiven, great sinners should not be preached to; but the gospel is to be preached to all. If they could not be forgiven, it were a dis-honour to Christ's blood; as if the wound were broader than the plaister. God has first made great sinners 'broken vessels;' he has broken their hearts for sin, and then he has made them 'golden vessels;' he has filled them with the golden oil of pardoning mercy. This may encourage great sinners to come in and repent. The sin indeed against the Holy Ghost is unpardonable, not but that there is mercy enough in God to forgive it, but because he who has committed it will not have pardon. He despises God, scorns his mercy, spills the cordial of Christ's blood, and tramples it under foot; he puts away salvation from him. When a poor sinner looks upon himself and sees his guilt, and then looks on God's justice and holiness, he falls down con-founded; but here is that which may be as a cork to the net, to keep him from despair – if he will leave his sins and come to Christ, mercy can seal his pardon.

(9) When God pardons a sinner, he forgives all sins. 'I will pardon all their iniquities.' Jer xxxiii 8. 'Having forgiven you all trespasses.' Col ii 13. The mercy-seat, which was a type of forgiveness, covered the whole ark, to show that God covers all our transgressions. He does not leave one sin upon the score; he does not take his pen and for fourscore sins write down fifty, but blots out all sin. 'Who forgiveth all thine iniquities.' Psa ciii 3. When I say, God forgives all sins, I understand it of sins past, for sins to come are not forgiven till they are repented of. Indeed God has decreed to pardon them; and when he forgives one sin, he will in time forgive all; but sins future are not actually pardoned till they are repented of. It is absurd to think sin should be forgiven before it is committed.

If all sins past and to come are at once forgiven, then what need to pray for the pardon of sin? It is a vain thing to pray for the pardon of that which is already forgiven. The opinion that sins to come, as well as past, are for-given, takes away and makes void Christ's intercession. He is an advocate to intercede for daily sins. 1 John ii 1. But if sin be forgiven before it be committed, what need is there of his daily intercession? What need have I of an advocate, if sin be pardoned before it be committed? So that, though God forgives all sins past to a believer, yet sins to come are not forgiven till repentance be renewed.

(10) Faith necessarily precedes forgiveness. There must be believing on our part before there is forgiving on God's part. 'To him give all the prophets witness, that through his name whosoever believeth in him shall receive remission of sins.' Acts x 43. So that faith is a necessary antecedent to forgiveness. There are two acts of faith, to accept Christ and to trust in Christ, to accept of his terms, to trust in his merits; and he who does neither of these, can have no forgiveness. He who does not accept Christ, cannot have his person; he who does not trust in him, cannot have benefit by his blood. So that, without faith, there is no remission.

(11) Though justification and sanctification are not the same, yet God never pardons a sinner but he sanctifies him. Justification and sanctification are not the same. Justification is without us, sanctification is within us. The one is by righteousness imputed, the other is by righteousness imparted. Justification is equal, sanctification is gradual. Sanctification is *recipere magis et minus* [to receive more and yet less]. One is sanctified more than another, but one is not justified more than another; one has more grace than another, but he is not more a believer than another. The matter of our justification is perfect, viz, Christ's righteousness; but our sanctification is imperfect, there are the spots of God's children. Deut xxxii 5. Our graces are mixed, our duties are defiled.

Thus justification and sanctification are not the same. Yet, for all that, they are not separated. God never pardons and justifies a sinner but he sanctifies him. 'But ye are sanctified, but ye are justified.' 1 Cor vi 11. 'This is he that came by water and blood, even Jesus Christ.' 1 John v 6. Christ comes to the soul by blood, which denotes remission; and by water, which denotes sanctification. Let no man say he is pardoned who is not made holy. This I urge against the Antinomians, who talk of their sin being forgiven, and having a part in Christ, and yet remain unconverted, and live in the grossest sins. Pardon and healing go together. 'I create the fruit of the lips, peace.' Isa lvii 19. Peace is the fruit of pardon, and then it follows, 'I will heal him.' Where God pardons, he purifies. As in the inauguration of kings, with the crown there is the oil to anoint; so when God crowns a man with forgiveness, he gives the anointing oil of grace to sanctify. 'I will give him a white stone, and in the stone a new name.' Rev ii 17. A 'white stone,' that is absolution; and a 'new name' in the stone, that is sanctification.

If God should pardon a man, and not sanctify him, it would be a reproach to him. He would love and be well pleased with men in their sins, which is diametrically contrary to his holy nature.

If God should pardon and not sanctify, he could have no glory from us. God's people are formed to show forth his praise; but if he should pardon and not sanctify us, how could we show forth his praise? Isa xliii 21. How could we glorify him? What glory can God have from a proud, ignorant, profane heart?

If God should pardon and not sanctify, that would enter heaven which defileth; but nothing shall enter that defileth. Rev xxi 27. God should then settle the inheritance upon men before they were fit for it. 'Which hath made us meet to be partakers of the inheritance.' Col i 12. How is that but by the divine unction? So that whoever God forgives, he transforms. Let no man say his sins are forgiven who does not find an inherent work of holiness in his heart.

(12) Where God remits sin, he imputes righteousness. This righteousness of Christ imputed is a salvo to God's law, and makes full satisfaction for the breaches of it. This righteousness procures God's favour. God cannot but love us when he sees us in his Son's robe, which both covers and adorns us. In this spotless robe of Christ we outshine the angels. Theirs is but the righteousness of creatures, this is the righteousness of God himself. 'That we might be made the righteousness of God in him.' 2 Cor v 21. How great a blessing then is forgiveness? With remission of sin is joined imputation of righteousness.

(13) They whose sins are forgiven must not omit praying for forgiveness. 'Forgive us our trespasses.' Believers who are pardoned must be continual suitors for pardon. When Nathan told David, 'The Lord hath put away thy sin,' David composed a penitential psalm for the pardon of his sin. 2 Sam xii 13. Sin, after pardon, rebels. Like Samson's hair, though it be cut, it will grow again. We sin daily, and must ask for daily pardon as well as for daily bread. Besides, a Christian's pardon is not so sure but he may desire to have a clearer evidence of it.

(14) A full absolution from all sin is not pronounced till the day of judgment. The day of judgment is called a time of refreshing, when sin shall be completely blotted out. Acts iii 19. Now God blots out sin truly, but then it shall be done in a more public way. God will openly pronounce the saints' absolution before men and angels. Their happiness is not completed till the day of judgment, because their pardon shall be solemnly pronounced, and there shall be the triumphs of the heavenly host. At that day it will be true indeed that God sees no sin in his children; they shall be as pure as the angels; then the church shall be presented without wrinkle. Eph v 27. She shall be as free from stain as guilt, Satan shall no more accuse. Christ will show the debt-book crossed in his blood. Therefore the church prays for Christ's coming to judgment. The bride says, 'Come, Lord Jesus:' light the lamps, then burn the incense. Rev xxii 20.

Use 1. For information.

(1) From this word, '*Forgive*,' we learn that if the debt of sin be no other way discharged but by being forgiven, we cannot satisfy for it. Among other damnable opinions of the church of Rome, one is, man's power to satisfy for sin. The Council of Trent holds that God is satisfied by our undergoing the penalty imposed by the censure of priests; and again, that we have works of our own by which we may satisfy for our wrongs done to God. By these opinions we judge what the Popish religion is. They intend to pay the debt they owe to God of themselves, to pay it in part, and do not look to have it all forgiven; but why did Christ teach us to pray, 'Forgive us our sins,' if we can of ourselves satisfy God for the wrong we have done him? This doctrine robs God of his glory, Christ of his merit, and the soul of salvation. Alas! is not the lock cut where the strength lay? Are not all our works fly-blown with sin, and can sin satisfy for sin? This doctrine makes men their own saviours; which is most absurd to hold, for can the obedience of a finite creature satisfy for an infinite offence? Sin being forgiven, clearly implies we cannot satisfy for it.

(2) From this word *us*, 'Forgive us,' we learn that pardon is chiefly to be sought for ourselves; for though we are to pray for the pardon of others, 'Pray one for another,' yet in the first place, we are to beg pardon for ourselves. James v 16. What! will another's pardon do us good? Everyone is to endeavour to have his own name in the pardon. A son may be made free by his father's freedom, but he cannot be pardoned by his father's pardon; he must have a pardon for himself. In this sense selfishness is lawful, everyone must be for himself and get a pardon for his own sins. 'Forgive us.'

(3) From this word *our*, 'our sins,' we learn how just God is in punishing us. The text says 'our sins;' we are not punished for other men's sins, but our own. *Nemo habet de proprio, nisi peccatum* [No one has anything of his own, except his sin]. Augustine. There is nothing we can call so properly ours as sin. Our daily bread we have from God, our daily sins we have from ourselves. Sin is our own act, a web of our own spinning. How righteous therefore is God in punishing us! We sow the seed, and God makes us reap what we sow. 'I give every man according to the fruit of his doings.' Jer xvii 10. When we are punished we but taste the fruit of our own grafting.

(4) From this word *sins*, see from hence the multitude of sin we stand guilty of. We pray not, forgive us our sin, as if it were only a single debt, but sins, in the plural. So vast is the catalogue of our sins that David cries out, 'Who can understand his errors?' Psa xix 12. Our sins are like the drops of the sea, like the atoms in the sun – they exceed all arithmetic. The debts we owe to God we can no more number than we can satisfy; which, as it should humble us to consider how full of black spots our souls are, so it should put us upon seeking after the pardon of our sins.

Use 2. For exhortation.

Let us labour for the forgiveness of sin, which is a main branch of the charter or covenant of grace. 'I will be merciful to their unrighteousness, and their sins and their iniquities will I remember no more.' Heb viii 12. It is mercy to feed us, but it is rich mercy to pardon us. Earthly things are no signs of God's love: he may give the venison, but not the blessing; but when he seals up forgiveness, he gives his love and heaven with it. 'Thou settest a crown of pure gold on his head.' Psa xxi 3. A crown of gold was a mercy; but if you look into Psa ciii you shall find a greater mercy: 'Who forgiveth all thine iniquities, who crowneth thee with lovingkindness;' ver 3, 4. To be crowned with forgiveness and lovingkindness is a far greater mercy than be have a crown of pure gold set upon the head. It was a mercy when Christ cured the palsied man; but when Christ said to him, 'Thy sins be forgiven,' it was more than to have his palsy healed. Mark ii 5. Forgiveness of sin is the chief thing to be sought after; and surely, if conscience be once touched with a sense of sin, there is nothing a man will thirst after more than forgiveness. 'My sin is ever before me.' Psa li 3. This made David so earnest for pardon. 'Have mercy upon me, O God; blot out my transgressions.' Psa li 1. If anyone should have come to David and asked him, Where is thy pain? What is it troubles thee? Is it the fear of shame which shall come upon thee and thy wives? Is it the fear of the sword which God has threatened shall not depart from thy house? He would have said, No, it is only my sin pains me: 'My sin is ever before me.' Were this removed by forgiveness, though the sword rode in circuit in my family, I would be well enough content. When the arrow of guilt sticks in the conscience, nothing is so desirable as to have it plucked out by forgiveness.

O therefore seek after forgiveness of sin. You may make a shift to live without it; but how will you die without it? Will not death have a sting to an unpardoned sinner? How do you think to get to heaven without forgiveness? As at some festivals there is no being admitted unless you bring a ticket; so unless you have this ticket to show, 'Forgiveness of sin', there is no being admitted into the holy place of heaven. Will God ever crown those that he will not forgive? O be ambitious of pardoning grace. When God had made Abraham great and large promises, Abraham replied, 'Lord, what wilt thou give me, seeing I go childless!' Gen xv 2. So, when God has given thee riches, and all thy heart can wish, say to him, Lord, what is all this, seeing I want forgiveness? Let my pardon be sealed in Christ's blood. A prisoner in the Tower is in an ill case, notwithstanding his brave diet, great attendance, soft bed to lie on, because, being impeached, he looks every day for his arraignment, and is afraid of the sentence of death. In such a case and worse is he who swims in the pleasures of the world, but his sins are not forgiven. A guilty conscience impeaches him, and he is in fear of being arraigned and condemned at God's judgment-seat. Give not then sleep to your eyes, or slumber to your eyelids, till you have gotten some well-grounded hope that your sins are blotted out. Before I come to press the exhortation to seek after forgiveness of sin, I shall propound one question.

If pardon of sin be so absolutely necessary, what is the reason that so few in the world seek after it? If they want health, they repair to the physician; if they want riches, they take a voyage to the Indies; but if they want forgiveness of sin, they seem to be unconcerned, and do not seek after it: whence is this?

Inadvertency, or want of consideration. They do not look into their spiritual estate, or cast up their accounts to see how matters stand between God and their souls. 'My people doth not consider:' they do not consider they are indebted to God in a debt of ten thousand talents, and that God will, ere long, call them to account. 'So, then, every one of us shall give account of himself to God.' Isa i 3; Rom xiv 12. But people shun serious thoughts: 'My people doth not consider.' Hence it is they do not look after pardon.

Men do not seek after forgiveness of sin for want of conviction. Few are convinced what a deadly evil sin is, that it is the spirits of mischief distilled, it turns a man's glory into shame, it brings all plagues on the body, and curses on the soul. Unless a man's sin be forgiven, there is not the vilest creature alive, the dog, serpent, or toad, but is in a better condition than the sinner; for when they die they go but to the earth; but he, dying without pardon, goes into hell torments for ever. Men are not convinced of this, but play with the viper of sin.

Men do not seek earnestly after forgiveness, because they are seeking other things. They seek the world immoderately. When Saul was seeking after the asses, he did not think of a kingdom. The world is a golden snare. *Divitiae saeculi sunt laquei diaboli* [The riches of the world are the snares of the devil]. Bernard. The wedge of gold hinders many from seeking after pardon. Ministers cry to the people, 'Get your pardon sealed;' but if you call to a man that is in a mill, the noise of the mill drowns the voice, that he cannot hear; so when the mill of a trade is going, it makes such a noise, that the people cannot hear the minister when he lifts up his voice like a trumpet, and cries to them to look after the sealing of their pardon. He who spends all his time about the world and does not mind forgiveness, will accuse himself of folly at last. You would judge that prisoner very unwise that should spend all his time with the cook to get his dinner ready, and should never mind getting a pardon.

Men seek not after forgiveness of sin, through a bold presumption of mercy; they conceive God to be made up all of mercy; and that he will indulge them, though they take little or no pains to sue for their pardon. True, God is merciful, but withal he is just, he will not wrong his justice by showing mercy. Read the proclamation: 'The Lord, the Lord God, merciful and gracious; and that will by no means clear the guilty.' Exod xxxiv 6, 7. Such as go on in sin, and are so slothful or wilful that they will not seek after forgiveness, though there be a whole ocean of mercy in the Lord, not one drop shall fall to their share. He 'will by no means clear the guilty.'

Men seek not earnestly after forgiveness out of hope of impunity. They flatter themselves in sin, and because they have been spared so long, therefore think God never intends to reckon with them. 'He hath said in his heart, God hath forgotten: he hideth his face; he will never see it.' Psa x 11. Atheists think either the judge is blind or forgetful; but let sinners know that long forbearance is no forgiveness. God bore with Sodom a long time, but at last rained down fire and brimstone upon them. The adjourning of the assizes does not acquit the prisoner. The longer God is taking the blow, the heavier it will be at last, if sinners repent not.

Men do not seek earnestly after forgiveness through mistake. They think getting a pardon is easy, it is but repenting at the last hour, a sigh, or a 'Lord, have mercy,' and a pardon will drop into their mouths. But is it so easy to repent, and have a pardon? Tell me, O sinner, is regeneration easy? Are there no pangs in the new birth? Is mortification easy? Is it nothing to pluck out the right eye? Is it easy to leap out of Delilah's lap into Abraham's bosom? This is the draw-net by which the devil drags millions to hell, the facility of repenting and getting a pardon.

Men do not look after forgiveness through despair. Oh, says the desponding soul, it is a vain thing for me to expect pardon; my sins are so many and heinous that surely God will not forgive me. 'And they said, There is no hope.' Jer xviii 12. My sins are huge mountains, and can they ever be cast into the sea? Despair cuts the sinews of endeavour. Who will use means that despairs of success? The devil shows some men their sins at the little end of the perspective-glass, and they seem little or none at all; but he shows others their sins at the great end of the perspective, and they fright them into despair. This is a soul-damning sin. Judas's despair was worse than his treason. Despair spills the cordial of Christ's blood. The voice of despair is, Christ's blood cannot pardon me. Thus you see whence it is that men seek no more earnestly after the forgiveness of sin. Having answered this question, I shall now come to press the exhortation upon every one of us, to seek earnestly after the forgiveness of our sins.

(1) Our very life lies in getting pardon. It is called the 'justification of life.' Rom v 18. Now, if our life lies in our pardon, and we are dead and damned

without it, does it not concern us above all things to labour after forgiveness of sin? 'For it is not a vain thing for you, because it is your life.' Deut xxxii 47. If a man be under a sentence of death, he will set his wits to work, and make use of all his friends to get the king to grant his pardon, because his life lies upon it; so we by reason of sin are under a sentence of damnation. There is one friend at court we may make use of to procure our pardon, namely, the Lord Jesus. How earnest then should we be with him to be our Advocate to the Father for us, that he would present the merit of his blood to the Father, as the price of our pardon!

(2) There is that in sin that should make us desire forgiveness. Sin is the only thing that disquiets the soul. It is a burden, it burdens the creation, it burdens the conscience. Rom viii 22; Psa xxxviii 4. A wicked man is not sensible of sin, he is dead in sin; and if you lay a thousand weight upon a dead man he feels it not. But to an awakened conscience sin is a burden. When a man seriously weighs with himself the glory and purity of that Majesty which sin has offended, the preciousness of that soul which sin has polluted, the loss of that happiness which sin has endangered, the greatness of that torment which sin has deserved, to lay all this together, surely must make sin burdensome: and should not we labour to have this burden removed by pardoning mercy? Sin is a debt, 'Forgive us our debts.' Matt vi 12. Every debt we owe, God has written down in his book. 'Behold, it is written before me,' and one day God's debt-book will be opened. 'The books were opened.' Isa lxv 6; Rev xx 12. And should not this make us look after forgiveness? Sin being such a debt as we must eternally lie in the prison of hell for, if it be not discharged, should we not be earnest with God to cross the debt-book with the blood of his Son? There is no way to look God in the face with comfort, but by having our debts either paid or pardoned.

(3) Nothing but forgiveness can give ease to a troubled conscience. There is a great difference between having the fancy pleased, and having the conscience eased. Worldly things may please the fancy, but not ease the conscience. Nothing but pardon can relieve a troubled soul. It is strange what shifts men will make for ease when conscience is pained, and how many false medicines they will use before they will take the right way for a cure. When conscience is troubled, they will try what merry company can do. They may perhaps drink away trouble of conscience; perhaps they may play it away at cards; perhaps a Lent-whipping will do the deed; perhaps multitude of business will so take up their time, that they shall have no leisure to hear the clamours and accusations of conscience; but how vain are all these attempts! Still the wound bleeds inwardly, their heart trembles, their conscience roars, and they can have no peace. Whence is it? The reason is they go not to the mercy of God, and the blood of Christ, for the pardon

of their sins; and hence they have no ease. Suppose a man has a thorn in his foot, which puts him to pain; let him anoint it, or wrap it up, and keep it warm; but till the thorn be plucked out, it aches and swells, and he has no ease; so when the thorn of sin is in a man's conscience, there is no ease till it be pulled out. When God removes iniquity, the thorn is plucked out. How was David's heart finely quieted, when Nathan the prophet told him, 'The Lord hath put away thy sin'! 2 Sam xii 13. How should we therefore labour for forgiveness! Till then we can have no ease in the mind. Nothing but pardon, sealed with the blood of the Redeemer, can ease a wounded spirit.

(4) Forgiveness of sin is feasible, and may be obtained. Impossibility destroys endeavour; but, 'There is hope in Israel concerning this.' Ezra x 2. The devils are past hope; a sentence of death is upon them, which is irrevocable; but there is hope for us of obtaining pardon. 'There is forgiveness with thee.' Psa cxxx 4. If pardon of sin were not possible, it were not to be prayed for; but it has been prayed for. 'I beseech thee, O Lord, take away the iniquity of thy servant.' 2 Sam xxiv 10. And Christ bids us pray for it, 'Forgive us our trespasses.' That is possible which God has promised, but God has promised pardon upon repentance. 'Let the wicked forsake his way and return unto the Lord, and he will have mercy upon him; and to our God, for he will abundantly pardon.' Isa lv 7. Hebrew, 'He will multiply to pardon.' That is possible which others have obtained; but others have arrived at forgiveness, therefore it is obtainable. Psa xxxii 5. 'Thou hast cast all my sins behind thy back.' Isa xxxviii 17.

(5) Forgiveness of sin is a choice and eminent blessing. To have the book cancelled, and God appeased, is worth obtaining, which may whet our endeavour after it. That it is a rare transcendent blessing, appears by three demonstrations:

First, if we consider how this blessing is purchased, namely, by the Lord Jesus. There are three things in reference to Christ which set forth the choiceness and preciousness of forgiveness:

[1] No mere created power in heaven or earth could expiate one sin, or procure a pardon, but Jesus Christ only. 'He is the propitiation for our sins.' 1 John ii 2. No merit can buy out a pardon. Paul had as much to boast of as any man, his high birth, his learning, his legal righteousness; but he disclaims all in point of justification, and lays them under Christ's feet to tread upon. No angel, with all his holiness, could lay down a price for the pardon of one sin. 'If a man sin against the Lord, who shall intreat for him?' 1 Sam ii 25. What angel durst be so bold as to open his mouth to God for a delinquent sinner? Only Jesus Christ, who is God-man, could deal with God's justice, and purchase forgiveness.

[2] Christ himself could not procure a pardon without dying. Every pardon is the price of blood. Christ's life was a rule of holiness, and a pattern of obedience. He fulfilled all righteousness. Matt iii 15. Certainly his active obedience was of great value and merit; but that which raises the worth of forgiveness, is that his active obedience had not fully procured a pardon for us without the shedding of his blood. Our justification therefore is ascribed to his blood. 'Being justified by his blood.' Rom v 9. Christ did bleed out our pardon. There is much ascribed to his intercession, but his intercession had not prevailed with God for the forgiveness of one sin had he not shed his blood. It is worthy of notice, that when Christ is described to John as an intercessor for his church, he is represented in the likeness of a Lamb slain, to show that Christ must die and be slain before he can be an intercessor. Rev v 6.

[3] Christ, by dying, had not purchased forgiveness for us if he had not died an accursed death. He endured the curse. Gal iii 13. All the agonies Christ endured in his soul, all the torments in his body, could not purchase a pardon except he had been made a curse for us. He must be cursed before we could be blessed with a pardon.

Secondly, forgiveness of sin is a choice blessing, if we consider what glorious attributes God puts forth in it. He puts forth infinite power. When Moses was pleading with God for the pardon of Israel's sin, he spoke thus: 'Let the power of my Lord be great.' Numb xiv 17. For God, forgiving sin is a work of as great power as to make heaven and earth, nay, a greater. When he made the world, he met with no opposition; but, when he pardons, Satan opposes, and the heart opposes. A sinner is desperate, and slights, yea, defies pardon, till God, by his mighty power, convinces him of his sin and danger, and makes him willing to accept of pardon. God, in forgiving sins, puts forth infinite mercy. 'Pardon, I beseech thee, the iniquity of this people, according unto the greatness of thy mercy.' Numb xiv 19. It is mercy to have a reprieve; and if there be mercy in sparing a sinner, what mercy is there in pardoning him! This is the *flos lactis*, the cream of mercy. For God to put up with so many injuries, to wipe so many debts off the score, is infinite favour.

Thirdly, forgiveness of sin is a choice blessing, as it lays a foundation for other mercies. It is a leading mercy. It makes way for temporal good things. It brings health. When Christ said to the palsied man, 'Thy sins are forgiven,' he made way for a bodily cure. 'Arise, take up thy bed and walk.' Matt ix 6. The pardon of his sin made way for the healing of his palsy. It brings prosperity. Jer xxxiii 8, 9. It makes way for spiritual good things. Forgiveness of sin never comes alone, but has other spiritual blessings attending it. Whom God pardons, he sanctifies, adopts, crowns. It is a voluminous mercy, it draws the silver link of grace, and the golden link of glory after it. It is a high act of indulgence. God seals the sinner's pardon with a kiss. And should not we, above all things, seek after so great a blessing as forgiveness?

(6) That which may make us seek after forgiveness of sin is God's inclinableness to pardon. 'Thou art a God ready to pardon.' Neh ix 17. In the Hebrew it is, 'A God of pardons.' We are apt to entertain wrong conceits of God, that he is inexorable, and will not forgive. 'I knew thee that thou art an hard man.' Matt xxv 24. But God is a sin-pardoning God. 'The Lord merciful and gracious, forgiving iniquity and transgression and sin.' Exod xxxiv 6, 7. Here is my name, says God, if you would know how I am called, I tell you my name, 'The Lord, the Lord God, merciful, forgiving iniquity.' A pirate or rebel, that knows there is a proclamation out against him, will never come in; but, if he hears that the prince is full of clemency, and there is a proclamation of pardon if he submit, it will be a great incentive to him to lay down his arms and become loyal to his prince. See God's proclamation to repenting sinners, in Jer iii 12: 'Go and proclaim these words, and say, Return, thou backsliding Israel, saith the Lord, and I will not cause mine anger to fall upon you, for I am merciful.' God's mercy is a tender mercy. The Hebrew word for mercy signifies bowels. God's mercy is full of sympathy, he is of a most sweet, indulgent nature. 'Thou, Lord, art good, and ready to forgive.' Psa lxxxvi 5. The bee does not more naturally give honey, than God shows mercy.

But does not God seem to delight in punitive acts, or acts of severity? 'I will laugh at your calamity.' Prov i 26.

To whom does God say this? See verse 25. 'Ye have set at nought all my counsel, and would none of my reproof.' God delights in the destruction of those who despise his instruction; but a humble penitent breaking off sin, and suing for pardon, he delights in. 'He delighteth in mercy.' Mic vii 18.

But though God be so full of mercy, and ready to forgive, yet his mercy reaches not to all; he forgives such only as are elected, and I question my election.

No man can say he is not elected. God has not revealed to any particular man that he is a reprobate, excepting him only who has sinned the sin against the Holy Ghost; which thou art far enough from who mournest for sin, and seekest after forgiveness.

The thought that we are not elected, and that there is no pardon for us, comes from Satan, and is the poisoned arrow he shoots. He is the accuser: he accuses us to God that we are great sinners; and he accuses God to us as if he were a tyrant, one that watches to destroy his creatures. These are diabolical suggestions; say, 'Get thee behind me, Satan.'

It is sinful for any to hold that he is not elected. It would take him off from the use of means, from praying and repenting; it would harden him, and make him desperate. Therefore pry not into the *arcana coeli*, secrets of heaven. Remember what befell the men of Bethshemesh, for looking into the ark. 1 Sam vi 19. Know that we are not to go by God's secret will, but by his revealed will. Let us look into God's revealed will, and there we shall find enough to cherish hope, and encourage us to go to God for the pardon of our sins. He has said in his Word, that he is 'rich in mercy,' and that he does not delight in the destruction of a sinner. Eph ii 4; Ezek xviii 32. *Jurat per essentiam.* Musculus. He swears by his essence. 'As I live, saith the Lord God, I have no pleasure in the death of the wicked.' Ezek xxxiii 11. Hence he waits long, and puts off the sessions from time to time, to see if sinners will repent and seek to him for pardon. Therefore, let God's tender mercies and precious promises encourage us to seek him for the forgiveness of our sins.

(7) Not to seek earnestly for pardon is unspeakable misery to such as need forgiveness. It must needs be ill with that malefactor that has not pardon.

The unpardoned sinner, who lives and dies such, is under the greatest loss and privation. Is there any happiness like the enjoyment of God in glory? This is the joy of angels, the crown of saints glorified; but the unforgiven sinner shall not behold God's smiling face; he shall see God as an enemy, not as a friend; he shall have an affrighting sight of God, not beatific; he shall see the black rod, not the mercy-seat. Sins unpardoned are like the angel with a flaming sword, who stopped the passage to paradise. They stop the way to the heavenly paradise. How doleful is the condition of that soul which is banished from the place of bliss, where the King of Glory keeps his court!

The unpardoned sinner has nothing to do with any promise. The promises are *mulctralia evangelii*, the breasts that hold the sincere milk of the word, which fill the soul with precious sweetness. They are the royal charter: but what has a stranger to do to meddle with the charter? It was the dove that plucked the olive branch; it is only the believer who plucks the tree of the promise. Till the condition of the promise be performed, no man can have right to the comfort of it; and how sad is it not to have one promise to show for heaven!

An unpardoned sinner is continually in danger of the outcry of an accusing conscience. An accusing conscience is a little hell. *Siculi non invenere tyranni tormentum majus* [The Sicilian tyrants devised no worse a torture]. We tremble to hear a lion roar: how terrible are the roarings of conscience! Judas hanged himself to quiet his conscience. A sinner's conscience at present is either asleep or seared; but when God shall awaken it, either by affliction or at death, how will the unpardoned sinner be affrighted! When a man shall have all his sins set before his eyes, and drawn out in their bloody colours, and the worm of conscience begins to gnaw, oh, what a trembling at heart will the sinner have!

All the curses of God stand in full force against an unpardoned sinner. His very blessings are cursed. 'I will curse your blessings.' Mal ii 2. His table is a snare; he eats and drinks a curse. What comfort could Dionysius have at his feast, when he imagined he saw a naked sword hanging by a twine-thread over his head? It is enough to spoil a sinner's banquet, that a curse, like a naked sword, hangs over his head. Caesar wondered to see one of his soldiers who was in debt so merry. One would wonder that man could be merry who is heir to all God's curses. He does not see these curses, but is blinder than Balaam's ass, who saw the angel's sword drawn.

The unpardoned sinner is in an ill case at death. Luther professed there were three things which he durst not think of without Christ; of his sins, of death, and of the day of judgment. Death to a Christless soul is the 'king of terrors.' As the prophet Ahijah said to Jeroboam's wife, 'I am sent to thee with heavy tidings' (1 Kings xiv 6); so death is sent to the unpardoned soul with heavy tidings; it is God's jailor to arrest him. Death is a prologue to damnation. It takes away all earthly comforts, it takes away sugared morsels; no more drinking wine in bowls, no more mirth or music. 'The voice of harpers and musicians shall be heard no more at all in thee.' Rev xviii 22. The sinner shall never taste of luscious delights more to all eternity; his honey shall be turned into the 'gall of asps.' Job xx 14. At death, an end shall be put to all reprieves. Now God reprieves a sinner, he spares him such a fit of sickness; he respites him many years; the sinner should have died at such a drinking bout, but God granted him a reprieve; he lengthened out the silver thread of patience to a miracle; but when the sinner dies without repentance, and unpardoned, the lease of God's patience is run out, and he must appear in person before the righteous God to receive his sentence; after which, there shall be none to bail him, nor shall he hear of a reprieve any more.

(6) The sinner dying unpardoned, must go into damnation; this is the second death, *mors sine morte* [an undying death]. The unpardoned soul must for ever bear the anger of a sin-revenging God. As long as God is God, so long the vial of his wrath shall be dropping upon the damned soul. This is a helpless condition. There is a time when a sinner will not be helped; Christ and salvation are offered to him, but he slights them, he will not be helped; and there is a time shortly coming when he cannot be helped; he calls out for mercy, Oh! a pardon, a pardon! but it is too late, the date of

mercy is expired. Oh! how sad, then, is it to live and die unpardoned! You may lay a grave-stone upon that man, and write this epitaph upon it, 'It had been good for that man that he had never been born.' Now, if the misery of an unpardoned state be so inexpressible, how should we labour for forgiveness, that we may not be engulfed in so dreadful a labyrinth of fire and brimstone to all eternity!

(7) Such as are unpardoned, must needs lead uncomfortable lives. 'Thy life shall hang in doubt before thee, and thou shalt fear day and night.' Deut xxviii 66. Thus the unpardoned sinner must needs have a palpitation and trembling at the heart; he fears every bush he sees. 'Fear hath torment.' 1 John iv 18. The Greek word for torment, *kolasis*, is used sometimes for hell: fear has hell in it. A man in debt fears, every step he goes, lest he should be arrested; so the unpardoned sinner fears, what if this night death, death which is God's sergeant, should arrest him! 'Why dost thou not pardon my transgression? For now shall I sleep in the dust:' as if Job had said, 'Lord, I shall shortly die, I shall sleep in the dust; and what shall I do if my sins be not pardoned?' Job vii 21. What comfort can an unpardoned soul take in anything? Surely no more than a prisoner can take in meat or music, that wants his pardon. Therefore, by all these powerful motives, let us labour for the forgiveness of sins.

But I am discouraged from going to God for pardon, for I am unworthy of forgiveness; what am I, that God should show such a favour to me?

God forgives, not because we are worthy, but because he is gracious. 'The Lord, the Lord God, merciful and gracious.' Exod xxxiv 6. He forgives out of his clemency; acts of pardon are acts of grace. What worthiness was there in Paul before conversion? He was a blasphemer, and so he sinned against the first table; he was a persecutor, and so he sinned against the second table; but free grace sealed his pardon. 'I obtained mercy;' I was all bestrewed with mercy. 1 Tim i 13. What worthiness was in the woman of Samaria? She was ignorant. John iv 22. She was unclean; ver 18. She was morose and churlish, she would not give Christ so much as a cup of cold water; ver 9. How is it that thou, being a Jew, askest drink of me which am a woman of Samaria? What worthiness was here? Yet Christ overlooked all, and pardoned her ingratitude; and though she denied him water out of the well, yet he gave her the water of life. *Gratia non invenit dignos, sed facit.* Free grace does not find us worthy, but makes us worthy. Therefore, notwithstanding unworthiness, seek to God, that your sins may be pardoned.

But I have been a great sinner, and surely God will not pardon me?

David brings it as an argument for pardon. 'Pardon mine iniquity, for it is great.' Psa xxv 11. When God forgives great sins, he does a work like himself. The desperateness of the wound the more sets forth the virtue of Christ's blood in curing it. Mary Magdalene, out of whom seven devils were cast, was a great sinner, yet she had her pardon. When some of the Jews, who had a hand in crucifying Christ, repented, the very blood they shed sealed their pardon. Consider sins either for their number as the sands of the sea, or for their weight as the rocks of the sea, yet there is mercy enough in God to forgive them. 'Though your sins be as scarlet, they shall be as white as snow.' Isa i 18. Scarlet signifies twice dipped, which no art of man can get out, yet God can wash out this scarlet dye. There is no sin exempted from pardon but that sin which despises pardon, the sin against the Holy Ghost. Matt xii 31. Therefore, O sinner, do not cast away thy anchor of hope, but go to God for forgiveness. The vast ocean has bounds set to it, but God's pardoning mercy is boundless. He can as well forgive great sins as little, as the sea can cover great rocks and little sands. Nothing hinders pardon but the sinner's not asking it.

That a great sinner should not despair of forgiveness, we may learn from this Scripture: 'I, even I, am he that blotteth out thy transgressions.' If you look on the foregoing words, you would wonder how this verse comes in. 'Thou hast made me to serve with thy sins, thou has wearied me with thine iniquities;' and then it follows, 'I, even I, am he that blotteth out thy transgressions.' Isa xliii 24, 25. One would have thought it should have run thus, 'Thou hast wearied me with thine iniquities; I, even I, am he that will punish thy iniquities;' but God comes in a mild loving strain, 'Thou hast wearied me with thine iniquities; I am he that blotteth out thy iniquities.' So that the greatness of our sins should not discourage us from going to God for forgiveness. Though thou hast committed acts of impiety, yet God can come with an act of indemnity, and say, 'I, even I, am he that blotteth out thy transgressions.' God counts it his glory to display free grace in its most brilliant colours. 'Where sin abounded, grace did much more abound.' Rom v 20. When sin becomes exceeding sinful, free grace becomes exceeding glorious. God's pardoning love can conquer the sinner, and triumph over the sin. Consider, thou almost despairing soul, there is not so much sin in man as there is mercy in God. Man's sin in comparison of God's mercy is but as a spark to the ocean; and who would doubt whether a spark could be quenched in an ocean?

But I have relapsed into the same sins, and how can I have the face to come to God for pardon of those sins into which I have more than once fallen?

I know the Novatians held that after a relapse there is no forgiveness by the church. But doubtless that was an error. Abraham twice equivocated;

Lot committed incest twice; Peter sinned thrice by carnal fear; but they repented, and they had absolution.

There is a twofold relapse, (1) A wilful relapse, when, after a man has solemnly vowed himself to God, he falls into a league with sin, and returns back to it. 'I have loved strangers, and after them will I go' (Jer ii 25); and (2) there is a relapse through infirmity, when the bent and resolution of a man's heart is against sin, but, through the violence of temptation, and withdrawing of God's grace, he is carried down the stream against his will. Now, though wilful and continued relapses are desperate, and tend *vastare conscientiam* (as Tertullian), to waste the conscience, and run men upon the precipice of damnation, yet if they are through infirmity, and we mourn for them, we may obtain forgiveness. A godly man does not march after sin as his general, but is led captive by it; and the Lord will pity a captive prisoner. Christ commands us to forgive a trespassing brother seventy-times seven. Matt xviii 22. If he bids us do it, much more will he forgive a relapsing sinner in case he repent. 'Return, thou backsliding Israel, for I am merciful, saith the Lord.' Jer iii 12. It is not falling once or twice into the mire that drowns, but lying there; it is not once relapsing into sin, but lying in sin impenitently that damns.

But God requires so much sorrow and humiliation before remission, that I fear I shall never arrive at it!

He requires no more humiliation than may fit a soul for mercy. Many a Christian thinks, because he has not filled God's bottle so full of tears as others, he is not humbled enough to receive pardon. But God's dealings are various; all have not the like pangs in the new birth. Some are won with love; the sense of God's mercy abused causes ingenuous tears to flow; others are more flagitious and hardened, and God deals with them more roughly. That soul is humbled enough to receive a pardon which is brought to a thorough sense of sin, and sees the need of a Saviour, and loves him as the fairest of ten thousand. Therefore be not discouraged, for if thy heart be bruised from sin and broken off from it, thy sin shall be blotted out. No sooner did Ephraim weep than God's bowels were working. 'My bowels are troubled for him; I will surely have mercy upon him.' Jer xxxi 20.

Having answered these objections, let me beseech you, above all things, labour for the forgiveness of sin. Think with yourselves how great a mercy it is: it is one of the richest jewels in the cabinet of the new covenant. 'Blessed is he whose transgression is forgiven.' Psa xxxii 1. In the Hebrew it is 'blessednesses'. And think of the unparalleled misery of those whose sins are not forgiven! Such as had not the blood of the paschal lamb sprinkled upon their door-posts, were destroyed by the angel. Exod xii. So they who have not Christ's blood sprinkled on them, to wash away the guilt of sin, will fall into the gulf of perdition. If you resolve to seek after forgiveness, do not delay.

Many say they will get their pardon, but they procrastinate and put it off so long that it is too late. When the shadows of the evening are stretched forth, and the night of death approaches, they begin to look after their pardon. This has been the undoing of millions. They purpose to look after their souls, but they stay so long till the lease of mercy is run out. Oh, therefore, hasten to get pardon! Think of the uncertainty of life. What security have you that you shall live another day? *Volat ambiguis mobilis alis hora* [The fleeting hour flies on fickle wings]. Our life is a taper soon blown out; it is made up of a few flying minutes. O thou dust and ashes! thou mayest fear every hour to be blown into thy grave; and what if death come to arrest thee before thy pardon be sealed? Plutarch reports of one Archias, who being among his cups when a letter was delivered to him, and he was desired to read it, as it was about serious business, *Seria cras*, he said, 'I will mind serious things to-morrow;' and that night he was slain. Thou that sayest, 'To-morrow I will repent, I will get my pardon,' thou mayest suddenly be slain; therefore to-day, while it is called to-day, look after the forgiveness of sin. After awhile, all the fountains of mercy will be stopped, there will not be one drop of Christ's blood to be had, there are no pardons after death.

Use 3. Let us labour to have the evidence that our sins are forgiven. A man may have his sins forgiven and not know it; he may have a pardon in the court of heaven when he has it not in the court of conscience. David's sin was forgiven soon as he repented. God sent Nathan the prophet to tell him so. 2 Sam xii 13. But David did not feel the comfort of it at once, as appears by the penitential Psalm composed afterwards. 'Make me to hear joy;' and 'Cast me not away from thy presence.' Psa li 8, 11. It is one thing to be pardoned and another to feel it. The evidence of pardon may not appear for a time, and this may be:

(1) From the imbecility and weakness of faith. Forgiveness of sin is so strange and infinite a blessing that a Christian can hardly persuade himself that God will extend such a favour to him. As it is said of the apostles when Christ first appeared to them, 'They believed not for joy, and wondered,' (Luke xxiv 41), so the soul may be so stricken with admiration that the wonder of pardon staggers its faith.

(2) A man may be pardoned and not know it from the strength of temptation. Satan accuses the godly of sin, and tells them that God does not love them; and should such sinners think of pardon? Believers are compared

to bruised reeds; and temptations to winds. Matt xii 20; chap vii 25. Now, a reed is easily shaken with the wind. Temptations shake the godly; and though they are pardoned, yet they know it not. Job in a temptation thought God his enemy, and yet he was then in a pardoned condition. Job xvi 9.

Why does God sometimes conceal the evidence of pardon?

Though he pardons, he may withhold the sense of it for a time: (1) Because he would lay us lower in contrition. He would have us see what an evil and bitter thing it is to offend him. Therefore we must lie longer in the briny tears of repentance before we have the sense of pardon. It was long before David's broken bones were set and his pardon sealed, that his heart might be more contrite; and this was a sacrifice which God delighted in. (2) Though God has forgiven sin, he may deny the manifestation of it for a time, to make us prize pardon and make it sweeter to us when it comes. The difficulty of obtaining a mercy enhances its value. When we have been a long time tugging at prayer for a pardon of sin, and still God withholds, but at last, after many sighs and tears, it comes, we esteem it the more, and it is sweeter. *Quo longius defertur eo suavius laetatur* [The longer the delay, the sweeter the rejoicing]. The longer mercy is in the birth the more welcome will the deliverance be.

Let us not be content however without the evidence and sense of pardon. He who is pardoned and knows it not, is like one who has an estate bequeathed to him, but knows it not. Our comfort consists in the knowledge of forgiveness. 'Make me to hear joy.' Psa li 8. There is a jubilee in the soul when we are able to read our pardon. To the witness of conscience God adds the witness of his Spirit; and in the mouth of these two witnesses our joy is confirmed. O labour for the evidence of forgiveness!

How shall we know that our sins are forgiven?

We must not be our own judges in this case. 'He that trusteth in his own heart is a fool.' Prov xxviii 26. 'The heart is deceitful.' Jer xvii 9. It is folly to trust a deceiver. The Lord only by his word must judge whether we are pardoned or not. As under the law no leper might judge himself to be clean, but the priest was to pronounce him clean, (Lev xiii 37); so we are not to judge ourselves to be clean from the guilt of sin till we are such as the word of God pronounces to be clean.

How shall we know by the word that our sins are pardoned?

(1) The pardoned sinner is a great weeper. The sense of God's love melts his heart. That free grace should ever look upon me; that such crimson sins

should be washed away in Christ's blood, makes the heart melt and the eyes drop with tears; never did any man read his pardon with dry eyes. 'She stood at his feet weeping.' Luke vii 38. Mary's tears were more precious to Christ than her ointment; her eyes, which before sparkled with lust, now became a fountain, and washed Christ's feet with her tears. She was a true penitent, and had her pardon. 'Wherefore, I say, her sins, which are many, are forgiven;' ver 47. A pardon will make the hardest heart relent and cause the stony heart to bleed. Is it thus with us? Have we been dissolved into tears for sin? God seals his pardons upon melting hearts.

(2) We may knows our sins are forgiven by having the grace of faith. 'To him give all the prophets witness, that whosoever believeth in him shall receive remission of sins.' Acts x 43. In saving faith there are two things – renunciation and recumbency: [1] Renunciation. A man renounces all opinion of himself; is digged out of his own burrow, and he is quite taken off from himself. Phil iii 9. He sees all his duties are but broken reeds; though he could weep a sea of tears; though he had all the grace of men and angels, it could not purchase his pardon. [2] Recumbency. Faith is an assent with affiance. The soul gets hold of Christ as Adonijah did of the horns of the altar. 1 Kings i 51. Faith casts itself into the stream of Christ's blood, and says, If I perish, I perish. If we have but the *minimum quod sic*, the least drachm of this precious faith, we have something to show for pardon. This faith is acceptable to God, it pleases him more than offering up ten thousand rivers of oil, than working miracles, than martyrdom, or the highest acts of obedience. This faith is profitable to us; it is our best certificate to show for pardon. No sooner does faith reach forth its hand to receive Christ, than Christ sets his hand to our pardon.

(3) The pardoned soul is an admirer of God. 'Who is a God like unto thee, that pardoneth iniquity?' Mic vii 18. Oh, that God should ever look upon me! I was a sinner, and nothing but a sinner, yet I obtained mercy! 'Who is a God like unto thee?' Mercy has been despised, and yet that mercy saves me. Christ has been crucified by me, yet his cross crowns me. God has displayed the ensigns of free grace, he has set up his mercy above my sin, nay, in spite of it. This causes admiration. 'Who is a God like thee?' A man that goes over a narrow bridge in the night, and next morning sees the danger he was in, how miraculously he escaped, is filled with admiration; so when God shows a man how near he was falling into hell, how that gulf is passed, and all his sins are pardoned, he is amazed, and cries out, 'Who is a God like unto thee, that pardoneth iniquity?' That God should pardon one and pass by another – one should be taken and another left – fills the soul with wonder and astonishment.

(4) Wherever God pardons sin, he subdues it. 'He will have compassion

on us, he will subdue our iniquities.' Mic vii 19. Where men's persons are justified, their lusts are mortified. There is in sin *vis imperatoria et damnatoria*, a commanding and a condemning power. The condemning power of sin is taken away when the commanding power of it is taken away. We know our sins are forgiven when they are subdued. If a malefactor be in prison, how shall he know that his prince has pardoned him? If the jailor come and knock off his chains and fetters, and lets him out of prison, then he knows he is pardoned: so we know God has pardoned us when the fetters of sin are broken off, and we walk at liberty in the ways of God. 'I will walk at liberty;' this is a blessed sign that we are pardoned. Psa cxix 45. Such as are washed in Christ's blood from guilt, are made kings to God. Rev i 6. As kings they rule over their sins.

(5) He whose sins are forgiven is full of love to God. Mary Magdalene's heart was fired with love. 'Her sins, which are many, are forgiven; for she loved much.' Luke vii 47. Her love was not the cause of her remission, but a sign of it. A pardoned soul is a monument of mercy, and he thinks he can never love God enough: he wishes he had a coal from God's altar to inflame his heart in love; he wishes he could borrow the wings of the cherubims that he might fly swifter in obedience; a pardoned soul is sick of love. He whose heart is like marble, locked up in impenitence, that does not melt in love, gives evidence that his pardon is yet unsealed.

(6) Where sin is pardoned, the nature is purified. 'I will heal their backslidings, I will love them.' Hos xiv 4. Every man, by nature, is both guilty and diseased. When God remits the guilt, he cures the disease. 'Who forgiveth all thine iniquities, who healeth all thy diseases.' Psa ciii 3. Herein God's pardon goes beyond the king's pardon; the king may forgive a malefactor, but he cannot change his heart, which may be a thievish heart still; but when God pardons, he changes the heart. 'A new heart also will I give you.' Ezek xxxvi 26. A pardoned soul is adorned and embellished with holiness. 'This is he that came by water and blood.' 1 John v 6. When Christ comes with blood to justify, he comes with water to cleanse. 'I have caused thine iniquity to pass from thee, and I will clothe thee with change of raiment.' Zech iii 4. I will cause thy iniquity to pass from thee, there is pardoning grace; and I will clothe thee with change of raiment, there is sanctifying grace. Let no one say, he has pardon who has not grace. Many tell us they hope they are pardoned, who were never sanctified. They believe in Christ; but what faith is it? A swearing faith, a whoring faith: the faith of devils is as good.

(7) Such as are in the number of God's people have forgiveness of sin. 'Comfort ye my people, cry unto her that her iniquity is pardoned.' Isa xl 1, 2.

How shall we know that we are God's elect people?

By three characters.

God's people are a humble people. The livery which all Christ's people wear is humility. 'Be clothed with humility.' 1 Pet v 5. A sight of God's glory humbles. Elijah wrapped his face in a mantle when God's glory passed by. 'Now mine eye seeth thee, wherefore I abhor myself.' Job xlii 5, 6. The stars vanish when the sun appears. A sight of sin humbles. In the glass of the word the godly see their spots, and they are humbling spots. Lo, says the soul, I can call nothing my own but sins and wants. A humble sinner is in a better condition than a proud angel.

God's people are a willing people. 'A people of willingness;' love constrains them; they serve God freely, and out of choice. Psa cx 3. They stick at no service; they will run through a sea, and a wilderness; they will follow the Lamb whithersoever he goeth.

God's people are a heavenly people. 'They are not of the world.' John xvii 16. As the *primum mobile* in the heavens has a motion of its own, contrary to the other orbs, so God's people have a heavenly motion of the soul, contrary to the men of the world. They use the world as their servant, but do not follow the world as their master. 'Our conversation is in heaven.' Phil iii 20. Such as have these three characters of God's people, have a good certificate to show that they are pardoned. Forgiveness of sin belongs to them. 'Comfort ye my people,' tell them their iniquity is forgiven.

(8) We are pardoned, if, after many storms, we have a sweet calm and peace within. 'Being justified we have peace.' Rom v 1. After many a bitter tear shed, and heart-breaking, the mind has been more sedate, and a sweet serenity or still music has followed; which brings the tidings that God is appeased. Before conscience accused, now it secretly whispers comforts, which is a blessed evidence that a man's sins are pardoned. If the bailiffs do not trouble and arrest the debtor, it is a sign his debt is compounded or forgiven; so if conscience does not vex or accuse, but upon good grounds whispers consolation, it is a sign that the debt is discharged, and the sin is forgiven.

(9) Sin is forgiven when we have hearts without guile. 'Blessed is he whose transgression is forgiven, unto whom the Lord imputeth not iniquity, and in whose spirit there is no guile.' Psa xxxii 1, 2.

What is it to be without guile?

He who is without guile has plainness of heart. He is without collusion, he has not *cor duplex*, a double heart; his heart is right with God. A man may do a right action, but not with a right heart. 'Amaziah did that which was right in the sight of the Lord, but not with a perfect heart.' 2 Chron xxv 2. To have the heart right with God, is to serve him from a right principle, which is love; by a right rule, the word; to a right end, the glory of God.

A heart without guile dares not allow itself in the least sin; it avoids secret sins. The man dares not hide any sin, as Rachel did her father's images, under her. Gen xxxi 34. He knows God sees him, which is more than if men and angels beheld him. He avoids besetting sins. 'I was also upright before him, and I kept myself from mine iniquity.' Psa xviii 23. As in the hive there is a master-bee, so in the heart there is a master-sin. A heart without guile takes the sacrificing knife of mortification, and runs it through its beloved sin.

A heart without guile desires to know the whole mind and will of God. An unsound heart is afraid of the light, it is not willing to know its duty. A sincere soul says (as Job xxxiv 32), 'That which I see not, teach thou me:' Lord, show me what is my duty, and wherein I offend; let me not sin for want of light; what I know not, teach thou me.

A heart without guile is uniform in religion. The man has an equal eye to all God's commands. He makes conscience of private duties; he worships God in his closet as well as in the temple. When Jacob was alone, he wrestled with the angel. Gen xxxii 23, 24. So a Christian, when alone, wrestles with God in prayer, and will not let him go till he has blessed him. He performs difficult duties, wherein the heart and spirit of religion lie, and which cross flesh and blood; he is much in self-humbling and self-examining. *Utitur speculis magis quam perspecillis.* Seneca. He rather uses the looking glass of the word to look into his own heart, than the broad spectacles of censure to spy the faults of others.

He who has a heart without guile is true to God's interest. He grieves to see it go ill with the church. Nehemiah, though the king's cupbearer, and wine so near, was sad when Zion's glory was eclipsed. Neh ii 3. Like the tree of which I have read, if any of the leaves of which are cut, the rest shrink up of themselves, and for a time hang down; so when God's church suffers, a sincere soul feels himself touched in his own person. He rejoices to see the cause of God get ground; to see truth triumph, piety lift up her head, and the flowers of Christ's crown flourish. This is a heart without guile, it is loyal and true to God's interest.

He who has a heart without guile is just in his dealings. As he is upright in his words, so he is in his weights. He makes conscience of the second table as well as the first; he is for equity as well as piety. 'That no man go beyond and defraud his brother in any matter.' 1 Thess iv 6. A sincere person thinks he may as well rob as defraud; his rule is to do to others what he would have them do to him. Matt vii 12.

He who has a heart without guile is true in his promises; his word is as good as his bond. If he has made a promise, though it be to his prejudice, and entrenches upon his profit, he will not go back. The hypocrite plays fast and loose, flees from his word; there is no more binding him with oaths and promises, than Samson could be bound with green withs. Judges xvi 7. A sincere soul saith as Jephthah, 'I have opened my mouth unto the Lord, and I cannot go back.' Judges xi 35.

He who has a heart without guile is faithful in his friendship; he is what he pretends; his heart goes along with his tongue, as a well-made dial goes with the sun. He cannot flatter and hate, commend and censure. Counterfeiting of love is hypocrisy. It is too usual to betray with a kiss. Joab took Abner by the beard to kiss him, and smote him in the fifth rib that he died. 2 Sam xx 9, 10. Many deceive with sugar words. Physicians judge of the health of the body by the tongue; if that look well, the body is in health; but we cannot judge of friendship by the tongue. The words may be full of honey, when the heart has the gall of malice. His heart is not true to God who is treacherous to his friend. Thus you see what a heart without guile is; and that to have such a heart is a sign that sin is pardoned. God will not impute sin to him 'in whose spirit there is no guile.' What a blessed thing is it not to have sin imputed! If our sins be not imputed, it is as if we had no sin; sins remitted are as if they had not been committed. This blessing belongs to a sincere soul. God imputes not iniquity to him in whose spirit is no guile.

(10) He whose sins are forgiven is willing to forgive others who have offended him. 'Forgiving one another, even as God for Christ's sake hath forgiven you.' Eph iv 32. A hypocrite will read, come to church, give alms, build hospitals, but cannot forgive wrongs; he will rather want forgiveness from God than he will forgive his enemies. A pardoned soul argues thus: 'Has God been so good to me to forgive me my sins, and shall I not imitate him in this? Has he forgiven me pounds, and shall I not forgive pence?' It is noted of Cranmer, *nihil oblivisci solet praeter injurias*. Cicero. He was of a forgiving spirit, and would do offices of love to all who had injured him; like the sun, which having drawn up black vapours from the earth, returns them back in sweet showers.

By this touchstone we may try whether our sins are pardoned. We need not climb up to heaven to see whether our sins are forgiven, but only look into our hearts. Are we of forgiving spirits? Can we bury injuries, requite good for evil? This would be a good sign that we are forgiven of God. If we can find all these things wrought in our souls, they are happy signs that our sins are pardoned, and are good letters testimonial to show for heaven.

Use 4. For consolation. I shall open a box of cordials, and show you some of the glorious privileges of a pardoned condition. This is a peculiar favour, it is a spring shut up, and unsealed for none but the elect. The wicked may have forbearing mercy, but an elect person only has forgiving mercy. Forgiveness of sin makes way for solid joy. 'Comfort ye, comfort ye my people, saith your God. Speak ye comfortably to Jerusalem;' or, as in the Hebrew, 'speak to her heart.' Isa xl 1, 2. What was to cheer her heart? 'Cry unto her, that her iniquity is pardoned.' If anything would comfort her the Lord knew it was this. When Christ would cheer the palsied man, he said, 'Son, be of good cheer, thy sins be forgiven thee.' Matt ix 2. It was a greater comfort to have his sins forgiven than to have his palsy healed. This made David put on his best clothes, and anoint himself. 2 Sam xii 20. His child was newly dead, and God had told him 'the sword shall never depart from thine house;' yet now he spruces up himself, puts on his best clothes, and anoints himself; whence was this? He had heard good news; God sent him pardon by Nathan the prophet. 'The Lord hath put away thy sin.' 2 Sam xii 13. This could not but revive his heart, and, in token of joy, he anointed himself. Philo says, it was an opinion of some of the philosophers, that among the heavenly spheres there was such sweet harmony, that if the sound of it could reach our ears it would affect us with wonder and delight. Surely he who is pardoned has such a divine melody in his soul as replenishes him with infinite delight. When Christ said to Mary Magdalene, 'Thy sins are forgiven,' he soon added, 'go in peace.' Luke vii 50. More particularly:

(1) God looks upon a pardoned soul as if he had never sinned. As cancelling a bond nulls the bond, and makes it as if the money had never been owing, so forgiving sin makes it not to be. Where sin is remitted, it is as if it had not been committed. So that, as Rachael wept because her children were not, so a child of God may rejoice because his sins are not. Jer l 20. God looks upon him as if he had never offended. Though sin remain in him after pardon, yet God does not look upon him as a sinner, but as a just man.

(2) God having pardoned sin, will pass an act of oblivion. 'I will forgive their iniquity, and I will remember their sin no more.' Jer xxxi 34. When a creditor has crossed the book, he does not call for the debt again. God will not reckon with the sinner in a judicial way. When our sins are laid upon the head of Christ, our scapegoat, they are carried into a land of forgetfulness.

(3) The pardoned soul is for ever secured from the wrath of God. How terrible is God's wrath! 'Who knoweth the power of thine anger?' Psa xc 11. If a spark of God's wrath lighting upon a man's conscience fills it with

horror, what is it to be always scorched in that torrid zone, to lie upon beds of flames! Now, from this avenging wrath of God every pardoned soul is freed. Though he may taste the bitter cup of affliction, he shall never drink of the sea of God's wrath. 'Being justified by his blood, we shall be saved from wrath through him.' Rom v 9. His blood quenches the flames of hell.

(4) Sin being pardoned, conscience has no more authority to accuse. Conscience roars against the unpardoned sinner, but it cannot terrify or accuse him that is pardoned. God has discharged the sinner, and if the creditor discharge the debtor, what right has the sergeant to arrest him? The truth is, if God absolves, conscience if rightly informed, absolves; if once God says, 'Thy sins are pardoned,' conscience says, 'Go in peace.' If the sky be clear, and no storms blow there, the sea is calm; so, if all be clear above, and God shines with pardoning mercy upon the soul, conscience is calm and serene.

(5) Nothing that befalls a pardoned soul shall hurt him. 'There shall no evil befall thee:' that is, no destructive evil. Psa xci 10. Everything to a wicked man is hurtful. Good things are for his hurt. His very blessings are turned into a curse. 'I will curse your blessings.' Mal ii 2. Riches and prosperity do him hurt. They are not *munera* [favours], but *insidiae* [snares]. Seneca. 'Gold snares.' 'Riches kept for the owners thereof to their hurt.' Eccl v 13. Like Haman's banquet, which ushered in his funeral. Ordinances do a sinner hurt; they are a 'savour of death.' 2 Cor ii 16. Cordials themselves kill. The best things hurt the wicked, but the worst things which befall a pardoned soul shall do him no hurt. The sting, the poison, the curse is gone. His soul is no more hurt, than David hurt Saul, when he cut off the lap of his garment.

(6) To a pardoned soul, everything has a commission to do him good. Afflictions do him good; poverty, reproach, persecution. 'Ye thought evil against me, but God meant it unto good.' Gen l 20. As the elements, though of contrary qualities, are so tempered that they work for the good of the universe, so the most cross providences work for good to a pardoned soul. Correction as a corrosive eats out sin; it cures the swelling of pride, the fever of lust, and the dropsy of avarice. It is a refining fire to purify grace, and make it sparkle as gold. Every cross providence, to a pardoned soul, is like Paul's Euroclydon or cross wind, which, though it broke the ship, yet Paul was brought to shore upon the broken pieces. Acts xxvii.

(7) A pardoned soul is not only exempted from wrath, but invested with dignity; as Joseph was not only freed from prison, but advanced to be second man in the kingdom.

(8) A pardoned soul is made a favourite of heaven. A king may pardon a traitor, but will not make him one of his privy council; but whom God

pardons, he receives into favour. I may say to him as the angel to the virgin Mary, 'Thou hast found favour with God.' Luke i 30. Hence, such as are forgiven, are said to be crowned with lovingkindness. Psa ciii 3, 4. Whom God pardons he crowns. Whom God absolves, he marries to himself. 'I am merciful, and I will not keep anger for ever;' Jer iii 12; there is forgiveness; and in the fourteenth verse, 'I am married to you;' and he who is matched into the crown of heaven, is as rich as the angels, as rich as heaven can make him.

(9) Sin being pardoned, we may come with humble boldness to God in prayer. Guilt makes us afraid to go to God. Adam having sinned, 'was afraid, and hid' himself. Gen iii 10. Guilt clips the wings of prayer, it fills the face with blushing; but forgiveness breeds confidence. We may look upon God as a Father of mercy, holding forth a golden sceptre. He that has got his pardon, can look upon his prince with comfort.

(10) Forgiveness of sin makes our services acceptable. God takes all we do in good part. A guilty person does nothing that is pleasing to God. His prayer is 'turned into sin;' but when sin is pardoned, God accepts his offering. We read of Joshua standing before the angel of the Lord: 'Joshua was clothed with filthy garments,' that is, he was guilty of divers sins; now, saith the Lord, 'Take away the filthy garments, I have caused thine iniquity to pass from thee;' and then he stood and ministered before the Lord, and his services were accepted. Zech iii 3, 4.

(11) Forgiveness of sin is the sauce which sweetens all the comforts of this life. As guilt embitters our comforts, and puts wormwood into our cup, so pardon sweetens all, and is like sugar to wine. Health and pardon, estate and pardon, relish well. Pardon of sin gives a sanctified title and a delicious taste to every comfort. As Naaman said to Gehazi, 'Take two talents,' so says God to the pardoned soul, Take two talents; take the venison, and take a blessing with it; take the oil in the cruse, and take my love with it; 'Take two talents.' 2 Kings v 23. It is observable that Christ joins these two together, 'Give us our daily bread, forgive us our trespasses,' as if Christ would teach us there is little comfort in daily bread unless sin be forgiven. Forgiveness perfumes and drops sweetness into every earthly enjoyment.

(12) If sin be forgiven, God will never upbraid us with former sins. When the prodigal came home to his father, the father received him into his loving embraces, and never mentioned his former luxury, or spending his estate among harlots; so God will not upbraid us with former sins – nay, he will entirely love us; we shall be his jewels, and he will put us in his bosom. To Mary Magdalene, a pardoned penitent, after Christ arose, he first appeared. Mark xvi 9. So far was he from upbraiding her, that he brought her the first news of his resurrection.

(13) Pardoned sin is a pillar of support in the loss of friends. God has taken away thy child, thy husband; but he has also taken away thy sins. He has given thee more than he has taken away; he has taken away a flower, and given thee a jewel. He has given thee Christ and the Spirit, and the earnest of glory. He hath given thee more than he has taken away.

(14) Where God pardons sins, he bestows righteousness. With remission of sin goes imputation of righteousness. 'I will greatly rejoice in the Lord: he hath covered me with the robe of righteousness.' Isa lxi 10. If a Christian can take any comfort in his inherent righteousness, which is so stained and mixed with sin, oh, what comfort may he take in Christ's righteousness, which is a better righteousness than that of Adam! Adam's righteousness was mutable; but suppose it had been unchangeable, it was but the righteousness of a man; but that which is imputed is the righteousness of him who is God. 'That we might be made the righteousness of God in him.' 2 Cor v 21. Oh, blessed privilege, to be reputed in the sight of God righteous as Christ, having his embroidered robe put upon the soul! This is the comfort of every one that is pardoned, he has a perfect righteousness; and now God says of him, 'Thou art all fair, my love; there is no spot in thee.' Cant iv 7.

(15) A pardoned soul needs not fear death. He may look on death with joy, who can look on forgiveness with faith. To a pardoned soul, death has lost his sting. Death, to a pardoned sinner, is like arresting a man after the debt is paid; it may arrest, but Christ will show the debt-book crossed in his blood. A pardoned soul may triumph over death, 'O death! where is thy sting? O grave! where is thy victory?' He who is pardoned need not fear death: it is not to him a destruction, but a deliverance; it is a day of jubilee or release; it releases him from all his sins. Death comes to a pardoned soul as the angel did to Peter, when he smote him, and beat off his chains, and carried him out of prison; it smites his body, and the chains of sin fall off. Death gives a pardoned soul a *quietus est* [he is at rest], it frees from all his labours. Rev xiv 13. *Felix transitus a labore ad requiem* [Happy is the passage from toil to rest]. Bernard. As it will wipe off our tears, so it will wipe off our sweat. It will do a pardoned Christian a good turn, therefore it is made a part of the inventory in 1 Cor iii 22; even death is yours. It is like the waggon which was sent for old Jacob, that came rattling with its wheels, but it was to carry Jacob to his son Joseph; so the wheels of death's chariot may rattle and make a noise, but they are to carry a believer to Christ. While a believer is here, he is absent from the Lord. 2 Cor v 6. He lives far from court, and cannot see him whom his soul loves; but death gives him a sight of the King of Glory, in whose presence is fulness of joy. To a pardoned soul, death is *transitus ad regnum* [a passage to the kingdom]; it removes him to the place of

bliss, where he shall hear the triumphs and anthems of praise sung in the choir of angels. No cause has a pardoned soul to fear death; what needs he fear to have his body buried in the earth who has his sins buried in Christ's wounds? What hurt can death do to him? It is but his ferryman to ferry him over to the land of promise. The day of death to a pardoned soul is his ascension-day to heaven, his coronation-day, when he shall be crowned with those delights of paradise which are unspeakable and full of glory. These are the rich consolations which belong to a pardoned sinner. Well might David proclaim him blessed. 'Blessed is he whose transgression is forgiven;' in the Hebrew it is in the plural, blessednesses. Psa xxxii 1. Here is a plurality of blessings. Forgiveness of sin is like the first link of a chain which draws all the links after it; it draws these fifteen privileges after it; it crowns with grace and glory. Who then would not labour to have his sins forgiven? 'Blessed is he whose transgression is forgiven, whose sin is covered.'

Use 5. Now follow the duties of those who have their sins forgiven.

(1) Be much in praise and doxology. 'Bless the Lord, O my soul, who forgiveth all thine iniquities.' Has God crowned you with pardoning mercy? set the crown of your praise upon the head of free grace. Pardon of sin is a discriminating mercy, a jewel hung only upon the elect, which calls for acclamations of praise. You give thanks for 'daily bread,' and will you not much more for pardon? You give thanks for deliverance from sickness, and will you not for deliverance from hell? God has done more for you in forgiving your sin than if he had given you a kingdom. That you may be more thankful, do but set the unpardoned condition before your eyes. How sad is it to want a pardon! All the curses of the law stand in full force against such a one. The unpardoned sinner dying drops into the grave and hell both at once; he must quarter among the damned; and will it not make you thankful that this is not your condition, but that you are 'delivered from the wrath to come'?

(2) Let God's pardoning love inflame your hearts with love to God. For God to pardon freely without any desert of yours; to pardon so many offences; to pardon you and pass by others; to take you out of the ruins of mankind, of a clod of dust and sin, and make you a jewel sparkling with heavenly glory; will not this make you love God much? If of three prisoners that deserve to die the king pardons one, and leaves the other two to the severity of the law, will not he that is pardoned love the prince who has been so full of clemency to him? How should your hearts be endeared in love to God! The schoolmen distinguish a twofold love, *amor gratuitus*, a love of bounty – that is, God's love to us in forgiving; and *amor debitus*, a

love of duty – that is, our love to God by way of return. We should show our love by admiring God, by sweetly solacing ourselves in him, and binding ourselves to him in a perpetual covenant.

(3) Let the sense of God's love in forgiving make you more cautious and fearful of sin for the future. 'There is forgiveness with thee that thou mayest be feared.' Psa cxxx 4. Oh, fear to offend the God who has been so forgiving to you. If a friend has done us a kindness, we shall not disoblige him or abuse his love. After Nathan had told David, 'The Lord hath put away thy sin,' how tender was his conscience! How fearful was he of staining his soul with the guilt of more blood! 'Deliver me from bloodguiltiness, O God.' Psa li 14. When men commit gross sins after pardon, God changes his carriage towards them, he turns his smile into a frown; they lie, as Jonah, in the 'belly of hell;' God's wrath falls into their conscience as a drop of scalding lead into the eye; the promises are as a fountain sealed, not a drop of comfort comes from them. O Christians, do you not remember what it cost before you got your pardon? how long it was before your 'broken bones' were set? and will you again venture to sin? You may be in such a condition that you may question whether you belong to God or not. Though God does not damn you, he may give you a taste of hell in this life.

(4) If God has given you good hope that you are pardoned, walk cheerfully. 'We joy in God, through our Lord Jesus Christ, by whom we have now received the atonement.' Rom v 11. Who should rejoice, if not he that has his pardon? God rejoices when he shows us mercy; and should not we rejoice when we receive mercy? In the saddest times, a pardoned soul may rejoice. Afflictions have a commission to do him good; every cross wind of providence shall blow him nearer to the haven of glory. Christian, God has pulled off your prison-fetters, and clothed you with the robe of righteousness, and crowned you with lovingkindness, and yet art thou sad? 'We rejoice in hope of the glory of God.' Rom v 2. Can the wicked rejoice who have only a short reprieve from hell, and not they who have a full pardon sealed?

(5) Has God pardoned you? Do all the service you can for God. 'Always abounding in the work of the Lord.' 1 Cor xv 58. Let your head study for God; let your hands work for him; let your tongue be the organ of his praise. When Paul got his pardon, and could say, 'I obtained mercy,' it was as oil to the wheels, it made him move faster in obedience. 1 Tim i 16. 'I laboured more abundantly than they all.' 1 Cor xv 10. Paul's obedience did not move slowly, as the sun on the dial; but swiftly, as the sun in the firmament. He did spend, and was spent for Christ. The pardoned soul thinks he can never love God enough, or serve him enough.

Use 6. Some rules or directions, how we may obtain forgiveness of sin.

(1) We must take heed of mistakes about pardon of sin; as the mistake that our sins are pardoned when they are not.

Whence is this mistake?

From two grounds. [1] Because God is merciful. God's being merciful shows that man's sins are pardonable. But there is a great deal of difference between sins pardonable and sins pardoned; thy sins may be pardonable, yet not pardoned. Though God be merciful, yet whom is God's mercy for? Not for the presuming sinner, but the repenting sinner. Such as go on in sin, cannot lay claim to it. God's mercy is like the ark, which none but the priests might touch; none but such as are spiritual priests, sacrificing their sins, may touch the ark of God's mercy. [2] Because Christ died for their sins, therefore they are forgiven. That Christ died for remission of sin is true; but that all have remission is false, for then Judas would be forgiven. Remission is limited to believers. 'By him all that believe are justified;' but all do not believe; some slight and trample Christ's blood under foot. Acts xiii 39; Heb x 29. Notwithstanding Christ's death, all are not pardoned. Take heed of this dangerous mistake. Who will seek after pardon that thinks he has it already?

Another mistake is, that pardon is easy to be had; it is but a sigh, or, Lord, have mercy; but how dearly has pardon cost those who have obtained it? How long was it ere David's broken bones were set! Happy are we if we have the pardon of sin sealed, though at the very last hour; but why do men think pardon of sin so easy to be obtained? Their sins are but small, therefore venial. The devil holds the small end of the perspective glass before their eyes. But there is no small sin against Deity. Why is he punished with death that clips the king's coin or defaces his statue, but because it is an abuse offered to the person of the king? Little sins, when multiplied, become great, as a little sum when multiplied, comes to millions. What is less than a grain of sand, but when the sand is multiplied, what heavier? Thy sins cost no small price. View them in the glass of Christ's sufferings, who veiled his glory, lost his joy, and poured out his soul an offering for the least sin. Little sins, unrepented of, will damn thee, as well as greater. Not only great rivers fall into the sea, but little brooks; not only greater sins carry men to hell, but less; therefore do not think pardon easy, because sin is small. Beware of mistakes.

(2) The second means for pardon of sin is to see yourselves guilty. Come to God as condemned men. 'They put ropes on their heads and came to the king of Israel.' 1 Kings xx 32. Let us come to God in profound humility; say not, Lord, my heart is good, and my life blameless. God hates this. Lie

in the dust, be covered with sackcloth: say as the centurion, 'Lord, I am not worthy that thou shouldest come under my roof;' I deserve not the least smile from heaven. Matt viii 8. This is the way for pardon.

(3) The third means for pardon is, hearty confession of sin. 'I said, I will confess my transgressions, and thou forgavest the iniquity of my sin.' Psa xxxii 5. Would we have God cover our sins, we must uncover them. 'If we confess our sins, he is just to forgive us our sins.' 1 John i 9. One would have thought it should have run thus, If we confess our sins, he is merciful to forgive them. Nay, but he is just to forgive them. Why just? Because he has bound himself by a promise to forgive humble confessors of sin. *Cum accusat excusat.* Tertullian. When we accuse ourselves, God absolves us. We are apt to hide our sins, which is as great a folly as for one to hide his disease from the physician; but when we open our sins to God by confessing, he opens his mercy to us by forgiving.

(4) Another means for pardon is sound repentance. Repentance and remission are put together. Luke xxiv 47. There is a promise of a fountain opened for washing away the guilt of sin. Zech xiii 1. But see what goes before: 'They shall look upon me whom they have pierced, and they shall mourn for him.' Zech xii 10. 'Wash you, make you clean;' that is, wash in the waters of repentance; and then follows a promise of forgiveness, 'Though your sins be as scarlet, they shall be as white as snow.' Isa i 16, 18. It is easy to turn white into scarlet, but not so easy to turn scarlet into white: yet, upon repentance, God has promised to make the scarlet sinner of a milk-like whiteness.

Think not, however, that repentance merits pardon, but it prepares for it. We set our seal on the wax when it melts; so God seals his pardons on melting hearts.

(5) The next means for pardon is faith in the blood of Christ. It is Christ's blood that washes away sin. Rev i 5. But this blood will not wash away sin, unless it be applied by faith. The apostle speaks of the sprinkling of the blood of Christ. 1 Pet i 2. Many are not pardoned, though Christ's blood be shed, because it is not sprinkled; now it is faith that sprinkles Christ's blood on the soul, for the remission of sin. As Thomas put his hands into Christ's sides, so faith puts its hands into Christ's wounds, and takes of the blood and sprinkles it upon the conscience, for the washing away of guilt. John xx 27. Hence in Scripture, we are said to obtain pardon through faith. 'By him all that believe are justified.' Acts xiii 39. 'Thy sins are forgiven.' Luke vii 48. Whence was this? 'Thy faith hath saved thee.' v 50. O let us labour for faith. Christ is a propitiation or atonement to take away sin; but how? 'Through faith in his blood.' Rom iii 25.

(6) The last means is to pray much for pardon. 'Take away all iniquity.'

Hos xiv 2. 'The publican smote upon his breast, saying, God be merciful to me a sinner.' Luke xviii 13. And the text says, he went away justified. Many pray for health, riches, children; but Christ has taught us to pray, *Dimitte nobis debita nostra*, 'Forgive us our sins.' Be earnest suitors for pardon; consider what guilt of sin is; it binds one over to the wrath of God; better thy house were haunted with devils than thy soul with guilt. He who is in the bond of iniquity, must needs be in the gall of bitterness. Acts viii 23. A guilty soul wears Cain's mark, which was a trembling at the heart, and a shaking in his flesh. Guilt makes the sinner afraid, lest every trouble he meets with should arrest him and bring him to judgment. If guilt be so dismal, and breed such convulsion fits in the conscience, how earnest should we be in prayer, that God would remove it, and so earnest as to resolve to take no denial! Plead hard with God for pardon, as a man would plead with a judge for his life. Fall upon thy knees, say, Lord, hear one word. God may say, What canst thou say for thyself, that thou shouldest not die? Lord, I can say but little, but I put in my Surety, Christ shall answer for me; O look upon that blood which speaks better things than that of Abel; Christ is my priest, his blood is my sacrifice, his divine nature is my altar. As Rahab was to show the scarlet thread in the window, that when Joshua saw it he might not destroy her, so show the Lord the scarlet thread of Christ's blood, for that is the way to have mercy. Josh ii 18, 21; vi 22, 23. God may say, Why should I pardon thee? Thou hast nowise obliged me. But, Lord, pardon me, because thou hast promised it; I urge thy covenant. When a man is about to die by the law, he calls for his book; so say, Lord, let me have the benefit of my book; thy word says, 'Let the wicked forsake his way and our God will abundantly pardon.' Isa lv 7. Lord, I have forsaken my sins, let me therefore have mercy; I plead the benefit of the book. But, for whose sake should I pardon? Thou canst not deserve it. Lord, for thy own name's sake; thou hast said, thou wilt blot out sin, for thy own name's sake. Isa xliii 25. It will not eclipse thy crown; thy mercy will shine forth, and all thy other attributes ride in triumph, if thou shalt pardon me! Thus plead with God in prayer, and resolve not to give over till thy pardon be sealed. God cannot deny importunity; he delights in mercy. As the mother, says Chrysostom, delights to have her breasts milked, so God delights to milk out the breast of mercy to the sinner. These means being used will procure this great blessedness, the forgiveness of sin.

IV. *The last part of this petition is the condition: 'As we forgive them that trespass against us.'* This word, As, is not a note of equality, but similitude; not that we equal God in forgiving, but imitate him. The great duty of forgiving others, is crossing the stream; it is contrary to flesh and blood.

R

Men forget kindnesses, but remember injuries. But it is an indispensable duty to forgive; we are not bound to trust an enemy; but we are bound to forgive him. We are naturally prone to revenge. Revenge, says Homer, is sweet as dropping honey. The heathen philosophers held revenge lawful. *Ulcisci te lacessitus potes* [When provoked you may avenge yourself]. Cicero. But we learn better things from the oracles of Scripture. 'When ye stand praying, forgive.' Mark xi 25. 'If any man have a quarrel against any: even as Christ forgave you, so also do ye.' Col iii 13.

How can we forgive others, when God only can forgive sin?

In every breach of the second table, there are two things: an offence against God, and a trespass against man. So far as it is an offence against God, he only can forgive; but so far as it is a trespass against man, we may forgive.

When do we forgive others?

When we strive against all thoughts of revenge; when we will not do our enemies mischief, but wish well to them, grieve at their calamities, pray for them, seek reconciliation with them, and show ourselves ready on all occasions to relieve them. This is gospel-forgiving.

But I have been much injured and abused, and to put up with it will be a stain to my reputation.

(1) To pass by an injury without revenge, is not eclipsing our honour. The Scripture says of a man, 'It is his glory to pass over a transgression.' Prov xix 11. It is more honour to bury an injury than to revenge it. Wrath denotes weakness; a noble heroic spirit overlooks a petty offence.

(2) Suppose a man's credit should be impaired with those whose censure is not to be regarded; consider the folly of challenging another to a duel. It is little wisdom for a man to redeem his credit by losing his life, and to run to hell to be counted valorous.

But the wrong he has done me is great.

But thy not forgiving him is a greater wrong. In injuring thee he has offended against man, but in not forgiving him thou offendest against God.

But if I forgive one injury, I shall occasion more.

If the more injuries you forgive, the more you meet with, it will make thy grace shine the more. Often forgiving will add more to the weight of thy glory. If any say, I strive to excel in other graces, but as for this forgiving, I cannot do it, I desire in this to be excused, what becomes of other graces?

The graces are *inter se connexae*, linked and chained together; when there is one, there is all. He that cannot forgive, his grace is counterfeit, his faith is fancy, his devotion is hypocrisy.

But suppose another has wronged me in my estate, may I not go to law for my debt?

Yes, else of what use were law courts? God has set judges to decide cases in law, and to give every one his right. It is with going to law, as it is with going to war; when the just rights of a nation are invaded, it is lawful to go to war; so when a man's estate is trespassed upon by another, he may go to law to recover it. But the law must be used in the last place; when no entreaties or arbitrations will prevail, then the chancery must decide it. Yet this is no revenge, it is not so much to injure another, as to right one's self; which may be, and yet we may live in charity.

Use 1. Here is a bill of indictment against such as study revenge, and cannot put up with the least discourtesy. They would have God forgive them, but they will not forgive others. They will pray, come to church, give alms; but, as Christ said, 'One thing thou lackest.' Mark x 21. They lack a forgiving spirit, they will rather want forgiveness from God than they will forgive their brother. How sad is it, that, for every slight wrong, or disgraceful word, men should let malice boil in their hearts! would there be so many duels, arrests, murders, if men had the art of forgiving? Revenge is the proper sin of the devil; he is no drunkard or adulterer, but this old serpent is full of the poison of malice: and what shall we say to those who make a profession of religion, but instead of forgiving, pursue others despitefully? It was prophesied, the 'wolf shall dwell with the lamb.' Isa xi 6. But what shall we say, when such as profess to be lambs become wolves? They open the mouths of the profane against religion who will say these are as full of rancour as any. O whither is love and mercy fled? If the son of man come, will he find charity on the earth? I fear but little. How can those who cherish anger and malice in their hearts, and will not forgive, pray, 'Forgive us, as we forgive others'? Either they must omit this petition, as Chrysostom says some did in his time, or they pray against themselves.

Use 2. Let us all be persuaded, if ever we hope for salvation, to pass by petty injuries and discourtesies, and labour to be of forgiving spirits. 'Forbearing one another, and forgiving one another.' Col iii 13.

(1) Herein we resemble God. He is ready to forgive. Psa lxxxvi 5. He befriends his enemies; he opens his hands to relieve those who open their mouths against him. It was Adam's pride to resemble God in omniscience;

but it is lawful to resemble God in forgiving enemies; this is a God-like disposition; and what is godliness, but God-likeness?

(2) To forgive is one of the highest evidences of grace. When grace comes into the heart, it makes a man, as Caleb, of another spirit. Numb xiv 24. It makes a great metamorphosis, it sweetens the heart, and fills it with love and candour. As a scion grafted into a stock, partakes of the nature and sap of the tree, and brings forth the same fruit, so he who was once of a sour crabby disposition, given to revenge, when ingrafted into Christ, partakes of the sap of the heavenly olive, and bears sweet and generous fruit; he is full of love to his enemies, and requites good for evil. As the sun draws up many thick noxious vapours from the earth, and returns them in sweet showers, so a gracious heart returns the unkindnesses of others with the sweet influences of love and mercifulness. 'They rewarded me evil for good; but as for me, when they were sick, my clothing was sackcloth, I humbled my soul with fasting.' Psa xxxv 12, 13. This is a good certificate to show for heaven.

(3) The blessed example of our Lord Jesus teaches this. He was of a forgiving spirit; his enemies reviled him, but he pitied them; their words were more bitter than the gall and vinegar they gave him, but his words were smoother than oil; they spat upon him, pierced him with the spear and nails, but he prayed for them, 'Father, forgive them.' He wept over his enemies, he shed tears for those that shed his blood. Never was there such a pattern of amazing kindness. Christ bids us learn of him. Matt xi 29. He doth not bid us learn of him to work miracles, but he would have us learn of him to forgive our enemies. If we do not imitate Christ's life, we cannot be saved by his death.

(4) The danger of an implacable unforgiving spirit. It hinders the efficacy of ordinances; it is like an obstruction in the body, which keeps it from thriving. A revengeful spirit poisons our sacrifice; our prayers are turned into sin. Will God receive prayer mingled with this strange fire? Our coming to the sacrament is sin if we come not in charity, so that ordinances are turned into sin. It were sad if all the meat we eat should turn to poison; but malice poisons the sacramental cup, men eat and drink their own damnation. Judas came to the passover in malice, and after the sop, Satan entered into him. John xiii 27.

(5) God has tied his mercy to the condition, that if we do not forgive, neither will he forgive us. 'If ye forgive not men their trespasses, neither will your Father forgive your trespasses.' Matt vi 15. A man may as well go to hell for not forgiving as for not believing. How can they expect mercy from God whose bowels are shut up and are merciless to their trespassing brethren? 'He shall have judgment without mercy that hath showed

no mercy.' James ii 13. 'I cannot forgive,' said one, 'though I go to hell.'

(6) The examples of the saints who have been of forgiving spirits. Joseph forgave his brethren, though they put him into a pit and sold him. 'Fear not; I will nourish you and your little ones.' Gen l 21. Stephen prayed for his persecutors. Moses was of a forgiving spirit. How many injuries and affronts did he put up with! The people of Israel dealt unkindly with him; they murmured against him at the waters of Marah, but he prayed for them. Exod xv 25. 'He cried unto the Lord, and the Lord shewed him a tree, which when he had cast into the waters, the waters were made sweet.' When they wanted water, they chided with him. 'Wherefore is this that thou hast brought us out of Egypt to kill us with thirst?' Exod xvii 3. As if they had said, 'If we die, we will lay our death to thy charge.' This was enough to have made Moses call for fire from heaven upon them; but he passes by this injury, and, to show he forgave them, he became an intercessor for them, and drew water from the rock for them; ver 4, 5, 6. The prophet Elisha feasted his enemies: he prepared a table for those who would have prepared his grave. 2 Kings vi 23. Cranmer was famous for forgiving injuries. When Luther had reviled Calvin, Calvin said, *Etiamsi millies me diabolum vocet:* 'Though he call me a devil a thousand times, yet I will love and honour him as a precious servant of Christ.' When one who had abused and wronged a Christian asked him what wonders his Master Christ had wrought, he said, 'He hath wrought this wonder, that though you have so injured me, I can forgive you and pray for you.'

(7) Forgiving and requiting good for evil is the best way to conquer and melt the heart of an enemy. When Saul had pursued David with malice and hunted him as a partridge upon the mountains, David would not do him mischief when it was in his power. David's kindness melted Saul's heart. 'Is this thy voice, my son David? And Saul lifted up his voice and wept, and said, Thou art more righteous than I, for thou hast rewarded me good.' 1 Sam xxiv 16, 17. Such forgiving is heaping coals which melt the enemy's heart. Rom xii 20. It is the most noble victory to overcome an enemy without striking a blow, to conquer him with love. When Philip of Macedon was told that one Nicanor openly railed against him, instead of putting him to death, he sent him a rich present, which so overcame the man, and made his heart relent, that he went up and down to recant what he had said against the king, and highly extolled the king's clemency.

(8) Forgiving others is the way to have forgiveness from God, and is a sign of that forgiveness.

[1] It is the way to have forgiveness. 'If ye forgive men their trespasses, your heavenly Father will also forgive you.' Matt vi 14. But one would

think other things should sooner procure forgiveness from God than our forgiving others. No, surely nothing like this to procure forgiveness; for all other acts of religion may have leaven in them. God forbade leaven in the sacrifice. Exod xxxiv 25. One may give alms, and there may be the leaven of vainglory in it. The Pharisees sounded a trumpet, when they gave alms, to gain applause. Matt vi 2. One may give his body to be burned, yet there may be the leaven of false zeal in this; but to forgive others that have offended us can have no leaven in it, no sinister aim. It is a duty wholly spiritual, and is done purely out of love to God; hence God annexes forgiveness to this rather than to the highest and most renowned works of charity which are cried up in the world.

[2] It is a sign of God's forgiving us. It is not a cause of God's forgiving us, but a sign. We need not climb up into heaven to see whether our sins are forgiven: let us look into our hearts, and see if we can forgive others. If we can, we need not doubt but God has forgiven us. Our loving others is the reflection of God's love to us. Oh, therefore, by all these arguments, let us be persuaded to forgive others. Christians, how many offences has God passed by in us! Our sins are innumerable and heinous. Is God willing to forgive us so many offences, and cannot we forgive a few? No man can do so much wrong to us all our life as we do to God in one day.

But how must we forgive?

As God forgives us. (1) Cordially. God not only makes a show of forgiveness, and keeps our sins by him; but he really forgives, he passes an act of oblivion. Jer xxxi 34. So we must not only say we forgive, but do it with the heart. 'If ye from your hearts forgive not.' Matt xviii 35.

(2) God forgives fully; he forgives all our sins. He does not for fourscore write down fifty. 'Who forgiveth all thine iniquities.' Psa ciii 3. Hypocrites pass by some offences, but retain others. Would we have God so deal with us as to remit only some trespasses, and call us to account for the rest?

(3) God forgives often. We run afresh upon the score, but God multiplies pardon. Isa lv 7. Peter asks the question, 'Lord, how oft shall my brother sin against me, and I forgive him? Till seven times? Jesus saith unto him, I say not until seven times, but until seventy times seven.' Matt xviii 21, 22. If he say, 'I repent,' you must say, 'I remit.'

But this is one of the highest acts of religion; flesh and blood cannot do it; how shall I attain to it?

(1) Let us consider how many wrongs and injuries we have done against God. What volume can hold our *errata*? Our sins are more than the sparks in a furnace.

(2) If we would forgive, let us see God's hand in all that men do or say against us. Did we look higher than instruments, our hearts would grow calm, and we should not meditate revenge. Shimei reproached David and cursed; but David looked higher. 'Let him alone, and let him curse, for the Lord hath bidden him.' 2 Sam xvi 11. What made Christ, when he was reviled, revile not again? He looked beyond Judas and Pilate, he saw his Father putting the bitter cup into his hand. As we must see God's hand in all the affronts and incivilities we receive from men, so we must believe God will do us good by all, if we belong to him. 'It may be the Lord will requite me good for his cursing this day.' 2 Sam xvi 12. *Quisquis detrahit famae meae addet mercedi meae.* Augustine. He that injures me shall add to my reward; he that clips my name to make it weigh lighter, shall make my crown weigh heavier. Well might Stephen pray for his enemies, 'Lord, lay not this sin to their charge.' Acts vii 60. He knew they did but increase his glory in heaven; every stone his enemies threw at him added a pearl to his crown.

(3) Lay up a stock of faith. 'If thy brother trespass against thee seven times in a day, and seven times in a day turn again to thee, saying, I repent, thou shalt forgive him.' Luke xvii 3, 4. The apostles said to the Lord, 'Increase our faith,' as if they had said, 'We can never do this without a great deal of faith; Lord, increase our faith.' Believe God has pardoned you, and you will pardon others; only faith can throw dust upon injuries, and bury them in the grave of forgetfulness.

(4) Think how thou hast sometimes wronged others; and may it not be just with God that the same measure you mete to others should be measured to you again? Hast thou not wronged others, if not in their goods, yet in their name? If thou hast not borne false witness against them, yet perhaps thou hast spoken falsely of them; the consideration of which may make Christians bury injuries in silence.

(5) Get humble hearts. A proud man thinks it a disgrace to put up with an injury. What causes so many duels and murders but pride? 'Be clothed with humility.' 1 Pet v 5. He who is low in his own eyes will not be troubled much though others lay him low; he knows there is a day coming when there shall be a resurrection of names as well as bodies, and God will avenge him of his adversaries. 'And shall not God avenge his own elect?' Luke xviii 7. The humble soul leaves all his wrongs to God to requite, who hath said, 'Vengeance is mine.' Rom xii 19.

Use 3. For comfort. Such as forgive, God will forgive them. You have a good argument to plead with God for forgiveness. Lo, I am willing to forgive him who makes me no satisfaction, and wilt not thou forgive me who hast received satisfaction in Christ my surety?

The Sixth Petition in the Lord's Prayer

'And lead us not into temptation, but deliver us from evil.' Matt vi 13

THIS petition consists of two parts. *First*, Deprecatory, 'Lead us not into temptation.' *Secondly*, Petitionary, 'But deliver us from evil.'

I. *'Lead us not into temptation.'* Does God lead into temptation? God tempts no man to sin. 'Let no man say when he is tempted, I am tempted of God: for God cannot be tempted with evil, neither tempteth he any man.' James i 13. He permits sin, but does not promote it. He who is an encourager of holiness cannot be a pattern of sin. God does not tempt to that to which he has an antipathy. What king will tempt his subjects to break laws which he himself has established?

But is it not said, God tempted Abraham? Gen xxii 1.

Tempting there was no more than trying. He tried Abraham's faith, as a goldsmith tries gold in the fire; but there is a great deal of difference between trying his people's grace and exciting their corruption; he tries their grace, but does not excite their corruption. Man's sin cannot be justly fathered on God. God tempts no man.

What then is the meaning of 'Lead us not into temptation'?

The meaning is, that God would not suffer us to be overcome by temptation; that we may not be given up to the power of temptation, and be drawn into sin.

Whence do temptations come?

(1) *Ab intra* [From within], from ourselves. The heart is *fomes peccati* [the kindling of sin], the breeder of all evil. Our own hearts are the greatest tempters: *quisque sibi Satan est* [everyone is Satan to himself]. 'Every man is tempted when he is drawn away of his own lust.' The heart is a perfect decoy. James i 14.

(2) Temptations come *ab extra* [from without], from Satan. He is called the Tempter. Matt iv 3. He lies in ambush to do us mischief: *stat in procinctu diabolus* [the devil stands girded for battle], the devil lays a train of temptation to blow up the fort of our grace. He is not yet fully cast into prison, but is like a prisoner under bail. The world is his diocese, where he is sure to

be found, whatever we are doing – reading, praying, or meditating. We find him within, but how he came there we know not; we are sure of his company, though uncertain how we came by it. A saint's whole life, says Augustine, is temptation. Elias, who could shut heaven by prayer, could not shut his heart from temptation. This is a great molestation to a child of God; as it is a trouble to a virgin to have her chastity daily assaulted. The more we are tempted to evil, the more we are hindered from good. We are in great danger of the 'Prince of the air;' and we need often pray, 'Lead us not into temptation.' That we may see in what danger we are from Satan's temptations:

Consider, [1] His malice in tempting. This hellish serpent is swelled with the poison of malice. Satan envies man's happiness. To see a clod of dust so near to God, and himself, once a glorious angel, cast out of the heavenly paradise, makes him pursue mankind with inveterate hatred. 'The devil is come down unto you, having great wrath.' Rev xii 12. If there be anything this infernal spirit can delight in, it is to ruin souls, and to bring them into the same condemnation with himself. This malice of Satan in tempting must needs be great, if we consider three things:

(1) That Satan, though full of torment, should tempt others. One would think that he would scarcely have a thought but of his own misery; and yet such is his rage and malice that, while God is punishing him, he is tempting others.

(2) His malice is great, because he will tempt where he knows he cannot prevail; he will put forth his sting, though he cannot hurt. He tempted Christ. 'If thou be the Son of God.' Matt iv 3. He knew well enough Christ was God as well as man, yet he would tempt him. Such was his malice against him that he would put an affront on him, though he knew he should be conquered by him. He tempts the elect to blasphemy; he knows he cannot prevail against them; and yet such is his malice, that though he cannot storm the garrison of their hearts, yet he will plant his pieces of ordnance against them.

(3) His malice is great, because though knowing his tempting men to sin will increase his own torment in hell, he will not leave it off. Every temptation makes his chain heavier and his fire hotter, and yet he will tempt. Therefore being such a malicious revengeful spirit, we need pray that God will not suffer him to prevail by his temptation. 'Lead us not into temptation.'

[2] Consider Satan's diligence in tempting. He 'walketh about.' 1 Pet v 8. He neglects no time; he who would have us idle is himself always busy. This lion is ever hunting after his prey, he compasses sea and land to make a

proselyte; he walks about – he walks not as a pilgrim, but a spy; he watches where he may throw in the fireball of temptation. He is a restless spirit; if we repulse him, he will not desist, but come again with a temptation. Like Marcellus, a Roman captain Hannibal speaks of, whether he conquered or was conquered, was never quiet. More particularly, Satan's diligence in tempting is seen in this:

(1) If he gets the least advantage by temptation, he pursues it to the utmost. If his motion to sin begins to take, he follows it close and presses to the act of sin. When he tempted Judas to betray Christ, and found him inclinable, and beginning to bite at the bait of thirty pieces of silver, he hurried him on, and never left him till he had betrayed his Lord and Master. When he tempted Spira to renounce his religion, and saw him begin to yield, he followed the temptation close, and never left off till he had made him go to the legate at Venice, and there abjure his faith in Christ.

(2) Satan's diligence in tempting is seen in the variety of temptations he uses. He does not confine himself to one sort of temptation, he has more plots than one. If he finds one temptation does not prevail, he will have another; if he cannot tempt to lust, he will tempt to pride; if temptation to covetousness does not prevail, he will tempt to profuseness; if he cannot frighten men to despair, he will see if he cannot draw them to presumption; if he cannot make them profane, he will see if he cannot make them formalists; if he cannot make them vicious, he will tempt them to be erroneous. He will tempt them to leave off ordinances; he will pretend revelations. Error damns as well as vice: the one pistols, the other poisons. Thus Satan's diligence in tempting is great: he will turn every stone; he has several tools to work with; if one temptation will not do he will make use of another. Had we not need then to pray, 'Lead us not into temptation'?

[3] Consider Satan's power in tempting. He is called 'the prince of this world' (John xiv 30), and the 'strong man' (Luke xi 21), and the 'great red dragon,' who with his tail cast down the third part of the stars. Rev xii 3, 4.' He is full of power, being an angel; though he has lost his holiness, yet not his strength. His power in tempting is seen several ways: (1) As a spirit he can convey himself into the fancy, and poison it with bad thoughts. As the Holy Ghost casts in good motions, so the devil does bad. He put it into Judas's heart to betray Christ. John xiii 2. (2) Though Satan cannot compel the will, he can present pleasing objects to the senses, which have great force in them. He set a 'wedge of gold' before Achan, and so enticed him with that golden bait. (3) He can excite and stir up the corruption within, and work some inclinableness in the heart to embrace the temptation. Thus he stirred up corruption in David's heart, and provoked him to number the people.

1 Chron xxi 1. He can blow a spark of lust into a flame. (4) Being a spirit, he can convey his temptations into our minds, so that we cannot easily discern whether they come from him or from ourselves. One bird may hatch the egg of another, thinking it to be her own: so we often hatch the devil's motions, thinking they come from our own hearts. When Peter dissuaded Christ from suffering, he thought it came from the good affection which he bore to his Master, little thinking that Satan had a hand in it. Matt xvi 22. Now, if the devil has such power to instil his temptations, that we hardly know whether they are his or ours, we are in great danger, and had need pray not to be led into temptation. Here, some are desirous to move the question:

How shall we perceive when a motion comes from our own hearts, and when from Satan?

It is hard, as Bernard says, to distinguish *inter morsum serpentis et morbum mentis* [between the bite of the serpent and the disease of the mind], between those suggestions which come from Satan, and which breed out of our own hearts. But I conceive there is this threefold difference:

First, such motions to evil as come from our own hearts spring up more leisurely, and by degrees. Sin is long concocted in the thoughts, ere consent be given; but usually we may know a motion comes from Satan by its suddenness. Temptation is compared to a dart, because it is shot suddenly. Eph vi 16. David's numbering the people was a motion which the devil injected suddenly.

Secondly, the motions to evil which come from our own hearts are not so terrible. Few are frightened at the sight of their own children; but motions coming from Satan are more ghastly and frightful, as motions to blasphemy and self-murder. Hence it is that temptations are compared to fiery darts, because, as flashes of fire, they startle and affright the soul. Eph vi 16.

Thirdly, when evil thoughts are thrown into the mind, when we loathe and have reluctance to them; when we strive against them, and flee from them, as Moses did from the serpent, it shows they are not the natural birth of our own heart, but the hand of Joab is in this. 2 Sam xiv 19. Satan has injected these impure motions.

(5) Satan's power in tempting appears by the long experience he has acquired in the art; he has been a tempter well nigh as long as he has been an angel. Who are fitter for action than men of experience? Who is fitter to steer a ship than an old, experienced pilot? Satan has gained much experience by being so long versed in the trade of tempting. Having such experience, he knows what are the temptations which have foiled others,

and are most likely to prevail; as the fowler lays those snares which have caught other birds. Satan having such power in tempting, increases our danger, and we had need pray, 'Lead us not into temptation.'

[4] Consider Satan's subtlety in tempting. The Greek word to tempt, signifies to deceive. Satan, in tempting, uses many subtle policies to deceive. We read of the depths of Satan (Rev ii 24), of his devices and stratagems (2 Cor ii 11), of his snares and darts. He is called a lion for his cruelty, and an old serpent for his subtlety. He has several sorts of subtlety in tempting.

1st subtlety. He observes the natural temper and constitution. *Omnium discutit mores* [He attacks the character of all]. He does not know the hearts of men, but he may feel their pulse, know their temper, and can apply himself accordingly. As the husbandman knows what seed is proper to sow in such a soil, so Satan, finding out the temper, knows what temptations are proper to sow in such a heart. The same way the tide of a man's constitution runs, the wind of temptation blows. Satan tempts the ambitious man with a crown, the sanguine man with beauty, the covetous man with a wedge of gold. He provides savoury meat, such as the sinner loves.

2nd subtlety. He chooses the fittest season to tempt in. As a cunning angler casts in his angle when the fish will bite best, so the devil can hit the very joint of time when temptation is likeliest to prevail. There are several seasons he tempts in.

1st season. He tempts us in our first initiation and entrance into religion, when we have newly given up our names to Christ. He will never disturb his vassals; but when we have broken his prison in conversion, he will pursue us with violent temptations. *Solet inter primordia conversionis acrius insurgere* [He is wont to attack more sharply at the first signs of conversion]. Bernard. When Israel were got a little out of Egypt, Pharaoh pursued them. Soon as Christ was born, Herod sent to destroy him; so when the child of grace is newly born, the devil labours to strangle it with temptation. When the first buddings and blossoms of grace begin to appear, the devil would nip the tender buds with the sharp blasts of temptation. At first conversion, grace is so weak, and temptation so strong, that one wonders how the young convert escapes with his life. Satan has a spite against the new creature.

2nd season. The devil tempts when he finds us unemployed. We do not sow seed in fallow ground; but Satan sows most of his seed in a person that lies fallow. When the fowler sees a bird sit still and perch upon the tree, he shoots it; so when Satan observes us sitting still, he shoots his fiery darts of temptation at us. 'While men slept, his enemy sowed tares;' so, while men sleep in sloth, Satan sows his tares. Matt xiii 25. When David was walking on the housetop unemployed, the devil set a tempting object before him, and it prevailed. 2 Sam xi 2, 3.

3rd season. When a person is reduced to outward wants and straits, the devil tempts him. When Christ has fasted forty days, and is hungry, the devil comes and tempts him with the glory of the world. Matt iv 8. When provisions grow short, Satan sets in with a temptation; What, wilt thou starve rather than steal? reach forth thy hand, and pluck the forbidden fruit. How often does this temptation prevail? How many do we see, who, instead of living by faith, live by their shifts, and will steal the venison, though they lose the blessing.

4th season. Satan tempts after an ordinance. When we have been hearing the word, or at prayer, or sacrament, Satan casts in the angle of temptation. When Christ had been fasting and praying, then came the tempter. Matt iv 2, 3.

Why does Satan choose time after an ordinance to tempt? We should think it to be the most disadvantageous time, when the soul is raised to a heavenly frame!

(1) Malice puts Satan upon it. The ordinances, which cause fervour in a saint, cause fury in Satan. He knows in every duty we have a design against him; in every prayer we put up a suit in heaven against him; in the Lord's Supper, we take an oath to fight under Christ's banner against him; therefore he is more enraged, and lays his snares and shoots his darts against us.

(2) Satan tempts after an ordinance, because he thinks he will find us more secure. After we have been at the solemn worship of God, we are apt to grow remiss, and leave off former strictness; like a soldier, who, after the battle, leaves off his armour. Satan watches his time. He does as David did to the Amalekites, who, when they had taken the spoil, and were secure, and they did eat and drink, and dance, fell upon them, and smote them. 1 Sam xxx 17. When we grow remiss after an ordinance, and indulge ourselves too much in carnal delights, Satan falls upon us by temptation, and often foils us. After a full meal, men are apt to grow drowsy; so, after we have had a full meal at an ordinance, we are apt to slumber and grow secure, and then Satan shoots his arrow of temptation, and hits us between the joints of our armour.

5th season. Satan tempts after some discoveries of God's love. Like a pirate who sets on a ship that is richly laden, when a soul has been laden with spiritual comforts, the devil shoots at him to rob him of all. He envies a soul feasted with spiritual joy. Joseph's party-coloured coat made his brethren envy him and plot against him. After David had the good news of the pardon of his sin, which must needs fill him with consolation, Satan tempted him to a new sin in numbering the people; and so all his comfort leaked out and was spilt.

6th season. Satan tempts when he sees us weakest. He breaks over the hedge where it is lowest; as the sons of Jacob came upon the Shechemites when they were sore, and could make no resistance. Gen xxxiv 25. On two occasions Satan comes upon us in our weakness: (1) When we are alone; as he came to Eve when her husband was away, and she the less able to resist his temptation. He has the policy to give his poison privately, when no one is by to discover the treachery. Like a cunning suitor who wooes the daughter when the parents are from home; when alone and none near, the devil comes wooing with a temptation, and hopes to have the match struck up. (2) When the hour of death approaches. As the crows peck at the poor sheep, when sick and weak, and can hardly help itself, so, when a saint is weak on his deathbed, the devil pecks at him with a temptation. He reserves his most furious assaults till the last. The people of Israel were never so fiercely assaulted as when they were going to take possession of the promised land; then all the kings of Canaan combined their forces against them; so, when the saints are leaving the world and going to set their foot on the heavenly Canaan, Satan sets upon them by temptation; he tells them they are hypocrites, and all their evidences are counterfeit. Like a coward, he strikes the saints when they are down; when death is striking at the body, he is striking at the soul.

3rd subtlety. Satan, in tempting, baits his hook with religion. He can hang out Christ's colours and tempt to sin under pretences of piety. Sometimes he is the white devil, and transforms himself into an angel of light. Celsus wrote a book full of error, and he entitled it, *Liber Veritatis*, The Book of Truth. So Satan can write the title of religion upon his worst temptation. He comes to Christ with Scripture in his mouth, 'It is written,' &c. So he comes to many and tempts them to sin, under the pretence of religion. He tempts to evil, that good may come of it; he tempts men to such unwarrantable actions, that they may be put into a capacity of honouring God the more. He tempts them to accept of preferment against conscience, that they may be in a condition of doing more good. He put Herod upon killing John the Baptist, that he might be kept from the violation of his oath. He tempts many to oppression and extortion, telling them they are bound to provide for their families. He tempts many to make away with themselves, that they may live no longer to sin against God. Thus he wraps his poisonous pills in sugar. Who would suspect him when he comes as a divine, and quotes Scripture?

4th subtlety. Satan tempts to sin gradually. The old serpent winds himself in by degrees: he tempts first to less sins, that so he may bring on greater. A small offence may occasion a great crime; as a little prick of an artery may occasion a mortal gangrene. Satan first tempted David to an impure glance of the eye to look upon Bathsheba, and that unclean look occasioned adultery and murder. First he tempts to go into the company of the wicked, then to twist into a cord of friendship, and so, by degrees, to be brought into the same condemnation with them. It is a great subtlety of Satan to tempt to less sins first, for these harden the heart, and fit men for committing more horrid and tremendous sins.

5th subtlety. Satan's policy is to hand over temptations to us by those whom we least suspect.

(1) By near friends. He tempts us by those who are near in blood. He tempted Job by a proxy, he handed over a temptation to him by his wife. 'Dost thou still retain thine integrity?' Job ii 9. As if he had said, Job, thou seest how, for all thy religion, God deals with thee, his hand is gone out sore against thee; what, and still pray and weep! Cast off all religion, turn atheist! 'Curse God, and die!' Thus Satan made use of Job's wife to do his work. The woman was made of the rib, and Satan made a bow of this rib, out of which to shoot the arrow of his temptation. *Per costam petit cor* [He aims at the heart through the rib]. The devil often stands behind the curtain – he will not be seen in the business, but puts others to do his work. As a man makes use of a sergeant to arrest another, so Satan makes use of a proxy to tempt; as he crept into a serpent, so he can creep into a near relation.

(2) He tempts sometimes by religious friends. He keeps out of sight, that his cloven foot may not be seen. Who would have thought to have found the devil in Peter? When he would have dissuaded Christ from suffering, saying, 'Master, spare thyself,' Christ spied Satan in the temptation. 'Get thee behind me, Satan.' When our religious friends would dissuade us from doing our duty, Satan is a lying spirit in their mouths, and would by them entice us to evil.

6th subtlety. Satan tempts some persons more than others. Some are like wet tinder, who will not so soon take the fire of temptation as others. Satan tempts most where he thinks his policies will most easily prevail. Some are fitter to receive the impression of temptations, as soft wax is fitter to take the stamp of the seal. The apostle speaks of 'vessels fitted to destruction,' so there are vessels fitted for temptation. Rom ix 22. Some, like the sponge, suck in Satan's temptations. There are five sorts of persons that Satan most broods upon by his temptations.

(1) Ignorant persons. The devil can lead these into any snare. You may lead a blind man any whither. God made a law that the Jews should not put a stumbling-block in the way of the blind. Lev xix 14. Satan knows it is easy to put a temptation in the way of the blind, at which they shall stumble into hell. When the Syrians were smitten with blindness, the prophet Elisha could lead them whither he would into the enemy's country. 2 Kings vi 20. The bird that is blind is soon shot by the fowler. Satan, the god of this world, blinds men and then shoots them. An ignorant man cannot see the devil's snares. Satan tells him such a thing is no sin, or but a little one, and he will do well enough; it is but repent.

(2) Satan tempts unbelievers. He who, with Diagoras, doubts a Deity, or with the Photinians, denies hell, what sin may he not be drawn into? He is like metal that Satan can cast into any mould; he can dye him of any colour. An unbeliever will stick at no sin, be it luxury, perjury, or injustice. Paul was afraid of none so much as those who did not believe. 'That I may be delivered from them that do not believe in Judæa.' Rom xv 31.

(3) Satan tempts proud persons: over these he has more power. None is in greater danger of falling by temptation than he who stands high in his own conceit. When David's heart was lifted up in pride, the devil stirred him up to number the people. 2 Sam xxiv 2. *Celsae graviore casu decidunt turres, feriuntque summos fulmina montes* [Lofty towers crash with a heavier fall, and lightning strikes the tops of mountains]. Horace. Satan made use of Haman's pride to be his shame.

(4) Melancholy persons. Melancholy is *atra bilis*, a black humour, seated chiefly in the brain. It clothes the mind in sable, and disturbs reason. Satan works much upon this humour. There are three things in melancholy which give the devil great advantage: [1] It unfits for duty, it pulls off the chariot-wheels; it dispirits a man. Lute strings that are wet, will not sound; so when the spirit is sad and melancholy, a Christian is out of tune for spiritual actions. [2] Melancholy sides often with Satan against God. The devil tells such a person God does not love him, there is no mercy for him; and the melancholy soul is apt to think so too, and sets his hand to the devil's lies. [3] Melancholy breeds discontent, and discontent is the cause of many sins, as unthankfulness, impatience, and often it ends in self-murder. Judge, then, what an advantage Satan has against a melancholy person, and how easily he may prevail with him by his temptation! A melancholy person tempts the devil to tempt him.

(5) Idle persons. The devil will find work for the idle to do. Jerome gave his friend this counsel, To be ever well employed, that when the tempter

came, he might find him working in the vineyard. If the hands be not working good, the head will be plotting evil. Mic ii 1.

7th subtlety. Satan gives some little respite, and seems to leave off tempting awhile, that he may come on after with more advantage; as Israel made as if they were beaten before the men of Ai, and fled; but it was a policy to draw them out of their fenced cities, and ensnare them by an ambush. Josh viii 15. The devil sometimes raises the siege, and feigns a flight, that he may the better obtain the victory. He goes away for a time, that he may return when he sees a better season. 'When the unclean spirit is gone out of a man, he walketh through dry places, seeking rest: and finding none, he saith, I will return unto my house, whence I came out.' Luke xi 24. Satan, by feigning a flight, and leaving off tempting awhile, causes security in persons; they think they are safe, and are become victors, when, on a sudden, Satan falls on and wounds them. As one that is going to leap, runs back a little, that he may take the greater jump, so Satan seems to retire and run back a little, that he may come on with a temptation more furiously and successfully. We need, therefore, always to watch, and have on our spiritual armour.

8th subtlety. The old serpent either takes men off from the use of means, or makes them miscarry in the use of them.

(1) He labours to take men off from duty, from praying and hearing, in order to discourage them; and, to do that, he has two artifices:

He discourages them from duty by suggesting to them their unworthiness; that they are not worthy to approach to God, or have any signals of his love and favour. They are sinful, and God is holy, how dare they presume to bring their impure offering to God? That we should see ourselves unworthy, is good, and argues humility; but to think we should not approach God because of unworthiness, is a conclusion of the devil's making. God says, Come, though unworthy. By this temptation, the devil takes many off from coming to the Lord's table. Oh, says he, this is a solemn ordinance, and requires much holiness: how darest thou so unworthily come? you will eat and drink unworthily. Thus, as Saul kept the people from eating honey, so the devil by this temptation, scares many from this ordinance, which is sweeter than honey and the honeycomb.

Satan endeavours to discourage from duty by objecting want of success. When men have waited upon God in the use of ordinances, and find not the comfort they desire, Satan disheartens them, and puts them upon resolves of declining all religion; they begin to say as a wicked king, 'What should I wait for the Lord any longer?' 2 Kings vi 33. When Saul saw God answered him not by dreams and visions, Satan tempted him to leave his worship, and seek to the witch of Endor. 1 Sam xxviii 6. No answer to prayer comes; therefore, says Satan, leave off praying; who will sow seed where no crop comes up? Thus the devil by his subtle logic would dispute a poor soul out of duty. But if he sees he cannot prevail this way, to take men off from the use of means, then he labours:

(2) To make them miscarry in the use of means. By this artifice he prevails over multitudes of professors. The devil stands, as he did at Joshua's right hand, to resist men. Zech iii 1. If he cannot hinder them from duty, he will be sure to hinder them in duty, two ways:

By causing distraction in the service of God; and this he does by proposing objects of vanity, or by whispering in men's ears, that they can scarcely know what they are doing.

He hinders, by putting men upon doing duties in a wrong manner. [1] In a dead formal manner, that so they may fail of the success. Satan knows duties done superficially were as good as left undone. That prayer which does not pierce the heart, will never pierce heaven. [2] He puts them upon doing duties for wrong ends. *Finis specificat actionem* [The end governs the action]; he will make them look asquint, and have by-ends in duty. 'Thou shalt not be as the hypocrites, for they love to pray standing in the corners of the streets, that they may be seen of men.' Matt vi 5. Prayer is good, but to pray to be seen of men, was a dead fly in the box of ointment. The oil of vainglory feeds the lamp; sinister aims corrupt and flyblow our holy things. Here is Satan's policy, either to prevent duty, or pervert it; either to take men off from the use of means, or make them miscarry in the use of them.

9th subtlety. Satan can colour over sin with the name and pretence of virtue. Alcibiades hung a curtain curiously embroidered over a foul picture of satyrs; so Satan can put the image of virtue over the foul picture of sin. He can cheat men with false wares; he can make them believe that presumption is faith, that intemperate passion is zeal, revenge is prudence, covetousness is frugality, and prodigality is good hospitality. 'Come, see my zeal for the Lord,' says Jehu. Satan persuaded him it was a fire from heaven, when it was nothing but the wildfire of his own ambition; it was not zeal, but state policy. This is a subtle art of Satan, to deceive by tempting, and put men off with the dead child, instead of the live child; to make men believe that is a grace which is a sin; as if one should write balm-water upon a glass of poison. If Satan has all these subtle artifices in tempting, are we not in great danger from this prince of the air? Have we not often need to pray, 'Lord, suffer us not to be led into temptation'? As the serpent beguiled Eve with his subtlety, let us not be beguiled by his hellish snares and policies. 2 Cor xi 3.

He has a dexterity in subtle contrivances. He hurts more as a fox than a lion; his snares are worse than his darts. 'We are not ignorant of his devices.' 2 Cor ii 11.

10th subtlety. He labours to ensnare us by lawful things, *in licitis perimus omnes* [we all perish through lawful things]. More are hurt by lawful things than unlawful, as more are killed with wine than poison. Gross sins affright, but how many take a surfeit and die, in using lawful things inordinately. Recreation is lawful, eating and drinking are lawful, but many offend by excess, and their table is a snare. Relations are lawful, but how often does Satan tempt to overlove! How often is the wife and child laid in God's room! Excess makes things lawful become sinful.

11th subtlety. He makes the duties of our general and particular calling hinder and jostle out one another. Our general calling is serving God, our particular calling is minding our employments in the world. It is wisdom to be regular in both these, when the particular calling does not eat out the time for God's service, nor the service of God hinder diligence in a calling. The devil's art is to make Christians defective in one of these two. Some spend all their time in hearing, reading, and under a pretence of living by faith, do not live in a calling; others Satan takes off from duties of religion, under a pretence that they must provide for their families; he makes them so careful for their bodies, that they quite neglect their souls. The subtlety of the old serpent is to make men negligent in the duties either of the first table or the second.

12th subtlety. He misrepresents true holiness that he may make others out of love with it. He paints the face of religion full of scars, and with seeming blemishes, that he may create in the minds of men prejudice against it. He represents religion as the most melancholy thing, and that he who embraces it must banish all joy out of his diocese, though the apostle speaks of 'joy in believing.' Rom xv 13. Satan suggests that religion exposes men to danger: he shows them the cross, but hides the crown from them; he labours to put all the disgrace he can upon holiness, that he may tempt them to renounce it; he abuses the good Christian, and gives him a wrong name. The truly zealous man he calls hot-headed and factious; the patient man that bears injuries without revenge, he represents as a coward; the humble man as low-spirited; the heavenly man he calls a fool. He lets things that are seen go for things that are not seen; and thus misrepresents religion to the world. As John Huss, that holy man, was painted with red devils, so Satan paints holiness with as deformed and mis-shapen a face as he can, that he may, by this temptation, draw men off from solid piety, and make them rather scorn than embrace it. The hand of Joab is in this. Satan is tempting persons to atheism, to cast off all religion.

13th subtlety. Satan draws men off from the love of the truth to embrace error. 'That they should believe a lie.' 2 Thess ii 11. He is called in Scripture not only an unclean spirit, but a lying spirit. As an unclean spirit he labours to defile the soul with lust, and as a lying spirit he labours to corrupt the mind with error. All this is dangerous, because many errors look so like the truth as gilt represents true gold. Satan thus beguiles souls. Though the Scripture blames heretics for being promoters of error, yet it charges Satan with being the chief contriver of it. They spread the error, but the devil is a lying spirit in their mouths. Satan's great temptation is to make men believe dangerous impostures to be glorious truths. He thus transforms himself into an angel of light. What is the meaning of Satan's sowing tares in the parable but sowing error instead of truth? Matt xiii 25. How quickly had the devil broached false doctrine in the apostles' times? That it was necessary to be circumcised, that angel worship was lawful, and that Christ was not come in the flesh. Acts xv 1; Col ii 18; 1 John iv 3. The devil tempts by drawing men to error, because he knows how deadly the snare is, and the great mischief it will do. (1) Error is of a spreading nature; it is compared to leaven because it sours, and to a gangrene because it spreads. Matt xvi 11; 2 Tim ii 17. One error spreads into more, like a circle in the water that multiplies into more circles; one error seldom goes alone. Error spreads from one person to another. It is like the plague, which infects all round about it. Satan by infecting one person with error infects more! The error of Pelagius spread on a sudden to Palestine, Africa, and Italy. The Arian error was at first but a single spark, but at last it set almost the whole world on fire. (2) The devil lays the snare of error, because it brings divisions into the church; and these bring opprobrium and scandal upon the ways of God. The devil dances at discord. Division destroys peace, which was Christ's legacy; and love, which is the bond of perfection. Not only has Christ's coat been rent, but his body, by the divisions which error has caused. In churches and families where error creeps in, what animosities and factions it makes! It sets the father against the son, and the son against the father. What slaughters and bloodshed have been occasioned by errors in the church! (3) The devil's policy in raising errors is to hinder reformation. He was never a friend to reformation. In the primitive times, after the apostles' days, the serpent cast out of his mouth water as a flood after the woman, which was a deluge of heresies, that so he might hinder the progress of the gospel. Rev xii 15. (4) Satan tempts to error, because error devours godliness. The Gnostics, as Epiphanius observes, were not only corrupted in their judgments, but in their morals; they were loose in their lives. 'Ungodly men, turning the grace of our God into lasciviousness.' Jude 4. The Familists afterwards turned Ranters, and gave themselves over to vices and immoralities; and this they did while boasting of the Spirit and of perfection. (5) The devil's design in seducing by error is, that he knows it is pernicious to souls. It damns as well as vice; poison kills as well as a pistol. 'Who privily shall bring in damnable heresies.' 2 Pet ii 1. If Satan be thus subtle in laying snares of error to deceive, had we not need to pray that God would not suffer us to be led into temptation; that he would make us wise to keep out of the snare of error; or, if we have fallen into it, that he would enable us to recover out of the snare by repentance?

14th subtlety. Satan bewitches and ensnares men by setting pleasing baits before them; as the riches, pleasures, and honours of the world. 'All these things will I give thee.' Matt iv 9. How many does he tempt with this golden apple? Pride, idleness, luxury, are the three worms which are bred by plenty. 'They that will be rich fall into temptation and a snare.' 1 Tim vi 9. Satan kills with these silver darts. How many surfeit on luscious delights! The pleasures of the world are the great engine by which Satan batters down men's souls. His policy is to tickle them to death, to damn them with delights. The flesh would fain be pleased, and Satan prevails by this temptation; he drowns them in the sweet waters of pleasure. Such as have abundance of the world walk in the midst of golden snares. We had need watch our hearts in prosperity, and pray not to be led into temptation. We have as much need to be careful that we are not endangered by prosperity as a man has to be careful at a feast where there are some poisoned dishes of meat.

15th subtlety. Satan in tempting pleads necessity. He knows that necessity may in some cases seem to palliate and excuse a sin. It may seem to make a less evil good to avoid a greater, as Lot offered to expose his daughters to the Sodomites, and was willing that they should be defiled, that he might preserve the angel strangers that were come into his house. Gen xix 8. Doubtless Satan had a hand in this temptation, and made Lot believe that the necessity of the action would excuse the sin. The tradesman pleads the necessity of unlawful gain, or he cannot live; another pleads a necessity of revenge, or his credit would be impaired. Thus Satan tempts men to sin by the plea of the necessity. He will quote Scripture to prove that in some extraordinary cases there may be a necessity of doing that which is not at other times justifiable. Did not David, in case of necessity, 'eat the shewbread, which was not lawful for him, but only the priests'? Matt xii 4. We do not read that he was blamed; then says Satan, Why may not you in cases extraordinary trespass a little and take the forbidden fruit? O beware of this temptation! Satan's cloven foot is in it. Nothing can warrant a thing in its own nature sinful: necessity will not justify impiety.

16th subtlety. Satan draws men to presumption. Presumption is a confidence without sufficient ground: it is made up of two ingredients – audacity and security. This temptation is common. There is a twofold presumption: (1) When men presume that they are better than they are; that they have grace when they have none. They will not take gold on trust, but they will take grace upon trust. The foolish virgins presumed that they had oil in their vessels when they had none. Here that rule of Epicharmus is good, 'Distrust a fallacious heart.' (2) When men presume on God's mercy; that though they are not so good as they should be, yet God is merciful. They look upon God's mercy with the broad spectacles of presumption. Satan soothes men in their sins; he preaches to them, 'All hope, no fear;' and deludes them with golden dreams. *Quam multi cum vana spe descendunt ad inferos* [How many with vain hope go down to hell]. Augustine. Presumption is Satan's draw-net, by which he drags millions to hell. By this temptation he often draws the godly to sin. They presume upon their privileges or graces, and so venture on occasions of sin. Jehoshaphat joined in a league of amity with king Ahab, presuming his grace would be an antidote strong enough against the infection. 2 Chron xviii 3. Satan tempted Peter to presume upon his own strength; and when it came to the trial he was foiled, and came off with shame. We had therefore need pray, that we may not be led into this temptation; and say with David, 'Keep back thy servant from presumptuous sins.' Psa xix 13.

17th subtlety. Satan carries on his designs against us under the highest pretences of friendship. He puts silver upon his bait, and dips his poisoned pills in sugar, as some courtiers who make the greatest pretences of love where they have the most deadly hatred. Satan puts off his lion's skin and comes in sheep's clothing; he pretends kindness and friendship, and would consult what might be for our good. Thus he came to Christ, 'Command that these stones be made bread.' Matt iv 3. As if he had said, 'I see thou art hungry, and here there is no table spread for thee in the wilderness; I, therefore, pitying thy condition, wish thee to get something to eat; turn stones to bread, that thy hunger may be satisfied:' but Christ spied the temptation, and with the sword of the Spirit wounded the old serpent. Thus Satan came to Eve, and tempted her under the notion of a friend: Eat, said he, of the forbidden fruit; for the Lord knows, 'that in the day ye eat thereof, ye shall be as gods:' as if he had said, I persuade you only to that which will put you into a better condition than you now are in; eat of this tree, and it will make you omniscient, 'Ye shall be as gods.' What a kind devil was here! But it was a subtle temptation. She greedily swallowed the bait, and ruined herself and all her posterity. Let us fear his fallacious flatteries. *Timeo Danaos et dona ferentes* [I distrust the Greeks even when they bring gifts].

18*th subtlety.* Satan tempts men to sin by persuading them to keep his counsel. They are like those that have some foul disease, and will rather die than tell the physician. It were wisdom, in case of sore temptation, to open one's mind to some experienced Christian, whose counsel might be an antidote against it. There is danger in concealing it, as in concealing a distemper that may prove mortal. How had we need renew the petition, 'Lead us not into temptation!'

19*th subtlety.* Satan makes use of fit tools and engines for carrying on his work – that is, he makes use of such persons as may be the most likely means to promote his designs. He lays the plot of a temptation, cuts out the work, and employs others to finish it.

(1) He makes use of such as are in places of dignity, men of renown. He knows, if he can get these on his side, they may draw others into snares. When the princes and heads of the tribes joined with Korah, they presently drew a multitude into the conspiracy. Numb xvi 2, 10.

(2) He carries on his designs by men of wit and parts, such as, if it were possible, should deceive the very elect. He must have a great deal of cunning that persuades a man to be out of love with his food; but the devil can make use of heretical spirits to persuade men to be out of love with the ordinances of God, in which they profess to have found comfort. Many who once seemed to be strict frequenters of the house of God are persuaded, by Satan's cunning instruments, to leave it off and to follow an *ignis fatuus*, the light within them. One great subtlety of the devil is to make use of such cunning, subtle-pated men as may be fit to carry on his tempting designs.

(3) He makes use of bad company to be instruments of tempting, especially to draw youth into sin. First they persuade them to come into their company, then to twist into a cord of friendship, then to drink with them, and, by degrees, debauch them. These are the devil's decoys to tempt others.

20*th subtlety.* Satan strikes at some grace more than others. He aims at some persons more than others; or at some grace more than others; and if he can prevail in this, he knows it will be an advantage to him. If you ask what grace it is that Satan most strikes at, I answer, it is the grace of faith. He lays the train of his temptation to blow up the fort of our faith. *Fidei scutum percutit* [He strikes the shield of faith]. Why did Christ pray more for Peter's faith than any other grace? Luke xxii 32. Because he saw that his faith was most in danger; the devil was striking at this grace. Satan, in tempting Eve, laboured to weaken her faith. 'Yea, hath God said, Ye shall not eat of every tree of the garden?' Gen iii 1. The devil would persuade her that God had not spoken truth; and when he had once brought her to distrust, she took of the tree. It is called *scutum fidei*, 'the shield of faith.' Eph vi 16. Satan, in tempting, strikes most at our shield, he assaults our faith. Though true faith cannot be wholly lost, it may suffer a great eclipse. Though the devil cannot by temptation take away the life of faith, yet he may hinder its growth. He cannot *gratiam diruere* [destroy grace], but he may *debilitare* [weaken it].

Why does Satan in tempting chiefly assault our faith?

'Fight neither with small nor great, save only with the king.' 1 Kings xxii 31. Faith is the king of the graces; it is a royal, princely grace, and puts forth the most majestic and noble acts; therefore Satan fights chiefly with this grace. I shall show you the devil's policy in assaulting faith most.

(1) It is the grace that does Satan most mischief; it makes the most resistance against him. 'Whom resist, stedfast in faith.' 1 Pet v 9. No grace more bruises the serpent's head than faith. It is both a shield and a sword, defensive and offensive. It is a shield to guard the head and defend the vitals. The shield of faith prevents the fiery darts of temptation from piercing us through. Faith is a sword that wounds the red dragon.

How comes faith to be so strong that it can resist Satan and put him to flight?

Because it brings the strength of Christ into the soul. Samson's strength lay in his hair, ours lies in Christ. If a child be assaulted, it runs and calls to its father for help: when faith is assaulted, it runs and calls Christ, and in his strength overcomes.

Faith furnishes itself with a store of promises. The promises are faith's weapons to fight with. As David, by five stones in his sling, wounded Goliath, so faith puts the promises, as stones, into its sling. 1 Sam xvii 40. 'I will never leave thee nor forsake thee.' Heb xiii 5. 'A bruised reed shall he not break.' Matt xii 20. 'Who will not suffer you to be tempted above that ye are able.' 1 Cor x 13. 'The God of peace shall bruise Satan under your feet shortly.' Rom xvi 20. 'No man is able to pluck them out of my Father's hand.' John x 29. Here are five promises, like five stones, put into the sling of faith, and with these a believer may wound the red dragon. Faith being such a grace to resist and wound Satan, he watches his opportunity to batter our shield, though he cannot break it.

(2) Satan strikes most at our faith, and would weaken and destroy it,

because it has a great influence upon all the other graces, and sets them to work. Like some rich clothier, that gives out a stock of wool to the poor, and sets them spinning, faith gives out a stock to all the other graces, and sets them to work. It sets love to work. 'Faith which worketh by love.' Gal v 6. When once the soul believes God's love, its love is kindled to God. The believing martyrs burned hotter in love than in fire. Faith sets repentance to work. When the soul believes there is mercy to be had, it sets the eyes weeping. Oh, says the soul, that ever I should offend such a gracious God! Repenting tears drop from the eye of faith. 'The father of the child cried out with tears, Lord, I believe.' Mark ix 24. If the devil cannot destroy our faith, yet if he can disturb it, if he can hinder and stop its actings, he knows all the other graces will be lame and inactive. If the spring in a watch be stopped, the motion of the wheels will be hindered: so if faith be down, all the other graces will be at a stand.

21st subtlety. Satan encourages those doctrines that are flesh-pleasing. He knows the flesh loves to be gratified, that it cries out for ease and liberty, and that it will not endure any yoke, unless it be lined and made soft. He will be sure, therefore, to lay his bait of temptation so as to please and humour the flesh. The word says, 'Strive as in an agony' to enter into glory; crucify the flesh; take the kingdom of heaven by holy violence. Satan, to enervate and weaken these Scriptures, flatters the flesh; tells man there needs no such strictness; nor so much zeal and violence; a softer pace will serve; sure there is an easier way to heaven; there needs no breaking the heart for sin: do but confess to a priest, or tell over a few beads, or say some Ave Marias, and that will procure you a pardon, and give you admission into paradise. Or he goes another way to work: if he sees men startle at Popery, he stirs up flattering Antinomianism, and says, 'What needs all this cost? what needs repenting tears? these are legal; what need to be so strict in your obedience? Christ hath done all for you: you should make use of your Christian liberty.' This temptation draws many away; it takes them off from strictness of life. He who sells cheapest shall have most customers; the devil knows that it is a cheap and easy doctrine which pleases the flesh, and he doubts not but he shall have customers enough.

22nd subtlety. Satan has his temptations in reference to holy duties. His policy is either to hinder from duty, or discourage in duty, or put men too far in duty.

(1) To hinder from duty, as (1 Thess ii 18), 'We would have come once and again, but Satan hindered us.' So many duties of religion would have been performed, but Satan hindered. The hand of Joab is in this. There are three duties which the devil is an enemy to, and labours to keep us from.

Meditation. He will let men profess, or pray and hear in a formal manner, which does him no hurt and them no good; but he opposes meditation, as being a means to compose the heart and make it serious. He can stand your small shot, if you do not put in this bullet. He cares not how much you hear, or how little you meditate. Meditation is chewing the cud; it makes the word digest and turn to nourishment; it is the bellows of the affections. The devil is an enemy to this. When Christ is alone in the wilderness, giving himself to divine contemplations, the devil comes and tempts him, to hinder him. He will thrust in worldly business, something or other to keep men off from holy meditation.

Mortification. This is as needful as heaven. 'Mortify your members which are upon the earth, uncleanness, inordinate affection.' Col iii 5. Satan will let men be angry with sin, exchange sin, or restrain sin, which keeps it a prisoner, that cannot break out; but when it comes to taking away the life of sin, he labours to stop the warrant and hinder the execution. When sin is mortifying, Satan is being crucified.

Self-examination. 'Examine yourselves:' a metaphor from metal that is pierced through, to see if there be gold within. 2 Cor xiii 5. Self-examination is a spiritual inquisition set up in the soul. Man must search his heart for sin, as one would search a house for a traitor; or, as Israel sought for leaven to burn it. Satan, if it be possible, will, by his temptations, keep men from this duty. He tells them their estate is good, and what need they put themselves to the trouble of examination? Though men will not take their money on trust, but will examine it by the touchstone, yet Satan persuades them to take their grace on trust. He persuaded the foolish virgins that they had oil in their lamps. He has another policy, which is to show men the faults of others, in order to keep them from searching their own. He will allow them spectacles to see what is amiss in others, but not a looking-glass to behold their own faces and see what is amiss in themselves.

(2) His policy is to discourage in duty. When any one has been performing holy duties, he tells him he has played the hypocrite; he has served God for money, he has had sinister ends: his duties have been full of distraction; they have been fly-blown with pride: he has offered the blind and the lame, and how can he expect a reward from God? He tells a Christian he has increased his sin by prayer, and endeavours to make him out of conceit with his duties, so he knows not whether he had better pray or not.

(3) If this plot will not take, he labours to put a Christian on too far in duty. If he cannot keep him from duty, he will run him on too far in it. Humiliation, or mourning for sin, is a duty, but Satan will push it too far; he will say, Thou art not humbled enough; and, indeed, he never thinks a

man is humbled enough till he despairs. He would make a Christian wade so far in the waters of repentance, that he should get beyond his depth, and be drowned in the gulf of despair. He comes thus to the soul, Thy sins have been great, and thy sorrows should be proportionate to thy sins. But is it so? Canst thou say thou hast been as great a mourner as thou hast been a sinner? Thou didst for many years drive no other trade but sin – and is a drop of sorrow enough for a sea of sin? No; thy soul must be more humbled, and lie steeping longer in the brinish waters of repentance. He would have a Christian weep himself blind, and in a desperate mood throw away the anchor of hope. Now, lest any be troubled with this temptation, let me say that this is a mere fallacy of Satan; for sorrow proportionable to sin is not attainable in this life, nor does God expect it. It is sufficient for thee, Christian, if thou hast a gospel-sorrow; if thou grievest so far as to see sin hateful, and Christ precious; if thou grievest so as to break off iniquity; if thy remorse end in divorce. This is to be humbled enough. The gold has lain long enough in the fire when the dross is purged out; so a Christian has lain long enough in humiliation when the love of sin is purged out. This is to be humbled enough for divine acceptation. God, for Christ's sake, will accept of this sorrow for sin; therefore let not Satan's temptations drive thee to despair. You see how subtle an enemy he is, to hinder from duty, or discourage in duty, or put men on too far in duty, that he may run them upon the rock of despair. Had we not need, then, who have such a subtle enemy, to pray, 'Lord, lead us not into temptation'? As the serpent beguiled Eve, let us not be beguiled by this hellish Machiavelli.

23rd subtlety. Satan tempts to sin by the hope of returning out of it by speedy repentance. It is easy for the bird to fly into the snare, but it is not so easy to get out of it. Is it so easy a thing to repent? Are there no pangs in the new birth? Is it easy to leap out of Delilah's lap into Abraham's bosom? How many has Satan flattered into hell by the policy, that if they sin, they may recover themselves by repentance! Alas! is repentance in our power? A springlock can shut of itself, but it cannot open without a key; so we can shut ourselves out from God, but we cannot open to him by repentance, till he opens our heart who has the key of David in his hand.

24th subtlety. Satan puts us upon doing that which is good, unseasonably. To mourn for sin is a duty; the sacrifices of God are a broken heart. But there is a time when it may not be so seasonable. Psa li 17. After some eminent deliverance, which calls for rejoicing, to have the spirit dyed of a sad colour, and to sit weeping, is not seasonable. There was a special time at the feast of tabernacles, when God called his people to cheerfulness. 'Seven days shalt thou keep a solemn feast unto the Lord thy God, thou shalt surely rejoice.' Deut xvi 15. Now, if at this time the Israelites had hung their harps upon the willows, and been disconsolate, it had been very unseasonable, like mourning at a wedding. When God, by his providence, calls us to thanksgiving, and we sit drooping, and, with Rachel, refuse to be comforted, it is very evil, and savours of ingratitude. It is Satan's temptation; the hand of Joab is in this.

To rejoice is a duty. 'Praise is comely for the upright.' Psa xxxiii 1. But when God, by his judgments, calls us to weeping, joy and mirth is unseasonable. 'In that day did the Lord call to weeping, and behold joy and gladness.' Isa xxii 12, 13. Oecolampadius, and other learned writers, think it was in the time of King Ahaz, when the signs of God's anger, like a blazing star, appeared. To be given to mirth at that time, was very unseasonable.

To read the word is a duty, but Satan sometimes puts men upon it when it is unseasonable. To read it at home when God's word is being preached, or the sacrament administered, is unseasonable, yea, sinful; as Hushai said, 'The counsel is not good at this time.' 2 Sam xvii 7. There was a set time enjoined for the passover, when the Jews were to bring their offering to the Lord. Numb ix 2. Had the people been reading the law at home in the time of the passover, it had not been in season, and God would have punished it for a contempt. It is the devil's subtle temptation either to keep us from duty, or to put us upon it when it is least in season. Duties of religion, not well timed, and done in season, are dangerous. Snow and hail are good for the ground when they come in their season; but in the harvest, when the corn is ripe, a storm of hail would do hurt.

25th subtlety. Satan persuades men to delay repenting and turning to God. He says (as Hag i 2), 'The time is not come.' Now youth is budding, or you are but in the flower of your age, it is too soon to repent: 'The time is not come.' This temptation is the devil's draw-net by which he draws millions to hell; it is a dangerous temptation. Sin is *dulce venenum* (a sweet poison). Bernard. The longer poison lies in the body, the more mortal; so, by delay of repentance, sin strengthens, and the heart hardens. The longer ice freezes, the harder it is to be broken; so the longer a man freezes in impenitency, the more difficult it will be to have his heart broken. When sin has gotten a haunt, it is not easily driven away. Besides, the danger of delaying repentance appears in this, that life is hazardous, and may on a sudden expire. What security have you that you shall live another day? Life is made up of a few flying minutes; it is a taper soon blown out. 'What is your life? It is even a vapour.' James iv 14. The body is like a vessel, tunned with a little breath; sickness broaches it, death draws it out. How dangerous therefore is it to procrastinate and put off turning to God by repentance! Many now in hell purposed to repent, but death surprised them.

26*th subtlety*. Satan, in tempting, assaults and weakens the saints' peace. If he cannot destroy their grace, he will disturb their peace. He envies the Christian his good day; and if he cannot keep him from a heaven hereafter, he will keep him from a heaven upon earth. There is nothing, next to holiness, a Christian prizes more than peace and tranquillity of mind. It is the cream of life, a bunch of grapes by the way. Now, Satan's great policy is to shake a Christian's peace; that, if he will go to heaven, he shall go thither through frights, and plenty of tears. He throws in his fire-balls of temptation, to set the saints' peace on fire. Of such great concern is spiritual peace, that no wonder if Satan would, by his intricate subtleties, rob us of that jewel. Spiritual peace is a token of God's favour. As Joseph had a special testimony of his father's kindness in the party-coloured coat, so have the saints a special token of God's good will to them, when he gives them the party-coloured coat of inward peace. No wonder then, if Satan rages so much against the saints' peace, and would tear off this comfortable robe from them. The devil troubles the waters of the saints' peace because hereby he hopes to have the more advantage of them.

(1) By perplexing their spirits, he takes off their chariot wheels; unfits them for the service of God; and puts body and mind out of temper, as an instrument out of tune. Sadness of spirit prevailing, a Christian can think of nothing but his troubles; his mind is full of doubts, fears, surmises, so that he is like a person distracted, and is scarcely himself; either he neglects the duties of religion, or his mind is taken off from them while he is doing them. There is one duty especially that melancholy and sadness of spirit unfits for, and that is thankfulness. Thankfulness is a tribute or quit-rent due to God. 'Let the saints be joyful, let the high praises of God be in their mouth.' Psa cxlix 5, 6. But when Satan has disturbed a Christian's spirit, and filled his mind full of black, and almost despairing thoughts, how can he be thankful? It rejoices Satan to see how his plot takes. By making God's children unquiet, he makes them unthankful.

(2) By troubling the saints' peace, Satan lays a stumbling block in the way of others. By this he gets occasion to render the ways of God unlovely to those who are looking heavenward. He sets before new beginners the perplexing thoughts, the tears, the groans of those who are wounded in spirit, to scare them from all seriousness in religion. He will object to new beginners: Do you not see how these sad souls torture themselves with melancholy thoughts, and will you change the comforts and pleasures of this life to sit always in the house of mourning? Will you espouse that religion

which makes you a terror to yourselves, and a burden to others? Can you be in love with a religion that is ready to fright you out of your wits? Thus the devil, by troubling the saints' peace, would discourage others who are looking towards heaven; he would beat them off from prayer, and hearing all soul-awakening sermons, by the fear lest they should fall into this black humour of melancholy, and end their days in despair.

(3) By this subtle policy of Satan, in disturbing the saints' peace, and making them believe God does not love them, he sometimes so far prevails as to make them begin to entertain hard thoughts of God. Through the black spectacles of melancholy, God's dealings look sad and ghastly. Satan tempts the godly to have strange thoughts of God; to think he has cast off all pity, and has forgotten to be gracious, and to make sad conclusions. Psa lxxvii 7, 8, 9. 'I reckoned, that as a lion, so will he break all my bones: from day even to night, wilt thou make an end of me.' Isa xxxviii 13. The devil, by melancholy, causes a sad eclipse in the soul, so that it begins to think God has shut up the springs of mercy, and there is no hope. Hereupon Satan gets further advantage of a troubled spirit. Sometimes he puts it upon sinful wishes and execrations against itself; as Job, who in distemper of mind, cursed his birthday. Job iii 3. Though he did not curse his God, yet he cursed his birthday. Thus you see what advantages the devil gets by raising storms and troubling the saints' peace. If the devil is capable of any delight, it is to see the saints' disquiets: their groans are his music. It is a sport to him to see them torture themselves upon the rack of melancholy, and almost drown themselves in tears. When the godly have unjust surmises of God, question his love, deny the work of grace, and fall to wishing they had never been born, Satan is ready to clap his hands, and shout for a victory.

By what arts and methods does Satan, in tempting, disturb the saints' peace?

He slily conveys evil thoughts, and makes a Christian believe they come from his own heart. The cup was found in Benjamin's sack, but it was of Joseph's putting there; so a child of God often finds atheistical and blasphemous thoughts in his mind, but Satan has put them there. As some lay their children at another's door, so Satan lays his temptations at our door, and fathers them upon us. We then trouble ourselves about them, and nurse them, as if they were our own.

Satan disturbs the saints' peace by drawing forth their sins in the black colours to affright them, and make them ready to give up the ghost. He is called the accuser of the brethren; not only because he accuses them to God, but accuses them to themselves. He tells them they are guilty of certain sins, and they are hypocrites; whereas the sins of a believer only show that grace is not perfect, not that he has no grace. When Satan comes with this temptation, show him that Scripture, 'The blood of Jesus Christ his Son cleanseth us from all sin.' 1 John i 7.

27th subtlety. Satan, by plausible arguments, tempts men to commit *felo de se*, to make away with themselves. This temptation not only crosses the current of Scripture, but it is abhorrent to nature to be one's own executioner. Yet such are the cunning artifices of Satan, that he persuades many to lay violent hands upon themselves, as the bills of mortality witness. He tempts some to do this in terror of conscience, telling them, All the hell they shall have is in their conscience, and death will give them present ease. He tempts others to make away with themselves that they may live no longer to sin against God. Others he tempts to make away with themselves, that they may presently arrive at happiness. He tells them, the best of the saints desire heaven, and the sooner they are there the better.

Augustine speaks of Cleombrotus, who hearing Plato read a lecture on the immortality of the soul, and the joys of the other world, *se in praecipitium dejecit*, threw himself down a steep precipice, or rock, and killed himself. This is Satan's plot; but we must not break prison by laying violent hands upon ourselves, but stay till God sends and opens the door. Let us pray, 'Lead us not into temptation.' Still bear in mind that Scripture, 'Thou shalt not kill.' Exod xx 13. *Clamitat in caelum vox sanguinis* [The voice of blood cries to heaven]. If we may not kill another, much less ourselves; and take heed of discontent, which often opens the door to self-murder.

Thus I have shown you twenty-seven subtleties of Satan in tempting, that you may the better know them, and avoid them. There is a story of a Jew who would have poisoned Luther, but a friend sent to Luther the picture of the Jew, warning him to take heed of such a man when he saw him; by which means he knew the murderer, and escaped his hands. I have told you the subtle devices of Satan in tempting; I have shown you the picture of him that would murder you. Being forewarned, I beseech you take heed of the murderer.

From the subtlety of Satan in tempting, let me draw three inferences.

(1) It may administer matter of wonder to us how any are saved. How amazing that Satan, this Abaddon, or angel of the bottomless pit (Rev ix 11), this Apollyon, this soul-devourer, does not ruin all mankind! What a wonder that some are preserved, that neither Satan's hidden snares prevail, nor his fiery darts: that neither the head of the serpent, nor the paw of the lion destroys them! Surely it will be matter of admiration to the saints, when they come to heaven, to think how strangely they came thither; that, notwithstanding all the force and fraud, the power and policy of hell, they should arrive safe at the heavenly port! This is owing to the safe conduct

of Christ, the Captain of our salvation. Michael is too hard for the dragon.

(2) Is Satan subtle? See what need we have to pray to God for wisdom to discern the snares of Satan, and strength to resist them. We cannot of ourselves stand against temptation; if we could, the prayer were needless, 'Lead us not,' &c. Let us not think we can be too cunning for the devil, or escape his wiles and darts. If David and Peter, who were pillars in God's temple, fell by temptation, how soon should such weak reeds as we are be blown down, if God should leave us! Take Christ's advice, 'Watch and pray, that ye enter not into temptation.' Matt xxvi 41.

(3) See how the end of all Satan's subtleties in tempting is, that he may be an accuser. He lays the plot, entices men to sin, and then brings in the indictment; as if one should make another drunk, and then complain of him to the magistrate for being drunk. The devil is first a tempter, and then an informer: first a liar and then a murderer.

Having shown the subtleties of Satan in tempting, I shall answer two questions:

Why does God suffer his saints to be buffeted by Satan's temptations?

He does it for many wise and holy ends.

(1) He lets them be tempted to try them. The Hebrew word signifies both to tempt and to try. Temptation is a touchstone to try what is in the heart. The devil tempts that he may deceive, but God lets us be tempted to try us. *Qui non tentatur, non probatur* [He who is not tempted is not tested]. Augustine.

Hereby God tries our sincerity. Job's sincerity was tried by temptation; the devil told God that Job was a hypocrite, and served him only for a livery; but, said he, 'Touch all that he hath (that is, let me tempt him) and he will curse thee to thy face!' Job i 11. Well, God did let the devil touch him by temptation, and yet Job remained holy, he worshipped God, and blessed God; ver 20, 21. Here Job's sincerity was proved; he had fiery temptations, but he came out of the fire a golden Christian. Temptation is a touchstone of sincerity.

By temptation God tries our love. The wife of Tigranes never showed her chastity and love to her husband, as when she was tempted by Cyrus, but did not yield; so, our love to God is seen when we can look a temptation in the face, and turn our back upon it. Though the devil come as a serpent subtly, and offers a golden apple, yet he will not touch the forbidden fruit. When the devil showed Christ all the kingdoms of the world, and the glory of them, such was Christ's love to his Father, that he abhorred the temptation. True love will not be bribed. When the devil's darts are most fiery, a saint's love to God is most fervent.

By temptation God tries our courage. 'Ephraim is a silly dove without heart.' Hos vii 11. So it may be said of many, they are *excordes*, without a heart; they have no heart to resist a temptation; no sooner does Satan come with his solicitations, but they yield; like a coward, who as soon as the thief approaches, delivers his purse. He is a valorous Christian that brandishes the sword of the Spirit against Satan, and will rather die than yield. The courage of the Romans was never more seen than when they were assaulted by the Carthaginians; so the heroic spirit of a saint is never more seen than in a battle-field, when he is fighting with the red dragon, and by the power of faith puts the devil to flight. *Fidei robur potest esse concussum, non excussum* [The strength of faith can be shaken, not destroyed]. Tertullian. One reason why God lets his people be tempted is, that their metal may be tried, their sincerity, love, and magnanimity. When grace is proved, the gospel is honoured.

(2) God suffers his children to be tempted, that they may be kept from pride. *Quos non gula superavit* [Those whom greed has not overcome]. Cyprian. Pride crept once into the angels, and into the apostles, when they disputed which of them should be greatest; and in Peter, when he said, 'Though all men forsake thee, yet I will not,' as if he had had more grace than all the apostles. Pride keeps grace low, that it cannot thrive; as the spleen swells, so the other parts of the body consume; as pride grows, so grace consumes. God resists pride; and, that he may keep his children humble, he suffers them sometimes to fall into temptation. 'Lest I should be exalted, there was given to me a thorn in the flesh, the messenger of Satan to buffet me.' 2 Cor xii 7. When Paul was lifted up by revelations, he was in danger of being lifted up with pride; then came the messenger of Satan to buffet him: that was some sore temptation to humble him. The thorn in the flesh was to prick the bladder of pride. Better is the temptation that humbles me than the duty that makes me proud. Rather than a Christian should be proud, God lets him fall into the devil's hands awhile, that he may be cured of his swelling.

(3) God lets his people be tempted that they may be fitter to comfort others who are in the same distress, and speak a word in due season to such as are weary. Paul was trained up in the fencing-school of temptation, and was able to acquaint others with Satan's wiles and stratagems, 2 Cor ii 11. A man that has ridden over a place where there are quicksands, is the fittest to guide others through that dangerous way; so he who has been buffeted by Satan, and has felt the claws of the roaring lion, is the fittest man to deal with one that is tempted.

(4) God lets his children be tempted to make them long more for heaven, where they shall be out of gunshot, and freed from the hissing of the old

serpent. Satan is not yet fully cast into prison, but like a prisoner who is under bail, he vexes and molests the saints; he lays his snares, throws his fire-balls, but it only makes the people of God long to be gone from hence, and pray that they had the wings of a dove, to fly away and be at rest. God suffered Israel to be vexed with the Egyptians, that they might long the more to be in Canaan. Heaven is the *centrum*, a place of rest, *centrum quietativum:* no bullets of temptation fly there. The eagle that soars aloft in the air, and sits perching upon the tops of high trees, is not troubled with the stinging of serpents; so, when believers have got into the heaven above, they shall not be stung with the old serpent. The devil is cast out of the heavenly paradise. Heaven is compared to an exceeding high mountain. Rev xxi 10. It is so high, that Satan's fiery darts cannot reach up to it. *Nullus ibi hostium metus, nullae insidiae daemonum* [There is no fear of enemies there, no snares of devils]. Bernard.

The temptations here are to make the saints long till death sound a retreat, and call them off the field where the bullets of temptation fly so thick, that they may receive a victorious crown.

What rocks of support are there, or what comfort for tempted souls?

(1) That it is not our case alone, but has been the case of God's most eminent saints. 'There hath no temptation taken you but such as is common to man,' yea, to the best men. 1 Cor x 13. Christ's lambs, which have had the mark of election upon them, have been set upon by the world. Elijah, that could shut heaven by prayer, could not shut his heart from temptation. 1 Kings xix 4. Job was tempted to curse God, Peter to deny Christ; and hardly ever any saint has got to heaven but has met with a lion by the way. *Sortem quam omnes sancti patiuntur nemo recusat* [No one escapes the lot which all the saints suffer]. Nay, Jesus Christ himself, though free from sin, yet was not free from temptation. We read of his baptism; then he was 'led into the wilderness to be tempted of the devil.' Matt iv 1. No sooner was Christ out of the water of baptism, but he was in the fire of temptation; and if the devil would set upon Christ, no wonder if he set upon us. There was no sin in Christ, no powder for the devil's fire. Temptation to him was like a burr on a crystal glass, which glides off; or like a spark of fire on a marble pillar, which will not stick: and yet Satan was bold to tempt him. It is some comfort that such as have been our betters have wrestled with temptations.

(2) Another rock of support that may comfort a tempted soul, is, that temptations (where they are burdens) evidence grace. Satan does not tempt God's children because they have sin in them, but because they have grace in them. Had they no grace he would not disturb them, for where he keeps possession all is in peace. Luke xi 21. His temptations are to rob the saints of

their grace. A thief will not assault an empty house, but where he thinks there is treasure; a pirate will not set upon an empty ship, but one that is full of spices and jewels; so the devil assaults most the people of God, because he thinks they have a rich treasure of grace in their hearts, and he would rob them of it. Why are so many cudgels thrown at a tree, but because there is much fruit upon it? The devil throws his temptations at you, because he sees you have much fruit of grace growing upon you. Though to be tempted is a trouble, yet to think why you are tempted is a comfort.

(3) Another rock of support or comfort is, that Jesus Christ is near at hand, and stands by us in all our temptations. Here take notice of two things:

[1] Christ's sympathy in our temptations. *Nobis compatitur Christus* [Christ suffers with us]. 'We have not an high priest which cannot be touched with the feeling of our infirmities.' Heb iv 15. Jesus Christ sympathises with us; he is so sensible of our temptations as if he himself lay under them, and did feel them in his own soul. As in music, when one string is touched, all the rest sound, so when we suffer Christ's bowels sound; we cannot be tempted but he is touched. If you saw a wolf worry your child, would you not pity it? You cannot pity it as Christ does tempted ones. He had a fellow feeling when upon earth, much more now in glory.

But how can it consist with Christ's glory now in heaven, to have a fellow feeling with our sufferings?

This fellow feeling in Christ arises not from an infirmity or passion, but from the mystic union between him and his members. 'He that toucheth you, toucheth the apple of his eye.' Zech ii 8. Every injury done to a saint he takes as done to him in heaven. Every temptation strikes at him, and he is touched with the feeling of them.

[2] Christ's succour in temptation. As the good Samaritan first had compassion on the wounded man, there was sympathy; then he poured in wine and oil, there was succour (Luke x 34); so when we are wounded by the red dragon, Christ is first touched with compassion, and then pours in wine and oil. 'In that he himself hath suffered being tempted, he is able to succour them that are tempted.' Heb ii 18. The Greek word for succour (*boethesia*) signifies to run speedily to one's help; so fierce is Satan, so frail is man, that Christ, who is God-man, runs speedily to his help. When Peter was ready to sink, and said, 'Lord, save me,' Christ presently stretched forth his hand, and caught him; so when a poor soul is tempted, and cries to heaven for help, 'Lord, save me,' Christ comes in with his auxiliary forces. *Noscit Christus*, our Lord Jesus knows what it is to be tempted, therefore he is ready to succour such as are tempted. It has been observed that child-bearing

women are more pitiful to others in their travails than such as are barren; so the Lord Jesus having been in travail by temptations and sufferings, is more ready to pity and succour such as are tempted.

Concerning Christ's succouring the tempted, consider two things: his ability, and his agility to succour. 'He is able to succour them that are tempted.' Heb ii 18. He is called Michael, which signifies, 'Who is like God.' Rev xii 7. Though the tempted soul is weak, yet he fights under a good Captain, the Lion of the tribe of Judah. When a tempted soul fights, Christ comes into the field as his second. Michael will be too hard for the dragon. When the devil lays the siege of a temptation, Christ can raise it when he pleases; he can beat through the enemy's quarters, and so rout Satan that he shall never be able to rally his forces any more. Jesus Christ is on the saint's side, and who would desire a better lifeguard than omnipotence? As Christ is able to succour the tempted, so he will certainly succour them. His power enables him, his love inclines him, his faithfulness engages him to succour tempted souls. It is a great comfort to a soul in temptation to have a succouring Saviour. God succoured Israel in the wilderness among fiery serpents. The rock sending forth water, the manna, the pillar of cloud, the brazen serpent, what were these but types of God's succouring poor souls in the wilderness of temptation, stung by the devil, that fiery serpent? Alexander being asked how he could sleep so securely, when his enemies were about him, said, 'Antipater is awake, who is always vigilant.' So when our tempting enemy is near us, Jesus Christ is awake, who is a wall of fire around us. There is a great deal of succour to the tempted in the names given to Christ. As Satan's names may terrify, so Christ's may succour. The devil is called *Apollyon*, the devourer. Rev ix 11. Christ is called a Saviour. The devil is called the 'strong man.' Matt xii 29. Christ is called *El Gibbor*, the mighty God. Isa ix 6. The devil is called the accuser. Rev xii 10. Christ is called the Advocate. 1 John ii 1. The devil is called the tempter. Matt iv 3. Christ is called the Comforter. Luke ii 25. The devil is called the prince of darkness. Christ is called the Sun of Righteousness. The devil is called the old serpent. Christ is called the Brazen Serpent that heals. John iii 14. Thus the very names of Christ have some succour in them for tempted souls.

How and in what manner does Christ succour them that are tempted?

He succours them by sending his Spirit, whose work it is to bring those promises to their mind which are fortifying. 'He shall bring all things to your remembrance.' John xiv 26. The Spirit furnishes us with promises as so many weapons to fight against the old serpent. 'The God of peace shall bruise Satan under your feet shortly.' Rom xvi 20. 'God will not suffer you to be tempted above that ye are able.' 1 Cor x 13. The seed of the woman shall bruise the serpent's head. Gen iii 15. We are often in times of temptation, as a man that has his house beset, and cannot find his weapons, his sword and gun, in which case Christ sends his Spirit, and brings things to our remembrance that help us in our combat. The Spirit of Christ does for the tempted what Aaron and Hur did for Moses, when they put a stone under him and held up his hands, and then Israel prevailed. The Spirit puts the promises under the hand of faith, and then the Christian overcomes the devil, that spiritual Amalek. The promise is to the soul, as the anchor to the ship, which keeps it steady in a storm.

Christ succours them that are tempted by 'interceding for them.' When the devil is tempting, Christ is praying. The prayer which Christ put up for Peter when he was tempted, extends to all his saints. Lord, said Christ, it is my child that is tempted; Father, pity him. Luke xxii 32. When a poor soul lies bleeding of the wounds the devil has given him, Christ presents his wounds to his Father, and, in the virtue of those, pleads for mercy. How powerful must his prayer be! He is a favourite. John xi 42. He is both High Priest and a Son. If God could forget that Christ were a Priest, he cannot forget that he is a Son. Besides, Christ prays for nothing but what is agreeable to his Father's will. If a king's son petitions only for that which his father has a mind to grant, his suit will not be denied.

Christ succours his people, by taking off the tempter. When the sheep begin to straggle, the shepherd sets the dog on them to bring them back to the fold, and then calls off the dog; so God takes off the tempter. He 'will with the temptation make a way to escape,' he will make an outlet. 1 Cor x 13. He will rebuke the tempter. 'The Lord rebuke thee, O Satan.' Zech iii 2. It is no small support, that Christ succours the tempted. The mother succours the child most when it is sick; she sits by its bedside, brings it cordials; so, when a soul is most assaulted, it shall be most assisted.

I have dealt unkindly with Christ and sinned against his love, and surely he will not succour me, but let me perish in the battle!

Christ is a merciful High Priest, and will succour thee notwithstanding thy failings. Joseph was a type of Christ; his brethren sold him away, and the 'irons entered into his soul;' yet afterwards, when his brethren were ready to die in the famine, he forgot their injuries, and succoured them with money and corn. 'I am,' said he, 'Joseph your brother.' So Christ will say to a tempted soul, 'I know thy unkindnesses, how thou hast distrusted my love, grieved my Spirit; but I am Joseph, I am Jesus, therefore I will succour thee when thou art tempted.'

(4) Another rock of support is that the best man may be most tempted. A

rich ship may be violently set upon by pirates; so he who is rich in faith may have the devil upon him with his battering-pieces. Job, an eminent saint, was fiercely assaulted. Satan smote his body that he might tempt him either to question God's providence or quarrel with it. Paul was a chosen vessel, but how was this vessel battered with temptation! 2 Cor xii 7.

Is it not said, 'He that is begotten of God, that wicked one toucheth him not'?
1 John v 18.

It is not meant that the devil does not tempt him, but he toucheth him not, that is, *tactu lethali*, Cajetan, with a deadly touch. 'There is a sin unto death.' 1 John v 16. Now, Satan with all his temptations does not make a child of God sin 'a sin unto death.' Thus he touches him not.

(5) Another rock of support is that Satan can go no further in tempting than God gives him leave. The power of the tempter is limited. A whole legion of devils could not touch one swine till Christ gave them leave. Satan would have sifted Peter till he sifted out all his grace, but Christ would not suffer him. 'I have prayed for thee,' &c. Christ binds the devil in a chain. Rex xx 1. If Satan's power were according to his malice, not one soul should be saved; but he is a chained enemy. It is a comfort that Satan cannot go a hair's breadth beyond God's permission. If an enemy could not touch a child further than the father appointed, he would do the child no great hurt.

(6) Another rock of support is that it is not having a temptation that makes guilty, but giving consent to it. We cannot hinder a temptation. If we abhor the temptation, it is our burden, not our sin. We read in the old law, that if one forced a virgin, and she cried out, she was reputed innocent; so if Satan by temptation would commit a rape upon a Christian, and he cries out, and does not consent, the Lord will charge it upon the devil's score. It is not laying the bait that hurts the fish if the fish do not bite.

(7) Another rock of support is, that our being tempted is no sign of God's hating us. A child of God often thinks God does not love him because he lets him be haunted by the devil. *Non sequitur*, this is a wrong conclusion. Was not Christ himself tempted, and yet by a voice from heaven proclaimed, 'This is my beloved Son'? Matt iii 17. Satan's tempting and God's loving may stand together. The goldsmith loves his gold in the fire; and God loves a saint, though shot at by fiery darts.

(8) Another rock of support is that Christ's temptation was for our consolation, *aqua ignis* [water to fire]. Jesus Christ is to be looked upon as a public person, as our head and representative; and what he did, he did for us: his prayer was for us, his suffering was for us; when he was tempted, and overcame the temptation, he overcame for us. Christ's conquering

Satan was to show that elect persons shall at last be conquerors over Satan. When Christ overcame Satan's temptation, it was not only to give us an example of courage, but an assurance of conquest. We have overcome Satan already in our covenant head, and we shall at last perfectly overcome.

(9) Another rock of support is that the saints' temptation shall not be above their strength. The harper will not stretch the strings of his harp too hard, lest they break. 'God is faithful, who will not suffer you to be tempted above that ye are able.' 1 Cor x 13. He will proportion our strength to the stroke. 'My grace is sufficient for thee.' 2 Cor xii 9. The torchlight of faith shall be kept burning, though all the winds of temptation are blowing.

(10) Another rock of support is that these temptations shall produce much good.

They quicken a spirit of prayer in the saints. They pray more and better. Temptation is *orationis flabellum* [fan], the exciter of prayer. Perhaps before, the saints came to God as cold suitors in prayer – they prayed as if they prayed not. Temptation is a medicine for security. When Paul had a messenger of Satan to buffet him, he was more earnest in prayer. 'For this thing I besought the Lord thrice.' 2 Cor xii 8. The thorn in his flesh was a spur in his sides to quicken him in prayer. The deer when shot with the dart runs faster to the water; so a soul that is shot with the fiery darts of temptation runs the faster to the throne of grace; and is earnest with God, either to take off the tempter, or to stand by him when he is tempted.

God makes the temptation to sin a means to prevent it. The more a Christian is tempted, the more he fights against the temptation. The more a chaste woman is assaulted, the more she abhors the attempt. The stronger Joseph's temptation was, the stronger was his opposition. The more the enemy attempts to storm a castle, the more is he repelled and beat back.

A godly man's temptations cause the increase of grace. *Unus Christianus temptatus mille;* 'one tempted Christian,' says Luther, 'is worth a thousand.' He grows more in grace. As the bellows increase the flame, so temptation increases the flame of grace.

By these temptations God makes way for comfort. After Christ was tempted, the angels came and ministered unto him. Matt iv 11. When Abraham had been warring, Melchizedek brought him bread and wine to revive his spirits. Gen xiv 18. So after the saints have been warring with Satan, God sends his Spirit to comfort them. Luther said that temptations were *amplexus Christi,* Christ's embraces, because he then manifests himself most sweetly to the soul.

That I may further comfort such as are tempted, let me speak to two particular cases.

I have horrid temptations to blasphemy, say some.

Did not the devil tempt Christ after this manner: 'All these things will I give thee, if thou wilt fall down and worship me'? Matt iv 9. What greater blasphemy can be imagined than that the God of heaven and earth should worship the devil? Yet Christ was tempted to this. If when blasphemous thoughts are injected, you tremble at them, and are in a cold sweat, they are not yours, Satan shall answer for them; let him that plots the treason suffer.

But my case is yet worse, say others; I have been tempted to such sins, and have yielded; the tempter has overcome me.

I grant that, through the withdrawing of God's grace, and the force of temptation, a child of God may be overcome. David was overcome by temptation in the case of Bathsheba, and in numbering the people. There is a party of grace in the heart true to Christ; but sometimes it may be over-voted by corruption, and then a Christian yields. It is sad thus to yield to the tempter. But yet let not a child of God be wholly discouraged, and say there is no hope. Let me pour in some balm of Gilead into this wounded soul.

(1) Though a Christian may fall by a temptation, yet the seed of God is in him. 'His seed remaineth in him.' 1 John iii 9. *Gratia concutitur, non excutitur* [Grace is shaken, not destroyed]. Augustine. A man may be bruised by a fall, yet there is life in him. A Christian foiled by Satan may be like the man going to Jericho, who fell among thieves, and was left 'wounded and half dead;' but still there is a vital principle of grace; his seed remains in him. Luke x 30.

(2) Though a child of God may be overcome *in praelio*, in a skirmish, yet not *in bello*, in the main battle; as an army may be worsted in a skirmish, but conquer at last. Though Satan may foil a child of God in a skirmish by a temptation, the believer shall overcome at last. A saint may be foiled, yet not conquered; he may lose ground, and not lose the victory.

(3) God does not judge his children by one action, but by the frame of the heart. As he does not judge a wicked man by one good action, so neither a godly man by one bad action. A holy person may be worsted by a temptation; but God does not measure him by that. Who measures milk when it seethes and boils up? God does not take the measure of a saint when the devil has boiled him up in a passion, but he judges of him by the pulse and temper of his heart. He would fear God; and when he fails he weeps. God looks which way the bias of his heart stands; if that be set against sin, God will pardon.

(4) God will make a saint's fall by temptation turn to his spiritual advantage.

He may let a regenerate person fall by a temptation to make him more watchful. Perhaps he walked loosely, and was decoyed into sin; but for the future he will grow more curious and cautious in his walking. The foiled Christian is a vigilant Christian; he will take care not to come within the lion's chain any more; he will be shy and fearful of the occasion of sin; he will not go abroad without his spiritual armour, and will gird on his armour by prayer. When a wild beast gets over the hedge and hurts the corn, the farmer will make his fence stronger; so, when the devil gets over the fence by temptation, and foils a Christian, he will be sure to mend his fence, and be more vigilant against temptation afterwards.

God sometimes lets his children be foiled by temptation that they may see their continual dependence on God, and may go to him for strength. We need not only habitual grace to stand against temptation, but auxiliary grace; as the boat needs not only the oars, but wind, to carry it against a strong tide. God lets his children sometimes fall by temptation, that, seeing their own weakness, they may rest more on Christ and free grace. Cant viii 5.

By suffering his children to be foiled by a temptation, God settles them the more in grace. They get strength by their falls. The poets feign that Antaeus the giant, in wrestling with Hercules, got strength by every fall to the ground; so a saint, when foiled in wrestling with Satan, gets more spiritual strength. Peter had never such strength of faith as after being foiled in the high priest's hall. How was he fired with zeal and steeled with courage! He who before was dashed out of countenance by the voice of a maid, now dares openly confess Christ before rulers and the councils. Acts ii 14. As the shaking of the tree settles it the more, God lets his children be shaken with the wind of temptation, that they may be more settled in grace afterwards. Let not those Christians whom God has suffered to be foiled by temptation, cast away their anchor, or give way to despairing thoughts.

May it not make Christians careless whether they fall into temptation or not, if God can make the temptation advantageous to them?

We must distinguish between being foiled through weakness and through wilfulness. If a soldier fights, but is foiled for want of strength, the general of the army will pity him, and bind up his wounds; but if he be wilfully foiled, and proves treacherous, he must expect no favour; so, if a Christian fight it out with Satan, but is foiled for want of strength, as it was with Peter, God will pity him and do him good by his being foiled; but if he be foiled wilfully and runs into temptation, as it was with Judas, God will show him no favour, but will execute martial law upon him.

The uses remain.

Use 1. See in what continual danger we are. Satan is an exquisite artist, a deep headpiece, he lies in ambush to ensnare; he is the tempter, it is his delight to make the saints sin; and he is subtle in tempting, he has ways and methods to deceive.

(1) He brings a saint into sin, by making him confide in his habitual graces. He makes him believe he has such a stock of grace as will secure him against all temptations. Thus he deceived Peter, he made him trust in his grace; he had such a cable of faith and strong tacklings, that though the winds of temptation blew ever so fierce, he could weather the point. 'Though all men forsake thee, yet will not I;' as if he had more grace than all the apostles. Thus he was led into temptation, and fell in the battle. Man may make an idol of grace. Habitual grace is not sufficient without auxiliary. The boat needs not only oars, but a gale of wind, to carry it against the tide; so we need not only habitual grace, but the gale of the Spirit, to carry us against a strong temptation.

(2) Satan tempts to sin by the baits and allurements of the world. *Faenus pecuniae funus animae* [The gain of money is the ruin of the soul]. One of Christ's own apostles was caught with a silver bait. Those whom the devil cannot debauch with vice, he will corrupt with money. 'All these things will I give thee,' was his last temptation. Matt iv 9. Achan was deluded by a wedge of gold. Sylvester II sold his soul to the devil for a popedom.

(3) Satan tempts to sin, *sub specie boni*, under a mask and show of good; his temptations seem gracious motions.

[1] He tempts men to duties of religion. You might think it strange that Satan should tempt to duty; but it is so. He tempts men to duty out of sinister ends. Thus he tempted the Pharisees to pray and give alms, that they might be seen of men. Matt vi 5. Prayer is a duty, but to look asquint in prayer, to do it for vainglory, turns prayer into sin. He tempts to duty when it is not in season. 'My offering and my bread for my sacrifices, shall ye offer unto me in their due season.' Numb xxviii 2. Satan tempts to duty when it is out of season; he tempts to read the word at home when we should be hearing the word. He tempts to one duty, that he may hinder another. He tempts some to duty that it may be a cloak for sin. He tempts them to frequency in duty that they may sin and be less suspected. He tempted the Pharisees to make long prayers that, under this pretence, they might devour widows' houses. Matt xxiii 14. Who would suspect him of false weights that so often holds a Bible in his hand?

[2] He tempts men to sin out of a show of love to Christ. You might think this strange, but there is truth in it. Many a good heart may think what he does is in love to Christ, and all the while he may be under temptation.

When Christ told Peter he must suffer at Jerusalem, Peter took him and rebuked him. 'Be it far from thee, Lord,' as if he had said, Lord, thou hast deserved no such shameful death, and this shall not be unto thee. Matt xvi 22. Peter did this, as he thought, out of love to Christ, but he was under temptation. What had become of us if Christ had hearkened to Peter, and had not suffered! So when Christ washed his disciples' feet, Peter was so mannerly that he said, 'Thou shalt never wash my feet.' John xiii 8. This he did, as he thought, out of love and respect to Christ. He thought Christ was too good to wash his feet, and therefore would have put him off, but it was a temptation; the devil put Peter upon this sinful modesty; he struck at Peter's salvation, insomuch that Christ said, 'If I wash thee not, thou hast no part with me.' So when the Samaritans would not receive Christ, the disciples James and John said, 'Lord, wilt thou that we command fire to come down from heaven and consume them?' Luke ix 54. They did this, as they thought, out of love to Christ; they wished for fire to consume his enemies, but they were under temptation; it was not zeal, but the wild fire of their own passion. 'Ye know not,' saith Christ, 'what manner of spirit ye are of.'

(4) Satan tempts to the sin to which a man's heart is naturally most inclinable. He will not tempt a civil man to a gross sin, which is abhorrent to the light of nature. Satan never sets a dish before men that they do not love. He will tempt a civil man to pride, and to trust in his own righteousness, and to make a Saviour of his civility. As the spider weaves a web out of her own bowels, the civil man would weave a web of salvation out of his own righteousness.

See, then, in what danger we are, when Satan is continually lying in ambush with his temptations!

See man's inability of himself to resist a temptation! Could he stand of himself against a temptation, the prayer were needless, 'Lead us not into temptation:' no man has power of himself to resist temptation, further than God gives him strength. 'O Lord, I know that the way of man is not in himself.' Jer x 23. If Peter, who had true grace, and Adam, who had perfect grace, could not stand against temptation, much less can any stand by the power of nature, which confutes the doctrine of free will. What freedom of will has man, when he cannot resist the least temptation?

Here is matter for humiliation, that there is in us such an aptitude and proneness to yield to temptation. We are as ready to swallow a temptation as the fish to swallow the bait. If the devil tempt to pride, lust, envy, revenge, how do we symbolise with Satan and embrace his snares! Like a woman that has a suitor, and does not need much wooing, but readily gives her consent, Satan comes wooing by temptation, and we soon yield; he strikes fire, and we are as dry tinder that catches the first spark; he knocks by temptation, and it is sad to think how soon we open the door to him, which is as if one should open the door to a thief.

See hence that a Christian's life is no easy life. It is military: he has a Goliath in the field to encounter with, one that is armed with power and subtlety, and has his wiles and darts. A Christian must be continually watching and fighting. Satan's designs carry death in the front. 'Seeking whom he may devour.' 1 Pet v 8. Therefore we had need always have our weapons in our hand. How few think their life a warfare! Though they have an enemy in the field, always laying snares, or shooting darts, yet they do not stand sentinel or get their spiritual artillery ready; they put on their jewels, but not their armour. 'They take the timbrel and harp, and rejoice at the sound of the organ,' as if they were rather in music than in battle. Job xxi 12. Many are asleep in sloth, when they should be fighting against Satan; and no wonder the devil shoots them when he finds them asleep.

Use 2. They are reproved who pray, 'Lead us not into temptation,' and yet run of themselves into temptation. Such are they who go to plays and masquerades, and hunt after strange flesh. Some go a slower pace to hell, but such as run themselves into temptation go galloping thither. We have too many of these in this debauched age, who, as if they thought they could not sin fast enough, tempt the devil to tempt them.

Use 3. Let us labour that we be not overcome by temptation.

What means should be used, that Satan's temptations may not prevail against us?

(1) Avoid solitariness. It is no wisdom, in fighting with an enemy, to give him the advantage of the ground. We give Satan advantage of the ground when we are alone. Eve was foiled in the absence of her husband. A virgin is not so soon set upon in company. 'Two are better than one.' Eccl iv 9. Get into the communion of saints, for that is a good remedy against temptation.

(2) If you would not be overcome by temptation, beware of the predominance of melancholy, which is *atra bilis*, a black humour seated chiefly in the brain. Melancholy disturbs reason and exposes to temptation. One calls melancholy *balneum diaboli*, the devil's bath; he bathes himself with delight in such a person. Melancholy clothes the mind in sable; it fills it with such dismal apprehensions as often end in self-murder.

(3) If you would not be overcome by temptation, study sobriety. 'Be sober, because your adversary walketh about.' 1 Pet v 8. Sober-mindedness consists in the moderate use of earthly things: an immoderate desire of these things often brings men into the snare of the devil. 'They that will be rich fall into a snare.' 1 Tim vi 9. He who loves riches inordinately, will purchase

them unjustly. Ahab would swim to Naboth's vineyard in blood. He who is drunk with the love of the world, is never free from temptation. He will pull down his soul to build up an estate. *Quid non mortalia pectora cogis, auri sacra fames?* [Oh cursèd hunger for gold, to what dost thou not drive the hearts of men?] Virgil. Be sober, take heed of being drunk with the love of the world, lest ye fall into temptation.

(4) Be always upon your guard, watch against Satan's wiles and subtleties. 'Be vigilant, because your adversary the devil walketh about.' 1 Pet v 8. A Christian must *excubias agere*, keep watch and ward; he must see where Satan labours to make a breach, see what grace he most strikes at, or what sin he most tempts to. 'I say unto all, Watch.' Mark xiii 37. Watch all the senses, the eye, the ear, the touch; for Satan can creep in by these. Oh, how needful is the spiritual watch! Shall Satan be watchful, and we drowsy? Does he watch to devour us, and shall not we watch to save ourselves? Let us see what sin our heart most naturally inclines to, and watch against it.

(5) Beware of idleness. Satan sows most of his seed in fallow ground. It was Jerome's counsel to his friend to be ever busied, that if the devil did come, he might find him working in the vineyard. Idleness tempts the devil to tempt. The bird that sits still is shot. He that wants employment never wants temptation. When a man has nothing to do, Satan will bring grist to the mill, and find him work enough.

(6) Make known thy case to some godly friend. Hiding a serpent in the bosom is not the way to be safe; when the old serpent has got into your bosom by temptation, do not hide him there by keeping his counsel. If a spark be got into the thatch, it is not wisdom to conceal it, it may set the house on fire. Conceal not temptation. Keeping secrets is for familiar friends: be not so great a friend to Satan as to keep his secrets. Reveal your temptations, which is the way to procure others' prayers and advice; let all see that you are not true to Satan's party, because you tell all his plots and reveal his treasons. Besides, telling your case to some experienced Christian, is the way to have ease; as the opening of a vein gives ease, so the opening of your case to a friend will give ease to the soul, and temptation will not so much inflame.

(7) Make use of the word. This the apostle calls the 'sword of the Spirit,' a fit weapon with which to fight against the tempter. Eph vi 17. This 'sword of the Spirit' is *gladius anceps*, a two-edged sword: it wounds carnal lust and it wounds Satan. He who travels a road where there is robbing will be sure to ride with his sword; we are travelling to heaven, and in this road there is a thief who always besets us in every place where we go. He meets us at church, he does not miss a sermon, he will be tempting us there; sometimes to drowsiness: when any sleep at sermon, the devil rocks them; sometimes

he tempts by distracting the mind in hearing, sometimes he tempts by questioning the truth of what is heard. He tempts in the shop to use collusion and deceit. 'The balances of deceit are in his hand.' Hos xii 7. Thus we meet with the tempter everywhere; therefore, this thief being in the road, we had need ride with a sword; we must have the 'sword of the Spirit' about us. We must have skill to use this sword, and have a heart to draw it out, and it will put the devil to flight. Thus when Satan tempted our blessed Saviour to distrust and blasphemy, he used a Scripture weapon, 'It is written.' Three times he wounded the old serpent with this sword. Christ, with his power and authority, could have rebuked the prince of the air as he did the winds; but he stopped the devil's mouth with Scripture, 'It is written.' It is not our vows and resolutions that will do it, it is not the Papist's holy water or charms that will drive away the devil; but let us bring the word of God against him: this is an argument that he cannot answer. It was a saying of Luther, 'I have had great troubles of mind; but so soon as I laid hold on any place of Scripture, and stayed myself upon it as upon my chief anchor, straightway my temptations vanished away.' There is no temptation but we have fit Scripture to answer it. If Satan tempts to Sabbath-breaking, answer him, ' "It is written, Remember to keep the Sabbath day holy." ' If he tempts to uncleanness, answer him, ' "It is written, whoremongers and adulterers God will judge." ' If he tempts to carnal fear, say, ' "It is written, Fear not them that kill the body, and after that, have no more that they can do." ' No such way to confute temptation as by Scripture; the arrows we shoot against Satan must be fetched out of this quiver. Many people want this sword of the Spirit, they have not a Bible; others seldom make use of it, but let it rust; they seldom look into it – no wonder, therefore, they are overcome by temptations. He who is well skilled in the word is like one who has a plaister ready to lay upon the wound as soon as it is made, and so the danger is prevented. O study the Scripture, and you will be too hard for the devil; he cannot stand against this.

(8) Let us be careful of our own hearts, that they do not decoy us into sin. The apostle says, 'A man is drawn away of his own lust, and enticed.' James i 14. *Quisque sibi Satan est* [Everyone is Satan to himself]. Bernard. Every man has a tempter in his own bosom. A traitor within the castle is dangerous. The heart can bring forth a temptation, though Satan do not midwife it into the world; if Satan were dead and buried, the heart could draw us to evil. As the ground of all diseases lies in the humours of the body, so the seed of all sin lies in the original lust. Look to your hearts.

(9) If you would not be overcome by temptation, flee the 'occasions of sin.' Occasions of sin have great force to awaken lust within. He that would keep himself free from infection will not come near an infected house; so if

you would be sober, avoid drunken company. When Joseph was enticed by his mistress, he shunned the occasion; the text says, 'He hearkened not unto her to be with her.' Gen xxxix 10. If you would not be ensnared with Popery, do not hear the mass. The Nazarite, who was forbid wine, might not eat grapes, which might occasion intemperance. Come not near the borders of temptation. Suppose any one had a body made of gunpowder, he would not come near the least spark of fire, lest he should be blown up. Many pray, 'Lead us not into temptation,' and yet run themselves into temptation.

(10) If you would not be overcome by temptation, make use of faith. 'Above all taking the shield of faith.' Eph vi 16. Faith wards off Satan's fiery darts, that they do not hurt. 'Whom resist, stedfast in the faith.' 1 Pet v 9. Mariners in a storm flee to their anchor; flee to your anchor of faith. Faith brings Christ with it. Duellers bring their seconds with them into the field; so faith brings Christ for its second. It puts us into Christ, and then the devil cannot hurt us. The chicken is safe from the birds of prey, under the wings of the hen; and we are secure from the tempter, under the wings of the Lord Jesus. Though other graces are of use to resist the impulses of Satan, yet faith is the conquering grace. It takes hold of Christ's merits, value and virtue; and so the Christian becomes too hard for the devil. As the stars vanish when the sun appears, so Satan vanishes when faith appears.

(11) If you would not be overcome by temptation, be much in prayer. Such as walk in infectious places, carry antidotes about them: prayer is the best antidote against temptation. When the apostle had exhorted, to 'put on the whole armour of God,' he adds, 'Praying with all prayer.' Eph vi 11, 18. Without this, *reliqua arma parum prosunt*. Zanchius. All other weapons will do little good. Christ prescribes this remedy, 'Watch and pray, lest ye enter into temptation.' Mark xiv 38. A Christian fetches down strength from heaven by prayer. Let us cry to God for help against the tempter, as Samson cried to heaven for help. 'O Lord God, remember me and strengthen me, I pray thee, that I may be avenged of the Philistines.' Judges xvi 28. 'The house fell upon the lords and upon all the people;' ver 30.

Prayer is *flagellum diaboli*, it whips and torments the devil. The apostle bids us 'pray without ceasing.' 1 Thess v 17. It was Luther's advice to a lady, when temptation came, to fall upon her knees in prayer. Prayer assuages the force of temptation. It is the best charm or spell we can use against the devil. Temptation may bruise our heel, but by prayer we wound the serpent's head. When Paul had a messenger of Satan to buffet him; what remedy did he use? He betook himself to prayer. 'For this thing I besought the Lord thrice, that it might depart from me.' 2 Cor xii 8. When Satan assaults furiously, let us pray fervently.

(12) If you would not be overcome by temptation, be humble in your own eyes. They are nearest falling who presume on their own strength. Pendleton said his fat flesh should melt in the fire; but instead of his fat melting, his heart melted, and he turned from the truth. When men grow into big conceit God lets them fall, to prick the bladder of pride. O be humble! They are likely to hold best out in temptation who have most grace; but God gives more grace to the humble. James iv 6. Beware of pride; an abscess is not more dangerous in the body than pride in the soul. The doves, says Pliny, take pride in their feathers, and in their flying high, till at last they fly so high, that they become a prey to the hawk; so when men fly high in pride and self-confidence, they become a prey to the tempter.

(13) If you would not be foiled by temptation, do not enter into a dispute with Satan. When Eve began to argue the case with the serpent, the serpent was too hard for her; the devil, by his logic, disputed her out of paradise. Satan can mince sin, make it small, and garnish it over, and make it look like virtue. He is too subtle a sophister for us to hold an argument with him. Dispute not, but fight. If you enter into a parley with him, you give him half the victory.

(14) If we would not be overcome by Satan, we must put on Christian fortitude. We must expect an enemy who is either shooting darts, or laying snares, therefore let us be armed with courage. 'Deal courageously, and the Lord shall be with the good.' 2 Chron xix 11. The coward never won a victory. To animate us in our combat with Satan, let us think, [1] We have a good Captain that marches before us. Christ is called the Captain of our salvation. Heb ii 10. [2] We have good armour. Grace is armour of God's making. Eph vi 11. [3] Satan is beaten in part already. Christ has given him his death-wound upon the cross. Col ii 15. [4] Satan is a chained enemy, his power is limited! he cannot force the will. Eve complained that the serpent deceived her, not constrained her. Gen iii 13. Satan has *astutiam suadendi* [guile to persuade], not *potentiam cogendi* [power to compel]; he may persuade, not compel. [5] He is a cursed enemy, and God's curse will blast him: therefore put on holy gallantry of spirit and magnanimity. Fear not Satan. Greater is he that is in you than he that is against you.

(15) If we would not be overcome by temptation, let us call in the help of others. If a house be on fire, would you not call in help? Satan tempts, that he may rob you of your soul; acquaint some friends with your case, and beg for their counsel and prayers. Who knows but Satan may be cast out by the joint prayers of others? In case of temptation, how exceeding hopeful is the communion of saints!

(16) If we would not be overcome by temptation, let us make use of all

the encouragements we can. If Satan be a roaring lion, Christ is the lion of the tribe of Judah. If Satan tempts, Christ prays. If Satan be a serpent to sting, Christ is a brazen serpent to heal. If the conflict be hard, look to the crown. James i 12. Whilst we are fighting, Christ will succour us; and when we overcome, he will crown us. What makes the soldier endure a bloody fight but the hope of a golden harvest? Think that shortly God will call us out of the field where the bullets of temptation fly so fast, and he will set a garland of glory upon our head. How will the case be altered then! Instead of fighting, singing; instead of a helmet, a diadem; instead of a sword, a palm branch of victory; instead of armour, white robes; instead of Satan's skirmishes, the kisses and embraces of a Saviour. These eternal recompenses should keep us from yielding to temptation. Who, to gratify a lust, would lose a crown?

Use 4. Let such as are tempted be wise to make good use of their temptations. As we should labour to improve our afflictions, so to improve our temptations. We should pick some good out of temptation, as Samson got honey out of the lion.

What good comes from temptation? Can there be any good in being set upon by an enemy? Can it be good to have fiery darts shot at us?

Yes! God can make his people get much good by their temptations. Hereby a Christian sees that corruption in his heart which he never saw before. Water in a glass looks pure, but set it on the fire, and the scum boils up; so in temptation a Christian sees the scum of sin boil up, of passion and distrust of God, which he thought had not been in his heart. Hereby a Christian sees more of the wiles of Satan, and is better able to withstand them. Paul had been in the fencing-school of temptation, and grew expert in finding out Satan's stratagems. 'We are not ignorant of his devices.' 2 Cor ii 11. Hereby a Christian grows more humble. God would rather let his children fall into the devil's hands than be proud. Temptation makes the plumes of pride fall. 'Lest I should be exalted above measure, there was given to me a thorn in the flesh.' 2 Cor xii 7. Better is that temptation that humbles than that duty which makes us proud. Thus a Christian may get much good by temptation, which made Luther say three things make a good divine, prayer, meditation, and temptation.

Use 5. Some have been under sore temptations and buffetings of Satan, to lust, revenge, self-murder, but God has stood by them, and given them strength to overcome the tempter.

(1) Let them be very thankful to God. 'Thanks be to God, which giveth us the victory.' 1 Cor xv 57. Be much in doxology. Why were we kept

more than others from falling into sin? Was it because temptation was not so strong? No, Satan shoots his darts with all his force. Was the cause in our will? No, such a broken shield would never have conquered Satan's temptations. Know that it was free grace that beat back the tempter, and brought us off with trophies of victory. O be thankful to God! Had you been overcome by temptation, you might have put black spots in the face of religion, and given occasion to the enemies of God to blaspheme. 2 Sam xii 14. Had you been overcome, you might have lain sick of a 'wounded spirit' and cried out, with David, of 'broken bones.' After David yielded to temptation, he lay for three quarters of a year in horror of mind; and some divines think he never recovered his full joy to the day of his death. Oh, therefore, what cause have they to stand upon mount Gerizim blessing God, who, in a field of battle have got the better of Satan, and been more than conquerors! Say as the Psalmist, 'Blessed be the Lord, who hath not given us as a prey to their teeth:' blessed be God, who hath not given us as a prey to Satan, that roaring lion. Psa cxxiv 6. When God puts mercy in the premises, we must put praise in the conclusion.

(2) You that have been tempted, and come off victors, be full of sympathy; pity tempted souls; show your piety in your pity. Do you see Satan's darts sticking in their sides? Do what you can to pull them out. Communicate your experiences to them; tell them how you broke the devil's snare, and your Saviour was your succourer. The apostle speaks of restoring others 'in the spirit of meekness.' Gal vi 1. The Greek word for restore alludes to surgeons, who set bones out of joint; so when we see such as are tempted, and Satan has, as it were, put their bones out of joint, labour to put them in again, with all love, meekness, and compassion. A word spoken in season may relieve a soul fainting in temptation; and you may, as the good Samaritan, drop oil and wine into the wound. Luke x 34. *Vir spiritualis consilia magis quam convicia meditatur* [The spiritual man thinks over advice rather than reproaches]. Augustine.

(3) You that have got the conquest over Satan, be not secure. Think not that you shall never be troubled with the tempter more. He is not like the Syrians, of whom it is said, 'The bands of Syria came no more into the land of Israel.' 2 Kings vi 23. If a cock be once made to run away, it will fight no more; but it is not so with Satan. He is a restless enemy; if you have beaten him back, he will make a fresh onset. Hannibal said of Marcellus, a Roman captain, that whether he beat or was beaten, he was never quiet.

When Satan was worsted by Christ, he went away, but *ad tempus*, for a season, as if he meant to come again. Luke iv 13. When we have got the better of Satan, we are apt to grow secure, to lay aside our armour, and leave off our watch; which, when he perceives, he comes upon us with a new temptation and wounds us. He deals with us as David did with the Amalekites, who, when they had taken the spoil and were secure, 'They were spread upon the earth eating, and drinking, and dancing' (1 Sam xxx 16); then 'David smote them, and there escaped not a man of them;' ver 17. Therefore, after we have got the better of the tempter, we must do as the mariners in a calm, mend our tackling, not knowing how soon another storm may come. Satan for a time may retreat, that he may afterwards come on more fiercely; he may go away awhile, and bring other seven spirits with him. Luke xi 26.

Therefore, be not secure, but stand upon your watch-tower; lie in your armour; always expect a fight. As he that has a short respite from an ague says, I look every day when my fit shall come, so say, I look every day when the tempter shall come; I will put myself into a warlike posture. When Satan is beaten out of the field, he is not beaten out of the heart; he will come again. He had little hope to prevail against Christ. Christ gave him three deadly wounds, and made him retreat; yet he departed 'only for a season.' If the devil cannot conquer us, he knows he can molest us; if he cannot destroy us, he will surely disturb us; therefore we must, with the pilot, have our compass ready, and be able to turn our needle to any point where temptation shall blow. If the tempter come not so soon as we expect, by putting ourselves in a defensive posture, we shall have the advantage of being always prepared.

To conclude all: let us often make this prayer, 'Lead us not into temptation.' If Satan woo us by a temptation, let us not give consent. In case a Christian has through weakness and not out of a design, yielded to temptation, let him not 'cast away his anchor;' but take heed of despair, which is worse than the fall itself.

Christian, steep thy soul in the brinish waters of repentance, and God will be appeased. Repentance gives the soul a vomit. Christ loved Peter after his denial of him, and sent the first news of his resurrection to him – 'Go tell the disciples and Peter.' It is an error to think that one act of sin can destroy the habit of grace. It is a wrong to God's mercy and to a Christian's comfort, to make the despairing conclusion, that after one has fallen by temptation, his estate is irrecoverable. Therefore, Christian, if thou hast fallen with Peter, repent with Peter, and God will be ready to seal thy pardon.

II. '*Deliver us from evil.*' There is more in this petition than is expressed. The thing expressed is, that we may be kept from evil: the thing further intended is, that we may make progress in piety. 'Denying ungodliness and worldly lusts;' there is being delivered from evil; 'we should live soberly, righteously, and godly;' there is progress in piety. Titus ii 12.

[1] In general, when we pray, 'Deliver us from evil,' we pray to be delivered from the evil of sin. Not that we pray to be delivered immediately from the presence and inbeing of sin, for that cannot be in this life, we cannot shake off this viper, but we pray that God would deliver us more and more from the power and practice, from the scandalous acts of sin which cast a reflection upon the gospel. Sin is the deadly evil we pray against. With what pencil shall I be able to draw the deformed face of sin? The devil would baptize sin with the name of virtue. It is easy to lay fair colours on a black face. I shall endeavour to show you what a prodigious monster sin is, and that there is great reason we should pray, 'Deliver us from evil.'

Sin, as the apostle says, is exceeding sinful. Rom vii 13. It is the very spirits of mischief distilled; it is called 'an accursed thing.' Josh vii 13. That sin is the most execrable evil, appears several ways: (1) Look upon sin in its origin. (2) Look upon sin in its nature. (3) Look upon sin in the judgment and opinion of the godly. (4) Look upon sin by comparison. (5) Look upon sin in the manner of its cure. (6) Look upon sin in its direful effects. When you have seen all these, you will apprehend what a horrid evil sin is, and what great reason we have to pray, 'Deliver us from evil.'

(1) Look upon sin in its origin. It fetches its pedigree from hell. It is of the devil. John viii 44. It calls the devil father. It is *serpentis venenum*, as Augustine says; it is the poison which the old serpent has spit into our virgin nature.

(2) Look upon sin in its nature, and it is evil. See what the Scripture compares it to. It has got a bad name. It is compared to the vomit of dogs (2 Pet ii 22); to a menstruous cloth (Isa xxx 22); which, as Jerome says, was the most unclean thing under the law; it is compared to the plague (1 Kings viii 38); and to a gangrene (2 Tim ii 17). Persons under these diseases we should be loth to eat and drink with.

Sin is evil in its nature, because it is transgression against God. It is a breach of his royal law. 'Sin is the transgression of the law.' 1 John iii 4. It is *crimen laesae majestatis*, high treason against heaven. What greater injury can be offered to a prince than to trample upon his royal edicts? 'They cast thy law behind their backs.' Neh ix 26. Sin is an affront to God, as it is walking contrary to him. Lev xxvi 40. The Hebrew word for sin signifies rebellion. It flies in the face of God. 'He stretcheth out his hand against God.' Job xv 25. We ought not to lift up a thought against God, much less to lift up a hand against him; but the sinner does both. Sin is *deicidium* [the killing of God]; it would not only unthrone God, but ungod him; if sin could help it, God should no longer be God.

Sin is an act of high ingratitude to God. He feeds a sinner, screens off many evils from him; and yet he not only forgets his mercies, but abuses them. 'I gave her corn, and wine, and oil, and multiplied her silver, which they prepared for Baal.' Hos ii 8. God may say, I gave thee wit, health, riches, which thou hast employed against me. A sinner makes an arrow of God's mercies, and shoots at him. 'Is this thy kindness to thy friend?' 2 Sam xvi 17. Did God give thee life to sin? Did he give thee wages to serve the devil? Oh, what an ungrateful thing is sin! Ingratitude forfeits mercy, as the merchant forfeits his goods by not paying custom.

Sin is evil in its nature, because it is a foolish thing. 'Thou fool, this night thy soul shall be required of thee.' Luke xii 20. Is it not foolish to prefer a short lease before an inheritance? A sinner prefers the pleasures of sin for a season before those pleasures which are at God's right hand for evermore. Is it not folly to gratify an enemy? Sin gratifies Satan. *Mortalium errores epulae sunt daemonum;* men's sins feast the devil. Is it not folly for a man to be *felo de se*, guilty of his own destruction, to give himself poison? A sinner has a hand in his own death. 'They lay wait for their own blood.' Prov i 18. No creature did ever willingly kill itself but man.

Sin is a polluting thing. It is not only a defection, but a pollution; it is as rust to gold, as a stain to beauty. It is called 'filthiness of flesh and spirit.' 2 Cor vii 1. It makes the soul red with guilt and black with filth. *Quanta foeditas vitiosae mentis!* [How great is the foulness of a corrupt mind!] Cicero. This filth of sin is inward. A spot in the face may easily be wiped off, but to have the liver and lungs tainted is far worse. Sin has got into the conscience. Titus i 15. It defiles all the faculties – the mind, memory, affections, as if the whole mass of blood were corrupted. It pollutes and fly-blows our holy things. If the leper under the law had touched the altar, the altar would not cleanse him, but he would pollute the altar, which is an emblem of sin's leprosy spotting our holy things.

Sin is a debasing thing, it degrades us of our honour. 'In his estate shall stand up a vile person.' Dan xi 21. This was spoken of Antiochus Epiphanes, who was a king, and whose name signifies illustrious; but sin made him vile. Sin blots a man's name. Nothing so turns a man's glory into shame as sin. It makes a man like a beast. Psa xlix 20. It is worse to be like a beast than to be a beast; it is no shame to be a beast, but it is a shame for a man to be like a beast. Lust makes a man brutish, and wrath makes him devilish.

Sin is an enslaving thing. A sinner is a slave when he sins most freely. *Grave servitutis jugum* [Heavy is the yoke of slavery]. Cicero. Sin makes men the devil's servants. Satan bids them sin, and they do it. He bid Judas betray Christ, and he did it; he bid Ananias tell a lie, and he did it. Acts v 3. When a man commits sin, he is the devil's lackey and runs on his errand. They who serve Satan have such a bad master that they will be afraid to receive their wages.

Sin is an unsavoury thing. 'They are all together become filthy;' in the Hebrew, they are become stinking. Psa xiv 3. Sin is very offensive to God. If he who worships in God's house lives in the sin of uncleanness, though he be perfumed with all the spices of Arabia, his prayers are unsavoury. 'Incense is an abomination to me' (Isa i 13); therefore 'the proud he knoweth afar off.' Psa cxxxviii 6. He will not come near the dunghill-sinner that has such offensive vapours coming from him.

Sin is a painful thing, it costs men much labour and pains to accomplish their wicked designs. 'They weary themselves to commit iniquity.' Jer ix 5. *Peccatum est sui ipsius poena* [Sin is its own punishment]. What pains did Judas take to bring about his treason! He goes to the high priest, then to the band of soldiers, and then back again to the garden! What pains did the powder-traitors take in digging through a thick stone wall! What pains in laying their barrels of powder, and then covering them with crows of iron! How they tired themselves out in sin's drudgery! Chrysostom says virtue is easier than vice. It is easier to be sober than intemperate; it is easier to serve God than to follow sin. A wicked man sweats at the devil's plough, and is at great pains to damn himself.

Sin is a disturbing thing. Whatever defiles disturbs. Sin breaks the peace of the soul. 'No peace to the wicked.' Isa lvii 21. When a man sins presumptuously, he stuffs his pillow with thorns, and his head will lie very uneasy when he comes to die. Sin causes a trembling at the heart. When Spira had sinned, he had a hell in his conscience; he was in such horror that he confessed he envied Cain and Judas. Charles IX, who was guilty of a massacre in Paris, was afterwards a terror to himself; he was frightened at every noise, and could not endure to be awaked out of his sleep without music. Sin breaks the peace of the soul. Cain in killing Abel stabbed half the world at a blow, but could not kill the worm of his own conscience. Thus you see what an evil sin is in the nature of it, and what need we have to pray, 'Deliver us from evil.'

(3) Look upon sin in the judgment and opinion of the godly, and it will appear to be the most prodigious evil.

It is so great an evil that the godly will rather do anything than sin. Moses chose 'rather to suffer with the people of God than to enjoy the pleasures of sin.' Heb xi 24. The primitive Christians said, *ad leonem potius quam lenonem* [to the lion rather than to the bawdy house], they chose rather to be devoured by lions without than lusts within. Irenaeus was carried to a place where a cross was on one side and an idol on the other, and he was put to his choice either to bow to the idol or suffer on the cross, and he chose the latter. A wise man will choose rather to have a rent in his coat than in his flesh; and the godly will rather endure outward sufferings than a rent in their conscience. So great an evil is sin that the godly will not sin for the greatest gain; they will not sin though they might purchase an estate by it – nay, though they were sure to promote God's glory by it.

The godly testify sin to be a great evil, in that they desire to die upon no account more than this, that they may be rid of sin. They are desirous to put off the clothing of the flesh, that they may be unclothed of sin. It is their greatest grief that they are troubled with such inmates as the stirrings of pride, lust, and envy. It was a cruel torment of Mezentius who tied a dead man to a living. Thus a child of God has corruption joined with grace; a dead man tied to a living. So hateful is this, that a believer desires to die for no reason more than this, that death shall free him from sin. Sin brought death into the world, and death shall carry sin out of the world.

(4) Judge of sin by comparison, and it will appear to be the most deadly evil. Compare what you will with it – afflictions, death, or hell, and still sin is worse.

First compare sin with affliction. There is more evil in a drop of sin than in a sea of affliction.

[1] Sin is the cause of affliction, and the cause is more than the effect. Sin brings all mischief: it has sickness, sword, famine, and all judgments in its womb. It rots the name, consumes the estate, and wastes the body. As the poets feigned of Pandora's box, that when opened it filled the world full of diseases, so when Adam broke the box of original righteousness, it caused all the penal evils in the world. Sin is the Phaeton that sets the world on fire. It turned the angels out of heaven, and Adam out of paradise. It causes mutinies, divisions, and massacres. 'O thou sword of the Lord, how long will it be ere thou be quiet?' Jer xlvii 6. The sword of God's justice lies quietly in the scabbard till sin draws it out and whets it against a nation. So that sin is worse than affliction, being the cause of it: and the cause is more than the effect.

[2] God is the author of affliction. 'Shall there be evil in a city, and the Lord hath not done it?' Amos iii 6. It is meant of the evil of affliction. God has a hand in affliction, but no hand in sin. He is the cause of every action, so far as it is natural, but not as it is sinful. He who makes an instrument of iron is not the cause of the rust and canker which corrupts it; so God made the instrument of our souls, but not the rust and canker of sin which corrupts them. *Peccatum Deus non fecit* [God is not the author of sin]. Augustine. God can no more act evil than the sun can darken. In this sense sin is worse than affliction. God has a hand in affliction, but disclaims having any hand in sin.

[3] Affliction reaches the body only, and makes that miserable, but sin makes the soul miserable. The soul is the most noble part. It is a diamond

set in a ring of clay; it is excellent in its essence, a spiritual, immortal substance; excellent in the price paid for it, redeemed with the blood of God. Acts xx 28. It is of more worth than a world. The world is of a coarser make, the soul of a finer spinning: in the world we see the finger of God, in the soul the image of God. To have the precious soul endangered is far worse than to have the body endangered. Sin wrongs the soul. Prov viii 36. It casts the jewel of the soul overboard. Affliction is but skin-deep; it can but take away the life, but sin takes away the soul. Luke xii 20. The loss of the soul is an unparalleled loss, it can never be made up again. 'God,' says Chrysostom, 'has given thee two eyes, if thou losest one, thou hast another; but thou hast but one soul, and if that be lost, it can never be repaired.' Thus sin is worse than affliction; the one can reach the body only, the other ruins the soul. Is there not great reason, then, that we should often put up this petition, 'Deliver us from evil'?

[4] Afflictions are good for us. 'It is good for me that I have been afflicted.' Psa cxix 71. Many can bless God for affliction. Affliction humbles. 'Remembering mine affliction, the wormwood and the gall, my soul hath them still in remembrance, and is humbled in me.' Lam iii 19. Afflictions are compared to thorns; these thorns are to prick the bladder of pride. Hos ii 6. Affliction is the school of repentance. 'Thou hast chastised me, and I was chastised; I repented.' Jer xxxi 18, 19. The fire being put under the distillery, makes the water drop from the roses; so the fire of affliction makes the water of repentance drop from the eyes. Affliction brings us nearer to God. The loadstone of mercy does not draw us so near to God as the cords of affliction. When the prodigal was pinched with want, he said, 'I will arise, and go to my Father.' Luke xv 18. Afflictions prepare for glory. 'Light affliction worketh for us an eternal weight of glory.' 2 Cor iv 17. The painter lays his gold upon dark colours; so God lays first the dark colours of affliction, and then the golden colour of glory. Thus affliction is for our good; but sin is not for our good; it keeps good things from us. 'Your sins have withholden good things from you.' Jer v 25. Sin stops the current of God's mercy; it precipitates men to ruin. Manasseh's affliction brought him to humiliation; but that of Judas brought him to desperation.

[5] A man may be afflicted, and his conscience be quiet. Paul's feet were in the stocks, yet he had the witness of his conscience. 2 Cor i 12. The head may ache, yet the heart may be well; the outward man may be afflicted, yet the soul may dwell at ease. Psa xxv 13. The hail may beat upon the tiles of the house when there is music within. In the midst of outward pain there may be inward peace. Thus, in affliction, conscience may be quiet; but when a man commits a presumptuous, scandalous sin, conscience is

troubled. By defiling the purity of conscience we lose the peace of conscience. When Spira had sinned and abjured the faith, he was a terror to himself; he had a hell within. Tiberius the emperor felt such a sting in his conscience, that he told the senate, he suffered death daily.

[6] In affliction we may have the love of God. Afflictions are love tokens. 'As many as I love I rebuke.' Rev iii 19. Afflictions are sharp arrows, but shot from the hand of a loving Father. If a man should throw a bag of money at another, and it should bruise him a little, and raise the skin, he would not be offended, but take it as a fruit of love; so, when God bruises us with affliction, it is to enrich us with the golden graces of his Spirit, and all is in love; but when we commit sin God withdraws his love; it is the sun overcast with a cloud; nothing appears but anger and displeasure. When David had sinned in the matter of Uriah, 'the thing that David had done displeased the Lord.' 2 Sam xi 27.

[7] There are many encouragements to suffer affliction. God himself suffers with us. 'In all their affliction he was afflicted.' Isa lxiii 9. God will strengthen us in our sufferings. 'He is their strength in the time of trouble.' Psa xxxvii 39. Either God makes our burden lighter, or our faith stronger. He will compensate and recompense our sufferings. 'Every one that hath forsaken houses or lands for my name's sake, shall receive an hundredfold, and inherit everlasting life.' Matt xix 29. Here are encouragements to suffer affliction, but there is no encouragement to sin. God has brandished a flaming sword of threatenings to deter us from sin. 'God shall wound the hairy scalp of such an one as goeth on still in his trespasses.' Psa lxviii 21. A flying-roll of curses enters into the house of a sinner. Zech v 4. If a man sin, be it at his peril. 'I will make mine arrows drunk with blood.' Deut xxxii 42. God will make men weary of their sins, or he will make them weary of their lives. Thus sin is worse than affliction. There are encouragements to suffer affliction, but no encouragement to sin.

[8] When a person is afflicted, he suffers alone; but by sinning openly he hurts others. He does hurt to the unconverted. One man's sin may lay a stone in another man's way, at which he may stumble and fall into hell. Oh, the evil of scandalous sin! Some are discouraged, others hardened. Thy sinning may be the cause of another's damning. The priests going wrong caused others to stumble. Mal ii 7, 8. He does hurt to the converted. By an open scandalous sin he offends weak believers, and so sins against Christ. 1 Cor viii 12. Thus sin is worse than affliction, because it does hurt to others.

[9] In affliction the saints may rejoice. 'Ye received the word in much affliction, with joy.' 1 Thess i 6. 'Ye took joyfully the spoiling of your

goods.' Heb x 34. Aristotle speaks of a bird that lives among thorns, and yet sings sweetly; so a child of God can rejoice in afflictions. Paul had his prison songs. 'We glory in tribulations.' Rom v 3. The Greek word signifies an exuberancy of joy, a joy with boasting and triumph. God often pours in those divine consolations that cause the saints to rejoice in afflictions, so that they had rather have their afflictions than be without their comforts. God candies their wormwood with sugar. Rom v 5. You have seen the sunshine when it rains: the saints have had the shinings of God's face when afflictions have rained and dropped upon them. Thus we may rejoice in affliction, but we cannot rejoice in sin. 'Rejoice not, O Israel, for joy, as other people, for thou hast gone a whoring from thy God.' Hos ix 1. Sin is matter of shame and grief, not of joy. David having sinned in numbering the people, his 'heart smote him.' 2 Sam xxiv 10. As pricking a vein lets out the blood, so, when sin has pricked the conscience, it lets out the joy.

[10] Affliction magnifies a person. 'What is man that thou shouldest magnify him, and visit him every morning?' Job vii 17, 18. That is, visit him with affliction.

How do afflictions magnify us?

(1) As they are signs of sonship. 'If ye endure chastening, God dealeth with you as with sons.' Heb xii 7. Every print of the rod is a badge of honour. (2) As the sufferings of the godly have raised their fame and renown in the world. The zeal and constancy of the martyrs in their sufferings have eternalized their name. Oh, how eminent was Job for his patience! 'Ye have heard of the patience of Job.' James v 11. Job the sufferer was more renowned than Alexander the conqueror. Thus afflictions magnify a person; but sin does not magnify, but vilifies him. When Eli's sons had sinned and profaned their priesthood, they turned their glory into shame; the text says they 'made themselves vile.' 1 Sam iii 13. Sin casts an indelible blot on a man's name. 'Whoso committeth adultery with a woman, a wound and dishonour shall he get, and his reproach shall not be wiped away.' Prov vi 32, 33.

[11] A man by suffering affliction may bring honour to religion. Paul's iron chain made the gospel wear a gold chain. Suffering credits and propagates the gospel; but committing sin brings dishonour and scandal upon the ways of God. Cyprian says, when in the primitive times a virgin, who vowed herself to religion, had defiled her chastity, *totum ecclesiae coetum erubescere*, shame and grief filled the face of the whole congregation. When scandalous sins are committed by a few, they bring a reproach upon many; as three or four brass shillings in a sum of money make all the rest suspected.

[12] When a man's afflictions are upon a good account, when he suffers for Christ, he has the prayers of God's people. It is no small privilege to have a stock of prayer going; it is like a merchant that has a part in several ships: and suffering saints have a large share in the prayers of others. 'Peter was in prison; but prayer was made without ceasing of the church unto God for him.' Acts xii 5. What greater happiness than to have God's promises and the saints' prayers! But when a man sins presumptuously and scandalously, he has the saints' bitter tears and just censures; he is a burden to all that know him, as David speaks in another case, 'They that did see me without fled from me.' Psa xxxi 11. So the people of God flee from a scandalous sinner; he is like an infected person, everyone shuns and avoids him.

[13] Affliction can hurt a man only while he is living, but sin hurts him when he is dead. As a man's virtues and alms may do good when he is dead, so his sins may do him mischief when he is dead. When a spider is killed, the poison of it may hurt; so the poison of an evil example may do much hurt when a man is in his grave. Affliction at most can but last a man's life, but sin lives and hurts when he is gone. Thus sin is far worse than affliction.

Secondly. Sin is worse than death. Aristotle calls death the terrible of terribles, and Job calls it 'the king of terrors,' but sin is more deadly than death itself. Job xviii 14. 1. Death, though painful, would not hurt but for sin; it is sin that embitters it and makes its sting. 'The sting of death is sin.' 1 Cor xv 56. Were it not for sin, though death might kill, it could not curse us. Sin poisons death's arrow, so that it is worse than death, because it puts a sting into death. 2. Death does but separate between the body and the soul; but sin, without repentance, separates between God and the soul. 'Ye have taken away my gods, and what have I more?' Judges xviii 24. Death does but take away our life, but sin takes away our God from us; so that it is worse than death.

Thirdly. Sin is worse than hell. In hell there is the worm and the fire, but sin is worse. 1. Hell is of God's making, but sin is none of his making; it is a monster of the devil's creating. 2. The torments of hell are a burden only to the sinner, but sin is a burden to God. 'I am pressed under you, as a cart is pressed that is full of sheaves.' Amos ii 13. 3. In hell torments there is something that is good: there is the execution of God's justice, there is justice in hell; but sin is the most unjust thing; it would rob God of his glory, Christ of his purchase, and the soul of its happiness; so that it is worse than hell.

(5) Look upon sin in the manner of its cure. It cost much to be done away; the guilt of sin could not be removed but by the blood of Christ; he who was God must die and be made a curse for us before sin could be remitted.

How horrid is sin, that no angel or archangel, nor all the powers of heaven, could procure its pardon, but the blood of God only! If a man should commit an offence, and all the nobles should kneel before the king for him, but no pardon could be had, unless the king's son be arraigned and suffer death for him, all would conceive it to be a horrible thing that was the cause of this. Such is the case here, the Son of God must die to satisfy God's justice for our sins. Oh, the agonies and sufferings of Christ! In his body: his head crowned with thorns, his face spit upon, his side pierced with the spear, his hands and feet nailed. *Totum pro vulnere corpus* [His whole body as one wound]. He suffered in his soul. 'My soul is exceeding sorrowful, even unto death.' Matt xxvi 38. He drank a bitter cup, mingled with curses, which made him, though sanctified by the Spirit, supported by the Deity, and comforted by angels, sweat drops of blood, and cry out upon the cross, 'My God, why hast thou forsaken me!' All this was to do away with our sin. View sin in Christ's blood, and it will appear of a crimson colour.

(6) Look upon sin in its dismal effects, and it will appear the most horrid and prodigious evil. 'The wages of sin is death,' that is, 'the second death.' Rom vi 23. Rev xxi 8. Sin has shame for its companion, and death for its wages. A wicked man knows what sin is in the pleasure of it, but does not know what sin is in the punishment of it. Sin is *scorpio pungens* [a stinging scorpion], it draws hell at the heels of it. This hellish torment consists of two parts:

Poena damni, the punishment of loss. 'Depart from me.' Matt vii 23. It was a great trouble to Absalom that he might not see the king's face; but to lose God's smiles, to be banished from his presence, in whose presence is fulness of joy, how sad and tremendous! That word, 'Depart,' said Chrysostom, is worse than the fire. Sure sin must be the greatest evil, which separates us from the greatest good.

Poena sensus, the punishment of sense. 'Depart from me, ye cursed, into everlasting fire, prepared for the devil and his angels.' Matt xxv 41. Why, sinners might plead, 'Lord, if we must depart from thee, let us have thy blessing.' 'No; go, ye cursed.' 'If we must depart from thee, let it be into some place of ease and rest.' 'No; go into fire.' 'If we must go into fire, let it be for a little time; let the fire be quickly put out.' 'No; go into everlasting fire.' 'If it be so, that we must be there, let us be with good company.' 'No; with the devil and his angels.' Oh, what an evil is sin! All the torments of this life are but *ludibrium et risus* [mockery and ridicule], a kind of sport to hell torments. What is a burning fever to the burning in hell! It is called, the 'wrath of Almighty God.' Rev xix 15. The Almighty God inflicts the punishment, therefore it will be heavy. A child cannot strike very hard, but if a giant strike, he kills with a blow; but to have the almighty God lay on the stroke, will be intolerable. Hell is the *emphasis* of misery. The body and soul, which have sinned together, shall suffer together; and those torments shall have no period put to them. They 'shall seek death, and shall not find it.' Rev ix 6. 'The smoke of their torment ascendeth up for ever and ever.' Rev xiv 11. Here the wicked thought a prayer long, a Sabbath long; but how long will it be to lie upon beds of flames for ever! That word, ever, breaks the heart. Surely, then, sin is the most deadly and execrable evil. Look upon it in its original, in its nature, in the judgment and estimate of the wise; look upon it comparatively, it is worse than affliction, death, and hell; look upon it in the manner of cure, and in the dismal effect, it brings eternal damnation. Is there not, then, great reason that we should make this prayer, 'Deliver us from evil'?

Use 1. For instruction. (1) Is sin such a deadly, pernicious evil, the evil of evils? See what we are to pray most to be delivered from, and that it is in reference to sin our Saviour has taught us to pray, 'Deliver us from evil.' Hypocrites pray more against temporal evils than spiritual. Pharaoh prayed more to have the plague of hail and thunder removed than his hard heart to be removed. Exod ix 28. The Israelites prayed, *Tolle serpentes*, take away the serpents from us, more than to have their sin taken away. Numb xxi 7. The hypocrite's prayer is carnal: he prays more to be cured of his deafness and lameness than of his unbelief; more that God would take away his pain than take away his sin. But our prayer should be, 'Deliver us from evil.' Spiritual prayers are best. Hast thou a diseased body? Pray more that the disease of thy soul may be removed than of thy body. 'Heal my soul, for I have sinned.' Psa xli 4. The plague of the heart is worse than a cancer in the breast. Hast thou a child that is crooked? Pray more to have its unholiness removed than its crookedness. Spiritual prayers are more pleasing to God, and are as music in his ears. Christ has here taught us to pray against sin, 'Deliver us from evil.'

(2) If sin be so great an evil, then admire the wonderful patience of God that bears with sinners. Sin is a breach of God's royal law, it strikes at his glory; for God to bear with sinners who provoke him, shows admirable patience. Well may he be called 'the God of patience.' Rom xv 5. It would tire the patience of the angels to bear with men's sins one day; but what does God bear! How many affronts and injuries he puts up with! He sees all the intrigues and horrid impieties committed in a nation. 'They have committed villainy in Israel, and have committed adultery; even I know, and am a witness, saith the Lord.' Jer xxix 23. God could strike men dead in their sins; but he forbears, and respites them. Methinks I see the justice of God with a flaming sword in his hand, ready to strike the stroke; and patience

steps in for the sinner and says, Lord, spare him awhile longer. Methinks I hear the angel saying to God, as the king of Israel to the prophet, 'Shall I smite them? Shall I smite them?' 2 Kings vi 21. Lord, here is such a sinner: shall I smite him? Shall I take off the head of such a drunkard, swearer, Sabbath-breaker? And God's patience says, as the dresser of the vineyard, 'Let him alone this year.' Luke xiii 8. Oh, the infinite patience of God, that he should bear with sinners so long! 'If a man find his enemy, will he let him go well away?' 1 Sam xxiv 19. God finds his enemies, yet he lets them go, he is not presently avenged on them. Every sin has a voice to cry to God for vengeance; as Sodom's sin cried. Gen xviii 20. God spares men; but let not sinners presume upon his patience. Long forbearance is not forgiveness; God's patience abused leaves men more inexcusable.

(3) If sin be so great an evil, there is no little sin. There is no little treason: every sin strikes at God's crown and dignity; and in this sense it may be said, Are not 'thine iniquities infinite?' Job xxii 5. The least sin, as the schoolmen say, is infinite objective, because it is committed against an infinite Majesty. Nothing can do away with sin but that which has infinity in it; for though the sufferings of Christ, as man, were not infinite, yet the divine nature shed forth an infinite value and merit upon his sufferings. No sin is little, and there is no little hell for sin. As we are not to think any of God's mercies little, because they are more than we can deserve, so neither are we to think any of our sins little, because they are more than we can answer for. The sin we esteem lightest, without Christ's blood, will be heavy enough to sink us into perdition.

(4) If sin be so great an evil, see whence all personal or national troubles come from. They come from the evil of sin. Sin grows high, which makes divisions grow wide. It is the Achan that troubles us, it is the cockatrice egg, out of which comes a fiery, flying serpent. It is like Phaeton, who, as the poets feign, driving the chariot of the sun, set the world on fire. Like the planet Saturn, it has a malignant influence. It brings us into straits. 'David said unto Gad, I am in a great strait.' 2 Sam xxiv 14. 'As keepers of a field are they against her round about;' as horses or deer in a field are so enclosed with hedges, and so narrowly watched, that they cannot get out, so Jerusalem was so close besieged with enemies and watched, that there was no escape for her. Jer iv 17. Whence was this? 'This is thy wickedness;' ver 18. All our evils are from the evil of sin. The cords that pinch us are of our own twisting. *Flagitium et flagellum sunt tanquam acus et filum* [Punishment follows wickedness as the thread the needle]. Sin raises all the storms in conscience. The sword of God's justice lies quiet till sin draws it out of the scabbard, and makes God whet it against a nation.

(5) If sin be so great an evil, how little reason has any one to be in love with

it! Some are so infatuated with it, that they delight in it. The devil can so cook and dress sin, that it pleases the sinner's palate. 'Though wickedness be sweet in his mouth.' Job xx 12. Sin is as delightful to corrupt nature as meat to the taste. It is a feast on which men feed their lusts; but there is little cause to be in love with it. 'Though wickedness be sweet in his mouth, it is the gall of asps within him.' Job xx 12, 14. To love sin is to hug an enemy. Sin puts a worm into conscience, a sting into death, a fire into hell. It is like those locusts in Rev ix 7: 'On their heads were as it were crowns like gold, and they had hair as the hair of women, and their teeth were as the teeth of lions, and they had tails like unto scorpions, and there were stings in their tails.' After the woman's hair comes in the scorpion's sting.

(6) If sin be so great an evil, what shall we say of them who make light of sin, as if there were no danger in it; as if God were not in earnest when he threatens sin; or as if ministers were about a needless work, when they preach against it? Some people make nothing of breaking a commandment; they make nothing of telling a lie, of cozening or slandering; nothing of living in the sin of uncleanness. If you weigh sin in the balance of some men's judgments, it is very light; but who are those that make light of sin? Solomon has described them. 'Fools make a mock at sin.' Prov xiv 9. *Stultus in vitia cito dilabitur* [The fool falls quickly into vices]. Isidore. Who but fools would make light of that which grieves the Spirit of God? Who but fools would put a viper in their bosom? Who but fools would laugh at their own calamity, and make sport while they give themselves poison?

(7) If sin be so great an evil, I infer that there is no good to be got by it. Of this thorn we cannot gather grapes. If sin be a deadly evil, we cannot get any profit by it; no man ever could thrive upon this trade. Atheists said, 'It is vain to serve God, and what profit is it?' Mal iii 14. But we may say more truly, what profit is there in sin? 'What fruit had ye then in those things whereof ye are now ashamed?' Rom vi 21. Where are your earnings? What have you got by sin? It has shame for its companion, and death for its wages. What profit had Achan of his wedge of gold? That wedge seemed to cleave asunder his soul from God. What profit had Ahab of the vineyard he got unjustly? The dogs licked his blood. 1 Kings xxi 19. What profit had Judas of his treason? For thirty pieces he sold his Saviour, and bought his own damnation. All the gain men get by their sins, they may put in their eye; nay, they must put it there and weep it out again.

(8) If sin be so great an evil, see the folly of those who venture upon it, because of the pleasure they have in it. 'Who had pleasure in unrighteousness.' 2 Thess ii 12. As for the pleasure of sin, it is but seeming; it is but a pleasant fancy; a golden dream. And besides, it is a mixed pleasure, it has bitterness intermingled with it. 'I have, says the harlot, perfumed my bed

with myrrh, aloes, and cinnamon.' Prov vii 17. For one sweet, here are two bitters; cinnamon is sweet, but myrrh and aloes are bitter; the harlot's pleasure is mixed. There are those inward fears and lashes of conscience, that embitter the pleasure. If there be any pleasure in sin, it is only to the body, the brutish part; the soul is not at all gratified by it. 'Soul, take thine ease;' he might have more properly said, 'Body, take thine ease;' the soul cannot feed on sensual objects. Luke xii 19. In short, the pleasure men talk of in sin, is their disease. Some take pleasure in eating chalk or coals, which is from disease; so when men talk of pleasure in eating the forbidden fruit, it is from the sickness and disease of their souls. They 'put bitter for sweet.' Isa v 20. Oh, what folly is it, for a cup of pleasure, to drink a sea of wrath! Sin will be bitter in the end. 'Look not upon the wine when it is red, when it giveth his colour in the cup; at the last it biteth like a serpent.' Prov xxiii 31, 32. Sin will prove like Ezekiel's roll, sweet in the mouth, but bitter in the belly, *mel in ore, fel in corde*. Ask Cain now how he likes his murder? Achan how he likes his golden wedge? O remember that saying of Augustine, *Momentaneum est quod delectat, aeternum quod cruciat* [The pleasure is momentary, the torture eternal]. The pleasure of sin is soon gone, but the sting remains.

(9) If sin be so great an evil, what wisdom is it to depart from it! 'To depart from evil is understanding.' Job xxviii 28. To sin is to do foolishly; therefore to depart from sin is to do wisely. Solomon says, 'In the transgression of an evil man there is a snare.' Prov xxix 6. Is it not wisdom to avoid a snare? Sin is a deceiver, it cheated our first parents. Instead of being as gods, they became as the beasts that perish. Psa xlix 20. Sin has cheated all that have meddled with it; and is it not wisdom to shun such a cheater? Sin has many fair pleas, and tells how it will gratify all the senses with pleasure; but, says a gracious soul, Christ's love is sweeter; peace of conscience is sweeter; what are the pleasures of sin to the pleasures of paradise? Well may the saints be called wise virgins, because they spy the deceits that are in sin, and avoid the snares. 'The fear of the Lord, that is wisdom; and to depart from evil is understanding.'

(10) If sin be so great an evil, how justifiable and commendable are all those means which are used to keep men from sin! How justifiable are a minister's admonitions and reproofs! 'Rebuke them sharply' (Titus i 13); cuttingly; a metaphor from a surgeon that searches a wound, and cuts out the proud flesh that the patient may be sound; so God's minister comes with a cutting reproof, but it is to keep from sin, and to save the soul. *Si merito objurgaverit te aliquis, scito quia profuit* [If anyone has reproved you justly, be sure that it was to your benefit]. Seneca. Esteem them your best friends who would keep you from sinning against God. If a man were going to poison

or drown himself, would he not be his friend who should hinder him from doing it? All a minister's reproofs are but to keep you from sin, and hinder from self-murder; all is in love. 'Knowing the terror of the Lord, we persuade men.' 2 Cor v 11. It is the passion of most to be angry with those who would reclaim them from sin. 'They hate him that rebuketh in the gate.' Amos v 10. Who is angry with the physician for prescribing a bitter potion, seeing it is to purge out the peccant humour? It is mercy to men's souls to tell them of their sins. And surely those are priests of the devil who see men go on in sin, and ready to drop into hell, and never pull them back by a reproof; nay, perhaps flatter them in their sins. God never made ministers to be false glasses, to make bad faces look fair; such make themselves guilty of other men's sins.

(11) If sin be so great an evil, the evil of evils, see what a bad choice they make who choose sin to avoid affliction! It is as if to save the coat from being rent, one should suffer his flesh to be rent. It was a false charge that Elihu brought against Job: 'This [iniquity] hast thou chosen rather than affliction.' Job xxxvi 21. This is a bad choice. Affliction has a promise made to it, but sin has no promise made to it. 2 Sam xxii 28. Affliction is for our good, but sin is not for our good; it would entail hell and damnation upon us. Spira chose iniquity rather than affliction, but it cost him dear; at last he repented of his choice. He who commits sin to avoid suffering, is like one that runs into a lion's den to avoid the stinging of a gnat.

(12) If sin be so great an evil, it should be a Christian's great care in this life to keep from it. 'Deliver us from evil.' Some make it all their care to keep out of trouble; they had rather keep their skin whole than their conscience pure; but our care should be chiefly to keep from sin. How careful are we to forbear such a dish as the physicians tell us is hurtful to us: it will bring the stone or gout! Much more should we be careful that we eat not the forbidden fruit, which will bring divine vengeance. 'Keep thyself pure.' 1 Tim v 22. It has always been the study of the saints to keep aloof from sin. 'How can I do this great wickedness, and sin against God?' Gen xxxix 9. 'Keep back thy servant from presumptuous sins.' Psa xix 13. It was a saying of Anselm, 'If sin were on one side, and hell on the other, I would rather leap into hell than willingly sin against my God.' Oh, what a mercy is it to be kept from sin! We count it a great mercy to be kept from the plague and fire; but what is it to be kept from sin!

(13) Is sin so great an evil? It should make us long for heaven, where we shall be perfectly freed from sin, not only from its outward acts, but from the inbeing of sin. In heaven we shall not need to pray this prayer, 'Deliver us from evil.' What a blessed time will it be when we shall never have a vain thought more! Then Christ's spouse shall be *sine macula et ruga*, without

w

spot or wrinkle. Eph v 27. Now there is a dead man tied to the living; we cannot do any holy duty, but we mix sin with it; we cannot pray without wandering; we cannot believe without doubting; but then our virgin souls shall not be capable of the least tincture of sin, but we shall all be as the angels of God.

In heaven we shall have no temptation to sin. The old serpent is cast out of paradise, and his fiery darts shall never come near to touch us.

Use 2. For exhortation.

First to all in general. If sin be so great and prodigious an evil, as you love your souls, take heed of sin. If you taste the forbidden fruit, it will cost you dear, it will cost you bitter tears, it may cost you lying in hell. O therefore flee from sin.

(1) Take heed of sins of omission. Matt xxiii 23. It is as really dangerous not to do things commanded, as to do things forbidden. Some think it no great matter to omit reading Scripture. The Bible lies by like rusty armour, which they never use. They think it no great matter to omit family or closet-prayer; they go several months, and God never hears from them. They have nothing sanctified to them; they feed upon a curse; 'for every creature is sanctified by prayer.' 1 Tim iv 4, 5. The bird which may shame many never takes a drop but its eye is lifted up towards heaven. O take heed of living in the neglect of any known duty. It was the prayer of a holy man on his death-bed, 'Lord, forgive my sins of omission.'

(2) Take heed of secret sins. Some are more modest than to sin openly in a balcony; but they will carry their sins under a canopy, they will sin in secret. Rachel would not let her father's images be seen, but she put them under her, 'and sat upon them.' Gen xxxi 34. Many will be drunk and unclean, if they may do it when nobody sees them; they are like one that shuts up his shop windows, but follows his trade within doors. If sin be so great an evil, let me warn you this day not to sin in secret; know that you can never sin so privately but that the two witnesses, God and conscience, are always by.

(3) Take heed of your besetting sin, that which your nature and constitution most incline to. As in the hive there is a master bee, so in the heart there is a master sin. 'I kept myself from mine iniquity.' Psa xviii 23. There is some sin that is a special favourite, the *peccatum in deliciis*, the darling sin that lies in the bosom, and this bewitches and draws away the heart. O beware of this!

[1] That sin which a man most cherishes, and to which all other sins are subservient, is the sin which is most tended and waited upon. The Pharisees' darling sin was vainglory, all they did was to feed the sin of pride. 'That they

may have glory of men;' when they gave alms they sounded a trumpet. Matt vi 2. If a stranger had asked the question, why does this trumpet sound? the answer was, The Pharisees are going to give alms to the poor. Their lamp of charity was filled with the oil of vainglory. Matt xxiii 5. All their works they did to be seen of men. Pride was their bosom sin. Oftentimes covetousness is the darling sin; all other sins are committed to maintain this. Why do men equivocate, oppress, defraud, take bribes, but to uphold covetousness?

[2] The sin which a man loves not to be reproved for is the darling sin. Herod could not endure to have his incest spoken against; if John the Baptist meddles with that sin, it shall cost him his head.

[3] That sin which has most power over a man, and most easily leads him captive, is the beloved of the soul. There are some sins which a man can better put off and repulse; but there is one sin, which, if it becomes a suitor, he cannot deny, but is overcome by it: this is the bosom sin. The young man in the gospel had a besetting sin which he could not resist, and that was the love of the world; his silver was dearer to him than his Saviour. It is a sad thing a man should be so bewitched by a lust that he will part with the kingdom of heaven to gratify it.

[4] The sin which men use arguments to defend is the darling sin. To plead for sin is to be the devil's attorney. If the sin be covetousness, and we vindicate it; if it be rash anger, and we justify it, saying (as Jonah iv 9), 'I do well to be angry,' this is the besetting sin.

[5] That sin which most troubles a man, and flies in his face in an hour of sickness and distress, is the beloved sin. When Joseph's brethren were distressed, their sin in selling their brother came to remembrance. Gen xlv 3. So, when a man is upon his sick-bed, conscience says, Dost not thou remember how thou hast lived in such a sin, though thou hast been often warned, yet thou wouldst not leave it? Conscience reads a curtain lecture upon the darling sin.

[6] The sin which a man is most unwilling to part with is the darling sin. Jacob could of all his sons, most hardly part with Benjamin. 'Joseph is not, and Simeon is not, and ye will take Benjamin away.' Gen xlii 36. So says the sinner, this and that sin have I parted with; but must Benjamin go? Must I part with this delightful sin? That goes to the heart. It is the Delilah, the beloved sin. Oh, if sin be such a deadly evil, dare not to indulge any bosom sin, which is the most dangerous of all; and, like a humour striking to the heart, which is mortal, leaves open but one gap for the wild beast to enter. One darling sin lived in, sets open a gap for Satan to enter.

(4) Take heed of the sins which attend your particular callings. A calling you must have. Adam in paradise tilled the ground. God never sealed warrants to idleness. But every calling has its snare; as some sin in living out of a calling, so others sin in a calling. Remember how deadly an evil sin is. Avoid those sins which you are exposed to in your trade. Take heed of all fraud and collusion in your dealings. 'Whatsoever ye would that men should do to you, do ye even so to them.' Matt vii 12.

Take heed of a sinful tongue in selling. The Scripture says of one that goes to heaven, 'He speaketh the truth in his heart.' Psa xv 2. It is the custom of many to say the commodity stands them more, and yet they take less. This is hardly creditable.

Beware of a deceitful balance. 'The balances of deceit are in his hand.' Hos xii 7. Men by making their weights lighter, make their accounts heavier.

Beware of sophisticating, mingling, and debasing commodities. 'We sell the refuse of the wheat.' Amos viii 6. They pick out the best grains of the wheat, and sell the worst at the same price as they did the best. To mix a coarse commodity with the fine, and sell it all for fine, is no better than deceit. Isa i 22.

Beware of stretching your consciences too far, or taking more for a commodity than it is worth. 'If thou sell ought unto thy neighbour, ye shall not oppress one another.' Lev xxv 14. There is a lawful gain allowed, yet one may not so advantage himself as to injure another. Let the tradesman's motto be, 'A conscience void of offence toward God and toward men.' Acts xxiv 16. He has a hard bargain that purchases the world with the loss of his soul.

(5) Sin being so deadly an evil, take heed of the appearance of sin. Abstain not only from apparent evil, but the appearance of evil; if it be not absolutely a sin, yet if it looks like sin, avoid it. He who is loyal to his prince, not only forbears to have his hand in treason, but he will take heed of that which has a show of treason. Joseph's mistress tempted him, and he fled and would not be with her. Gen xxxix 12. An appearance of good is too little, and an appearance of evil is too much.

The appearance of evil is often an occasion of evil. Dalliance is an appearance of evil, and oftentimes occasions evil. Touching the forbidden fruit occasions tasting. Dancing in masquerades has often been the occasion of uncleanness.

The appearance of evil may scandalize another. 'When ye sin against the brethren, and wound their weak conscience, ye sin against Christ.' 1 Cor viii 12. Sinning against a member of Christ is sinning against Christ himself.

What means shall we use to be kept from acts of sin?

(1) If you would be preserved from actual and scandalous sins, labour to mortify original sin. If you would not have the branches bud and blossom, smite at the root. I know that original sin cannot in this life be removed, but labour to have it subdued. Why do men break forth into actual sins but because they do not mortify heart sins? Suppress the first risings of pride, lust, and passion. Original sin unmortified will prove such a root of bitterness as will bring forth the cursed root of scandalous sin.

(2) If you would be kept from actual sins, think what an odious thing sin is. Besides what you have heard, remember sin is the accursed thing. Josh vii 13. It is the abominable thing God hates. 'Oh do not this abominable thing that I hate.' Jer xliv 4. Sin is the spirit of witchcraft; it is the devil's excrement; it is called filthiness. James i 21. If all the evils in the world were put together, and their essence strained out, they could not make a thing so filthy as sin is. So odious is a sinner that God loathes the sight of him. 'My soul lothed them.' Zech xi 8. He who defiles himself with avarice, what is he but a serpent licking the dust? He who defiles himself with the lust of uncleanness, what is he but a swine with a man's head? He who defiles himself with pride, what is he but a bladder which the devil has blown up? He who defiles himself with drunkenness, what is he but a beast that has got the staggers? To consider how odious and base a thing sin is, would be a means of keeping us from sinning.

(3) If you would be kept from actual sins, get the fear of God planted in your hearts. 'By the fear of the Lord men depart from evil.' Prov xvi 6. *Cavebis si pavebis* [You will take care if you fear]; fear is a bridle to sin and a spur to holiness. Fear puts a holy awe upon the heart and binds it to its good behaviour. By the fear of the Lord men depart from evil. When the Empress Eudoxia threatened to banish Chrysostom, 'Tell her,' said he, 'I fear nothing but sin.' Fear is *janitor animae*; it stands as a porter at the door of the soul and keeps sin from entering. All sin is committed for want of the fear of God. 'Whose mouth is full of cursing and bitterness; their feet are swift to shed blood; there is no fear of God before their eyes.' Rom iii 14, 15, 18. Holy fear stands sentinel, and is ever watching against security, pride, and wantonness. Fear is a Christian's lifeguard to defend him against the fiery darts of temptation. *Si vis esse securus, semper time.* The way to be safe is always to fear.

(4) If we would be kept from actual sins, let us be careful to avoid all the inlets and occasions of sin. Run not into evil company. He that would not have the plague will not go into an infected house. Guard your senses, which may be the inlets to sin. Keep the two portals, the eye and the ear;

especially look to your eyes. Much sin comes in by the eye; the eye is often an inlet to sin; sin takes fire at the eye; the first sin in the world began at the eye. 'When the woman saw that the tree was good for food, and was pleasant to the eyes, she took of the fruit thereof.' Gen iii 6. Looking begat lusting. Intemperance begins at the eye. Looking on the wine when it is red and gives its colour in the glass, causes excess of drinking. Prov xxiii 31. Covetousness begins at the eye. 'When I saw among the spoils a goodly Babylonish garment, and a wedge of gold, I coveted and took them.' Josh vii 21. The fire of lust begins to kindle at the eye. David walking upon the roof of his house saw a woman washing herself, and she was, says the text, 'beautiful to look upon,' and he sent messengers and took her, and defiled himself with her. 2 Sam xi 2. O therefore look to your eyes! Job made a covenant with his eyes. Job xxxi 1. If the eye be once inflamed, it will be hard to stand out long against sin. If the outworks are taken by the enemy, there is great danger of the whole castle being taken.

(5) If you would be kept from actual gross sin, study sobriety and temperance. 1 Pet v 8. *Sobrii este*, be sober. Check the inordinance of appetite, for sin frequently makes its entrance this way. By gratifying the sensitive appetite, the soul, that is akin to angels, is enslaved to the brutish part. Many drink to drowsiness, if not to drunkenness. Not denying the sensitive appetite, makes men's consciences full of guilt, and the world full of scandal. If you would be kept from running into sin, lay restraint upon the flesh. For what has God given reason and conscience but to be a bridle to check inordinate desires?

(6) If you would be kept from actual sins, be continually upon your spiritual watch.

Watch your thoughts. 'How long shall thy vain thoughts lodge within thee?' Jer iv 14. Sin begins at the thoughts. First, men cherish revengeful thoughts, then they dip their hands in blood. Set a spy over your thoughts.

Watch your passions of anger and passions of lust. The heart is ready to be destroyed by its own passions, as a vessel to be overturned by its sails. Passion transports beyond the bounds of reason; it is *brevis insania* (Seneca), a short frenzy. Moses in a passion 'spake unadvisedly with his lips.' Psa cvi 33. The disciples in a passion called fire from heaven. A man in a passion is like a ship in a storm that has neither pilot nor sails to help it, but is exposed to waves and rocks.

Watch your temptations. Satan continually lies in ambush, and watches to draw us to sin; *stat in procinctu diabolus* [the devil stands girded for battle]. He is fishing for our souls; he is either laying snares, or shooting darts. Therefore we had need watch him, that we be not decoyed into sin. Most sin is committed for want of watchfulness.

(7) If you would be kept from the evil of sin, consult the oracles of God; be well versed in Scripture. 'Thy word have I hid in my heart, that I might not sin against thee.' Psa cxix 11. The word is *anceps gladius*, a two-edged sword, to cut asunder men's lusts. When the fogs and vapours of sin begin to rise, let but the light of Scripture shine in the soul, and it dispels them. 'Let the word of Christ dwell in you richly.' Col iii 16. Alphonsus, king of Arragon, read over the Bible fourteen times. The word shows the damnable evil of sin; it furnishes us with precepts, which are so many recipes and antidotes against sin. When Christ had a temptation to sin, he beat back the tempter, and wounded him three times with the sword of the Spirit: 'It is written.' Why do men live in sin, but because they either do not read the word or do not believe it?

(8) If you would be preserved from gross, presumptuous sin, get your hearts fired with love to God. Love has great force in it; it is 'strong as death;' it breaks the league between the heart and sin. Two things in God cause love.

[1] His glorious beauty. Moses desired to see some glimpse of it. 'Lord, show me thy glory.' [2] His amazing love. What a prodigy of love was it, to give his Son out of his bosom, and lay such a jewel to pawn for our redemption! The glories of God's beauty, and the magnitude of his love, like two loadstones, draw our love to God; and if we love him, we shall not sin against him: he that loves his friend, will not by any means displease him. I have read of four men meeting together, who asked one another what it was that kept them from sinning? One said, the fear of hell; another said, the joys of heaven; the third said, the odiousness of sin; the fourth said, that which keeps me from sin is love to God; shall I sin against so good a God? shall I abuse love? Love to God is the best curbing-bit to keep from sin.

(9) If you would be kept from the evil of sin, be diligent in a calling. *Dii laboribus omnia vendunt* [Work buys all things from the gods]. Adam in paradise must till the ground. Such as live idly, expose themselves to sin. If we have no work to do, Satan will find us work; he sows most of his seed in fallow ground. A woman being much tempted to sin, came to the reverend Mr Greenham, and asked him what she should do to resist temptation? He answered, Be always well employed, that when Satan comes he may find thee busied in thy calling, and not at leisure to listen to his temptation.

(10) If you would be kept from sin, fix the eye of your mind upon the 'beauty of holiness.' Holiness consists in conformity to God. It is the sparkling of the divine nature, a beam of God shining in the soul. How lovely is Christ's bride when decked and bespangled with the jewels of

holiness! What makes the seraphims angels of light, but their holiness? Do but think with yourselves what a splendid, glorious thing holiness is, and it will cause a disgust and hatred of sin, which is so contrary to it. The beholding of beauty will make us out of love with deformity.

(11) If you would keep from the evil of sin, meditate frequently on death. Think of the unavoidableness of it. Heb ix 27. *Statutum est*, 'It is appointed unto men once to die.' We are not so sure to lie down this night in bed as to lie down in the grave. Think of the uncertainty of the time. We are but tenants at will. We hold our life at the will of our landlord, and how soon may God turn us out of this house of clay! Death often comes when we least look for it. The flood, as some learned writers observe, came in the month *Ziph*, or April, in the spring; when the trees were blossoming, and the birds singing, and men least looked for it; so, often in the spring of youth, when the body is most healthy, and the spirits most sprightly and vigorous, and it is least thought on, then death comes. Could we think often and seriously of death, it would give a death's wound to sin. *Nihil sic revocat peccata quam crebra mortis contemplatio* [Nothing restrains from sin so much as the frequent thought of death]. Augustine. No stronger antidote against sin than the thought I am now sinning, and to-morrow may be dying. What if death should find me doing the devil's work, would it not send me to him to receive my wages? Would the adulterer but think, I am now in the act of sin, but how soon may death come, and then I who have burned in lust, must burn in hell! it would strike a damp into his soul, and make him afraid of going after strange flesh.

(12) If you would be kept from gross, scandalous sins, beware of a covetous heart. Covetousness is a dry drunkenness. He who thirsts insatiably after the world will stick at no sin; he will betray Christ and a good cause for money. *Cui nihil satis, eidem nihil turpe* [The man for whom nothing is enough holds nothing shameful]. Tacitus. 'The love of money is the root of all evil.' 1 Tim vi 10. From this root comes theft. Achan's covetous humour made him steal the wedge of gold. Josh vii 21. Covetousness makes the gaols full. From this root comes murder. Why did Ahab stone Naboth to death but to possess his vineyard? 1 Kings xxi 13. Covetousness has made many swim to the crown in blood. From this bitter root of covetousness proceeds fraud. It is the covetous hand that holds false weights. From this root of covetousness comes uncleanness. You read of the hire of a whore. Deut xxiii 18. For money she would let both her conscience and chastity be set to sale. Oh, if you would be kept from the evil of sin, beware of covetousness, which is the inlet to so many sins!

(13) Let us be much in prayer to God, to keep us from engulfing our-

selves in sin. 'Keep back thy servant from presumptuous sins.' Psa xix 13. We have no power inherent to keep us from evil. Arnoldus says, that man in his corrupt estate, has *aliquas reliquias vitae spiritualis*, some relics of spiritual life left. And Arminius says, man has a sufficiency of grace within himself whereby he may *abstinere a malo*, abstain from evil; that freewill is a sufficient curb to check and pull him back from sin. But what needed Christ to have taught us this prayer: *Libera nos a malo*, 'Deliver us from evil'? If we have power of ourselves to keep from sin, why pray to God for power? Alas! if David and Peter, who in a habit of grace fell, for want of a fresh gale of the Spirit to hold them up, much more will they be in danger of falling who have only the power of freewill to hold them.

Let us therefore sue to God for strength to keep us from sinning! Let us pray the prayer of David, 'Hold thou me up, and I shall be safe' (Psa cxix 117); and that other prayer, 'Hold up my goings in thy paths, that my footsteps slip not.' Psa xvii 5. Lord, keep me from dishonouring thee; keep me from the defiling sins of the age, that I may not be worse for the times, nor the times the worse for me. 'Keep back thy servant from presumptuous sins.' Lord, whatever I suffer, keep me from sin. The child is safe in the nurse's arms; and we are only safe from falling into sin while we are held up in the arms of Christ and free grace.

Secondly, this exhortation has an aspect to God's children. You that are professors, and carry Christ's colours, I beseech you, above all others, to take heed of sin; beware of any action that is scandalous and unbecoming the gospel. You have heard what a prodigious hyperbolical evil sin is. Come not near the forbidden fruit. 'Though Israel play the harlot, yet let not Judah offend.' Hos iv 15. So, though wicked men run into sin, yet let not the spouse of Christ defile the breasts of her virginity. Sin ill becomes any, but least becomes professors. Dung is unsightly in the street; but to see it in the temple is much more offensive. Leprosy in the foot is ill, but to see a leprous sore in the face is much worse: to see sin break forth in those who have a face of religion, is most to be abominated. The sins of the wicked are not so much to be wondered at. 'The wicked shall do wickedly.' Dan xii 10. It is no wonder to see a toad spit poison. It was not so wonderful to see Cain or Ahab sin; but to see Lot's incest, to see David's hands stained with blood, was strange indeed. When the sun is eclipsed every one stands and looks at it; so when a child of light is eclipsed by scandalous sin, all stand and gaze at such an eclipse.

The sins of God's people do, in some sense, provoke him more than the sins of the wicked! We read of the provocations of his sons and daughters. Deut xxxii 19. The sins of the wicked anger God, but the sins of his people grieve him. The sins of God's people have a more malignant aspect, and are

x

of a blacker dye than others. There are aggravations in the sins of his people, which are not to be found in the sins of the unregenerate, in eight particulars:

(1) The godly have something which may *ponere obicem* [set up a barrier], restrain them from sin. When wicked men sin, they have no principle to r estrain them; they have wind and tide to carry them, they have nothing to pull them back from sin; but a child of God has a principle of grace to give check to sin; he has the impulses of God's Spirit dissuading him from evil. For him, therefore, to commit sin is far worse than for others. It is to sin more desperately; it is as if a woman should go about to kill the babe in her womb. Christian, when thou sinnest presumptuously, thou doest what in thee liest to kill the babe of grace in thy soul.

(2) The sins of God's people are greater than others, because they sin against more mercy. It is like a weight put in a scale to make sin weigh heavier. God has given Christ to a believer; he has cut him off from the wild stock of nature, and grafted him into the true olive; and for him to abuse all this mercy is to outdo the wicked, and to sin with a higher aggravation, because it is to sin against greater love. How was Peter's sin enhanced and accented, by Christ having done more for him than others! He had dropped some of the holy oil upon him; he had taken him into the number of the apostles; he had carried him up into the mount of transfiguration, and shown him the glory of heaven in a vision. For Peter to deny Christ after all this mercy was heinous, and could not be forgiven but by a miracle and prodigy of love.

(3) The sins of the godly have this aggravation in them, that they sin against clearer illumination than the wicked. 'They are of those that rebel against the light.' Job xxiv 13. Light is there taken figuratively for knowledge. It cannot be denied, but the wicked sin knowingly; but the godly have a light beyond them, such a divine, penetrating light as no hypocrite can attain to. They have better eyes to see sin than others; and for them to meddle with sin and embrace this dunghill, must needs provoke God, and make the fury rise up in his face. O therefore, you that are the people of God, flee from sin; your sins are more enhanced, and have worse aggravations in them, than the sins of the unregenerate.

(4) The sins of the godly are worse than the unregenerate; for, when they sin, it is against great experiences. They have felt the bitterness of sin in the pangs of the new birth, and afterwards God has spoken peace, and they have had an experimental taste how sweet the Lord is; and yet, after these experiences, that they should touch the forbidden fruit, and venture upon a presumptuous sin, enhances and aggravates their guilt, and is like putting a weight more in the scale to make their sin weigh heavier. The wicked have never tasted the sweetness of a heavenly life; they have never known what

it is to have any smiles from God; they have never tasted anything sweeter than corn and wine; therefore no wonder if they sin: but for a child of God, who has had such love-tokens from heaven, and signal experiences from God, for him to gratify a lust, how horrid is this! It was an aggravation of Solomon's sin, that his heart was turned from the Lord, who had appeared to him twice. 1 Kings xi 9.

(5) The sins of the godly are greater than others, because they sin against their sonship. When wicked men sin, they sin against the command; but when the godly sin, they sin against a privilege; they abuse their sonship. The godly are adopted into the family of heaven, they have a new name. Is it a light thing, said David, to be son-in-law to a king? So, to be called the sons of God, to be heirs of the promises, is no small honour. For such to run into an open offence, is sinning against their adoption. They hereby make themselves vile, as if a king's son should be tumbling in the mire, or lie among swine.

(6) The sins of the godly are worse than others, because they are committed against more vows and engagements. They have given up their names to God; they have bound themselves solemnly to God by oath. 'I have sworn that I will keep thy righteous judgments.' Psa cxix 106. In the supper of the Lord, they have renewed this sacred vow; and, after this, to run into presumptuous sin, is a breach of vow, a kind of perjury, which dyes the sin of a crimson colour.

(7) The sins of the godly are worse than others, because they bring a greater reproach upon religion. For the wicked to sin, must be expected from them, as swine will wallow in the mire; but when sheep do so, when the godly sin, it redounds to the dishonour of the gospel. 'By this deed thou hast given great occasion to the enemies of the Lord to blaspheme.' 2 Sam xii 14. Every one's eye is upon a stain in scarlet; for the godly to sin, is like a spot in scarlet, it is more taken notice of, and reflects greater dishonour upon the ways of God. When the sun is eclipsed, every one stands and looks upon it; so, when a child of light is eclipsed by scandalous sin, all stand and gaze at it. How does the gospel suffer by the miscarriages of the godly! Their blood can never wash off the stain they bring upon religion.

(8) The sins of the godly are worse, because they encourage and harden wicked men in sin. If the wicked see the godly loose and uncircumspect in their lives, they think they may do so too. The wicked make the godly their pattern, not in imitating their virtues, but their vices; and is it not fearful to be the means to damn others? These are the aggravations of the sins of the godly. You, therefore, above all others, beware of presumptuous sin. Your sins wound conscience, weaken grace, and do more highly provoke God than the sins of others, and God will be sure to punish you. Whoever

escapes, you shall not. 'You only have I known of all the families of the earth: therefore I will punish you for all your iniquities.' Amos iii 2. If God does not damn you, he may send you to hell in this life; he may cause such agonies and tremblings of heart, that you will be a terror to yourselves. You may draw nigh to despair, and be ready to look upon yourselves as castaways. When David had stained himself with adultery and murder, he complained of his broken bones. Psa li 8. This metaphor sets forth the grief and agony of his soul; he lay in sore desertion three quarters of a year, and it is thought he never recovered his full joy to his dying day. O, therefore, you who belong to God and are enrolled in his family, take heed of blemishing your profession with scandalous sin; you will pay dear for it. Think of the broken bones. Though God does not blot you out of his book, yet he may cast you out of his presence. Psa li 11. He may keep you in long desertion. You may feel such lashes in your conscience, that you may roar out and think yourselves half in hell.

[2] We also pray in a special sense, 'Deliver us from evil.' We pray to be delivered from evil under a threefold notion. 1. From the evil of our heart, which is called an evil heart. Heb iii 12. 2. From the evil of Satan, who is called the 'wicked one.' Matt xiii 19. 3. From the evil of the world, which is called an 'evil world.' Gal i 4.

(1) In the petition, 'Deliver us from evil,' we pray to be delivered from the evil of our heart, that it may not entice us to sin. The heart is the poisoned fountain, from whence all actual sins flow. 'Out of the heart proceed evil thoughts, fornications, murders.' Mark vii 21. The cause of all evil lies in a man's own breast, all sin begins at the heart. Lust is first conceived in the heart, and then it is midwifed into the world. Whence comes rash anger? The heart sets the tongue on fire. The heart is a shop or workhouse, where all sin is contrived and hammered out. How needful, therefore, is this prayer, deliver us from the evil of our hearts! The heart is the greatest seducer, therefore the apostle James says, 'Every man is drawn away of his own lust, and enticed.' James i 14. The devil could not hurt us, if our own hearts did not give consent. All that he can do is to lay the bait, but it is our fault to swallow it.

O let us pray to be delivered from the lusts and deceits of our own heart. 'Deliver us from evil.' Luther feared his heart more than the pope or cardinal; and it was Augustine's prayer, *Libera me, Domine, a meipso;* Lord, deliver me from myself. It was good advice one gave to his friend, *Caveas teipsum* [Beware of yourself]. Beware of the bosom traitor, the flesh. The heart of a man is the Trojan horse, out of which comes a whole army of lusts.

(2) In this petition, 'Deliver us from evil,' we pray to be delivered from the evil of Satan. He is 'the wicked one.' Matt xiii 19.

In what respect is Satan the wicked one?

He was the first inventor of evil. He plotted the first treason. John viii 44.

His inclination is only to evil. Eph vi 12.

His constant practice is doing evil. 1 Pet v 8.

He has some hand in all the evils and mischiefs that fall out in the world.

He hinders from good. 'He shewed me Joshua the high priest standing before the angel of the Lord, and Satan standing at his right hand to resist him.' Zech iii 1.

He provokes to evil. He put it into Ananias' heart to lie. 'Why hath Satan filled thine heart to lie to the Holy Ghost?' Acts v 3. The devil blows the fire of lust and strife. When men are proud, the old serpent has poisoned them, and makes them swell. Thus he is the evil one; and well may we pray, 'Lord, deliver us from the evil one.' The word Satan in the Hebrew signifies an opponent or adversary.

He is a restless adversary, he never sleeps. Spirits need no sleep. He is a peripatetic. He 'walketh about.' 1 Pet v 8. And how does he walk? Not as a pilgrim, but as a spy. He narrowly observes where he may plant his pieces of battery, and make his assaults with most advantage against us. Satan is a subtle engineer; there is no place that can secure us from his assaults and inroads. While we are praying, hearing, and meditating, we are of his company, though uncertain how we came by it.

Satan is a mighty adversary, he is armed with power. He is called the 'strong man.' Luke xi 21. He takes men captive at his pleasure. 'Who are taken captive by him at his will,' who are taken alive by him. 2 Tim ii 26. It alludes to a bird that is taken alive in the snare. The devil's work is to angle for men's souls; he lays suitable baits; he allures the ambitious man with honour, the covetous man with riches; he hooks his bait with silver; he allures the lustful man with beauty, he tempts men to Delilah's lap to keep them from Abraham's bosom. The devil glories in the damnation of souls. How needful then is this prayer, 'Deliver us from evil!' Lord, keep us from the evil one. Though Satan may solicit us to sin, suffer us not to give consent; though he may assault the castle of our hearts, yet let us not deliver up the keys of the castle to our mortal enemy.

(3) In this petition, 'Deliver us from evil,' we pray to be delivered from the evil of the world. It is called an evil world, not but that the world, as God made it, is good, but through our corruption it becomes evil, and we had need pray, deliver us from an evil world. Gal i 4.

In what sense is it an evil world?

(1) It is a defiling world. It is like living in an infectious air, it requires a high degree of grace to keep ourselves 'unspotted from the world.' James i 27. It is as hard to live in the world and not be defiled, as to go much in the sun and not be tanned.

The opinions of the world are defiling; as that a little religion will serve the turn; that like leaf gold, it must be spread but thin; that morality runs parallel with grace; that to be zealous is to be righteous over much; that it is better to keep the skin whole than the conscience pure; that the flesh is rather to be gratified than mortified. These opinions of the world are defiling.

The examples of the world are defiling. Examples have great force to draw us to evil. *Princeps imperio magnus exemplo major* [A prince great in power is greater by his example]. Princes are looking-glasses by which we dress ourselves; if they do evil, we are apt to imitate them. Great men are copies we set before us, and usually we write most like the copy when it is blotted. There is great proneness in us to follow the examples of the world; therefore God has put in a caveat against it. 'Thou shalt not follow a multitude to do evil.' Exod xxiii 2. How easily are we hurried to sin, when we have the tide of natural corruption and the wind of example to carry us! Lot was the world's wonder; the complexion of his soul kept pure in Sodom's infectious air. The river of Peru, in America, after running into the main sea, keeps fresh, and does not mingle with the salt waters; to which Lot might be compared, whose piety kept fresh in Sodom's salt water. Bad examples are catching. 'They were mingled among the heathen, and learned their works.' Psa cvi 35. Had we not need then pray, Lord, deliver us from this evil world? Living in the world is like travelling in a dirty road.

(2) It is an evil world, as it is an ensnaring world. The world is full of snares. Company is a snare, recreation is a snare, oaths are snares, riches are golden snares. *Opes irritamenta malorum* [Riches are incitements to sin]. The apostle speaks of 'the lust of the flesh, and the lust of the eyes and the pride of life.' 1 John ii 16. The lust of the flesh is beauty, the lust of the eye is money, the pride of life is honour; these are the natural man's trinity. *In mundo splendor opum, gloriae majestas, voluptatum illecebrae ab amore Dei nos abstrahunt* [In the world, the splendour of wealth, the greatness of high reputation and the allurements of pleasure draw us away from the love of God]. The world is a flattering enemy; whom it kisses it betrays; it is a silken halter. The pleasures of the world, like opium, cast men into the sleep of security. Lysimachus sold his crown for a draught of water; so, many part with heaven for the world. The king of Armenia was sent prisoner to queen

Cleopatra in golden fetters. Too many are enslaved with the world's golden fetters. The world bewitched Demas. 2 Tim iv 10. One of Christ's own apostles was caught with a silver bait. It is hard to drink the wine of prosperity and not be giddy. The world, through our innate corruption, is evil, as it is a snare. 'They that will be rich fall into temptation and a snare.' 1 Tim vi 9. If an angel were to live here, there were no danger of the world's ensnaring him, because he has no principle within to receive the temptation; but we have a corrupt principle that suits the temptation, and that makes us always in danger.

(3) It is an evil world as it is a discouraging world. It casts scorn and reproach upon those who live virtuously. What, will you be holier than others, wiser than your ancestors? The world deals with the professors of religion, as Sanballat did with the Jews when they were building. 'He mocked the Jews, and said, What do these feeble Jews? Will they fortify themselves? Will they revive the stones out of the heaps of the rubbish which are burned?' Neh iv 1. So the wicked world casts out squibs of reproach at the godly. What, will ye build for heaven? What needs all this cost? What profit is it to serve the Almighty? Thus the world would pluck off our chariot wheels when we are driving towards heaven. These are called cruel mockings. Heb xi 36. It requires a great measure of sanctity to withstand the discouragements of the world, to dance among serpents, to laugh at reproaches, and bind them as a crown about our head.

(4) It is an evil world as it is a deadening world. It dulls and deadens the affections to heavenly objects. It cools holy motions, like a damp in a silver mine, which puts out the light. Earthly things choke the seed of the word. A man entangled in the world is so taken up with secular concerns that he can no more mind the things above than the earth can ascend, or the elephant fly in the air. And even such as have grace in them, when their affections are belimed with the earth, they find themselves much indisposed to meditation and prayer; it is like swimming with a stone about the neck.

(5) It is an evil world as it is a maligning world. It hates the people of God. 'Because ye are not of the world, therefore the world hateth you.' John xv 19. Hatred, as Aristotle says, is against the whole kind. Haman's hatred was against the seed of the whole Jews. When you can find a serpent without a sting, or a leopard without spots, then you may expect to find a wicked world without hatred. The mark that is shot at is piety. 'They are mine adversaries, because I follow the thing that good is.' Psa xxxviii 20. The world pretends to hate the godly for something else, but the ground of the quarrel is holiness. The world's hatred is implacable; anger may be reconciled, hatred cannot. You may as well reconcile heaven and hell, as the two seeds. If the world hated Christ, no wonder it hates us. 'The world hated me before it

hated you.' John xv 18. Why should any hate Christ? This blessed Dove had no gall, this Rose of Sharon sent forth the sweetest perfume; but it shows the world's baseness, that it is a Christ-hating and a saint-hating world. Had we not need to pray, deliver us from this evil world?

(6) It is an evil world, as it is a deceitful world.

There is deceit in dealing. 'He is a merchant, the balances of deceit are in his hand.' Hos xii 7. The Hebrew word *rimmah* signifies both to deceive and oppress. He who dares use deceit will not spare to oppress.

There is a deceit in friendship. 'But a faithful man who can find?' Prov xx 6. *Trita frequensque via est per amici fallere nomen.* Some use too much courtship in friendship; they are like trumpets which make a great noise, but within they are hollow. Some can flatter and hate, commend and censure. *Mel in ore, fel in corde* [Honey on the tongue, gall in the heart]. Dissembled love is worse than hatred.

There is deceit in riches. 'The deceitfulness of riches.' Matt xiii 22. The world makes us believe it will satisfy our desires, and it does but increase them; it makes us believe it will stay with us, and it takes wings. Prov xxiii 5.

(7) It is an evil world, as it is a disquieting world. It is full of trouble. John xvi 33. The world is like a beehive; when, having tasted a little honey, we have been stung with a thousand bees. Basil was of opinion that before the fall the rose grew without prickles; but now every sweet flower of our life has its thorns. There are many things which cause disquiet—loss of friends, law-suits, crosses in estate. Relations are not without their troubles; some are troubled that they have no children, others that they have children: the world is a vexing vanity. If a man be poor, he is despised by the rich; if he be rich, he is envied by the poor. If we do not find an ensnaring world, we shall find it an afflicting world; it has more in it to wean us than tempt us. The world is a sea, where we are tossed upon the surging waves of sorrow, and often in danger of shipwreck. It is a wilderness, full of fiery serpents. What storms of persecution are raised against the righteous! 2 Tim iii 12. The wicked are briers, where Christ's sheep lose some of their golden fleece. Mic vii 4. Then had we not need pray, Lord, deliver us from being hurt by this evil world? Why should we be forbidden to love the world? Though we are commanded to love our enemies, yet this is an enemy we must not love. 'Love not the world.' 1 John ii 15.

[3] Let it be observed, however, that abstaining from, or forbearing the external acts of sin, is not sufficient to entitle us to salvation. When we pray, 'Deliver us from evil,' more is implied in it, as that we make progress in holiness. Being divorced from sin is not enough, unless we are espoused to

virtue; therefore in Scripture these two are joined. 'Depart from evil, and do good.' Psa xxxiv 14; Rom xii 9. 'Cease to do evil, learn to do well.' Isa i 16, 17. 'Let us cleanse ourselves from all filthiness of the flesh and spirit, perfecting holiness.' 2 Cor vii 1. Leaving sin is not enough, unless we embrace righteousness. *Virtutis est magis honesta agere quam non turpia* [The mark of righteousness is rather to do good than not to do evil]. As it is in the body, it is not enough that the disease be stopped, but it must grow in health; so in the soul, it is not enough that acts of sin be forborne, which is stopping a disease, but it must be healthy, and grow in holiness.

Use 1. Those are reproved who labour only to suppress the outward acts of sin, but do not press on to holiness; they cease from doing evil, but do not learn to do well. Their religion lies only in negatives; they glory in this, that they are given to no vice, none can charge them with any foul miscarriages. 'God, I thank thee that I am not as other men are; extortioners, unjust, adulterers.' Luke xviii 11. This is not enough, you must advance a step further in solid piety. It is not enough that a field be not sown with tares or hemlock, but it must be sown with good seed. Consider two things:

(1) If that you are not guilty of gross sins be the best certificate you have to show, God makes no account of you. Though a piece of brass be not so bad as clay, yet not being so good as silver, it will not pass for current coin; so, though you are not grossly profane, yet not being of the right metal, wanting the stamp of holiness, you will never pass current in heaven.

(2) A man may abstain from evil, yet he may go to hell for not doing good. 'Every tree which bringeth not forth good fruit, is hewn down, and cast into the fire.' Matt iii 10. Why were the foolish virgins shut out? They had done no hurt, they had not broken their lamps: yea, but their fault was, there was no goodness in them, they had no oil in their lamps. O therefore, let us not content ourselves in being free from gross acts of sin, but let us launch forth further in holiness; let us cleanse ourselves from all pollution, perfecting holiness.

[4] 'Deliver us from evil,' may be from temporal evil. We pray that God will either prevent temporal evils or deliver us out of them.

(1) We pray that God will prevent temporal evils; that he will be our screen, to stand between us and danger. 'Save me from them that persecute me.' Psa vii 1. We may lawfully pray against the plots of the wicked, that they may prove abortive, that, though they have a design upon us, they may not have their desire upon us. 'Keep me from the snares which they have laid for me.' Psa cxli 9.

(2) We pray that God will deliver us out of temporal evils; that he will remove his judgments from us, whether famine, sword, or pestilence.

'Remove thy stroke away from me.' Psa xxxix 10. Yet may we pray to be delivered from temporal evils, only so far as God sees it good for us. We may pray to be delivered from the evil of sin absolutely, but we must pray to be delivered from temporal evils conditionally, so far as God sees fit for us, and may stand with his glory.

Use 2. In all the troubles that lie upon us, let us look up to God for ease and succour. 'Should not a people seek unto their God?' Isa viii 19. The Papists, then, are to blame who knock at the wrong door. When they are in any trouble, they pray to the saints to deliver them. When they are in danger of shipwreck, they pray to St Nicholas; when they are in the fit of a fever, they pray to St Petronilla! when they are in travail, they pray to St Margaret. How unlawful it is to invocate saints in prayer I will prove from one Scripture: 'How then shall they call on him in whom they have not believed?' Rom x 14. We may pray to none but such as we believe in; but we ought not to believe in any saint, therefore we may not pray to him. The Papists have, in their Lady's Psalter, directed their prayers for deliverance to the Virgin Mary; Deliver me, O Lady. *Benedicta Domina, in manibus tuis reposita est nostra salus;* O thou blessed Lady, in thy hands our salvation is laid up. But 'Abraham be ignorant of us.' Isa lxiii 16. The saints and Virgin Mary are ignorant of us.

To pray to saints is idolatry advanced to blasphemy. Our Saviour has taught us in all our distresses to pray to God for a cure. 'Deliver us from evil.' He only knows what our troubles are, and can give us help from trouble; he only that laid the burden on can take it off. David went to God: 'O bring thou me out of my distresses.' Psa xxv 17. God with a word can heal. 'He sent his word, and healed them.' Psa cvii 20. He delivered the three children out of the fiery furnace, Joseph out of prison, Daniel out of the lions' den; which proves him to be God, because none can deliver as he does. 'There is no other God that can deliver after this sort.' Dan iii 29. Let us, then, in all our straits and exigencies, look to God, and say, 'Deliver us from evil.'

SOME OTHER
THOMAS WATSON
TITLES
BY
BANNER OF TRUTH

A BODY OF DIVINITY

Thomas Watson

The first book published by the Trust, this has been one of the best sellers and consistently the most useful and influential of our publications. There are several reasons for this:

1. *The subject of the book.* It deals with the foremost doctrinal and experimental truths of the Christian Faith.

2. *The means of instruction used.* It is based on the Westminster Assembly's *Shorter Catechism*, in which the main principles of Christianity that lie scattered in the Scriptures are brought together and set forth in the form of question and answer. This Catechism is unsurpassed for its 'terse exactitude of definition' and 'logical elaboration' of the fundamentals.

3. *The style of the author.* Watson conveys his thorough doctrinal and experimental knowledge of the truth in such an original, concise, pithy, pungent, racy, rich and illustrative style that he is rightly regarded as the most readable of the Puritans.

ISBN 978 0 85151 383 6
328pp. Large paperback

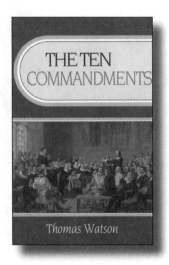

THE TEN COMMANDMENTS

Thomas Watson

In this book Thomas Watson (c.1620-1686) continues his exposition of the *Shorter Catechism* drawn up by the Westminster Assembly. Watson was one of the most popular preachers in London during the Puritan era. His writings are characterised by clarity, raciness and spiritual richness. The series of three volumes, of which this is the second, makes an ideal introduction to Puritan literature.

There are few matters about which the Puritans differ more from present-day Christians than in their assessment of the importance of the ten commandments. The commandments, they held, are the first thing in Christ-ianity which the natural man needs to be taught and they should be the daily concern of the Christian to the last.

In *The Ten Commandments* Watson examines the moral law as a whole as well as bringing out the meaning and force of each particular commandment. In view of the most important function of the law in Christian life and evangelism this is a most valuable volume.

ISBN 978 0 85151 146 7
288pp. Large paperback

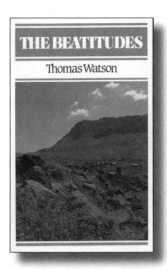

THE BEATITUDES

Thomas Watson

The opening verses of the best-known of all Christ's sermons were handled by many Puritans for the Beatitudes gave full scope to the combination of sound doctrine, practical wisdom and heart-searching application which characterised their preaching. To these general Puritan characteristics Watson added certain of his own: a master of a terse, vigorous style and of a beauty of expression, he could speak not only to win men's understanding but also to secure a place for the truth in their memories. More than most of his generation he sought to follow the example of Christ's teaching by employing all manner of illustrative material from common life, and with simplicity and charm he spoke words not easy to forget. Two hundred years after Thomas Watson's death, William Jay of Bath said that he could go to anyone of his books and 'find it ever fresh, pointed and instructive.'

The Beatitudes has been one of the rarest of Watson's works. In this edition the layout has been entirely revised and editorial notes supplied.

ISBN 978 0 85151 035 4
398pp. Large paperback

For more information about our publications, or to order, please visit our website.

THE BANNER OF TRUTH TRUST

3 Murrayfield Road, Edinburgh EH12 6EL UK P O Box 621, Carlisle, PA 17013, USA

www.banneroftruth.co.uk